Curriculum Studies
Guidebooks

Studies in the
Postmodern Theory of Education

Shirley R. Steinberg
General Editor

Vol. 499

The Counterpoints series is part of the Peter Lang Education list.
Every volume is peer reviewed and meets
the highest quality standards for content and production.

PETER LANG
New York • Bern • Frankfurt • Berlin
Brussels • Vienna • Oxford • Warsaw

Marla Morris

Curriculum Studies Guidebooks

VOLUME 2

Concepts and Theoretical Frameworks

PETER LANG
New York • Bern • Frankfurt • Berlin
Brussels • Vienna • Oxford • Warsaw

Library of Congress Cataloging-in-Publication Data

Morris, Marla.
Curriculum studies guidebooks: concepts and theoretical frameworks / Marla Morris.
volumes; cm. — (Counterpoints: studies in the
postmodern theory of education; vols. 498–499)
Includes bibliographical references and index.
Contents: v. 1. Introduction—Historical Curriculum Concepts, Part One—
Historical Curriculum Concepts, Part Two—Historical Curriculum Concepts,
Part Three—Political Curriculum Concepts—Multicultural Curriculum Concepts—
Gender Curriculum Concepts—Literary Curriculum Concepts—
v. 2. Introduction—Aesthetic curriculum concepts—Spiritual curriculum concepts—
Cosmopolitan curriculum concepts—Ecological curriculum concepts—
Cultural studies curriculum concepts—Postcolonial curriculum concepts—
Poststructural curriculum concepts—Psychoanalytic curriculum concepts.
1. Education—Curricula—United States—Philosophy. I. Title.
LB1570.M685   375'.001—dc23   2015022031
ISBN 978-1-4331-3126-4 (v. 1, hardcover)
ISBN 978-1-4331-3125-7 (v. 1, paperback)
ISBN 978-1-4539-1658-2 (v. 1, e-book)
ISBN 978-1-4331-3128-8 (v. 2, hardcover)
ISBN 978-1-4331-3127-1 (v. 2, paperback)
ISBN 978-1-4539-1659-9 (v. 2, e-book)
ISSN 1058-1634

Bibliographic information published by **Die Deutsche Nationalbibliothek**.
Die Deutsche Nationalbibliothek lists this publication in the "Deutsche
Nationalbibliografie"; detailed bibliographic data are available
on the Internet at http://dnb.d-nb.de/.

Cover image: ©iStock.com/gemenacom

© 2016 Peter Lang Publishing, Inc., New York
29 Broadway, 18th floor, New York, NY 10006
www.peterlang.com

DEDICATION

To Mary Aswell Doll, the love of my life

TABLE OF CONTENTS

ACKNOWLEDGMENTS

Special thanks to Chris Myers, who was there for me all along the way. To Shirley Steinberg, who has always believed in my work. To William F. Pinar, who always inspires me. To John Weaver, my friend and colleague. To Naomi Rucker, who listened to me hours on end about the progress of the book. To the late Dennis Carlson, who generously gave much time to read both volumes and make helpful comments along the way. To the reviewers who made my work stronger. To the copy editor who helped in the final stages of the book.

· 1 ·

INTRODUCTION

This book is the second volume of *Curriculum Studies Guidebooks: Concepts and Theoretical Frameworks*. This book is an introduction to current curricular issues that students of education, curriculum studies scholars, educationists, teachers, and policymakers might find useful when trying to understand the current field of curriculum studies.

In the first volume of the *Guidebooks* I explore curriculum studies in the interstices of history, politics, multiculturalism, gender, and literature. In this volume, I examine curriculum studies in the interstices of aesthetics, spirituality, cosmopolitanism, ecology, cultural studies, postcolonialism, poststructuralism, and psychoanalytic theory. Many of these theoretical frameworks were in their early stages or were hinted at in Pinar et al. (1995). Today these frameworks have emerged in new ways, which is what I explore in these *Guidebooks*. At the close of this introduction I offer brief outlines of the chapters.

A Debt of Gratitude

Alberto Manguel (2015) says, "There are always models for any new literary [or curriculum studies] venture" (p. 20). Indeed, there are many models of current curriculum studies scholarship. There are many schools of thought about what curriculum studies means. These *Guidebooks* are written in the tradition of the reconceptualization that began in the early 1970s. Today, though, curriculum studies scholarship has moved into what is dubbed the (post)reconceptualization. The field has moved and changed over the years but the basic structure of the field has not changed. There is continuity between what was done in the 1970s and what is going on today in the field. And, too, there are differences in the field; there are new models—or what I would call "theoretical frameworks"—that have emerged since the 1970s.

I would like to say a word of thanks to others who have paved the way for scholars to do curriculum work in new ways. Books are not written in a vacuum. Other curricularists have certainly influenced my work. I owe a debt of gratitude to Connelly, He, and Phillon (2008); Flinders and Thornton (2004); J. Dan Marshall et al. (2007); Schubert et al. (2002); Kridel (2010) and Pinar et al. (1995). All of these scholars have opened up what I call vistas-of-curriculum that make it possible to think about the field of curriculum studies differently. All of these scholars have advanced the field significantly.

Although indebted to many of the scholars above, the organization and structure of both *Guidebooks* were most influenced by Pinar et al. (1995). With the exception of poststructuralism and aesthetics, the theoretical frameworks I examine in this *Guidebook* were either hinted at in Pinar et al. (1995) or are new to the field of curriculum studies. In this *Guidebook* I explore different concepts, different content, and, in my writing, I take a different approach to any of the books I mention above.

Voice

Ben Yagoda (2005) comments,

> Critic Roman Jakobson said that language has two basic functions: the communicative and the poetic. Strictly communicative writing includes business memos, instruction manuals, news articles, college textbooks. (p. 166).

I must make clear from the outset that this college textbook is not written in a "communicative" style. The communicative style is the style of no style. On the other hand, this college textbook is not written in a poetic style either. I am not a poet. However, my style is closer to poetics than a communicative style. As much of my background comes out of the humanities, I write more like a humanities scholar than a social scientist. I am interested in issues of voice, the process of writing, and style much as a fiction writer might be. Unlike creative writers (i.e., poets, novelists, playwrights), many academics—especially if they are social scientists who are not curriculum theorists—are not much interested in developing voice, pay little attention to the process of writing, and have little interest in developing style.

Thaisa Frank and Dorothy Wall (1994) contend

> Nobody but you has your voice. Yet voice isn't unchanging, nor is it a static, precious commodity. It's always shifting in response to an immediate moment, an intention, an audience. Just as you aren't a static, singular entity, neither is your voice. (p. 6)

Both *Guidebooks* were written over a very long period of time. These books took years to complete. And during those years my life changed. My interests changed. I changed as a person. And more than likely—in my writing—my voice changed over time. I do think that much of our work as scholars is driven by the unconscious. And, at bottom, it is the unconscious that drives the writing. Voice, therefore, is mostly unconscious.

Wendy Lesser (2014) contends, "The good writer remains vitally present in every line he [sic] writes, and even when the mortal author dies, the voice on the page is still alive with that individuality" (p. 92). For many academics the scholar's voice remains absent. Much conservative scholarship sounds like it has been written by a computer or a machine. There is no trace of the author to be found. But most poststructural scholars do, indeed, take the concept of voice seriously. Jacques Derrida and Michel Serres, for example, take voice seriously. Each has a distinct voice that is immediately recognizable. Like artists, these scholars craft their texts in such a way that their voices are heard. Michael Collier (2007) tells us

> We believe that voice develops, that it's a product of maturation, but we also believe that it involves listening to something inside of us that's unique. It's also supposed to have the quality of a signature and we don't quite know what that is until we see or hear it. Voice contains tone and mood. In other words, it comprises an atmosphere. (p. 142)

It is important to note that Collier is a poet. These ideas that he talks about above are important not only to poets but to all artists and academics. In order to be discovered or to get published, artists have to develop their own voice or signature. I think that scholars, too, need to develop their own voices and signatures. But this isn't the way most academics think. Perhaps these concerns are generational. Older generations of scholars were taught to write in the formal "we," never to use "I," and never insert personality into the text. I think for my generation things are very different. Conversational tone, personal narrative, and autobiographical reflections are encouraged—but still risky. In curriculum studies, William Pinar—who introduced autobiography to the field—changed the way curriculum scholars do their work. He opened the door to all kinds of writing, including autobiographical and personal narrative.

In contradistinction to an autobiographical style, more conservative scholars report, argue, and are absent in the text—especially if they are writing handbooks, research reports, grants, and even, yes, guidebooks. My *Guidebooks* are not written in this fashion. These books are not encyclopedias or research reports. My *Guidebooks* are explorations, adventures. The concepts explored in these books are experimental, open ended, and dialogic. Throughout the books, I think, my voice is evident.

The Process of Writing

Many academics do not think much about the process of writing. They simply write, not giving writing a thought. But I think about the process of writing all the time because it is a subject that I find engaging. There was a process to writing these *Guidebooks*. I think the process is as important to discuss as the final product. Annie Dillard (2013) says, "Every book has an intrinsic impossibility" (p. 72). This impossibility has to do with the process of writing. Students are often told by their mentors to write about what they know. But knowledge—on the part of the individual—is limited. One simply cannot know everything! The impossibility of these *Guidebooks* turned on stretching my knowledge base beyond what is seemingly possible. That is part of the reason that it took me years to finish these books. My studies took me to new lands, open horizons where I encountered difficulties and challenges. Nonetheless, I took on the challenge and what a challenge it was.

The chapters went through numerous revisions. William Zinsser (1985) tells us, "Rewriting is the essence of writing. I pointed out that professional writers rewrite their sentences repeatedly and then rewrite what they have rewritten" (p. 4). I do not know exactly how many times I revised my work. There were many, many rewrites. In some cases entire chapters were thrown out and completely rewritten from different angles. Clearly, these were the hardest books I have ever written.

Part of the difficulty of writing academic books has to do with the use of citations. As William Pinar says, "We work from the work of others" (personal communication). In other words, scholars work from citations. There is a certain rhythm to using citations. However, it is not enough to merely cite other scholars. One has to do something with the citations. Scholars must make the work their own by advancing the discussion. Sometimes I felt it was necessary to use more citations in some chapters than in others because the subject matter was so difficult to comprehend.

As I worked my way through the chapters for final edits, I cut huge amounts of material that I thought was not needed. Francine Prose (2007) explains

> For any writer, the ability to look at a sentence and see what's superfluous, what can be altered, revised, expanded, and, especially, cut is essential. It's satisfying to see that sentence shrink, snap into place, and ultimately emerge in a more polished form: clear, economical, sharp. (p. 2)

Cutting material and sharpening focus are crucial to good writing, as Prose suggests. Toward the end of the writing and revising I was my harshest critic. I struggled mostly with getting the sentences to "snap into place," by making them as clear as possible so that readers could better understand my points. But being clear does not mean writing like a machine. Good writing—at least for me—is musical, lyrical. And dare I say poetic—even though I do not consider myself a poet! Raymond Carver (2006) tells readers

> Evan Connell said once that he knew when he was finished with a short story when he found himself going through it and taking out commas and then going through the story again and putting commas back in the same place. (p. 104)

I found myself, too, putting in commas, taking them out and then putting them back again—for the sake of clarity. Although these *Guidebooks* are not short stories, they are writings—prose—that demand attention to punctuation. One of the most important things to me, as a scholar, is to be clear in my writing. And clarity has a lot to do with the art of punctuation. Clarity does not mean losing your voice; it means strengthening voice by making meaning clear. Only readers, though, can judge whether the writing is clear or not. Writers are too in the thick of it to be certain that meanings will be made via clarity.

Writing is not merely about technique. It is also, first and foremost, "the subject of invention" (Bawarshi, 2003, p. 1). The way in which scholars use citations, leave things out, put things back in place, and think creatively about the subject at hand is—at the end of the day—about invention. Scholarship is as much as an invention as is creative writing, poetry, fiction, short stories, and so on. Scholars invent narratives.

Susan Cahill (2004) states, "Some writers challenge the reader to change her life, or at least to rethink its assumptions, not to get stuck. Subversive points of view, though never soothing, are always invigorating, the voice strong" (p. xiii). I think that "subversive points of view" only come about through a dialogic relation with texts. Scholars must dance with the text, as it were, to be able to change the way readers think about things. Scholarship is not merely reporting, it is making new meaning from old ideas. And making the old new requires dance, dialogue. It is for the reader to judge, though, whether the positions taken by the writer are subversive or not.

It is important to note that curriculum scholars are not all in agreement on things. We are not cut out of the same cloth. The positions that I take throughout the *Guidebooks* might differ from the positions that another scholar might take. Some might think the nature of a guidebook is not to take positions but to merely report on the state of knowledge. But I think otherwise. The scholar takes an idea, does something with it, takes a position and hopefully—as Cahill (2004) suggests—makes readers think differently about the subject at hand.

A Few Points about Style

When I approach an idea, or a concept, I do so with what I call an "open horizon." That is, after working on a concept, that concept takes on its own life and I follow it wherever it goes—into an open horizon. This does not mean that my writing has little structure. My writing is highly structured. The work at hand must be highly structured in order to get entangled in an open horizon. Open horizons are made up of tangents and meanderings. This is the style of what some might consider to be bricolage. I would venture to say that most guidebooks or handbooks do not wander or meander or celebrate tangents or bricolage. But I think that scholarship is made interesting on the edges of horizons. One comes to those edges through wandering, getting entangled in tangents, and working in the style of a bricoleur. I see my work—overall—as postmodern. The postmoderns meander, embrace tangents, and engage in bricolage. Although I have a basic thesis for each chapter, my work is hardly linear. If anything my writing is circular and labyrinthine.

William Zinsser (1985) says, "Style, of course, is ultimately tied to the psyche, and writing has deep psychological roots" (p. 24). The psyche is not the master of its own house. Much of the psyche is unconscious, as I stated earlier. Much of the process of writing—the voice, the content, and the style—is driven by the unconscious. Thus, why we write about what we do—at the end of the day—is a mystery.

Ben Yagoda (2005) remarks,

> Style in the deepest sense is not a set of techniques, devices, and habits of expression that just happen to be associated with a particular person, but a presentation or representation of something essential about him or her. (p. xvii)

One's style cannot be detached from one's personality. As Yagoda points out, style reflects "something essential" about the writer. To remove one's personality from the writing is to, in effect, destroy the writing. But in much academic writing, the personality of the writer vanishes. Academics suggest—Yagoda tells us—that style "will cloud the waters and shift the focus of the piece away from the issues at hand, toward something literary or personal" (p. 167). On the contrary, I think that concepts and theoretical frameworks are better understood when the writer's personality and voice are made clear. Students who read dead textbooks written by committees—who agree to offend no one—get bored and stop reading. Students should be engaged in their reading by writers who are engaged with their materials. I do not think that personal styles "cloud the waters" (Yagoda, p. 167). Authentically presenting to the reader one's own voice, style, and position is a more clear and honest approach to doing scholarship.

Brief Chapter Outlines

In chapter 2, "Aesthetic Curriculum Concepts," I begin with a general introduction to aesthetics and its relation to curriculum studies. I explore music, dance, reader's theater, the visual arts, and drama. I argue that aesthetics in these art forms raises psychoanalytic, philosophical, postmodern, posthuman, and political questions. I explore these questions in relation to curriculum studies.

In chapter 3, "Spiritual Curriculum Concepts," I begin with a general introduction to spirituality in its relation to religion, aesthetics, ecology, and depth psychology. Then I examine concepts that emerge in the interstices of curriculum studies and spirituality such as soul, holy sparks, mysticism, eco-spirituality, the spiritual in its relation to social activism, and I explore the emergence of Jewish scholarship in its relation to curriculum studies.

In chapter 4, "Cosmopolitan Curriculum Concepts," I ask what it means to think the world, to think, in other words, on a universal level. Then I explore what it means to think on a national level. I explore what it means to think about borders between nations and the permeability of those borders. I ask readers to think the universal and particular (or the international and the national) together. I ask readers to consider what it means to move toward having more international conversations.

In chapter 5, "Ecological Curriculum Concepts," I explore the naturalists and their decline. Then I move into a section on human-animal studies. I explore what is called "environmental education," issues of ecojustice education, and environmental justice education. Finally, I examine ecology, and in this context I explore the concept of home (or being in place) and homelessness (or being displaced.)

In chapter 6, "Cultural Studies Curriculum Concepts," I discuss what is meant by the concept of "youth cultures." Then I examine what it means for youth cultures to express themselves in the realm of the popular. That is, I contextualize my study on youth cultures as they engage in music, graffiti, sports, and more. I argue in this chapter that youth is raced, classed, and gendered. I look at various ways that the concept of the popular is deconstructed through a variety of theoretical frameworks.

In chapter 7, "Postcolonial Curriculum Concepts," I look at the debate over the concept of "post" in postcolonial literature. I examine issues of colonialism and racism and the ways in which education has been complicit in colonization. I also talk about the problems of the concepts of the "canon" and "tradition." I argue that these are political concepts. I also examine the ways in which colonial peoples have resisted colonization. I explore psychological problems brought on by colonialism. Finally, I talk about what is called "anticolonial scholarship."

In chapter 8, "Poststructural Curriculum Concepts," I argue that curriculum theorists have carved out at least four areas in relation to poststructuralism. These are chaos and complexity theory, posthumanism, postformalism, and poststructural ethics and politics. Three major poststructural writers upon whom curriculum theorists draw are Michel Foucault, Jacques Derrida, and Emmanuel Levinas. I discuss curriculum studies scholars' recent commentaries on these thinkers.

In chapter 9, "Psychoanalytic Curriculum Concepts," I offer brief discussions on some key concepts of psychoanalysts Sigmund Freud, Melanie Klein, and Anna Freud. In the second part of the chapter I explore the work of psychoanalyst and educationist Deborah Britzman. In the last part of the chapter I explore a variety of curriculum scholars who have done psychoanalytically oriented work in relation to curriculum studies.

· 2 ·

AESTHETIC
CURRICULUM CONCEPTS

Introduction

This chapter begins with a general and brief introduction to aesthetics and its relation to curriculum studies. I will discuss such art forms as music, dance, reader's theater, the visual arts, and drama. Aesthetics and these various art forms raise psychoanalytic, philosophical, postmodern, posthuman, and political questions. My aim in this chapter is to explore these questions in their relation to curriculum studies.

What Is Aesthetics?

Boyd White (2009) points out that according to Andrew Irving's "review of Schneider and Wright's (2006) *Contemporary Art and Anthropology*":

> *Aishitikos* is the ancient Greek word for that which is "perceptive by feeling" and as Susan Buck-Moss (1992) suggests, the original semantic field of aesthetics was not art but reality—or rather a **corporeality**: a discourse of the body or form of knowledge whereby taste, touch, hearing, seeing and smell are the means by which we come to know and understand the world. (p. 3).

Aesthetics originally was not about art but about perception and living in the everyday world. The Greeks were interested in living aesthetically by paying attention to the way in which the world was experienced through the senses. Interestingly enough this position dovetails with Dewey (2005) as he too believed that aesthetic living meant living well in the everyday. Likewise, Mark Johnson (2007) writes about aesthetics as it has to do with living well in the everyday world. Boyd White points out,

> A contemporary understanding of aesthetics should not be constrained to discussions of beauty, or taste, or limited to the art world. Rather, as [Mark] Johnson insists, "aesthetics becomes the study of everything that goes into the human capacity to make and experience meaning" (x). (p. 5)

Aesthetics, however, was not always defined by meaning making in the everyday. Paul Oskar Kristeller (2008) suggests that in the 18th century Alexander Baumgarten was "famous for having coined the term aesthetics" (p. 11). Baumgarten believed, as Boyd White points out, that the "linking of art and beauty and the necessity for attention to taste as the arbiter of beauty" also meant that art was separated from the everyday world (p. 121). And it was this separation that Dewey later critiqued.

According to Kristeller, Kant "was the first major philosopher who included aesthetics and the philosophical theory of the arts as an integral part of his system" (p. 13). For Kant, aesthetics was a form of thought. Mark Johnson tells us that Dewey wrote that "an experience of thinking has its own esthetic quality" (p. 103). Scholarship—as a form of thought—should be a sensual experience. Johnson also points out that for Dewey thinking is always already embodied (p. 103). Johnson and White concur. Johnson, White, and Dewey all suggest that aesthetics concerns both emotions and thought and has everything to do with living well in the world. Hence, their positions are closer to the ancient Greeks than to Baumgarten or Kant.

Aesthetics and Curriculum Studies

Here I will explore curriculum studies scholars who work in aesthetics. Of course there are many approaches one might take when writing about aesthetics and curriculum. One approach is Freudian. I take a Freudian approach in my book called *On Not Being Able to Play: Scholars, Musicians and the Crisis of Psyche* (2009). I suggest, "Artistic expression is a projection of unconscious conflict" (p. 17). In this context, I write about playing music, which is the least written about of the arts in curriculum studies. I note:

> Michael Eigen (2005) points out in his book *Emotional Storm* that "[t]here are creative as well as destructive storms" (p. 11). For some, creativity and destruction are of a piece. Eigen (2005) talks much of "psychic annihilation" (p. 23) throughout his work. Music can be made in the service of psychic annihilation...One might write or play music to obliterate the self, or to obliterate others symbolically. One plays an instrument, in some cases, to make the self disappear. (p. 17)

This psychoanalytic interpretation of aesthetics—in this case music—is unusual because most curriculum studies scholars who analyze the arts do not use this theoretical framework. Most curriculum studies scholars write about aesthetics in a more positive light. Most of the discussion of aesthetics in curriculum studies turns on the notion of beauty, not destruction. But I (2009) argue that many artists are depressives and live destructive lives or live on the brink of disaster and it is this disaster that artists are expressing. Mark Rothko (2004)—the well-known painter—tells us,

> Pain, frustration, and the fear of death seem the most common binder between human beings, and we know that a common enemy is a much better coalescer of energies and a much more efficient eraser of particularities than is a common positive end. (p. 35)

When one looks at a Rothko painting, one might not understand his work because it is abstract. But reading his text helps us to understand what he might be trying to express. Clearly it is a sense of disaster that drives his work.

Artistic expression—for many—comes out of a place of pain, not beauty. S. Brent Plate (2005) comments that one of Walter Benjamin's "much valued possession[s]" (p. 23) was a painting by Paul Klee titled *Angelus Novus*. Richard Wolin (1994) explains that Benjamin discusses this painting and calls the discussion "legendary" as he tells us,

> In his legendary discussion of the "angel of history" [which is Paul Klee's painting *Angelus Novus*]—perhaps the defining image of his entire work—Benjamin affirms that "Where we perceive a chain of events [the angel] sees one single catastrophe which keeps piling wreckage upon wreckage and hurls it in front of his feet." (p. xxi)

Art expresses catastrophe. Think of Dylan Thomas, Anne Sexton. These poets wrote out of a sense of misery, pain, and catastrophe. Of course there are happy artists and happy poets but a deeper analysis of the why of creation seems to suggest that much art comes from a place of pain. Not all would agree on this point.

Delores Liston (2001), in her book *Joy as a Metaphor of Convergence: A Phenomenological and Aesthetic Investigation of Social and Educational Change*, argues that aesthetics expresses joy. But this joy, says Liston,

> has been trivialized and sentimentalized. As noted…I use the term joy to refer to a way of "coming" to view, hear, and feel the world. Thus, joy is a state of awareness through which the senses interpret the world. (p. 19)

Liston goes on to tie joy into the idea of beauty. But this too she qualifies as she states,

> As an aesthetic metaphor, Joy calls our attention to beauty. Beauty here is not representative of any particular culture. The beauty is not the beauty of a beauty queen or even the beauty of a work of art. Instead, beauty here refers to "beauty of being," the aesthetics of being. (p. 20)

The talk of beauty—even if it is about the beauty of lived experience—is a more traditional way of talking about art. Aesthetics traditionally has been about the study of beauty. This traditional view, though, is highly problematic, especially now living in a post-9/11 world. Still, most commentators in curriculum studies on aesthetics couch their discussions in terms of beauty. There are more abstract ways of talking about aesthetics as a way of experiencing the world—but still this experiencing seems always to take on a positive light. Can we experience the world aesthetically through a negative light?

Drawing on Dewey (2005), many curriculum scholars write about aesthetic experience. Shaun McNiff (2004) writes about "the everyday nature of aesthetic experience" (p. ix) as a form of "authentic wonder" (p. xii). Aristotle describes philosophy as beginning in wonder. Does aesthetic experience too begin in wonder, as McNiff suggests? What is "authentic wonder" in a post-9/11 world? Perhaps scholars need to think more in terms of anxiety. Living anxiously is another way of seeing the world and another way of creating art. Remember that Freud suggested that anxiety is the seat of all problems; anxiety is also the seat of most art. Aesthetics as it is connected to states of anxiety is not a new idea. The notion of the sublime—which encompasses states of anxiety, dread, and awe—can be traced back to writings that date somewhere between 213–273 CE. Patrick Frierson and Paul Guyer (2011) explain:

> The sublime, and the contrast between the beautiful and the sublime, were a constant theme in European letters after the republication of the ancient treatise *Peri hypsous*, falsely attributed to the rhetorician Dionysius Cassius Longinus (c. 213–73 CE), translated into English as early as 1652. (p. 14)

The notion of the sublime is an aporia. Opposite feelings are felt together without resolution. The sublime is the feeling that both negative and positive emotions occur at once. Awe and terror, for example, are felt simultaneously. Robert Rosenblum (2010) explains further:

> The Sublime was fervently explored in the later eighteenth and early nineteenth centuries and recurs constantly in the aesthetics of such writers as Burke, Reynolds, Kant, Diderot and Delacroix....the Sublime provided a flexible semantic container for the...experiences of awe, terror, boundlessness and divinity....the Sublime could be extended to art as well as to nature. (p. 108)

The sublime is an unsettling concept. It is important to note that the sublime is usually contrasted with the notion of beauty. It is not beauty. The sublime is horror and awe at once. How is it possible to feel two very different emotions at once? Kant (2001) explains,

> Since the mind is not simply attracted by the object but is alternately repelled thereby, the delight in the sublime does not so much involve positive pleasure as admiration and respect; i.e., merits the name of a negative pleasure. (p. 307)

For Kant these feelings emerge in response to art and nature. These are overwhelming feelings that cannot easily be explained. In fact, Simon Morley (2010) points out that Kant

> observed, that sometimes we cannot present to ourselves an account of an experience that is in any way coherent. We cannot encompass it by thinking, and so it remains indiscernible or unnamable, undecidable, indeterminate and unpresentable. (p. 16)

This description of the sublime sounds almost postmodern. Derrida often writes about the undecidable. Samuel Beckett—who could be considered a postmodern novelist and playwright—writes about the unnamable. The question here is can there be a postmodern sublime? Some seem to think so. Simon Morley suggests

> The experience of modern life itself has been viewed by such thinkers as Jean-Fran-cois Lyotard and Fredric Jameson in terms of the sublime, as the extreme space-time compressions produced by globalized communication technologies give rise to a per-ception of the everyday as fundamentally destabilizing and excessive. (p. 12)

Is the experience of using technology a sublime experience? This is debatable. But living in a post-9/11 world might lead to feelings such as terror. However, 9/11 is in no way sublime. The awe of life fades into the background when thinking of such horrific catastrophes.

Few scholars in curriculum studies describe the arts in a negative way or describe the everyday as terror-filled and simultaneously full of awe. Few of the curriculum scholars I review here write about the sublime or frame their work in terms of the sublime. The arts for most curriculum scholars are seen as creative, beautiful, meaningful but not terror filled. However, Sylvia Wilson (2004) is an exception.

Sylvia Wilson tells us that aesthetic experience is like a "contemplative practice" or after James Macdonald "a prayerful act" (p. 57). Art in the service of contemplation and prayer again harkens back to the traditional notion of beauty. To live prayerfully is to live beautifully. But for Wilson this isn't the whole story. Wilson creates art out of negativity too—which reminds us of the experience of the sublime—as she remarks that in one of her works she expresses "raising my son who is multiply disabled, grief has coloured my life… Death and loss and grief, like autumn leaves in the dying become brilliant and magnificent, lend a richness and intensity to life" (p. 52). Certainly death and loss add intensity to life. Wilson's work, by combining the contemplative and the horrors of death, could be considered to be sublime. But to romanticize death, though, is problematic.

I (2008) write much about these issues in *Teaching Through the Ill Body: A Spiritual and Aesthetic Approach to Pedagogy and Illness*. I suggest that we must be careful not to turn something awful into something good. What is awful is awful. We may choose to make art out of the awful—and that art might be beautiful—but still the experience remains awful. Creation and destruction, as Michael Eigen (2005) points out, occur throughout our lives as he says, "There are creative as well as destructive storms" (cited in Morris, 2009, p. 17). These storms to which Eigen refers are what he calls "emotional storms," as the title of his book suggests. The question is, do most people experience emotion as a storm? Some people do and some do not. People who lack affect hardly ever experience life in highly dramatic ways. Now, Beethoven, on the other hand, lived an "emotional storm," as Eigen would put it. In my book, *Teaching Through the Ill Body*, I state:

> In a letter to Dr. Von Schaden written early in his life (1787) Beethoven complains, "I have been troubled with asthma and I much fear that it will lead to consumption. I also suffer from melancholy which is as great an evil as my illness itself." (p. 17).

Beethoven suffered the cruelest of fates as a composer with the onset of his deafness. To suffer from illness, depression, and deafness has got to make for a stormy life. Beethoven wrote from a sense of destruction most of the time, although he did write a piece titled "Ode to Joy." But Beethoven was not a very joyful fellow.

Aesthetics, Meditation, and Prayer

Like Sylvia Wilson (2004), Margaret Macintyre Latta (2001) writes about the intersection of aesthetics, the contemplative and the prayerful, although Latta uses the word "meditative" rather than contemplative or prayerful (p. 3). To meditate is almost a religious act. Some use meditation in the service of the spiritual. Others use meditation in the service of art as Latta suggests. And still others use the meditative in the service of psychoanalysis. Mark Epstein (2007) writes about meditation and psychoanalysis. But for Epstein the point is to do "psychotherapy without the self," as the title of his book suggests. Epstein is a Buddhist so he is talking here not about literally obliterating the self but rather attaining a state of both mindfulness and egolessness simultaneously. This is certainly an artful way to live a life.

Two comments are at hand. First, on mindfulness. Being mindful is paying attention to the everyday in a more heightened way. This is what Maxine Greene (1995) calls "wide-awakenness." Certainly, when performing a piece of music the musician must be ever so mindful of the phrasing and transitions in the music. Listening is key to good musicianship. The only way to really listen is to develop a sense of mindfulness. Second, the good performance, ironically, is one where the performer disappears and becomes egoless. This is a rare occasion in performance. But the musician must be mindful in order to get rid of the ever-watching censor of the superego. If too much superego is present during a performance, the performance could be ruined because the superego gets in the way of the performer losing herself in the music (egolessness through mindfulness). Mindfulness is listening, careful listening. Deep listening actually makes the superego vanish.

The Dance of Aesthetics

Donald Blumenfeld-Jones (2008) writes about dance when he suggests that aesthetic experience—like dancing—helps in "extending our understanding" (p. 179). Blumenfeld-Jones is thinking of understanding in the philosophical sense of the word. Understanding the world via dance is understanding the world through movement as Blumenfeld-Jones remarks, that "The choreographer develops the motional, spatial, and temporal themes of the dance either alone or with dancers, and then begins to compose the movements for the dance" (p. 177). Choreography is an interesting way to think about understanding the world. To understand the world through the composition of movement—which is what choreography is—is not the way in which most people think about their everyday lives. Many take for granted the fact that we can move at all. Those with disabilities, however, know all too well what it means to have trouble moving.

Most people in their everyday lives do not think about issues of time and space—as Blumenfeld-Jones points out in the above citation—but choreographers think about these things. How can we be more cognizant of moving in time and space in our everyday lives? Perhaps this too is a way to become—in the Buddhist sense—mindful. Mindfulness in dance has to do with listening because dancers dance to music and they have to learn to listen to know when and where to move. A good dancer is also a good listener. A good listener is also mindful.

Reader's Theater

While dance and music may evoke "emotional storms," as Michael Eigen (2005) puts it, Robert and June Yennie Donmoyer (2008) suggest that when engaging in reader's theater the script—according to Brecht—acts as a distancing device that allows the audience not only to feel and listen but also to think. The Donmoyers say,

> For Brecht, in other words, theater should never be escapist or tie things up in neat and tidy packages; rather it should encourage thought as well as emotion, not just empathy. Brecht, in fact, employed various distancing strategies to break the spell created by the illusion of reality on stage. (p. 213)

Reader's theater—as an art form—is Brechtian because readers use scripts rather than memorize their lines. The use of scripts, the Donmoyers suggest, is a way to make people think because, like Brechtian theater, it "break[s] the spell" (p. 213) of being on stage. Does a script really "break the spell" of the magic of theater? In the music world, since the standardization of classical music, solo performers were—and still are—forbidden to use scripts, or in this case scores. Soloists are supposed to memorize their music. But before the advent of the classical period, soloists played by reading the score on stage. For some reason, this fell out of fashion. Today a soloist who reads from a score is thought to be second rate. However, for more liberal musicians and composers, reading scores does not seem to be a problem. Both Philip Glass and Laurie Anderson, on occasion, read from scores.

It is questionable whether reading a script or score distances an audience in order to make them think. Is getting distance—intellectually and emotionally—part of an aesthetic experience? Certainly, Brecht thought so. Did the painter Rothko intend for his work to distance people? Is there a certain sense of alienation when viewing paintings by Rothko? Is alienation the same as distance? Are alienation and distance aesthetic experiences? Perhaps. Are alienation and distance part of a sublime experience? Perhaps. In music, when a composer reads a score and plays from that score, does the audience get a sense of distance? Does the reading of the score by the composer make the audience think more than if the composer memorized the score? The purpose of music is to allow people to listen. Listening can cause many emotional and intellectual responses. I do not think that the emotional and intellectual can be neatly separated. As against Brecht, I think that an audience is little affected whether or not someone reads from a score or script.

Susan H. Gere, Tsoi Hoshmand, and Rick Reinkraut (2002) write about the way in which we might experience being with people in a more aesthetic fashion if we thought of them as "characters in a play" (p. 163). This needs more explanation. Gere, Hoshmand, and Reinkraut suggest,

> Regarding a person aesthetically is clearly a different enterprise from regarding a painting or a piece of sculpture. The aesthetic regarding of a person is much more akin to the aesthetic regard that is extended to a character in a play. The writer, in creating her/his characters, is challenged to create a personage whose inner world is compelling to the viewer, a "person" to whom the audience responds. (p. 163)

To consider people characters in plays, to consider their inner lives compelling, is an interesting idea. Some people are more compelling than others. There are some very engaging people in this world, indeed. But then there are others who are not. Dewey (2005) wrote about the "enemies of the esthetic[s]" as the "humdrum" (p. 42). Certainly, many people are humdrum. Teachers see this in the faces of some of their students who do not want to be in their classes. These students are bored and would rather be playing on the computer than studying; these students are what Dewey called the "humdrum." Can teachers transform students who are humdrum and get them more interested and become more like compelling "characters in a play," as Gere et al. (2002) suggest? Perhaps a good teacher could turn humdrum students into interesting characters or try to draw out of them whatever interesting character traits they might be hiding under their masks of boredom and complacency. The role of the teacher—who also can be considered a character in a play—is to turn humdrums into characters. However, it is interesting to note that playwright Arthur Miller (2010) says, "No human being feels he's a character in a play....No human being I ever heard of. He's just living his life" (p. 161).

The Difficulty with Art

Psychoanalysis—as Freud told us—is an impossible profession. Likewise, Donald Blumenfeld-Jones (2002) tells us that there is a certain "impossibility of art" and an impossibility of speaking about it (p. 90). First, art is an impossible profession. Creating is impossible; that is, it is very difficult to create something out of nothing. In scholarship—which I consider a creative endeavor—we draw on the work of others, like dance, music, painting, or acting. But to make that work our own becomes the impossible. How to make things your own is possible only if you let go of ego and simultaneously become mindful of what you are doing. This is what Mark Epstein (2007) suggests. Composing a new piece of music is not exactly new. Composers draw on music that has been handed down to them in the past and try to make something new from something old. The same problem arises in dance, scholarship, or painting. We do not create out of a vacuum.

The second point about Blumenfeld-Jones's (2008) claim—that art is impossible to speak—raises a different issue. There are art forms that have nothing to do with words, like music, unless we are talking about singing. Instrumental music has little to do with words. How to "speak" an art form that has little to do with language? Music is formed through phrasing and breath—like speaking—but this is a different kind of speaking, almost a preverbal speaking (Morris, 2009). How to speak the preverbal? That is impossible. But for some, preverbal feelings get expressed in music. But one must be able to listen—to really listen—to perform music. In the listening is a speaking. The two are not separated. Listening speaks. The audience, too, must listen and all kinds of strange things happen when people listen to music. Sometimes music puts them to sleep; other times, it makes them pensive. Sometimes it makes them drift in a state of reverie. Interestingly enough, Maxine Greene (2004), who has done much to bring to our attention the importance of aesthetics and education, feels that if a listener falls into a state of reverie she is simply not paying attention. Greene says, "A Bach cantata cannot be realized as a work of art if the listener slips into reverie after the first fingering of the strings" (p. 21). Greene, rather, calls for "attentiveness and active participation" (p. 21). Conversely, I feel that people can appreciate a Bach cantata if it allows listeners to drift. Music can reach people on all kinds of psychological registers including drifting and reverie. I understand Greene's concern for attentiveness to the music, but this attentiveness does not have to be wholly intellectual; it can also be emotional. In fact, attentiveness involves both intellect and emotion. Of all the arts, music brings emotion up more so than, say, painting. Perhaps the emotions that are brought up are painful. Painful emotions cannot always be intellectualized. But to feel pain in the music is another way to experience art.

Greene (2001) writes about the arts and the bringing about of what she calls an "intensified consciousness" (p. 30). The performer—and here too I am thinking of the musician—must take her work with the utmost seriousness and intensity, otherwise the experience for the listener will not be intense. This intensity (of the performer) has to be somehow translated and projected out into the audience. Not an easy task. Translating and projecting a piece of music is a form of speaking without words, that is, if we are talking about strictly instrumental music. This intensity can be felt and projected to others; when this happens it is a remarkable occurrence. The intensity is not something that is willed onto the audience but is transferred onto the audience by feeling, more than anything else. If music makes one emotional, it just does and there it is: the ego cannot control it because if it is truly intense it overpowers the ego. Gary Rasberry (2002) says that "working words" helps us to enact dreams (p. 107). Music, too, helps us to dream and dreaming is not the same as intellectualizing.

The Trace

Walter Benjamin (1999), long before Derrida arrived on the scene, wrote about works of art having a "trace and aura" (p. 447). The trace is the emotional resonance that is left over after the end of a concert. There is a trace of the experience that gets encrypted in the memory of the listener. This trace might affect someone for a few days or perhaps for several weeks. When people keep thinking about what they heard, the trace of that music is permeating psyche. Also, the notion of aura—as Benjamin puts it—is another idea left out of most discussions on music. There is an aura at hand when musicians perform. The space, the instrument, the sounds, the resonances, the response of the audience all contribute to the aura of a performance. When one receives a standing ovation, the aura in that room is good. But when nobody claps or when people boo, that creates a bad aura.

Perhaps when Maxine Greene (2001) talks about active engagement with a work of art, the intellectualizing of it comes later. After listening to a concert it might take days to unpack what happened. So being "actively engaged," as Greene suggests, can be a delayed and deferred engagement because we do not always understand what we experience. Isn't there always a lag time between what we hear and what we understand?

Donald Blumenfeld-Jones (2002) suggests that dance involves both "FEELING" (p. 93) and "intellectual engagement…below the threshold" (p. 93). But what is "below the threshold?" Emotionality happens below the threshold, and when intensity is translated and projected out onto the audience then something mysterious happens that cannot be spoken. Blumenfeld-Jones suggests that the "FEELING" just is and "cannot be described" (p. 93). If the concert has little impact on us, then it wasn't a good concert. But if the concert was a good one, we are left speechless. Being left speechless is a kind of speaking. Perhaps we can't speak our feelings but we can feel them. For Blumenfeld-Jones (2008) dancing does not involve speaking, but certainly a good dancer speaks the dance through gesture and movement. Yet, like music, there is a certain ineffability about dance that cannot be spoken. This is what Blumenfeld-Jones might mean when he talks about the impossibility of speaking about the arts.

Interiority and the Arts

Ineffability also has something to do with the difficulty of expressing interiority. Elliot Eisner (2002) suggests, "The arts are means of exploring our own interior landscape. When the arts generally move us, we discover what it is that we are capable of experiencing" (p. 11). This "interior landscape," about which Eisner speaks, is hard to get at because much of it is unconscious. What moves us might be something that we do not understand. Why we are moved is a mystery. Some art forms move us more than others. Being moved is always a sensuous experience. S. Brent Plate (2005) comments, "The sensual roots of aesthetics are largely forgotten today" (p. 20). But this sensuousness is not lost on Eric Lott, who Amitava Kumar (1999) comments on when he says that "Lott's mix of memoir and music criticism…[is a form of] sensuous noise-making" (p. 2). This sensuous quality of dance is certainly not lost on Celeste Snowber (2002) who says that "bodydance" (p. 20) is a form of "sensuous knowledge" (p. 21).

Art and Empathy

Tom Barone (2000) suggests that the arts can help us to develop a more "empathic understanding" (p. 21). When someone is truly moved by a performance—as Eisner (2002) points out—empathic understanding, as Barone suggests, might become possible. There is a connection that is made sometimes—perhaps an empathic one—between, say, the musician and the audience.

But there is a counterexample to empathy and the arts. The arts do not always lead to empathy. This demands explanation. The book titled *The Reader* by Bernhard Schlink (1997) is about a woman who likes being read to because she cannot read. The problem is that she had been a Nazi camp guard and liked being read to by inmates who are soon to be gassed to death. This book was later turned into a film. We watch as years later a young boy reads to this former Nazi camp guard without knowing that she was once a Nazi. At the end of the film she is sent to prison for her complicity in the Holocaust. This is highly unlikely because hardly anybody was prosecuted (see Morris, 2001). At any rate, while in prison she teaches herself to read. Now, the question here is did her appreciation and love for literature make her more empathic? No. So we wonder why we teach the humanities if they do not serve to humanize. Not everyone can be empathic or even human. Clearly, the woman who became "the reader" in Schlink's novel never became empathic. Here I am also thinking of what is called the Heidegger Affair (see Morris, 2002b). The greatest philosopher of the 20th century was also a Nazi. Heidegger never apologized. In fact, he said very little about the Holocaust. It was his silence that condemned him in the end. Did his work in philosophy humanize him? Obviously not.

The film *The Pianist* (2002) is the story of a famous Polish pianist named Szpilman (meaning the man who plays) who escapes being murdered during the Holocaust partly because people helped him but mostly because he was lucky. A high-ranking Nazi officer is moved by Szpilman's playing of a Chopin nocturne. He was so moved that he helped to hide Szpilman. Here we have a hardened heart becoming more empathic. The scene in the film is moving as we see this very blond black-booted German nearly in tears at Szpilman's playing. He was what is termed a righteous Gentile because he saved a Jew from being murdered. Holocaust literature suggests that there were some righteous Gentiles who did in fact hide Jews from the Nazis, but they were few and far between. The upshot of this discussion is to show how complicated the idea of empathy is when talking about the arts. Sometimes the arts evoke empathy, other times not. Recall, it is Tom Barone (2000) who allows us to think through the idea of "empathic understanding" (p. 21) and the arts.

Thought and the Arts

The notion of understanding has something to do with thought. Let us think on this for a moment when it comes to the arts. To write a composition or choreograph a dance takes thought. Transitions, harmonies, tonal relations, phrases, movement, and sound all require a great deal of thought. The same can be said for the painter or the novelist. John Dewey (2005) points out that there is "the odd notion that an artist does not think" (p. 14). Creating art or performing works of art are emotional experiences but they also require thought. Performing music means that one must think about what one is doing. Thought and emotion go together when performing or composing a piece of music, acting in a play, dancing, or painting. Elliot Eisner (2008), like Dewey, says that historically the arts have not been understood as "a form of knowledge" (p. 3). Eisner explains,

> The idea that art can be regarded as a form of knowledge does not have a secure history in contemporary philosophical thought. The arts traditionally have been regarded as ornamental or emotional in character. Their connection to epistemological issues, at least in the modern day, has not been a strong one. Are the arts merely ornamental aspects of human production and experience or do they have a more significant role to play in enlarging human understanding? (p. 3)

One of the reasons that the first cuts made to school curriculum are the arts is probably because people still think of art courses as "merely ornamental," to use Eisner's words. American culture is particularly problematic because the arts are not highly valued. What we have seen in recent years is the collapsing of symphony orchestras all over the country. One wonders about the future of classical music. Is there a future in it? Conservatories across the country still draw students and turn out performers. But it is hard to make a living being a classical musician, and many symphony musicians have had to take deep cuts in salaries within the last few years. Artists in general are not supported in American culture as they are in Europe because they are not valued the way businessmen are. In American culture it seems that an individual's worth is measured by how much money he makes. Musicians do not make much money unless they are opera stars at the Met. Some musicians who play in major symphony orchestras can make good money, but most make average salaries.

The issue, as Eisner suggests, is that the arts are considered fluff. Attending a concert is a luxury in hard times. Who can afford that? Well, people still go to concerts in hard times. Music and the other arts are not merely fluff; they are the heart and soul of culture. If we cut the heart and soul out of the curriculum, our children's education is impoverished. Imagine life without music. Imagine life without art.

Most of what is on TV is what Eisner (2002) calls the "anesthetic" (p. 81). Eisner explains,

> The hallmark of the aesthetic is perhaps best known by contrast with its opposite, the *anesthetic*. An anesthetic suppresses feeling: It dulls the senses. It renders you numb to feeling. What is aesthetic heightens feelings. What is aesthetic is pervaded by an emotional tone made possible by being engaged in a world of art. (p. 81)

TV programs are dumbed down (at least on mainstream television) because they serve to suppress feelings. They make for a dull culture. Now, there are some good programs on TV but they are few and far between. Attending live concerts or live theater are ways to heighten the senses and bring heart and soul back into life.

Aesthetics and the Obscure

Here, I want to think about more obscure aspects of the aesthetic experience. Theodor Adorno (1997) captures the obscurity of aesthetics when he suggests that "art's substance could be its transitoriness" (p. 3). This is especially true with music. Music happens in time and what takes months to compose is over in thirty minutes. Music is a transitory art because it happens in time. Performing happens in time and the music as it is listened to is a momentary experience. The music floats by and the audience listens in time to notes written in time. Sounds happen in time and then disappear, leaving only—as Benjamin (1999) would put it—a "trace and aura" (p. 447). Adorno has more to say on this issue:

> Every artwork is an instant; every successful work is a cessation, a suspended moment of the process, as which it reveals itself to the unwavering eye. If artworks are answers to their own questions, they themselves thereby truly become questions. (p. 6)

The disappearance of the sound during a musical performance is a strange phenomenon, indeed. The performer has control over the dynamics of the sound produced. A good performer nuances the sounds made and makes the audience listen. The intensity of the performer will draw in the listeners. But the intensity of the sound, as Adorno puts it, always ends in a cessation. Music allows for suspended moments in time. It seems that time is drawn out by sound. Sound happens in time and time changes as the music changes.

Philip Jackson (1998), in his book titled *John Dewey and the Lessons of Art*, declares that when attending to a work of art "both the experiencer… and the object of experience have changed" (p. 5). This is not an easy idea to understand. There is an uncanny connection between the performer and the audience; if all goes right perceptions change. The audience is changed by listening. The musician is changed by performing. Then there is the space between the musician and the audience where the sound is produced. What happens in that space between the sound, the musician who produces the sound and the audience's perception of it, is a mystery and, as Adorno suggests above, raises only more questions.

The interpretation of the music by the audience is another strange event. One person interprets the music to mean one thing, while another person interprets the music differently. It is as if the music brings up images and people try to put those images into story form or into some kind of form that they can grasp, even though the music is ungraspable. Jacques Derrida (1987) suggests,

> In order to think art in general, one thus accredits a series of oppositions (meaning/ form, inside/outside, content/container, signified/signifier, represented/representer,

etc.) which, precisely structure the traditional interpretation of works of art. (p. 22)

Music heard in time seems to be formless, but there is a form because, when written down, notes are followed in succession through time and form time as they are written, even if there is a feeling of free flowingness about the music. Music is performed in some kind of form unless it is totally improvised, but still there is a form to the improvisation.

We do not really know where music comes from: it just does. Certain people have a gift for music, while others do not. Certain people have a gift for painting while others do not. We do not know where that gift comes from. But when we talk about someone like the painter Andrew Wyeth, we say he had a gift. When we see clips of Horowitz playing we say he had a gift. Still, people need to study their crafts to fine-tune them, if you will. This is the purpose of conservatories. Having a gift is not enough. One learns how to paint or how to be a musician through study. But what is this gift? We do not know. Adorno (1997) says, "It is self-evident that nothing concerning art is self-evident anymore, not its inner life, not its relation to the world, not even its right to exist" (p. 1). Maxine Greene (2001) thinks otherwise. She suggests that we can develop "the ability to feel from the inside what the arts are like and how they mean" (p. 8).

Adorno suggests, contrarily, that people do not understand "the inner life" of art (p. 1). Here I am thinking of comments Christopher Rothko (2004), Mark Rothko's son, makes about his father's paintings. Christopher Rothko comments, "He [Mark Rothko] cannot tell you what his paintings, or anyone else's, are about. You have to experience them" (p. xii). So, if the artist cannot tell you what his paintings mean how can we know—as Adorno puts it—"the inner life" (p. 1) of art? Even if the artist understood what he was doing when painting, still that does not mean that the art can easily be translated by the viewer. Interpretations of a particular painting differ no matter what the artist meant. Paintings and instrumental music have this in common—they are nonverbal. How to verbalize what is not verbal? Impossible. Christopher Rothko says that his father's paintings were preverbal (p. xi). What is preverbal cannot be made verbal. What is preverbal gets expressed through gesture, emotion. But we cannot quite put our finger on what it is that is being expressed. So when one looks at a Rothko painting, one might be dumbfounded.

What Is Art?

Elizabeth Grosz (2008) suggests, "Art is, for Deleuze, the extension of the architectural imperative to organize the space of the earth" (p. 10). Art, in other words, is a way to put our dwelling places in order, the spaces into which we are thrown. Art is a way to make order out of disorder. The world is disordered; our ego orders it. Art is a way for the ego to make sense of what is nonsensical. Art orders the Id. But the Id always has the last word. If, as Freud suggests, we are not the masters of our psychic houses, then how can we order our dwelling spaces and places through art? Again, try as we may, the Id has the last say. The order that is made from art is not order at all. The Id is the mystery. So the attempt "to organize the space of the earth" as Grosz puts it—when speaking about Deleuze and his interpretation of what art is—will always already fail. We simply cannot organize what is beyond organization. The Id drives us into the unknown, and art comes out of the Id or the unconscious and so we can never really get at what art is.

Mark Epstein (2007), in talking about the way in which D. W. Winnicott has influenced his work, quotes Winnicott, who asks about children playing with toys or people creating things: "Where are we (if anywhere at all)?" (p. 188). If we are nowhere, then how can we create an architectural space that houses our art or organizes our world? When composing where is the composer? Where is the painter when he is painting, "if anywhere at all?" Epstein also cites Christopher Bollas who talks about the "aesthetic moment" (p. 186). Epstein says,

> Another, more contemporary psychoanalyst, Christopher Bollas (1987), refers to this as an "aesthetic moment" in which "the subject feels, held in symmetry and solitude by the spirit of the object" (p. 16). These are "fundamentally wordless occasions," Bollas insists. (p. 186)

If there are no words to describe "where we are, if we are anywhere at all," as Winnicott puts it, if these are in fact "wordless occasions," as Bollas says, then how do we even begin to write about aesthetics? Can we write about aesthetics at all? Or is this a futile attempt to try to capture what simply cannot be captured in words? The arts are perhaps the most difficult subjects to talk about because the arts are mysterious. How does one come to paint? How does one become a concert pianist? How does that happen? And what happens when one plays? These questions have no answers and that is the interesting thing about writing about aesthetics.

Elitism and the Arts

There is much talk in curriculum circles about the elitist nature of the arts. Dewey and Benjamin (1999) began the conversation about moving the arts from the museum onto the streets. Most people in curriculum studies draw on Dewey's *Art as Experience* but do not much cite Benjamin's (1999) *Arcades Project*. Although Dewey and Benjamin are very different in their approach to aesthetic experience both suggest that the everyday could be considered a place to find art. Most curriculum studies scholars are troubled by the elitist tendency of the arts: the separation of the fine arts from popular culture, the separation of the arts as they get sequestered in museums and conservatories. These ideas spring from Dewey who wrote about taking the arts out of these sequestered places and thinking about the arts differently as everyday experiences. To understand what it is that many in curriculum studies are doing in what is called "arts-based education," scholars must return to Dewey, who suggests,

> Art is remitted to a separate realm, where it is cut off from the association with the materials and aims of every other form of human effort, undergoing, and achievement. A primary task is thus imposed upon one who undertakes to write upon the philosophy of the fine arts. The task is to restore continuity between the refined and intensified forms of experience that are works of art and the everyday events, doings, and sufferings that are universally recognized to constitute experience. (p. 2)

Dewey wants to integrate the arts into the everyday and make everyday life more artful. This is a way to democratize the arts so that everybody can be engaged in more artful living. When the arts are sequestered in museums and conservatories, only the elite get to contribute or be engaged in artistic undertakings. On a different level Walter Benjamin (1999) suggests,

> Streets are the dwelling places of the collective. The collective is an eternally unquiet, eternally agitated being that—in the space between building fronts—experiences, learns, understands, and invents as much as individuals do within the privacy of their own four walls. For this collective, glossy enameled shop signs are a wall of decoration as good as, if not better than, an oil painting in the drawing room of the bourgeois; walls with their "Post No Bills" are its writing desk, newspaper stands its libraries, mailboxes its bronze bust, benches its bedroom furniture, and the café terrace is the balcony from which it looks down on its household. (p. 423)

So the flaneur takes in the cityscape as if it were an artistic landscape. Dwelling in cities can become an artistic experience if one is open to it. Benjamin was one of the first to engage in cultural studies because he valued popular culture and considered everything worthy of study and engagement. Billboards, storefronts, arcades are all places where one could find the artful. Not many in curriculum studies draw on the work of Benjamin but there is much to learn from him, especially in his work on arcades. Many scholars in curriculum studies who do work on art are in some way derivative of Dewey as they suggest that art should be brought down to earth and put back in place with everyday people in everyday experiences. Most curriculum studies scholars are highly critical of the elite mentality of fine arts. Many curriculum scholars make little distinction between the fine arts and other art forms since they want to collapse the fine with the everyday. Everything can be considered art. Popular culture and high culture are two abstractions that get collapsed by curriculum studies scholars. The question about who decides what is "fine" versus what is not fine or "popular" is a political question. Still, colleges of fine arts exist in the United States and still museums abound.

Here, I want to briefly explore what it is some are saying about the collapse of the distinction between the fine and the everyday as these terms relate to artful experience. Celeste Snowber (2004) suggests,

> Each day we are invited to taste life, to drink in the colors, textures, sounds, gestures, and poetry of everyday living. Aesthetic experience does not only come in the form of theater, dance performances, literary genres, visual arts or musical compositions, but is fused into the threads and fibers of our days....Living aesthetically is intrinsic to what it means to be human on this richly textured earth. (p. 115)

Snowber is a most eloquent writer; it is obvious that she takes great care with language and is a true wordsmith. She crafts her words as if every word were a work of art. The aesthetic can be experienced by everybody at any time and anywhere. But one has to be open to these kinds of experiences. This is like the Zen tea ceremony where every sound, every sip, every swallow of tea is made mindful. Recall, this is what Buddhists term "mindfulness." And this mindfulness is what is necessary if one is to embrace a more artful way of living. Sheng Kuan Chung (2004) remarks,

> In the East, arts and aesthetics are integrated into all aspects of everyday life and are interpreted in a much broader sense. The boundary between the art object and the everyday item is not clearly drawn. An ordinary household item may possess a certain aesthetic quality depending on how the user or viewer approaches it. Using this view, the scope of the arts includes not only music and poetry, drama, painting, and calligraphy, but also other unconventional practices, such as fighting, gardening,

flower arrangement, tea drinking, and meditation....Cultivation of the mind is an-other form of art. (p. 37)

There are several things here worthy of comment. The first is that Dewey's ideas on the democratization of the arts are not dissimilar to Eastern ways of thinking. But as Chung points out, Eastern ways of thinking about aesthetics are even broader than those of Dewey or even Benjamin. In the West, people tend not to think of everyday life as artful at all because—especially in America—we are the country of fast food and business. Business deals are hardly artful since their goal is making money. Most Americans are about making money, not art.

At any rate, what is remarkable about Dewey's take on art and the every-day is that he suggests that we might even consider "bodily scarification" as an art form (p. 5). Today scarification has become popular but it is actually an ancient ritual; it is a form of marking sacred turning points. Tattooing is a form of scarification and, too, it has regained its popularity, although it is an ancient art form as well.

Where Do We Find Art?

Like other writers in curriculum studies, Maxine Greene (2001) suggests that the world can be seen as a more artful place if people are "wide awake" to it (p. 11). Greene talks about developing a way to "break through the 'cotton wool' of dailyness and passivity and boredom to the colored, sound-ing, problematic world" (p. 7). Greene directs our attention not so much to the flaneur, or to the streets, but to paintings, poems, works of literature, and music. Greene does not believe that everything is art, or that art is found on a billboard as Benjamin (1999) suggested. Greene separates art-ists from nonartists. To try to democratize the arts and make everyday life artful is one thing, but to suggest that everybody is an artist is something that Greene finds problematic. However, many arts-based educators suggest that everybody is an artist and everybody can produce works of art. Dewey's idea that artful living is a possibility for everyone is a good one. But to say that anyone can be an artist troubles. The other problem with arts-based education—which I will talk more about later—is that people who are not artists tend to romanticize the arts. There is nothing romantic about being a classical pianist. Preparing, practicing, and working on pieces is hard work. Getting to the point where you can actually perform on the stage takes years and years of concentrated study and concentrated work.

Art as Interruption

A major contribution to the field of curriculum studies as it relates to art and aesthetics is, of course, the work of Maxine Greene. She has devoted her life's work to introducing aesthetics to teachers and sharing her thoughts with readers about all kinds of things from literature to music, from film to painting. I would suggest students of curriculum studies read especially her books *Releasing the Imagination: Essays on Education, the Arts and Social Change* (1995) and *Variations on a Blue Guitar: The Lincoln Center Institute Lectures on Aesthetic Education* (2001). It is important for students to know the important work that Maxine Greene did at the Lincoln Center Institute, which is affiliated with the Juilliard Conservatory. Scott Noppe-Brandon and Madeleine Holzer (2001) explain:

> To better fulfill the new expectations, in 1975 the Institute established a partnership with Teachers College, Columbia University. A faculty committee worked out the details of the collaborations, and the college President, Lawrence Cremin, appointed one key faculty member, Dr. Maxine Greene, distinguished philosopher and authority in the field of aesthetic education, to serve as liaison with the Institute. When the Institute's Summer Session for teachers and administrators was established a year later, a series of workshops and lectures by Dr. Greene dealing with the philosophy of aesthetic education…became an integral part. (p. 3)

Students of aesthetics should read Greene's lectures that are found in her book *Variations on a Blue Guitar*. They are perhaps the most important pieces in the field of curriculum studies that deal with thinking about aesthetics philosophically. Greene suggests that she is interested in breakthroughs and certainly her book breaks ground when thinking through and thinking about the arts. One of the major themes of Greene's work concerns the blue guitar, which is part of the title of her book on lectures to teachers at the Lincoln Center Institute, but this issue is also discussed in her other work as well. In *Releasing the Imagination*, Green explains,

> I think of Wallace Stevens's "man with the blue guitar," the guitar that symbolizes imagination. The guitarist speaks of throwing away "the lights, the definitions" and challenges his listeners to "say of what you see in the dark"…These are the listeners who have been asking him to "play things as they are," because it is disruptive to look at things as if they could be otherwise. (p. 15)

Greene's brilliant use of Stevens's poetry expresses her understanding of the arts as a form of interruption or disruption. A blue guitar is not expected—especially in Wallace Stevens's day when guitars were mostly made of brown woods. The point here about Greene's work is that she suggests that aesthetics is about interruption. Most people do not like to be interrupted, as Wallace Stevens points out in his poem: people want to hear what they've always heard. Play things the way they are. And of course the larger meaning that Greene makes, drawing on Stevens's poem, is that thought is about interrupting our—as Dewey (2005) put it—"humdrum" frames of mind (p. 42). Most people do not like interference or interruption. Thinking differently is about being interrupted, Greene suggests. The arts help us to learn new things about the world by interrupting us and taking us to other places so that we can "release the imagination," as the title of Greene's book (1995) suggests. It is interesting to note that many writers on aesthetics and the arts talk about this notion of interruption. I trace this idea back to Walter Benjamin (1999) who says "to interrupt the course of the world—that was Baudelaire's deepest intention" (p. 318). Now, certain interruptions like Baudelaire's might shock. Interruptions are not necessarily shocking though. They could be ways of making us think differently; perhaps they could be ways of making us float in a space of reverie. We might be stunned by the sheer beauty of a piece of art or made to think differently by reading a historical novel that teaches us about horror, like slavery for instance. Toni Morrison's work does just that.

Richard Wolin (1994), writing about Benjamin, suggests that Benjamin was concerned with what he calls "aesthetics of horror" (p. xxvii). Wolin explains here:

> Fascism, too, placed great emphasis on the need to destroy; an avowedly nihilistic "aesthetics of horror" formed a key component of the fascist worldview. Hence, Benjamin saw the need to distance his own "conservative revolutionary" tendencies—his inclination to view radical destruction as a necessary prerequisite for cultural renewal—from those of his proto-fascist contemporaries, such as Gottfried Benn, C. J. Jung, Ernst Junger, Ludwig Klages, and Carl Schmitt. (p. xxvii)

To interrupt one's worldview is to destroy and unlearn the status quo. But this is very different from aesthetics of horror where entire peoples are murdered in order to bring in a new order. Benjamin committed suicide because he was Jewish and saw no escape from Hitler's henchmen. Interruption does not literally mean killing people who get in your way. Interruption has other meanings as well. To think differently does not necessarily entail destruction, not in a literal way. Metaphorically, we do need to destroy ideas or emotions inside of us that get in the way of our lives, like the overuse of defense mechanisms, or the overuse of the superego (which can make people sadistic) or—in contradistinction—the underutilization of the ego, where the ego has deteriorated. For schizophrenics, ego needs to be rebuilt. But for neurotics the ego needs to be, in a way, torn down because it builds walls around the psyche that prevent the introjection of the new.

Howard Eiland (2006) says, "Benjamin lays emphasis on the principle of interruption" (p. 4). And the title of Eiland's chapter "Reception in Distraction" captures what Benjamin was doing in his own work. As his life was constantly interrupted: running from the Nazis, never landing an academic position—probably because of anti-Semitism—living as a flaneur, taking in the city streets and discovering the aliveness of the city. His writing also reads like one interruption after another. For the reader who is unfamiliar with Benjamin's style, his writing can be impenetrable. He juts off from this topic to another without any transition or introduction; he was one of the first to do a form of writing called "montage."

Contained in the title of Eiland's piece on Benjamin is the word "distraction." This is what an interruption is for Benjamin, a distraction. To constantly be distracted is to be taken off guard. We think of distractions as negative experiences. But Benjamin used his own distractions in his life—being constantly on the run from the Nazis—to think through the ways in which distractions can actually help to think about art and life differently. Maxine Greene's use of Stevens's blue guitar metaphor is a distracting metaphor. We are taken off guard because when we think of a guitar it is usually not blue. When we think of art that is not distracting or art that does not serve to interrupt our humdrumness as Dewey puts it, we think of painters of the nostalgic. Art critics, according to Henry Adams (2009), took Thomas Hart Benton to task because they thought his subject matter was merely sentimental, nostalgic, and conservative. The ironic thing about Benton is that he was Jackson Pollock's teacher, and Pollock's art certainly differs from that of his teacher with his paint blobs and splotches and abstractions. The art world embraced Pollock but did not embrace Benton (Adams). An extreme example of nostalgic art is Thomas Kinkade—who most artists frown on. Kinkade's whole theme is nostalgia. Kinkade's paintings are reproduced in factory-like style.

In any event, in her book titled *Line Dancing: An Atlas of Geography Curriculum and Poetic Possibilities*, Wanda Hurren (2000) tells us, "My travel notes are interruptions. They perform a refusal to construct a smooth linear journey out of travels that have often been along winding, maze-like trails" (p. 3). Contextualization is needed here. Hurren's book is about the intersection of geography, curriculum, and dance. She explains,

> Geography can be thought of as *geo-graphy*, that is "earth-writing." It is my belief that how we *graphy* the *geo* affects and reflects in the same instant how we live in the world….I want to write/dance in the spaces between the lines that are written about the world and about curriculum; to consider how dancing, in effect, writes the world and curriculum. (p. xiv)

Dancing is an interesting metaphor for the way we move about through life. Good writing is like dancing. The dance of the writer is the ability to play with ideas and craft words just as a dancer crafts movement. Writing is about movement and good writers move sentences along to capture attention. Curriculum—as lived experience—is this dance and that is Hurren's point. Our lives could be made more artful if we thought about moving around the earth in a dancelike way. It is also interesting to note that her travel notes are not nostalgic memories but serve to interrupt her thinking.

Chess is a game of geography as the whole point is to move things around on a board. If a chess player can surprise—that is, disrupt the opponent—winning is at hand. The surprise is always about making the familiar strange. It is an interruption. Elliot Eisner (2002) has something to say about that in the context of art. Eisner states,

> Surprise is one of the rewards of work in the arts. In addition, it is from surprise that we are most likely to learn something. What is learned can then become a part of the individual's repertoire, and once it is part of that repertoire, new and more complex problems can be generated. (p. 8)

Eisner is right to talk about the importance of surprise and the way in which surprises can generate "more complex problems" (p. 8). Think of Rothko's paintings. They are surprising because it seems that nothing is happening in them. His paintings consist of huge blocks of colors, and that is it. But in that nothingness, much is going on. There is something spiritual about Rothko. It is no accident that he has a permanent installation in the Rothko Chapel in Houston. His paintings evoke a Buddhist experience of the sacredness of nothingness. The colors of his paintings stun. But one expects more. That is the problem. Expectation. As the Buddhists say, expect nothing. Rothko's paintings interrupt our notion of what a painting should be. Should a painting be a representation of something? Or nothing at all? This is hard to think. Almost a koan.

On the other hand, interruptions are not always good. Philip Jackson (1998) remarks,

> Interruptions may also occur mundanely in the form of overhead planes at an outdoor performance, talkativeness on the part of other patrons in the darkened theater, crinkling candy wrappers in the concert hall. (p. 5)

These are bad interruptions and do not generate anything but annoyance. So one mustn't romanticize the notion of interruption.

Chaos and Discontinuities

The postmoderns are not the first ones to embrace chaos and discontinuities. Walter Benjamin's work—much of it having to do with the aesthetic—preceded the postmoderns in the way he approached his subject matter. Richard Wolin (1994) explains,

> The continuity of Benjamin's lifework can only be discovered by way of discontinuities....He drew upon theoretical traditions as diverse as Jewish Kabbalist Abraham Abulafia's theological philosophy of language and the Marxist playwright Bertolt Brecht's theory of epic theater....His perpetual refusal to respect the traditional boundaries of the intellectual division of labor resulted in a work in whose fusion and subtlety and scope would be nearly unthinkable under the climate of spiritual life [or academic life] today. (p. xv)

Again, although Benjamin wrote on many different subjects, aesthetics seems to permeate his work. For Benjamin, the aesthetic experience of the world is captured only in discontinuities, as Wolin points out above. The flaneur is the anyman of the streets, not the elitist in the museum. Walking through city streets and taking in all the sights and sounds can be an aesthetic experience for the anyman or anywoman (what the Marxists might call the proletariat). The anyman who hasn't enough money to go to a museum can simply appreciate the wonders of city dwelling. This is Benjamin's major contribution to aesthetics. But the flaneur does not take things in in a logical order but in a more discontinuous way and this is perhaps why Benjamin's writing style seems discontinuous. As Richard Wolin points out his style was "intentionally asystematic [and had a] fragmentary nature [about it]" (p. xi). Is this not what the postmoderns also do in their work? Think of Deleuze and Guattari, Derrida, Zizek, and Lacan for a moment. Their work too is discontinuous, fragmentary, and hardly logical. So can one consider Benjamin a precursor to the postmoderns? Perhaps.

Stephanie Springgay (2004) too talks about art as fragments. She explains,

> Understanding the complexity of art and its relationship with fragments is a pedagogic process that serves to deepen our understanding of how identities are formed, artwork produced, and responsibilities engaged so as to enable the possibilities of generativity and transformation. (pp. 60–61)

Life is a fragmentary experience. It seems that the clock moves along linearly but what we experience is hardly linear. So too with the production of art as Springgay points out. If art reflects lived experience and the artist attempts to express her experience in the world, then thinking in terms of fragments makes sense. Our thought process is mostly fragmentary. The difficulty with writing is putting those fragments together in paragraphs that make sense to others. Academic writing is difficult because scholars have to straighten out the fragments and present words in a seemingly logical order. But as novelists like Virginia Woolf understood—or James Joyce and Samuel Beckett for that matter—stream of consciousness breaks open thought and is closer to the way people experience life. Life is not experienced as linear and logical. Philosophers, up until, say, Nietzsche, tried to straighten out fragmentary thought and make logical arguments about the world. But the world is not logical and so philosophers who tried to develop systems of philosophy failed to do so, at the end of the day, because there is no system to experience. Life is chaotic. This is what Benjamin and the postmoderns try to suggest through their writing style and subject matter.

Collage/Montage

Many curriculum studies scholars who work in aesthetics talk about the use of collage and montage, which are forms of fragmentary thought. Some might drive a wedge between the terms "collage" and "montage," but here I use the terms interchangeably. Collage and montage are not new by any means. Recall that Walter Benjamin's work is stylistically collage or montage. Richard Wolin

(1994) comments, "As Adorno has remarked, Benjamin's thought often takes on the form of a rebus; his discourse becomes a collage of images which, like a work of art that kindles one's fascination, beseeches interpretation or decipherment" (p. xi). Benjamin was perhaps one of the first writers—beside Nietzsche—to write in the style of a collage, or montage. Much of his writing is hard to understand—like Nietzsche's—but then again he is nothing like Nietzsche. One of the reasons Benjamin could write in this style is that he was not affiliated with a university. Academic writing is policed. The formal five-paragraph essay writ large is the style that journal editors want to see. The style of collage is simply not acceptable in most traditional academic journals. Curriculum theorists, however, have taken the leap into collage and write about the value of collage, aesthetics, and writing. Here I am especially thinking of Toby Daspit and Morna McDermott's (2002) work in collage. They suggest, "Each 'scrap' [in a collage] has emotional, geographical, and/or temporal significance…as the scraps were gathered during our 'trips' to personally significant places at significant times in our own shared lives" (p. 182). What is striking about this citation is that these so-called scraps of life are both emotional and have geographical significance—as Daspit and McDermott point out. What else is life beside scraps of this and that? If we think about all the moves we've made in our lives both emotionally and geographically we can better understand what they mean here. The scraps of things we leave behind are important. Scraps left behind could be associated with loss and/or regret. Scraps can also be considered our notes that we take when we are getting ready to write academic papers. Our notes are scraps of thought that are put here and there, maybe written down on napkins, in notebooks, or on dog-eared pages in books. These thought-scraps are then synthesized into a manuscript that sometimes surprises. It is amazing the way that scraps seem to have a mind of their own and come together as if by some strange force from within.

Margaret Macintyre Latta (2001) speaks to the issue of collage. She states,

> I turn to the artistic form of a collage to examine the aesthetic. A collage combines and arranges fragments into a related whole. Therefore, the collage form provides a means to pursue aspects of the aesthetic in teaching/learning/researching from varying perspectives, working towards a coherent whole. (p. 1)

Latta, twice in the above citation, makes reference to "a coherent whole." Do fragments ever become coherent or whole? For the postmoderns, no. Scholars want their writing to be coherent and whole so as to make sense to readers. However, thought remains fragmented and probably—at the end of the day—

incoherent, even to ourselves. This is what the unconscious is all about, the incoherent and hallucinatory. If we think about our dreams, this is exactly what they are. Dreams—as a product of the unconscious—are an example of what Freud calls "primary process thought." Secondary process thought is what the ego filters and connects to what Freud calls the "reality principle." But secondary process thought is only part of the picture. Most of thought is fragmented. A collage is formless and boundless. This is why it is so hard to understand Benjamin—his writing is formless and boundless. We want order but do not get it. The frame of a painting—as Derrida (1987) points out—is perhaps a delusion. The binding of a book, too, Derrida suggests, is also a delusion. The binding seems to close off our thought and wrap up the thinking into a neat tidy package—which is the purpose of a book. But really, as Derrida suggests, all of our books could be thought of as of a piece.

Other writers in curriculum studies remark on the process of collage. Gene Diaz (2002) notes, "Here I juxtapose these disparate discourses, specifically those of ethnography and painting, through a discursive collage of meaning-making in my words as ethnographer and those of John Dehlinger, painter" (p. 148). Can ethnography be thought of as a form of painting-in-words? Or can ethnography be thought of in terms of a collage? Diaz raises some interesting questions here. A modernist ethnography cannot be thought of in these terms. But a postmodern ethnography can. One could do an ethnography of a painter or paint an ethnography through words. Susan Finley (2002) tells us:

> As an educator and collagist, I have constructed life history paintings/collages of teachers, teacher educators, and homeless youth participants in my educational inquiry. Constructing collages requires a peculiar level of intimacy with images in popular culture and a critical approach to understanding. (p. 165)

Here Finley raises some interesting questions about the possibilities of life history and intersections that life history narratives might have with the arts. Can the art of history writing be thought of as an art form? Most traditional historians would say no. Most traditional historians see themselves as social scientists trying to get at some level of truth.

Imagery and Photography

I suggest that students study Nicholas Paley's (1995) book *Finding Art's Place: Experiments in Contemporary Education and Culture*. Paley writes about photography in the context of helping children who are having trouble in school or who have dropped out of school. Paley explains,

> Because it is in the city where I work, I learned about Jim Hubbard and his efforts in photography with homeless and "at risk" children in Washington D.C. at the Shooting Back Education and Media Center. I also heard about "Voices From the Streets," an acting troupe of inner-city children and adults in Washington D.C. whose performances were linked to a socially active agenda....It was at the Video Data Bank at the School of the Art Institute also in Chicago that I came across the work of Branda Miller (a video artist, curator, and editor) [who does]...video projects that engage city youth in actively examining issues such as drug use, teenage pregnancy, and school attendance. (p. 5)

It is interesting to note that Hubbard's project—which Paley mentions above—uses the word "shooting" to describe photography. Shooting is also about guns and killing. Shooting Back is a brilliant phrase that helps explain the ways in which photography can be an alternative to killing. Shooting photos is a way to still an image and capture it in time. But this stilling of the image via shooting ironically brings it to life as photos help youth better understand their world through an artistic lens. Creativity with photography is a great way for youth to express their emotions and do something that is not destructive.

Hybridization and Aesthetics: Posthuman Art

In relation to collage and montage, hybridization is another key idea that relates to aesthetics. The hybrid and collage are related, but hybridity differs in that it is a more intensified mixture of genres than collage. Donna Haraway (1997) writes about the posthuman—which ties directly into hybridization—and it is through Haraway that one can better understand aesthetics in a more posthuman and hybridized fashion. Haraway says that the posthuman is about the

> imploded germinal entities, densely packed condensations of worlds, shocked into being from the force of the implosions of the natural and the artificial, nature and culture, subject and object, machine and organic, body, money and lives, narrative and reality. (p. 14)

Posthuman aesthetics would incorporate these "densely packed condensations of worlds" that Haraway talks about here. Some scholars in curriculum studies are interested in aesthetics working in these "densely packed condensations of [art] worlds," as Haraway puts it. A good example of the posthuman aesthetic of "densely packed condensations of worlds" is jan jagodzinski's (1997) book titled *Postmodern Dilemmas: Outrageous Essays in Art & Art Education*. I would recommend students read his book if they are especially interested in the intersections of postmodern theory and art. jagodzinski writes about hybrid forms of art as he states,

> To work in the space of the "in between," postmodern art-texts have become "hybrid" texts not easily fitting into one category or another, e.g., weaved sculpture, collaged photographs and paintings—the so-called "mixed media" art-texts, performance art, earth sculpture, and actual walk-in gallery environments. (p. 86)

Here, jagodzniski mentions performance art and later mentions the work of Laurie Anderson (p. 82). I have (2009) also written on Laurie Anderson in *On Not Being Able to Play*. I state,

> While attending the Spoleto Festival in Charleston, I had the opportunity to see Laurie Anderson perform....It was truly an amazing experience. What I learned from this [performance] is that she is NOT monolingual in any sense. She is a performance artist and does a variety of things. As I see it she is a poet, a storyteller, a musician, a visual artist, a cultural critic, a cultural studies scholar in fact. She sings, plays the electric violin, plays keyboards, does multimedia visuals, tells stories and comments on politics. (p. 278)

Laurie Anderson has been doing performance art since at least the early 1980s. She has collaborated with such notables as Philip Glass, William Burroughs, Lou Reed, and more. She is artistic, creative, and highly critical of American politics. Anderson is what I would call a posthuman artist as her work crosses boundaries and mixes genres.

Toby Daspit and Morna McDermott (2002) engage in a posthuman aesthetic. They state,

> Following that conversation [with Wanda Hurren], we continuously return her words, tumbling over the visual, aural, and spatial ideas in our heads, turning concepts over, inverting frameworks; how to hear spaces; how to see sounds? A question emerges and begins to gnaw at the periphery of our brains: How can performance and representation be hybridized across the context of time and space? (p. 179)

Notice here the use of the word "hybridized" and also note the mixing up of sounds and spaces, seeing sounds and hearing spaces; this is a more posthuman way of understanding the "densely packed condensations" of art that Haraway talks about. When art causes our senses to mix and merge, our perceptions are altered and everything becomes more "densely packed" and mixed up. The posthuman is the mixing up of everything, machine, nonhuman animal, human animal, but also the mixing up of genres, realities, and even hallucinatory realities. Isn't hearing spaces hallucinatory? Seeing sounds is another form of mixed-up reality. When a composer hears music in her head, is she not hallucinating those sounds? Where are they coming from? Music takes up space in the mind—and here I am thinking of the question that Daspit and McDermott raise about hearing spaces. Isn't composing about putting sound in space and time and also the ability to capture what is heard in that space in the mind? Artists are able to mix up senses and use that mix to make something, to create something. Musicians talk about the color of a pitch, or the colors that are generated by certain chord structures. Overtones produce auras, some grating, others beautiful. Overtones are also associated with colors. Musicians intuit that overtones produce the richness and density of sound that are needed in order to break through the deadness of the everyday.

Another posthuman aesthetic is the work of Sandra Weber (2008) as she writes about "a wide range of visual forms, films, video, photographs, drawings, cartoons, graffiti, maps, diagrams, cyber graphics, signs, and symbols" (p. 43). It is interesting that Weber considers cartoons and graffiti as art. Of course this is not new. Still many people consider cartoons as junk and graffiti as a crime. At any rate, it would take someone very talented to work across genres to do this. Alex F. de Cosson (2008) comes to mind here as he says,

> I build a sculpture out of text. This text is textu(r)al, a hybrid text, built from words and print fonts. I conceive of fonts as similar to various bits of string or wire that I use to build a sculpture. These are visual connecting devices that help compose the texture (a fundamental sculpture reality). (p. 277)

The title of de Cosson's piece is also of note as it signifies hybridization. His piece is titled "Textu(r)al Walking/Writing Through Sculpture." Let us deconstruct this title for a moment to think through what he is doing. Text, of course, can be anything, not only writing. A billboard can serve as text—as we learned from Walter Benjamin—the entire city can be text; it is all grist for the mill when thinking about aesthetics. The idea of walking in De Cosson's title is of interest because walking can also be thought of as an art form. Dance is a form of walking, walking can be dance-like.

How does one "write through sculpture" as de Cosson puts it? Does the artist write a three-dimensional art form (the sculpture) in space? Does writing about sculpture change the work through the writing? De Cosson raises some fascinating questions in this piece.

A posthuman aesthetic is evident in the work of Mary Beth Cancienne (2008) who tells us, "For more than fifteen years, I have choreographed dance performances based on literary pieces, curriculum theory writings, and autobiographical reflections" (p. 397). Notable are the intersections of many different genres blurring together: dance, choreography, literature, curriculum theory and autobiography. Choreography is an interesting word. It sounds like geography and is like geography as it deals with movement through space. But that movement must be written and so the choreo part of the geography becomes text. But the text that a dancer follows is different from, say, the score that a composer follows. Both are text, but they lead to different forms of art. Dance, though, is usually performed to music so the dancer must have a musical ear as well as a sense of bodily movement in time and across space. That is where geography comes in. Recall Wanda Hurren (2000) is the scholar who speaks to these issues of geography as a way of dancing through the world. Cancienne adds to Hurren's work because she also includes the use of literature. Dancing to literature is an interesting hybridization. In the dance, Cancienne suggests, is the autobiographical element upon which she draws to express her art. Is all art somewhat autobiographical? T. S. Eliot would say no. Adam Kirsch (2005) tells us, "Eliot set the tone for an era when he proclaimed that poetry must be impersonal" (p. xiii). Does the muse speak from an impersonal source, such as the objective psyche or what the Jungians call the collective unconscious? Or not? Nicholas Basbanes (2010) interviews literary critic Alfred Kazin who talks about his own books and says,

> A lot of my books came out of deep personal urgency, which had nothing to do with anything but my own problems or my own interests…I wrote *On Native Grounds* and published it in 1942 because that was the time for me to write it for me. *For Me*. (p. 121)

Do we write mostly for ourselves? Kazin does. Many of us write out of our own personal histories. So how T. S. Eliot thought he could write from an objective muse is curious.

Rita Irwin (2004) has another way of expressing what I call the posthuman aesthetic. In "A/r/tography: A Metonymic Metissage," the introduction to her co-edited collection with Alex de Cosson, she says,

> Over the last decade, we have witnessed the growth of arts-based forms of research through narrative, autobiography, performative ethnography, reader's theater, poetic inquiry, and self-study, among many other forms of creative inquiry. (p. 28)

Think all of these art forms together and what emerges is a posthuman aesthetic. Most people, however, focus on one form of art over/against another and do not blend genres. But what if we were to bend genres? Playwright Arthur Miller (2010) says that he is "in a sense…always bending time" (p. 162). Time does bend and so, too, does the universe. But to be aware of the bending of time or the blending of genres, which is a form of bending, is something that takes much talent and intuition. Rita Irwin tells us,

> From a socio-cultural perspective, metissage is a language of the borderlands, of English-French, of autobiography-ethnography, of male-female. Metaphorically, these borderlands are acts of metissage that strategically erase the borders and barriers once sustained between the colonizer and the colonized. (p. 29)

"Metissage" is another term for hybridization. Can we think these things together as Irwin suggests? Thinking things together is what hybridization is; confusing all the categories is what the posthuman is about. When most people talk about the posthuman they only include discussions of cyborgs. But when we speak of metissage—in the sense that Rita Irwin discusses it—we can extend our discussion of the posthuman to include art that blends things together. What strikes me about Irwin's citation above is that she talks about the colonizer and the colonized in the context of intellectual policing. Colonizers police intellectual borders. The academy is certainly colonizing in that way. Can you be both scholar and musician? Does composing count toward tenure if one is a curriculum theorist? Does documentary filmmaking count if one is a curriculum studies scholar going up for tenure? Rishma Dunlop (2004) speaks to these issues as she states,

> My life as an academic includes my life as an artist, a poet and fiction writer. In an era when women artists continue to be underrepresented in the art world and in the domains of scholarly activity, our collective aims will be to increase awareness of the immense educational possibilities in the links between cognition and artistic creation. When I ask women scholars who are artists to reflect on their artistic practices and

their identities as artists and teachers, I frequently discover they have felt pressured to suppress their identities as artists. (p. 149)

Dunlop speaks for many women artists who are also academics, and she worries that women especially need to be concerned when it comes to the tenure process if they include in their materials their creative works.

Dance the Dance

Male dancers are shunned, not only in aesthetic education but also in the dance world itself. Michael Gard (2006) has written a fascinating study of male dancers that gives us a historical overview of men and dance in his book titled *Men Who Dance: Aesthetics, Athletics & the Art of Masculinity*. Gard states early on in the book that his "focus is on those Western forms of dance which appear to have been at odds with Western masculinity" (p. 5). Gard also states, "Little scholarly attention has been paid to the experience of male dancers. Within the growth of dance scholarship over the last 20 years, dance research has, not unreasonably, concentrated on the experiences of women" (p. 5). The art of dance, perhaps more so than other arts, is gendered. Men who dance, says Gard, are always already suspect. Here is what Gard has to say about why this might be so: "A dancing son may represent a potentially unmanageable threat to the internal cohesion, public respectability and cultural legitimacy of this family" (p. 41). The real fear about this "unmanageableness" concerns "the assumption of homosexuality" (p. 42). This might be the case but when we think of famous ballet dancers mostly men come to mind, for example, Vaslav Nijinsky and Mikhail Baryshnikov. For most laypeople, the only famous female dancer who comes to mind is the modern dancer Martha Graham. So even though homophobia plays a role in the way the West has viewed male dancers, it seems—still—that only male dancers get famous, gay or not. Interestingly enough, Gard points out that "it is noticeable that much of the writing about Nijinsky (and male dancers more generally) appears to ignore or excuse his sexuality" (p. 55). Recently Broadway put on a production of *Billy Elliot*, which originally was a 2000 film. Billy Elliot is born into a working-class rough-and-tumble British family and has a hard time convincing them, especially his father, that dance is an okay thing to do for a boy. Much of the musical deals with Billy's Oedipal drama with his father, but there is little in the play that would suggest anything about Billy's sexuality. Broadway skirted the issue of homosexuality.

Drama

Another interesting art form that is highly gendered (and also suspect) is drama, as Kathleen Gallagher (2000) points out in her important book titled *Drama Education in the Lives of Girls: Imagining Possibilities*. Gallagher states that drama is thought to be a soft subject and is associated with femininity. She states,

> I have always found it curious that in schools (and most markedly in high schools) drama is considered a "lightweight subject, soft, of the emotions—in essence for girls. Drama is a gendered subject, not masculine like math and sciences, which are hard, of the mind and *not for girls*." (p. 5)

The irony here is that when we think of famous playwrights who do we think of? Men. What famous women playwrights can we think of? When it comes to making it in the real world of drama, the men seem to win out again. So it seems that the arts—like mostly every other field—are sexist. There have been thousands of women composers, for example, throughout history but few of them are known or performed. Nadia Boulanger was perhaps the most famous female composer but she was only known as a teacher. She also was one of the first women to conduct a symphony orchestra, but many of the male orchestra members were highly disrespectful toward her (Morris, 2009). Still, today, it is rare to hear the work of women composers played in the classical music world. The classical music world, too, is highly sexist. There are few women conductors still. And most of the winners of the Van Cliburn Competition are males because the judges tend to be misogynist (personal communication, Raymond Gitz). Most of the successful concert pianists are men—think of all the names that come to mind: Vladimir Horowitz, Arthur Rubenstein, Misha Dichter, Gary Graffman, and Alfred Brendel. Martha Argerich is one of the few women pianists to make it big. But most women concert pianists—if they make it that far—fade into the background and are forgotten in the dustbin of history.

What Art Form Counts as Art?

Not all the arts are valued the same. For some, the visual arts seem to take on more importance than, say, dance, drama, or music. Some scholars of art, such as Walter Benjamin, had no use for music. Benjamin (1994) says in a letter dated 1917 to one Ernst Schoen:

> Yesterday we saw a young musician whom I met several years ago when he first arrived from Wickerdorf. I knew him as a charming and quiet boy who, even then, was completely absorbed in music…but what I found was a young man who…had lost the singular beauty that had characterized him.…But let me speak frankly: he had developed a hump. The spiritual impression he made on me was concentrated on this image.…the hump suddenly seemed to me to be a characteristic of most modern people who devote themselves to music. It is as if they are seemingly deformed; as if they were carrying something heavy on top of something hollow. (p. 95)

This is an astonishing admission on Benjamin's part. For a man who so appreciated his walks through the city and saw art in everything, his distaste for music seems rather—well—appalling. There are some people who are tone deaf and perhaps to them music is little more than noise. Perhaps Benjamin was tone deaf. He certainly found music irritating, to say the least. Freud felt the same way and only attended the Vienna Opera to further work on his scholarly papers. He had no use for music either (Morris, 2009). I note in *On Not Being Able to Play* that in the field of curriculum studies music tends to be overlooked as an art form. There are some articles and book chapters written on music and there is only one edited book on the subject, titled *Sound Identities: Popular Music and the Cultural Politics of Education* (McCarthy, Hudak, Miklaucic, & Saukko, 1999). My 2009 book is the only full-length book that treats music in a psychoanalytic fashion. Most of the work being done in arts-based education is on visual art, not music. One must wonder why visual arts seem more acceptable to write about in arts-based education. Why is music still a marginalized subject?

Art and Politics

Some scholars argue that art and politics are natural bedfellows. Historically, one can trace this discussion—at least in the 20th century—back to Walter Benjamin. Andrew Benjamin (2006) states,

> Central to any discussion of the work of art in the contemporary period…is Walter Benjamin's text "The Work of Art in the Age of its Technological Reproduction".…The history of the work's production provides an important glimpse into the contested nature between art and politics in the late 1930s. More exactly, the final version provides a way into an understanding of the role of art in any analysis of fascism as well as in finding possible avenues of response to its emergence. (p. 1)

What is missing from Andrew Benjamin's article is the larger historical back-drop of Nazism around which Walter Benjamin was trying to flee. The Nazis embraced certain artists while excoriated others—mainly for being Jewish. Certain musicians were considered Hitler's musicians, like Carl Orff. While on the other hand, Gustav Mahler—who at the time was writing music and conducting the Vienna Philharmonic—left his position because his music was thought to be degenerate. After Mahler left Vienna, nearly all of the Jew-ish musicians who worked under him were let go (Morris, 2009). Artists had choices to make with the rise of the Third Reich. If they were not Jewish, they could stay on, but they could have chosen also to quit out of protest because all music production was controlled by Hitler's henchmen. Clearly in the case of Carl Orff, he chose to stay. Pablo Casals, on the other hand, was dubbed the cellist of conscience because he refused to play in Spain—his own country—while Franco was dictator. Casals played elsewhere, but chose self-exile as a political statement (Morris, 2009).

Many curriculum theorists tie together art and politics in a variety of ways that I would like to briefly explore here. Americans and Canadians have had a different history than the Europeans; thus, their interests in art and politics differ from that of the Europeans. History and geography make a difference in the way that people view these matters. One of the best theorists on politics and the arts is the late Landon Beyer (2000). His book, *The Arts, Popular Culture, and Social Change*, is one of the most important texts in the field of curriculum studies that deal with the connections between art and politics. Here, I will comment on a few things that strike me in Beyer's text. Beyer states early on:

> Moreover, as we have become more aware in the recent past—and as this book demonstrates—in order to understand the meaning and value of the arts, we must situate them within the cultural, social, political, economic, and ideological contexts out of which they emerge....This perspective places the arts within a complex, often contradictory set of tendencies...making the understanding of any particular work of art much more complicated than its meaning when filtered through, say, theories that hold significant form or beauty as the central foci. (p. x)

As was mentioned earlier, traditional theories of aesthetics are about the-ories of beauty. But political scholars, like Beyer, point out that this focus is not only too narrow but also misses the larger sociopolitical context into which the artwork is produced. Like art, scholarly work might also be better understood against the larger sociopolitical context in which it is produced.

Political scholars like Beyer might argue that training in classical music is elitist and even the word "classical" takes on a political hue. Who decides what is "classic" and what isn't? Why is jazz not considered classic or why is some rock called "classic rock?" Some political theorists would argue that performing classical music or composing in the classical genre is highly conservative. The music conservatory is a highly conservative institution. Where do students learn about popular music? Certainly not in most conservatories.

Beyer tells us,

> Issues in philosophical aesthetics have misunderstood the relationship between politics and culture, the arts and meaning, in society and in schools; and how they have constricted the nature of aesthetic value. (p. 25)

Many philosophers who work in aesthetics have skipped over the political as it intersects with art but instead focus on the traditional notion of beauty. The idea of the Beautiful is like the philosophical idea of the Truth or the idea of the Good. All of these notions are problematic but throughout the history of Western philosophy these ideas dominated the writings of most philosophers. Since the advent of postmodernism, all of these ideas have been turned on their heads. Postmodernism is at loggerheads with the Platonic notion of Ideals such as Truth, Beauty, and the Good. These are reified ideals that have little to do with the way we experience the world, especially since WWI, the Holocaust, the dropping of atom bombs, Vietnam, 9/11, and other hideous atrocities. Landon Beyer, though, does not want to claim the postmodern, but rather he engages in Marxist (p. 9) aesthetics. His primary interest is the way that the arts are an issue of class and elitism. But there is more to it than that. The arts have everything to do with race, gender, and class as we've been discussing throughout this chapter. The postmodern theorists on art, like Deleuze and Guattari, however, are not so much concerned about race, class, and gender as they are interested in more abstract notions of chaos and discontinuity as a form of political thinking. They too talk of art in a "constricted" manner—to use Beyer's term—because they do not deal much with race, class, and gender.

Susan Finley (2008) addresses race, class, and gender when talking about the intersection of the arts and politics, as she states,

> Arts-based education is uniquely positioned as a methodology for radical, ethical, and revolutionary research that is futuristic, socially responsible, and useful in addressing social inequities by its integration of multiple methodologies used in the arts with

the postmodern ethics of performative, action-oriented, and politically situated perspectives for human social inquiry, arts-based inquiry has the potential to facilitate
critical race, indigenous, queer, feminist, and boarder theories. (p. 71)

Finley's tightly packed citation covers all the bases. Like Finley, Stephanie
Springgay (2004) states, "I paint and sew, collage and create as an act of violence, as a form of political resistance" (p. 73). Like Springgay, Kathleen Gallagher (2007), in her book titled *The Theater of Urban: Youth and Schooling in
Dangerous Times*, reminds us of the political work of drama. Gallagher states,

> Drama, born in the writings of Augusto Boal and theatre of the oppressed, transforms
> the space. Even in tired spaces of urban schooling, bad lights, graffitied desks, broken
> chairs and dreams "there is always the possibility of both identification with and
> distance from the drama." Indeed, the drama class offers "an aesthetic experience that
> resides in the connection between what a person already knows…feels, and desires
> with what a new experience might offer." This contrasts so fundamentally with the
> everyday praxis of schooling and social life, where urban youth are cast routinely as
> dangerous or invisible. (p. xii)

Giving youth the chance to act in plays would enable them to express their
frustrations, desires, loves, and disturbances. Acting is a great outlet for all
kinds of expression. Gallagher rightly points out that the experience of being
part of a dramatic production gives youth a new sense of themselves and makes
them feel like they are somebody. The irony about the perceived dangers of
urban youth is that most school violence has happened in upper-middle-class
white suburban areas. The perceived dangers of urban youth have everything
to do with racism. However, the majority of school shootings in the United
States has been committed by white children.

If drama, however, is seen as a soft and a feminine form of expression—as
Gallagher (2000) points out in her other work—I wonder how the boys in
these classrooms take to acting out parts in a play? Are they resistant to doing this? Who is theater of the oppressed for, boys or girls? And who are the
oppressed? Youth at large? Black youth? Girls? White suburban boys? If boys
acting in plays are being perceived as effeminate, does this make them turn
to violence to deal with their own crisis of masculinity? Many questions are
raised by reading Gallagher's (2000; 2007) important and interesting work on
drama in the classroom.

Another kind of political form of art is art that offends. Here I am thinking of the work of Karel Rose and the late Joe Kincheloe (2004) in their important book titled *Art, Culture, and Education: Artful Teaching in a Fractured*

Landscape. Kincheloe (2004a) examines the response to what was called the Sensation Exhibit in New York City. This exhibit was offensive to some—especially Mayor Rudy Giuliani. Kincheloe (2004a) tells us,

> Portraying himself as a cultural cop, the mayor sought to cultivate the image of a brave crusader fighting the lonely battle for decency in a corrupt world. In the years preceding the "Sensation exhibit" Giuliani sought out transgressive artists, often ordering their arrest and confiscation of their art. Indeed, in the first four years of his administration Giuliani ordered over 700 illegal arrests. (p. 15)

This is shocking to those of us who know little about New York City politics. It gets worse. Kincheloe (2004a) goes on to say that this scandal was aired on national TV when

> again, "Giuliani versus the art world" became a national story; Jay Leno on the *Tonight Show* referred to the mayor as a fascist. The comedian was not alone as numerous Giuliani-Hitler comparisons erupted around the country. Leno delineated the Fuhrer's efforts to rid Germany of what he called degenerate art. (p. 16)

This incident raises many questions about art, indeed. In Nazi Germany degenerate art was usually considered Jewish art. "Degenerate" was also a word bandied about during the Eugenics craze in the United States, another code word for racism. The thing that strikes me the most about Giuliani's responses to art is that he was in some way threatened by it. Is art so powerful as to be threatening? Does arresting people keep them from creating more art? Think of the case of Antonio Gramsci whose writings were so threatening to the Fascists that they talked about shutting off his brain so he could never write again—but that attempt failed because his manuscripts were smuggled out of prison and we have them today in his *Prison Notebooks*. You simply cannot suppress the creative spirit. The repressed will find a way back.

What offends one person might not offend another. And even if the art is offensive to some, why would you throw someone in prison for that? Drawing a picture is not the same as killing someone. Murderers should be thrown in prison, not artists or writers (in the case of Gramsci). What this suggests is that art (of any genre) is powerful and affects people in ways that are too complex to even describe. For a mayor to arrest artists because he thought that the content of their art offensive is absurd and criminal. The mayor's job is not to police art but to govern a city.

Amitava Kumar (1999) argues "for a poetics that is political" (p. 2). Kumar's use of the word "poetics" is rather broad as he considers all of the arts as a form of poetics. He cites two interesting examples of the ways in which music as a form of the poetic can be political. He talks about the work of Eric Lott and Samir Gandesha as political—poetic musicians. Kumar notes

> Eric Lott's mix of memoir and music criticism wherein he looks closely at what he calls "the political richness of sensuous noise-making." Or Samir Gandesha's exploration of Punk as a model of multiculturalism when mapped against the larger contradictions of the postcolonial city. (p. 2)

My impression of punk music is that it has to do with the crisis of white masculinity. There is a spectrum of punk that has moved beyond this crisis though. Students will learn more about this in the chapter on cultural studies curriculum concepts.

Amitava Kumar also talks about the potential of dance to become a more political art form. He states,

> More recently, Randy Martin…published his *Critical Moves: Dance Studies in Theory and Politics*, which deploys dance as language of political mobilization to counter the notion of arrested motion that has too often, and perhaps too conveniently, served as the image of the crisis of left politics. (p. 5)

I am compelled to read Randy Martin's work on dance that might jumpstart—if you will—the left. Dance, too, then can be a political art form. One could argue that all art is political, that everything is political. But some would disagree.

Integrating the Arts into the Curriculum

This is the last brief section of this chapter and here I will be looking at what some curriculum scholars have to say about integrating the arts into the curriculum. Tom Barone (2000) comes to mind as he suggests that students become engaged in what he calls "aesthetic projects" (p. 128). Barone states,

> Aesthetic projects can be fashioned almost anywhere: in the science corner, in the library, in the nearby community, in the studio. They occur as students embark on the production of a class play, on an investigation of the political history of their town, on the creation of an essay about a facet of the natural world. (p. 128)

Reading Barone brings to mind once again Dewey's (2005) call for the democratization of art. Bringing art out of sequestered places like museums is a step toward the democratization of the arts. But there is more to it than that.

What Barone is suggesting here—much like Dewey—is that being more artful means experiencing life more aesthetically. That is, anything can be experienced more aesthetically if we are open to it. What strikes me in Barone's quote above is that he talks about science as being an opening to aesthetics. How many scientists also think of themselves as artists? Is there an art to science? Well, maybe so. But more traditional scientists probably do not think that art has anything to do with science. But then again when we think about medicine as a science we think about the medical arts. There is an art to medicine, there is an art to diagnosis. There is an art to treating patients. But again, some doctors do not treat patients artfully or tactfully.

Like Tom Barone, Madeleine Grumet (2004) talks specifically about school programs that have integrated the arts into the curriculum. She states,

> The arts integration programs of the Chicago Arts Partnerships in Education (CAPE), Arts for Academic Achievement (AAA) in Minneapolis, the Conservatory Lab Charter School in Boston, North Carolina's A plus Schools and Curriculum Music, and Community Project (CMC), and the Lincoln Center Institute in New York grow from the conviction that the strong emotions which inform both art and academic work cannot be isolated from the relationships of students to each other, to their teachers, and to their communities. (p. 51)

I have already discussed Maxine Greene's work with the Lincoln Center Institute that Grumet mentions here. That there are these other programs across the country signifies that art is a part of the curriculum here and there, but as Tom Barone points out most Americans think that art is frivolous and is not really an academic subject. Barone says

> Despite the lip service sometimes paid to the arts, the American public (including legislators and many educators) obviously does not share our devotion to a belief in their intrinsic worth. Perhaps a generally low level of aesthetic literacy prevents a sizable number from appreciating the profundity of the life-enhancing capacities of the arts; perhaps not. (p. 95)

So the art programs that Grumet mentions are few and far between. Most of American public education has little room in the curriculum for the arts. And as I mentioned earlier, when budgets shrink the first things to get cut are the arts. Nick Rabkin (2004) argues that there are "deep structural connections between the arts and other subjects" (p. 8), and he too calls for the arts to be more integrated into and across the curriculum. And jan jagodzinski (1997) argues, "Art and art education should make its way to the interdisciplinary field of cultural studies rather than continue to confine itself to the fine arts tradition as a 'discipline'" (p. xiv). But if art becomes a part of cultural studies, does that not water down art as a field of study? Music can be treated through the lens of cultural studies but I do not think that it constitutes cultural studies. Dance is a field of study, it is not cultural studies, but I suggest that dance can be studied through a cultural studies perspective. If one moves the arts into cultural studies, the integrity of these various fields of study suffer. Being interdisciplinary is fine and perhaps everything should be treated in an interdisciplinary fashion so as to deepen the discussion, but there is such a thing as disciplinarity. Curriculum studies is a discipline, a field with a history that can be studied through different theoretical frameworks but curriculum is not cultural studies. If scholars say that curriculum studies is really cultural studies then what happens to the field? It disintegrates. So too with the various fields of music, art, dance, painting. These fields of study all have their own histories and are all disciplines in and of themselves. But I agree that these fields should be studied in a broader fashion.

· 3 ·

SPIRITUAL
CURRICULUM CONCEPTS

Introduction

In this chapter I begin with a general introduction to spirituality in its connection to religion, aesthetics, ecology, and depth psychology. I then explore
some major concepts emerging in the interstices of curriculum studies and
spirituality such as soul, holy sparks, interiority, mysticism, ecospirituality,
spiritual and social activism, and bearing witness to Jewish identity.

Spirituality and Religion

A debate in the field of religious studies turns on whether or not one can de-
tach spirituality from a particular religion. Most religious studies scholars will
say no. Spirituality is always connected to a tradition. Spirituality does not
come out of nowhere. The two earliest curriculum theorists who worked in
the area of spirituality were Dwayne Huebner (1999) and James Macdonald
(1996). Both of these curriculum theorists' writings on spirituality are steeped
in the Christian tradition. Current curriculum theorists who write on spirituality are indebted to both Macdonald and Huebner because they opened the
door for this kind of work to be done in the field of curriculum studies.

Spirituality, Aesthetics, Ecology, and Depth Psychology

The spiritual ties both into aesthetics and ecology. According to Edmund Morris (2005) Beethoven "insisted on kneeling prayers in the morning and evening" (p. 199). He considered his Pastorale Symphony "a religious utterance" (pp. 199–200). Morris also suggests that Beethoven was a sort of pantheist (p. 199). His pantheism (that God is everywhere and in everything) was steeped in the Christian tradition. Spinoza's (2002) version of pantheism is different because he was Jewish so his pantheism reflects the Jewish tradition. There are all kinds of pantheisms. For example, the Hindus have millions of gods and goddesses, but not all Hindus see Hinduism this way.

There are, likewise, scholars in ecology who talk of ecospirituality, especially the Jungians. Depth psychology as it was initially formulated by Jung has spiritual overtones. One of the most important books on this issue is by Gary Lachman (2010), called *Jung the Mystic*. Jung also has many nature writings as well. So Jung could be considered an ecologist, a spiritual writer, and the founder of depth psychology. The spiritual, the aesthetic, the ecological, and the psychological all intertwine. But each of these areas has its own history and is a field in and of itself, but there certainly is a lot of crossover.

Major Themes

What I propose to do here is share with readers some of the major themes that come up in the current literature on the interstices of curriculum theory and spirituality. This is a fascinating area of study. A layperson might think that spirituality is a natural fit for the discipline of religious studies. But, in fact, it is not. The field of religious studies is at loggerheads with the notion of the spiritual. Religious studies—although interdisciplinary—is mostly based on theology, which is very different from spirituality. Theology is based on systems of thought much like philosophy but the focus is more narrow than philosophy. Scholars of pastoral studies are more likely to take the issue of spirituality seriously. Pastoral studies and religious studies are two different fields within theology. Jungian depth psychologists also take the issue of spirituality seriously and so too do curriculum theorists.

Spirituality, in both the Jewish and Christian traditions, has always been on the margins of thought. There are Christian mystics and Jewish mystics, Sufi mystics, and so forth. But these mystics have always been seen as outliers or even heretics. So it makes sense that curriculum studies scholars are interested in spirituality because it is an issue that falls on the outside of tradition. Curriculum studies in general is interested in looking at things differently and looking at what has been left out of the tradition, or left out of the traditional canon.

What is also interesting about spirituality is that it can fall either to the left or the right politically and so we have to be careful to understand who it is we are studying. Here, I am exploring writers of the spiritual who are to the left politically. Spirituality can easily turn into dogma and cultism and take a rightward turn. That is dangerous. There is a fine line we walk here and scholars must be careful to know who it is they are reading and what their political position is because—as Philip Wexler (2008) so aptly points out—politics and spirituality are of a piece. Wexler states, "Perhaps more importantly, the current interest in spirituality has to be understood politically, as part of that very same quest to undermine the alienating effects of global capitalist social organization" (pp. 2–3). Like Wexler, David Purpel (2004), Roger I. Simon, Sharon Rosenberg, and Claudia Eppert (2000), and H. Svi Shapiro (2006; 2010) write in the intersections of spirituality and politics. It is an interesting thought that one can be both a critical theorist and spiritual thinker. Students must not forget that Paulo Freire was one of the earliest educational theorists who was both Marxist and deeply Christian. Of course liberation theology— the movement out of which Freire worked—was all about the intersection between Marxism and Christianity. Many writers on spirituality tend to separate politics from the spiritual and focus only on notions of soul, heart, and the divine. However, scholars need to think the spiritual and the political together as Wexler, Purpel, Simon, Freire, and Shapiro all suggest.

Spirit and Soul

Some writers on spirituality prefer the word "soul" to "spirit" or the word "spirit" to "soul," or some collapse the two. In the Jewish tradition there is no holy ghost or what is sometimes called spirit. But often, Jewish writers talk both of spirit and soul. In the Buddhist tradition, generally speaking, there is no notion of soul, self, or God. One must be careful not to generalize religious terms across traditions.

Christianity, Judaism, and Buddhism

What are mostly reflected in the writings of curriculum scholars are basically three traditions: Christianity, Judaism, and Buddhism. There have been some writings on Taoism, Sufism, and Sikhism but mostly the work has centered on Christianity, Judaism, and Buddhism; therefore, I will be working mostly with these three traditions. When studying religious traditions, too, one must be careful when comparing not to think that religious traditions are all the same because they are not. The world religions (Hinduism, Buddhism, Christianity, Islam, Judaism, Ba'hi, Sikhism, Taoism, Confucianism, and more) are all vastly different from each other. The danger with any comparative study is that some scholars tend to focus on similarities and not differences. Focusing on similarities flattens out traditions. I think that scholars must focus on the differences because the more one studies, say, Christianity—in all its varieties—one better understands how vastly different its history is from, say, Judaism, even though the roots of Christianity are found in Judaism. And all variations of Christianity are not the same. In Judaism there are at least three different branches if you will: reformed, conservative, and orthodox. All three of these branches differ. In Buddhism there is the Mahayana and Theravadan traditions and these are very different from each other.

Soul as Energy

The notion of soul is not exactly postmodern if it is thought of as a core or substance. But there are other ways of thinking of the soul in a more postmodern way. John Miller (2000) thinks of soul in this more postmodern sense as he states,

> Another way of seeing ourselves as part of Sophia [a word that also means wisdom] is to imagine, as Jung did, that the soul is mostly outside the body. In other words, we can see our souls as not localized within ourselves but as an energy field that extends beyond our physical Being. This concept is similar to Heidegger's notion of *Dasein*, or "force field." (p. 37)

If we can imagine soul as something that moves beyond our own interiority it helps us to better understand how interconnected we are, not just with other humans but also with nonhuman animals and objects. Object-relations theory—founded by Melanie Klein—is all about the interrelation between self and other, but only the Jungians—in the field of depth psychology—talk in terms of soul. However, Jung's notion of the soul tends to be impersonal because it pervades all things. In contradistinction to Jung, Freud does not use the word "soul." Freud had no truck with spirituality and shied away from words like soul because of the religious overtones of the term. Freud considered himself a scientist—so too did Jung—but unlike Jung, Freud did not use the term "soul" to describe the inner workings of the psyche.

If the soul is like a force field of energy—as Miller puts it— physics comes to mind. Physicist Jeremy Hayward (1999) talks in terms of the soul in connection with

> [a] spectrum of finer and finer "energy," but it is not just physical energy. There is an inner aspect to this spectrum as well. Energy is very closely related to awareness in direct experience....I would call it "awareness-energy" or "psycho/spiritual/material energy." Something to show the unity of material with mental/spiritual, outer with inner. So there is a continuous spectrum of finer and finer, subtler and subtler, levels of energy....Even at the level of rocks. (p. 67)

Jung (2005) also suggested that rocks had soul-like energy. Gary Lachman (2010) explains,

> Throughout his life, stone, like water, had a mystical effect on Jung, and one near the "fire wall" became *his* stone. Jung would sit on it and fall into a metaphysical reverie. "I am sitting on this stone," he would think but immediately the thought would come to him that perhaps the stone is thinking. (p. 23)

This might sound like the words of a psychotic. And there was a psychotic side to Jung; see, for instance, *The Red Book* (2009) by Jung. Does a stone think? What did Jung mean? This is an open question.

Like Jung and Hayward—who obviously felt that stones are more than merely stones—Gaston Bachelard (2002), who in his masterwork on the earth, claims that the earth is a living creature and is not a dead thing and all things related to the earth—including rocks—are alive and full of energy. Bachelard was a scientist, philosopher, and poet and has been embraced mostly by Jungians and those interested in ecospirituality.

On the matter of soul, I (2008) state,

> Drawing on Rupert Sheldrake (1996), the divine [or the soul] might be conceptualized better as a mysterious field. For Sheldrake the soul is a field, not a stand-alone thing. And this soul is not anthropocentric, but it is spread through all of creation. (p. 108)

The soul leaks out of the head. Think of auras. What are those? Soul leaks? When we say that someone has "bad vibes" what does that mean? Bad vibes are connected to soul. According to string theory, the world is composed of strings (like musical instruments) and they vibrate. These vibrations hold the chaos of the world together. Bad vibes are connected to the vibrations of the world. Good vibes are connected to the soul and they are also connected to the vibrations of the world. Perhaps our current ecodisaster is related to our disrespect of the fundamental things that make up the soul of the world (i.e., auras, bad vibes, and chaos).

Energy—like vibrations—is all about movement. Beings are always on the move even when sitting still. The brain changes all the time, the skin sheds, our hearts beat. All is energy. Energy moves through time-space. Matter is energy. Bachelard (2002) points this out in his book on the earth. Earth is matter is energy. Things move in time. One can say that things change over time—but what does time mean? I (2008) draw on the work of Edward Casey to flesh out the problem of time and the soul:

> I want to get back to thinking about the mystical as a moment in time. And this brings up issues around duration. Edward Casey (1991) talks of the connection between the soul and time and the soul in time. Casey says, "time and the soul are profoundly linked, in the depths of, in the interiority of each" (p. 279). (p. 114)

What if Casey is wrong? What if the whole idea of time is wrong? Does time really exist? Maybe there is no such thing as time. Kant thought that time was a category in our heads, like space. Do we have internal time clocks? Perhaps, at night most of us sleep; during the day we get up and go to work or school. Some scientists suggest that working a night shift takes at least 10 years off of your life because it interrupts your natural clock. Working night shift changes your perception of time. Time has little meaning working night shift. Now, interestingly enough Philip Wexler (2000), who has written one of the most important books on spirituality in the field of curriculum studies called *Mystical Society: An Emerging Social Vision*, which I will discuss in more detail as we move along here, suggests that a mystical experience is not about time but rather about "a lived timelessness" (p. 24). Writers, artists, dancers, and musicians experience timelessness during the perfect performance. When things go well, it seems that the event happens by itself. Freud suggested that the unconscious has no sense of time. That is, when you dream of something that happened long ago, say, in childhood, it seems like it happened yesterday. In the dream world, time is all mixed up.

Old Souls

The idea of soul is a very old one indeed. It is an old word from the old world that Americans have inherited and many of us have held onto this concept even into the postmodern era. Even Foucault (1979) uses the term "soul." Now, many would argue that people do not have souls. The Dali Lama (1999)—who is Buddhist—describes the good life without reference to soul:

> When you have devoted your life to meaningful activities [which we would call soul-ful]—have been motivated by a sense of caring—then I think that when the last moments of your life comes, you will have no regrets. (p. 89)

Buddhists do not believe in the notion of soul, but rather that what is is nothingness. Soul is not a concept in Buddhism. Neither is god. What is more important to Buddhists is to grapple with suffering and care for others.

Holy Sparks

Another way to think about the soul comes from the Jewish mystical tradition about which Wexler (1996) writes in his book *Holy Sparks: Social Theory, Education and Religion*. Think of the soul as a "holy spark" when reading Wexler's words:

> I struggle not only to rekindle the "holy sparks" of light and energy [think of soul here] remaining from the primal creative destruction (sparks that, according to the Kabbalistic narrative of universal beginning, remain indwelling [in] worldly places for creativity). I also struggle to recollect such sparks in the interests of a vivifying social theory and socioeducational practice. (p. 17)

A sparkle in the eye suggests intelligence. A light in the eye suggests energy, movement. But that is not all. Wexler points out that sparks are partly destructive. In the Kabbala they fall to earth like shards of glass that we have to pick up—this is called *Tikkun Olam*, which H. Svi Shapiro (2006) points out means "the imperative to heal and repair the world" (p. xix). Later, I want to spend more time on issues of healing, but for now students should know that these holy sparks contain both the seeds of destruction and healing. Holy sparks smash down to earth like broken shards of glass. The task for us is to pick them up to heal the wounds of the world. This is the main message of mystical Judaism. But remember that the Kabbala is a mystical text that is not often talked about in traditional Judaism. There is an interesting parallel to this creation myth. Mark Epstein (2007) who is an MD, Buddhist, and practicing psychoanalyst tells us about Achaan Chah who

> motioned to a glass sitting to one side of him. "Do you see the glass?," he asked us. "I love this glass. It holds water admirably. When the sun shines on it, it reflects the light beautifully. When I tap it, it has a lovely ring. Yet, for me, this glass is already broken." (p. 7)

We are that glass and we are beautiful but yet we are "already broken" (p. 7). There is a parallel between the Jewish Kabbalist text of the holy sparks breaking and the Buddhist's glass breaking. The holy sparks are in us and we are like broken glass because glass breaks easily and so too do we. The soul, then, easily shatters. And perhaps the birthing experience is a shattering one. Leaving the warmth of the womb for the coldness of a new world is a shattering experience. Let us be like T. S. Eliot's "wounded surgeon." Beings are always already wounded but still work to heal (as a surgeon does) the world. This, too, is the task of the Buddhist Bodhisattva. The Bodhisattva goes out into the world to heal others. The task of being is ultimately to help others. And that is what teaching is about. Teaching is a healing and soulful profession. But at the end of the day, the soul remains a mystery. Martin Buber (2002) points out:

> Yet it can happen that we venture to respond, stammering perhaps—the soul is but rarely able to attain to surer articulation—but it is an honest stammering as when sense and throat are united about what is to be said, but the throat is too horrified at it to utter purely the already composed sense. The words of our response are spoken in the speech, untranslatable like the address, of doing and letting. (pp. 19–20)

Twice in Buber's passage above he uses the word "stammering." This is an interesting word that suggests struggle. Scholars struggle to articulate issues. Soul is a concept that does not make for easy definition. The problem with religious dogma, on the other hand, is that there is little stammering. Dogma is too sure of itself, whereas spirituality and talk of the soul, as Buber points out, is a stammering and something that is untranslatable. Buber sounds postmodern here and echoes in many ways the writings of Deleuze and Guattari, as well as Jacques Derrida.

Interiority

Talk of the soul and of spirituality is always about interiority. Interiority is what Buber calls "the untranslatable" (p. 20). This dovetails with the writings of William Pinar (2012) as he states that scholars must work from within—from the space of interiority—to think historically and socially. William Pinar was the first person to bring autobiography—or the study of interiority—to the field of curriculum studies in the 1970s. John Miller (2000) suggests

> a soulful curriculum recognizes and gives priority to the inner life. It seeks a balance and connection between our inner and outer lives. Traditionally, schools have ignored the child's inner life, in fact, our whole culture tends to ignore the inner life. (p. 49)

The United States is a culture that is mostly about business and making money. This is the culture of fast food and fast money. Fast food and fast money have little to do with soul.

So much of teaching at the public school level is scripted and has little to do with the inner lives of children. And, too, even in college, the readings that students are assigned are to be memorized for answers on tests. This is hardly helpful to the cultivation of the inner life. Children should be reading and studying meaningful things, not memorizing junk for a multiple-choice test.

Reading good literature means taking it in, not to memorize it, but to make something of it, to be nourished by it. However, America is hardly a literary culture. So to try and instill good reading practices in our students is a struggle because they come to us, even in college, mostly unread and unprepared to read. One could argue that children read things on the Internet, Facebook. But are these activities really reading? William Pinar (2012) thinks not. Reading good literature takes time and one must go into one's interior to concentrate on the text at hand and this takes time and commitment. Reading posts on Facebook takes two seconds and is hardly literary and rarely leads to serious introspection. A "soulful curriculum" as John Miller points out begins with developing good reading practices and reading good literatures. The aim of reading should not be to memorize either. The aim of reading is to enrich the soul. Why else do we read? Reading scholarly books—if they are good—should serve to enrich the soul. Why do we do scholarship in the first place? To enrich our lives, to make us think, feel, and have something to contribute to the culture into which we are thrown. The art of thinking and the contemplative life are all about the cultivation of interiority. Dwelling in the house of the self is necessary in order to foster the contemplative art of study and reading. Then comes writing. Writing is a highly contemplative and solitary act—although we draw on the works of others. But in order to be a good writer, one must be a good thinker, and in order to be a good thinker one must have a sense of one's own interiority; the depth of the inner self must be cultivated. Parker Palmer (1999) comments, "Attention to the inner life is not romanticism. It involves the real world, and it is what is desperately needed in so many sectors of American education" (p. 16). As long as the assessment craze takes precedence over what really counts as education—like love, heart, soul, and cultivating the interior life—we are lost. The American education system—especially public education—is in shambles and it has been for decades. Memorizing facts for tests hardly counts as education. But that is most of what children do in schools and even in universities. Parker Palmer makes an important point that when we are talking about interiority we are also talking about "the real world" (p. 16). The world out there is the world in here and the world in here is the world out there. Contemplative life, although solitary, should lead to deeper engagement with others in that real world. Whatever the "real" means. The problem with understanding one's own interiority, of course, is that much of it is unconscious.

The mystical experience begins with the exploration of interiority but does not stop there. Philip Wexler (2000) states,

> Mysticism is *defined* by practices that recompose the inner self to transcend time and space; aim to create a more fluid self, if not to dissolve it entirely; show how the individual can simultaneously be present in this and other worlds; and attune the self to become relationally receptive and tied to a larger absolute universe, which generates meaning and vitality. (pp. 23–24).

Wexler is not alone in thinking about cultivating a "more fluid self." Kathleen Kesson (2002) similarly suggests, "These contemplative paths share an understanding of the self as a nondualistic continuum of fluid experience, ranging from the dense expression of the body to the more subtle and ephemeral expressions of mind and spirit" (p. 52). Interiority, then, is about fluidity for both Wexler and Kesson. But what exactly does this mean and how to achieve this and why? What are we being more fluid with? The outer world? Does the sense of fluidity help us understand that the outer world and the inner world are of a piece? Fluidity suggests connectivity. If human beings think of themselves as connected with the outer world perhaps people wouldn't be engaged in the ruination of the earth. Jung has an interesting thing to say on this matter and certainly gives us food for thought. Jung (2005) says, "Do you think that somewhere we are not Nature, that we are different from Nature? No, we are Nature and think exactly like Nature" (p. 24). This is a good example of just how fluid beings are with nature. As Jung suggests there is no separation between us and the outside world: we are the outside world. But we are miseducated to think that what is out there is separate from us. And this idea that what is out there is utterly different from us allows people to think that they can ruin, scar, and maim the earth because it has little to do with us. But the earth is not an "it"; rather, "it" is us and we are not its. We are souls and so too is the earth—the earth has a soul because we are the earth and we have souls. This is one way, then, to think of fluidity between ourselves and the world.

Wexler (2000) writes about the importance of the inner self in relationality to the world (pp. 23–24). The inner self is always in relation to others and to the world. We are not alone, even if we live solitary lives. Although much of our time as academics is spent writing—which is a solitary act—we are in relation to our students, to our colleagues, and we are in relation to the texts we study. This being-in-relation also cultivates the idea of a "more fluid self," as Wexler puts it (pp. 23–24). We are fluid in our relationships with others as we must speak with others, help others, and work with others.

The Fluid Self and Dreams

Another way to think of this fluid self, too, is to think of our own intellectual lives. The more scholars are able to make connections among ideas, the more fluid our writing becomes. The more connections scholars can make, the more fluid are our thoughts. Writing becomes fluid, though, after much study and much work. And then there is the fluidity of the mind itself. If we are in touch with our unconscious, that is, if we pay attention to dreams, the dreams tell us things and help us to make sense of what troubles. Mary Doll (1995) has done extensive work on dreams and what they can teach. It is interesting to note that most curriculum studies scholars who work in the field of psychoanalysis—if they are neo-Freudians—do not write about dreams. Mostly they write about defense mechanisms. The only way to undo defense mechanisms is to unpack the unconscious through freely associating dreams. Mary Doll's writing is Jungian and not Freudian and perhaps she is more comfortable talking about dreams than Freudians. John Miller (2000) says, "Dreamwork is based on the assumption that within each person there is a 'source of wisdom' that allows the person to work with dreams and internal images"(p. 66). It is interesting that this "source of wisdom" comes to us not through rationality and intellect but through what is irrational and unconscious. The difficulty is to get at that which is unconscious. Can one ever get at that stuff that is buried deeply in the psyche? Maybe not. But through work and free association one can get at some of what is unconscious and that is where wisdom comes. But most people ignore dreams and think they are irrelevant or have nothing to do with our real lives. Dreams, however, are another way to go deeper into our interiority—and also deeply into what is spiritual—and make connections with that part of the self that is often ignored. Thomas Moore (2005) says,

> A dream is a perfect example of soul speech. It usually connects strongly with the dreamer's daily life, it is full of obscure imagery and it hints at far broader, collective, and eternal issues. It demands a poetic sensitivity if we are to take any insight from it. (pp. 10–11)

"Day residue" is Freud's term for dreams that reflect the previous day's events. But there are other kinds of dreams that do not reflect this at all. Many dreams are mixed up with past issues that could stem from childhood. Thomas Moore—who is more Jungian than Freudian—is also talking here about the collective unconscious and how dreams capture things that are deep in the culture into which we are thrown. So dreams are also culturally constructed. Dreams speak to us, Moore suggests, as "soul speech." The soul, then, is mostly unconscious. Dreams reflect what is going on in our unconscious and that is why they are so hard to interpret. Even if you develop what Moore calls "a poetic sensitivity" in order to interpret your dreams, still they elude. The elusive nature of dreams is what is so fascinating about them. We know little about what is going on inside of us. And when we are able to freely associate, Freud suggests, it is not so much the dream that matters but what we do with those associations from the dream. But free association is difficult because the ego tends to block thought. The interesting thing about the unconscious is that although it is seemingly fluid—because dreams mix everything up—Freud suggests that the unconscious is rigid. It is the rigidity that causes us problems. The more rigid we are in our daily lives the more problems we have making our way through the world. The building up of defense mechanisms, although necessary to survive, can get in the way of our lives by making us become too rigid. Rigidity in thought leads to dogma. Rigidity in emotion leads to breakdown. The more rigid you are emotionally the more likely you are to have a breakdown. Coming to a fluidity of self—as Wexler

(2000) and Kesson (2002) suggest—takes work. It is easier to be rigid than to be fluid. People who are dogmatic are rigid and see the world one way. This can be very dangerous and can lead to fundamentalism, nationalism, and even war.

To Transcend or Descend

Wexler suggests that the inner self should "transcend space and time" (2000, pp. 23–24). Conversely, for Jungians, the point of the inner life is not transcendence but descending deeper into earthly matters. Going into the unconscious is to descend down into an unknown world. To get at that which is unconscious one needs to go down into it. Jungians (see, for instance, the work of Mary Doll, James Hillman, Patrick Dennis Slattery, and David Miller) often speak of the descent into the underworld—much like Greek myth. The descent into the underworld is a spiritual undertaking.

Another curriculum theorist who talks about transcendence is Dwayne Huebner (1999). In fact, the title of his collected essays is *Lure of the Transcendent*. So both Wexler and Huebner are in agreement on the point of transcendence. Certainly the idea of the transcendent has a long history in Judaism and Christianity as god in the traditional sense is thought to be transcendent. But there are other ways to think of the divine. The divine can be thought of as immanent—within all living things (which is called pantheism)—or the divine can be thought of as both immanent and transcendent (which is called pan-en-theism). Pan-en-theism is the best of both worlds.

Mysticism

Mysticism is a natural fit for curriculum studies scholars because it is an outlier. Mysticism is not part of traditional studies on religion. Most academic theology programs do not focus on mysticism but rather on systematic theology. Mysticism is hardly systematic. But there is a rich literature on mysticism and many religions have a mystical branch, if you will. There are many kinds of mysticisms. There are indigenous mysticisms. There is Christian mysticism. Many Christian mystics have been women. But even still, Christian mysticism is patriarchal. There is Jewish mysticism. Indigenous mysticisms are different from Christian mysticisms, and Sufi mysticism is different from both Christian and indigenous mysticism. It is crucial not to essentialize mystical experience because mysticisms are variegated. Michael Eigen (1998) states,

> There are mysticisms of emptiness and fullness, difference and union, transcendence and immanence. One meets the Super personal beyond opposites or opens to the void and formless infinite. There are mystical moments of shattering and wholeness— many kinds of shattering, many kinds of wholeness. In moments of illumination, not only one's flaws stand out, one's virtues become a hindrance. (p. 13)

What Eigen suggests is that mystical experience is an aporia. These constant contradictions and opposites cannot be resolved. Contradictions just are. Now, many people think that mystical experience is irrelevant. People who are rationalists probably think this. But if you are opened to the universe you can experience the mystical and you do not need a church to do so. This is why the medieval Christian mystics were seen as heretical because they did not follow church dogma. Mystical experience has little to do with church law or theological systems. If you do not need a church to have mystical experiences, then what happens to the church? If you do not need a church, the church ceases to exist. And this is what the patriarchs of Christianity feared most.

What fascinates me about Michael Eigen is that he is a psychoanalyst, not a religious scholar. Mark Epstein, too, is interested in the intersections of psychoanalysis and religion as he is a practicing Buddhist. Many Jungians practice what is called "spiritual depth psychology." However, Jung denied that he was, in fact, a mystic. Although after reading Jung's (2009) *Red Book*, I do not see how he could make such a claim. This book is highly mystical. Gary Lachman (2010), in his book titled *Jung the Mystic*, asks,

> Was Jung a mystic? Jung didn't think so and he thought little of those who did. In a filmed interview in 1957 with Richard I. Evans, Professor of psychology at the University of Houston, Jung, then in his eighties, remarked, "Everyone who says that I am a mystic is just an idiot." By that time, this would have included quite a few people, not the least of whom was Sigmund Freud. (p. 1)

Jung might not have considered himself a mystic, but his writings certainly lead the reader to believe otherwise. Perhaps Jung thought that if he told people he was a mystic they might think he was a kook! Even today, if you tell people that you have had a mystical experience they probably will think you are a kook. American culture, in particular, is pragmatic, highly Protestant, and conservative. Of course there is right-wing mysticism that veers straight into fundamentalism. I am certainly not endorsing right-wing fundamentalism. The mysticisms that most curriculum theorists are interested in are to the left of the political spectrum.

Historical Study of Mysticism(s)

Philip Wexler (2000) suggests that if scholars are interested in studying mysticism, a return to ancient traditions is necessary. Scholars must study mysticism historically. Wexler states,

> Just as social theory has always drawn from the wider, general culture in the work of creating more specialized cultures of systematic understanding, so now do esoteric religious traditions provide the cultural resources for historically novel forms of social understanding, particularly their affinity with mysticism. (p. 7)

Wexler works out of Jewish mysticism and it is this "esoteric religious tradition" upon which he draws. Wexler's book, *Mystical Society: An Emerging Social Vision*, is one of the most important texts on mysticism and education today. Students interested in mysticism should read Wexler's book in its entirety. Wexler couches mysticism within the larger sociocultural society and he also situates mysticism historically. Many writers on mysticism do not do this and do not talk about the social in relation to the personal because mystical experience is highly personal. But Wexler insists that scholars must connect the personal with the social. He calls this social movement of mysticism the coming "mystical society" (p. 3). Wexler explains,

> Against the disorientation, decathexis, and desensitization that I suggest characterize modernity and postmodernity, the emerging form of life in a mystical society is characterized by unification rather than dispersion; holistic relationality rather than functional specialization; release of historically pent up emotion rather than cool instrumental calculation; faith against skepticism; and joy rather than mourning. (p. 3)

"Holistic relationality" in academics means interdisciplinarity. Holistic relationality is possible between teachers and students only if teachers and students hold mutual respect for each other. But often there is a disconnect and the teacher-student relationship can become more like a battleground. Further, the relations between teachers and students become asymmetrical when grades and standardized tests make students fear the teacher and make the students hate learning. It is difficult also to not be skeptical in a post-9/11 world. It is difficult to find joy in a world where there is so much hatred and discontent and where there are so many ecological disasters. But in our own worlds there are spaces where people can make holistic relationality happen; joy is possible if people are leading lives that are meaningful. But so many academics get caught up in petty squabbles that life in the academy becomes a battlefield of egos, jealousy, and even hatred. How to make the university a more "mystical society"—as Wexler suggests—is a difficult question. The university should be a place of solitude and work, a place not unlike a monastery where scholars work like monks in the stacks of the library trying to find things out, trying to make meaning of a world that can be at times cruel and seemingly meaningless. But the university is often a place that is highly anti-intellectual and fosters little intellectual discussion between colleagues (Morris, 2006).

The university reflects the larger sociocultural society and—in contradistinction to Wexler—I do not think that American society is, generally speaking, mystical and probably is not moving in that direction. What I see is an ever-deepening path into meaninglessness and consumerism. Americans love their gadgets. Why are Americans addicted to their gadgets? And where is the mysticism in gadgets? The love of gadgets is hardly spiritual. Wexler talks about the "release of pent up emotion" (p. 3) in this "emerging mystical society." Perhaps Wexler is looking for a utopia when there is none. I (2001) argue that society is dystopic and scholars must concentrate on these dystopic elements in the world—not on joy—because there is little joy in the world. Scholars must focus on ecodisasters and try to learn how to help the victims of oil spill catastrophes, disease, war, terrorism, and unhappiness.

Ecospirituality

Elaine Riley-Taylor (2002) calls for a more ecospiritual understanding of the world. Like Wexler (2000), Riley-Taylor talks about mysticism in connection to education. She explains,

> It is my opinion that to be a truly generative, creative process, education must recognize the interconnection between all areas of human capacity: [this would be Wexler's holistic relationality] not only those born of the rational mind but also those emanating from the energetic drive of the physical body, the seat of mystical intuition, the source of heartfelt emotions, the shimmering seeds of a personal-communal spirit. (p. 60)

What strikes me in Riley-Taylor's citation above is that she posits that mystical experience emanates from the body and not from intellect alone. She suggests that the body—as the "seat of mystical intuition"—is what people should be focusing on. Also, here, for Riley-Taylor mysticism is a kind of intuition. Intuition is one of the hardest concepts to define because people do not really understand what it is. Intuition is something that, according to Aristotle, one can develop. But I am not so certain about this. Intuition is something you either have or you do not. Now, if you have it, you might be able to fine-tune it. What blocks the capacity to become more intuitive is addiction to money and gadgets. If your only purpose in life is to make a lot of money and own a lot of gadgets, intuition is the least of your interests.

Is mystical intuition different from intuition in and of itself? Or is all intuition mystical? When most people think of the mystical—whether it is intuition or just a way of being in the world—they think of someone with their head in the clouds. But recall, Riley-Taylor points out that mysticism is embodied. This is an important point for her. If meditation leads to mystical experience, then that meditation cannot be an out-of-body experience but an experience of deepening bodily feeling. Like Riley-Taylor, I (2008) argue that mystical experience is a bodily experience, but there is more. For me, the aesthetic and mystical are interconnected and so I argue that bodyart (tattoos) can allow one to deepen bodily experience and deepen the mystical. I argue,

> Bodyart [is] a site of mystical experience. Looking at a painting or reading poetry can also lead to the mystical, but when the artform is put into you and put on you literally [i.e., tattoos] the mystical becomes enfleshed. The royal road to the mystical is enfleshed. Crossing into another state of consciousness is an experience of the mystical....One need not be a monk, saint, or Bodhisattva to experience the mystical. The mystical experience is an experience for those who are open to it. (p. 107)

My point here is that artwork can lead to mystical experience. Painting, playing a musical instrument, reading poetry, getting tattooed can all open the door to the mystical. But still, you have to be open to the idea of the mystical in the first place in order to have a mystical experience. Some feel that mysticism is just kooky and thus they will never open the door to this other world. This is Riley-Taylor's point also. You do not need to go to another world (like outer space) to have a mystical experience; you need only be cognizant of the workings of your body. Now, if your body does not work right, say, if you suffer from illness, disease, or disability, you can still have mystical experiences through the illness. I do not mean to romanticize illness, disease, and disability, all I mean to say is that the body does not need to be healthy in order to experience the mystical. The body can be broken down and still there are portals to the mystical, if one is open to it. Most people who are healthy do not give death a thought. But perhaps people should always live on the near side of death; this nearness to the thought of not being opens the door to mysticism. The mundane world can block the mystical because the mundane world is the world of taking the bus to work, cleaning up the sink after dinner. It is in the mundane that the mystical can open up. You do not have to go to church to have a mystical experience. Thoughts come in the most unexpected places. In the literature on mysticism it has long been said that the sacred is the profane and that the profane is the sacred.

Mindfulness

One thing that helps us get at the sacred-in-the-profane is what many Buddhists call "mindfulness," which is something that Riley-Taylor (2002, p. 21) writes much about. To be mindful of what one is doing when sweeping the floor, for example, one must pay attention to the sweeping as if it were an art form. The more we pay attention to the activity at hand—even if it is completely mundane and boring—the more mindful we become. Thich Nhat Hanh (2006) comments on Buddhists sweeping the floor and what that mundane activity meant to them. Hanh says

> A philosopher asked the Buddha what his monks did all day long. The Buddha replied that they walked, stood, lay down, sat, ate, washed their bowls, and swept the floor. How, then, asked the philosopher, were they any different from people in the world? The Buddha replied that the difference was that the monks did these things in mindfulness, guarding their six senses. Whatever we are doing, we can be mindful. We can recognize all the phenomena in our body, our feelings, our mind, and the objects of our mind. (p. 224)

I do not know if we can "recognize *all* [emphasis mine] the phenomena in our body," as Hanh puts it. Much of what goes on within us is unconscious, what we do know is only the tip of the iceberg. Still, we can be more mindful and aware of our daily activities, and daily awareness can lead to a more nuanced understanding of ourselves and the world into which we are thrown. Matthew Fox (2006) says,

> A mindful education would, for example, increase our capabilities for silence, for stillness and contemplation. It would enhance our capacity for grappling with chaos and for living with stress; our capacity for letting go, for letting be, and for forgiveness. (pp. 27–28)

Too much of education is about busywork that is meaningless or rote memorization that is pointless and instills fear into the hearts of our children. Children do not get intellectual nourishment in school. There will never be a capacity for stillness, as Fox suggests, when teachers are forced to give children tests all the time that have nothing to do with their lives and make them fear teachers and the world, and, worst of all, to fear learning. "Stillness and contemplation," as Fox puts it, can be acquired through reading, thinking, and writing. The reason we read, think, and write is to better understand what we cannot. The reason we read, think, and write is to better understand our purpose in the world. But schooling is not about these things. It is about torture. Test-taking and firing teachers because test scores do not meet state "standards" are akin to torture.

Revitalizing Education Through Religiosity

Alan A. Block (2009) has written an important book on education and ways to revitalize it through thinking more religiously. His book is titled *Ethics and Teaching: A Religious Perspective on Revitalizing Education*. What strikes me the most in Block's book is the following sentence: "Study is equivalent to prayer" (p. 116). And in another important book, titled *Pedagogy, Religion, and Practice: Reflections on Ethics and Teaching*, Block (2007) states, "In study, we find the practice of study; in the practice of study we discover the life we want to live" (p. 39). Studying for Block is a religious imperative. This echoes James Macdonald's (1996) work as he said that theory is a prayerful act. But schooling is hardly prayerful. Jung, according to Gary Lachman (2010),

> fainted when asked to do homework…Jung fainted every time the issue of school came up.…For six months he was left to himself. He indulged in an orgy of reading, daydreaming, and solitary walks in the woods by the water. (p. 27)

Today psychologists might call these fainting spells that Jung had panic attacks. Anxiety leads to panic and panic leads to fainting. The mind just collapses onto itself. Jung found a way, though, to escape the drudgeries of school. And in fact, when he finally split from Freud's circle he developed an entire new school of thought that today we call depth psychology or Jungian psychology. Still, today, Jungian psychology is considered a fringe psychology. Jung's ideas veer too close to the mystical and more scientific psychologists have no truck with him. Lachman comments, "This ambiguity [of whether or not Jung was a kook, mystic or scientist] is…one reason why most members of the scientific community are unwilling to grant him acceptance" (p. 3).

Still, there are Jungian institutes around the country and depth psychology flourishes even though it is still on the fringe.

The Spiritual and the Social

One of the misconceptions about mysticism is that it is only a personal feeling. However, many mystics historically have also been social activists. Although some religious scholars might not consider the Jewish prophets to be mystics, I do. These mystical prophets were engaged in social activism. Abraham Heschel (1969) comments,

> By insisting on the absolutely objective and supernatural nature of prophecy, dogmatic theology has disregarded the prophet's nature in the prophetic act. Stressing revelation, it has ignored the response; isolating inspiration, it has lost sight of the human situation. (p. ix)

The "prophetic act" is, for one thing, not supernatural. Mysticism is not supernatural either. Prophetic acts are a response to a cruel and unjust world. There is nothing supernatural about that. Prophets are mystics who act in the world to help others. H. Svi Shapiro (2010) comments,

> My own concerns as an educator are shaped by what is sometimes referred to as the prophetic tradition, after the role of the ancient Hebrew prophets....They were the relentless voices of conscience that spoke truth to power, even in the face of their own isolation or the hostility of their audience. (p. 17)

As Shapiro points out, the Hebrew prophets were social activists and he models his own work after them. In Buddhism these prophets are called Bodhisattvas who go out into the world to help others. Responding to the other is what Levinas spent his entire life writing about. Derrida too. In their own ways, these two thinkers were also mystical prophets who understood the idea of prophetic understanding, as Heschel explains it. Heschel writes: "Understanding prophecy is an understanding of an understanding rather than an understanding of knowledge; it is exegesis of exegesis" (p. xiv). William Pinar et al. (1995) call for understanding curriculum. But understanding is more than understanding. To understand curriculum scholars have to understand the concept of understanding. And for Heschel understanding the concept of understanding is more akin to prophecy than to the gathering of knowledge. Knowledge might be the compilation of facts without the understanding that these facts are socially constructed. To get underneath what is going on in the world understanding must be thought of in a prophetic way. That is, understanding is a form of "exegesis of exegesis" (Heschel, p. xiv). The image that comes to mind is digging. In music we say, dig into that phrase. In scholarly work we might say dig into that thought. This is also an archaeological image. Digging into thought means tearing it apart (which is what the prophets did) to come to some new understanding of old ideas. Derrida is the master of "exegesis of exegesis." Derrida had a prophetic understanding of the world. Interestingly enough, his Hebrew name was Elijah, who was a prophet in the Hebrew Scriptures. Scholars must allow themselves to let go of ego and work with Derrida. Dig into his texts. Studying Derrida's scholarship might open onto a horizon of new ideas; scholars might better understand what work is involved in understanding what understanding means. Understanding the concept of understanding is difficult. Understanding is standing under the idea and looking at it upside down. Tearing the idea apart and digging deeply into it is what analysis is all about. It is not enough to report on what people say, but scholars must dig deeper into their phrases to come to their own ideas.

Mystical thought is prophetic if it takes up the notion of understanding in this sense. And writing through new understandings is a prophetic act. Writing is an act. It is a form of social activism. Social activism is not just standing on the frontlines. But social activism or mystical-prophetic thought is also understanding that writing is key. Writing changes the world—if it is truly prophetic. To write is to think. Intellectual ideas that are prophetic can change the world.

The point I want to make here is that mystics who write prophetically are always already engaged in the social. The mystic who is not involved in intellectual activity or who is not interested in helping others is not prophetic. Curriculum theorists who focus on spirituality also focus on social change. Recall, Philip Wexler (1996) writes about "holy sparks" (out of Jewish mysticism) and argues that holy sparks are not incompatible with social change. Wexler insists that scholars must attempt to make "changes in our systematic understanding" (p. 5). To change ideas is to change the world. This is Wexler's point. Wexler is a social theorist and couches his work in Jewish mysticism in the larger social and historical scene. Wexler contextualizes his work on mysticism in larger social change and sees social movement as a result of new understanding. Wexler argues that mysticism should not be "world-fleeing" (p. 11). Levinas, Buber, and Derrida (all three Jewish writers) argue that the spiritual is in this world, not in another, and the spiritual moves us to respond to the Other in a worldly way. Mysticism must not collapse onto itself and become a self-preoccupation only. Mystical feeling can lead to writing that grapples with social issues.

David Purpel (2004), another Jewish writer in education, critiques what he calls "the trivialization and vulgarization of education in America" (p. 19). In the tradition of mystical prophecy, Purpel calls for a study of "more critical topics [which include]…social, political, and moral issues" (p. 19). These are prophetic issues. Like Purpel, Alan Block (2009) says, "To teach is to assume an ethical position in an immoral world. To teach is to not suffer silently, but to suffer nonetheless. To teach is to change the world student by student and paper by paper" (p. 38). The spiritual is contextualized in the social, and as Block puts it, the spiritual is also contextualized in the ethical. Thinking spiritually means thinking about social change for the better and this change, as Block points out, might happen slowly "student by student." Revolutions happen person by person. Mass movements start with a few people and grow from there. The seed is planted in the garden and grows slowly. Social change happens slowly. And change can begin in our own classrooms, Block insists. Like Wexler, Block, and Purpel, H. Svi Shapiro's (2006) work is in this same prophetic tradition. Shapiro remarks, "We have made a Faustian bargain for our kids—a schooling that promises higher standards and test scores, instead of an education that enlivens and enriches how children engage their world" (p. 7). To engage the world. That is prophetic thought. Children are taught to be passive observers of the world, they are taught obedience. But they are not taught to think and so they cannot "engage their world," as Shapiro puts it. You have to be able to think in order to engage the world and change that world for the better. Spiritual people do not have to have their heads in the clouds all day. They can be engaged in the world and help children to engage as well.

Thomas Oldenski and the late Dennis Carlson (2002) suggest,

> We want to view spirituality in ways that do not separate the spiritual from the material, the "soul" from the body, subjectivity from spirituality, in ways that are consistent with the notions of the democratic spirit and the human spirit, a spirit in the process of historical transformation. (p. 5)

For Oldenski and Carlson a more grounded and worldly spirituality is key to changing the world for the better. This more democratic spirituality is neo-Marxist in the tradition of Paulo Freire.

Freire (2005) talks about the importance of testimony (p. 103). Testimony is what education is all about. Testimony is a word that brings up religiosity and Freire's work can be read in this way because his entire life project was to help the Other. To testify to suffering is the work of the prophet. Freire's work falls within the prophetic tradition as he remarks,

> It is my conviction that there are no themes or values of which one cannot speak, no areas in which one must be silent. We can talk about everything, and we can give testimony about everything. The language that we use to talk about this or that and the way we give testimony are, nevertheless, influenced by the social, cultural, and historical conditions of the context in which we speak and testify. (p. 103)

Most people think of Freire as a political thinker. He was that. But he was also a deeply spiritual man, something that is often overlooked in commentaries on his work. For Freire, people are called to testify to the suffering of others and try to help those who suffer. This is the heart and soul of education.

Education as Healing and Redemption

Education should be about healing and redemption according to many curriculum theorists. The current state of public education is hardly about healing. It is more about wounding. Alan Block (2009) states: "I have argued… that education is redemptive." (p. 116). Education should be redemptive but, for the most part, it is not. Likewise, Philip Wexler (1996) says that "social theory [should be]…redemptive" (p. 88). Social theory about schooling should be redemptive but schooling is not. Schooling is wounding. Parker Palmer (1999) says, "Education is about healing" (p. 19). Education should be about healing but education is damaging, not healing. Philip Wexler (2000) calls for a "resacralized mystical society" (p. 7). Education should be "resacralized." Where is this possible? Probably not in public schools. John Miller (2000) suggests, "By being more attentive to our inner life, or soul life, we can perhaps help in the process of healing ourselves and the planet" (p. 6). But public schooling has little to do with the self, the soul, healing, or redemption. So why, if so many educational scholars write about this, is no one listening? Why are we never consulted by government officials who set public policy? Public policy is set by people who know nothing about education. What government officials do know is how to build smart bombs and how to send young people to war. David Purpel (2004) calls for a "vitalization of a vision of meaning" when it comes to educating our children (p. 42). This call echoes Wexler's resacralized vision of education. Thomas

Moore (1996) suggests that "we educate our hearts" (p. 6). H. Svi Shaprio (2006) says likewise that he has a

> passion for *Tikkun Olam*—the imperative to heal and repair the world. We need, I believe, to find, and "tap into," those wellsprings that feed all of our deepest impulses for a better world for ourselves and our children. (p. xix)

The underlying idea of all of these scholars I have quoted is that education should be about healing and redemption but obviously it is not—at this current time. But still educationists write about healing wounds caused by public schooling.

Education Has Lost Its Soul

One of the reasons scholars write about spirituality and education is because public schooling and even university education lack spirituality, for the most part. Public school is in shambles because of high-stakes testing. In this short section I would like to explore what scholars are saying about the loss of soul in the context of education.

Molly Quinn (2001), in her book titled *Going Out, Not Knowing Whither: Education, the Upward Journey and the Faith of Reason*, has much to say on the loss of soul and education. Quinn says, "I am seeking to address the issue of this loss of depth or soul in our society: the denial of the mysteriousness" (p. 5). Quinn draws on theologian Paul Tillich who, according to Quinn,

> describes our world situation, our historically constitutive interpretation of existence, as one of crisis, marked by this loss of "soul." The relation of the human subject and of human society to a transcendent reality, which historically has served as the center of meaning for humanity, is gone or no longer has power. (p. 2)

Tillich was not primarily concerned with educational institutions but with Western theology and Western religious institutions. But Quinn makes the connection between what Tillich says here and the state of current public schooling and the university. As against Tillich, I do not think all of society embraces the notion of the transcendent. The transcendent is certainly not the center of many world religions. Certainly indigenous peoples and Eastern traditions think differently about the divine.

American schooling has probably never had a soul; we didn't lose something we never had. Eastern and Central European educational systems are similarly problematic. I (2006) state,

> It is important to note that the academic institutions in which Freud and Buber were schooled were by no means democratic places. In fact, Eastern and Central European high schools were known for being highly authoritarian and rigid, not unlike many American institutions. What is notorious about educational institutions, especially during the reign of the Habsburg Empire, is that they were oppressive. (p. 94)

These institutions never had a soul. The oppressive nature of schooling is nothing new. But standardized tests and constant testing of children are historically relatively new. The constant testing of children is cruel and psychically damaging.

Molly Quinn suggests that scholars might think of

> education as a project of faith…referential of the spiritual journey of humanity… Such is also education in its classical sense, the upward journey of the soul, in the words of Plato, concerning freedom and transcendence. (p. 11)

I do not find the concept of transcendence helpful. Freud talked about the archaeology of the psyche and digging down into the unconscious to find out what is going on. Let us think more in terms of going down into the unconscious of public schooling and universities to find out what is wrong. The soul is found not by an upward motion but by a downward one. Or from a different angle, studying Buddhist writings—even though Buddhists have no notion of soul—one reads in Thich Nhat Hanh (2006) that one must dig into garbage (p. 221). When you go into psychic garbage you go down into the depths.

Plato's *Republic* is, in part, about transcending emotions. In the parable of the cave, people are caught up in their emotions, intuitions, and feelings; they cannot see the light of day and cannot find their way out of the darkness. The way out of the darkness and the way out of the cave are through the intellect, through reason, and the symbol for reason is the sun and the light. Those who try to escape their emotions (in the cave of the self) and try to leave the cave too soon, before they are ready, become blinded by the light of the sun. So the cave people have to *transcend* the darkness of emotions and move upward (transcend) away from their emotions, bodily feelings, and intuitions into the light of reason and the light of the sun. The Enlightenment (the light) is a continuation of Plato's parable of the cave. The sun is up in the sky, you have to look up (transcendence is an upward movement) and look to reason in order to understand the world. I am not so sure this metaphor works anymore. Reasonable people do unreasonable things. The unreasonable things people do are because they have not gone into what Thich Nhat Hanh calls "garbage" (p. 221). It is ironic and tragic that reason, rationality, and science led to the dropping of the atom bombs. In this postmodern era scholars are more interested in questioning the meaning of reason, progress, and rationality.

Quinn (2001) discusses the "soul sickness at the heart of humanity" (p. 15). The "soul sickness" of America—if I might generalize for a moment—has mostly to do with consumer capitalism, xenophobia, racism, homophobia, and heteronormativity. There is also an anti-intellectual strain in American culture that leads to all of these problems. Nonthinking and nonreading people find it easier to hate than to understand others. Understanding as I said earlier is a way of getting-under-what-we-stand-for, getting underneath the (intellectual, emotional, spiritual) ground upon which we walk. Quinn comments, too, that she is concerned with "trivialization...dissociation, repression, reduction" (p. 22). Repression buries the garbage that Thich Nhat Hanh talks about. How to undo that repression? Not an easy task.

Quinn comments on trivialization (p. 22) in American culture. All you have to do is turn on mainstream TV and you will be saturated with trivial programming. There are educational programs out there, but most of what we see on TV trivializes everything. There is nothing trivial about life, but so many people are caught up in trivia that they lose their soul, they lose their way, they lose direction. Spiritual people, truly spiritual people, are able to somehow maneuver around the trivial to stay focused on their life tasks. But it is so easy to fall into the trap of the trivial.

Clifford Mayes (2005) remarks, "American education is becoming ever more heartless" (p. 11). H. Svi Shapiro's (2006) book on spirituality and education is, in fact, titled *Losing Heart: The Moral and Spiritual Miseducation of America's Children.* And Matthew Fox (2006) says, "Education becomes a kind of vile medicine to take until you can escape school. Or a punishment for our sins...education is punitive, therefore" (p. 16). If the medicine of school is vile, as Fox suggests, there is nothing about it that serves to cure. Recall, Derrida (1991) in "Plato's Pharmacy" talks about medicine as both a poison and a cure. Well, schooling, for Fox, has no curative value whatsoever. School just makes children and teachers sick. H. Svi Shapiro suggests,

> What we provide them with now [in public schools] in no way helps them develop the things that they need most in their lives—the capability to discern meaning and purpose in their lives; the ability to question and challenge the dehumanizing di-

mensions of our culture....The crisis of culture is not hard to detect and is felt, if not always understood, throughout society, and experienced in our daily lives. (p. xviii)

The spiritual dimension of education, as Shapiro reminds us, is about finding "meaning and purpose" in our lives. He argues contrarily that we are miseducating our children. This miseducation will take years to undo, if it can ever be undone. Public schools have been in a continual state of crisis for decades in this country and it seems that things have only gotten worse. Schooling is worse with the onslaught of more and more standardized tests (which only serve to dehumanize, as Shapiro puts it). What kind of a world are we sending our children into once they "escape" school? One of the most important points Shapiro makes is that educators are not preparing children to cope with this kind of world. Not only that, schooling does not teach them how to think so that they can make this a better world. Changing the world begins with thought. Children are not taught to think, they are taught to obey and fill in the blanks. This is not a fill-in-the-blank world. Molly Quinn (2001) also speaks to these issues as she says,

> As the crisis of our day can be described as a crisis of faith, which is also a *breakdown* of meaning and of intelligibility productive of alienation, then it can also be characterized as a crisis of story and of understanding and of the imagination and of language. (p. 7)

What strikes me in Quinn's passage above is that she feels that the crisis of culture is one of story. What stories are educators teaching children in school? What stories can children tell us about their own lives? Or are they even allowed to think about their own lives? If children do not have stories to tell, how will they negotiate a complex world? Schooling erases children's stories. By erasing stories, subjectivity and human feeling fade. The story of a life is an autobiography. Children are not taught to think about who they are. They are taught to memorize junk and fill in the bubbles on a Scantron Test. Teachers are now being fired as their jobs are directly tied to standardized test scores. I thought No Child Left Behind would go away with the Obama administration. But things have only gotten worse with Arne Duncan's Race to the Top. The crisis of culture starts in childhood. And that crisis scars people for a lifetime. We are ruining our children. We are ruining generations of children. So where do children really learn anything? If they do not take up reading on their own, if they do not study the arts or take up music or dance or theater on their own, what do they think about? A foundation is needed to support a house or the house will collapse. What is the foundation we are teaching our children? How are their interior psyches being shaped? Interiority does not seem to be a priority in public schooling. H. Svi Shapiro (2006) comments,

> When Mother Teresa visited the United States to receive an Honorary degree it is reported that she said. "This is the poorest place I've ever been in my life." As John De Graff and his fellow authors point out in their wonderful book *Affluenza*, she was not talking about our extraordinary abundance of material goods or monetary wealth. She was talking about "poverty of the soul." (p. 23)

Drive through any town in the United States and you will see this "poverty of the soul." Strip malls. Drive-through fast food restaurants. Pawn shops. Title Bucks. Children want to hurry up and get out of school—"escape school," as Matthew Fox (2006) puts it—only to be thrown into a world of junk and drive-through jobs. Children are in a hurry to go nowhere, because this world of junk and horrible jobs robs people of their souls. If young people are lucky enough they can get into good colleges where they are taught meaningful things, but getting into a good college costs money and today, with the economy the way it is, only the well-to-do can send their kids to good colleges. If youth go to mediocre colleges, they will only get a mediocre education and perpetuate mediocrity after they graduate. Abraham Heschel (1969) speaks of the work of the Hebrew prophets; he offers clues to a more prophetic education. Heschel states, "Insight is a breakthrough, requiring much intellectual dismantling and dislocation. It begins with a mental interim, with the cultivation of a feeling for the unfamiliar, unparalled, incredible" (p. xii). "Intellectual dismantling" is especially important. To unlearn. To counter miseducation. The house of the self must be dismantled; the junk of standardization must be dismantled in order to build a new house of the soul and intellect. A good education is a dislocation or unease. Reading good literature means dislocating someone, getting them to think anew. Reading good literature means getting away from reading junk. What you read is what you become. If you read junk, you become junk. Souls are destroyed by this culture of junk. Again, these critiques of culture are not new. Philip Wexler (2000) points out that Max Weber echoed these sentiments decades ago. Wexler remarks,

> Weber's social criticism was also about the modern societal destruction of being. The bureaucratic world was one of excessive rationality, leading to a numbing of feeling and a loss of spiritual vitality. Not alienation but, relatedly, "mechanical petrification" was the upshot of secularization and the demagnification and "disenchantment of the world." As Weber put it, modern society becomes an "iron cage." (p. 6)

Americans still live in that "iron cage." Schools are becoming more and more like prisons (Giroux, 2003). Schools are run with an iron fist, an invisible iron fist. Who demands these standardized tests? Who demands the removal of arts programs from public education? The invisible hand rules with an iron fist in the iron cage of schooling to use Weber's phrase. The result, as Wexler points out, is what Weber called "mechanical petrification." Kids come out of schools petrified. What they learn is to mechanically memorize junk for no purpose whatsoever. A petrified forest is a dead forest. Petrified students are the walking dead. Thomas Oldenski and Dennis Carlson (2002) call for a "reenchantment of the world" (p. 3). But was the world ever enchanting? History teaches us that the world is one of wars, violence, and more wars. Thomas Merton (1976), in 1948, said,

> I became the complete twentieth-century man. I now belonged to the world in which I lived. I became a true citizen of my own disgusting century: the century of poison gas and atomic bombs. A man living on the doorsill of the Apocalypse, a man with veins full of poison, living in death. (p. 85)

The 20th century was bad. The 21st century is not starting off on a good note either. 9/11 shocked. This was the most horrific catastrophe on American soil. Ours, too, is a disgusting century already. How can we make a disgusting century enchanting? History teaches us that oppression, abuse, colonization, and miseducation are to be found everywhere. Racism, terrorism, xenophobia, the hatred of women, homophobia, Islamophobia, and classism abound. But still we must try to change this world for the better. David Purpel (2004) comments on these terrible situations we face today in the 21st century. Purpel states,

> We face major political and economic instability across the world, serious regional disputes, the proliferation of weapons of mass destruction, mass hunger, and a domestic economy and a job market of unusual volatility and cruelty. We also face a number of relatively recent crises of enormous difficulty and import, e.g., the AIDS epidemic; violence among and between children; and the emerging consequences of a global economy. (p. 18)

Discussions, then, on spirituality, mysticism, religiosity have to be understood against the realities we are facing, otherwise we sound naïve. Being spiritual or being a mystic does not mean that you do not live in the world; it means you live more deeply in the world. Rather than transcending the world through mystical ideas, one should move more deeply into the mess that is our reality. Prophetic thought is not ungrounded thought. If mystical experience makes you forget history, then you are being led astray. There are all kinds of mysticisms, and I suggest that whatever you experience in your personal life—for example, a mystical transformation—you must use that experience to work in the world to help others. If mysticism is used only to escape the world, then it is not in any way generative or generous. Generosity is a lost art. How to teach people to be more generous? How to become a more generous spirit? To be generous means to listen, to help, to take care of others, to take care of animals, to help our students become more learned and more grounded. The true mystic is generous. The Dali Lama is generous. Of course we cannot all be Dali Lamas but we can try in our own small ways to be more generous—and hence, more mystical, more prophetic. Prophecy has nothing to do with predicting the future or knowing things others do not know. There is nothing magical about prophetic knowing. Knowing the current realities we face against the backdrop of history is important in developing a more prophetic way of understanding the world. Being a spiritual person does not mean ignoring the horrors of history. It means studying the horrors more closely and trying to stop future horrors. Grace Feuerverger (2007) says in her book titled *Teaching, Learning and Other Miracles,*

> I also wrote this book for the many children in our classrooms today who have experienced violence, war, abuse, poverty, and other traumas and oppressions, and for the many teachers who teach them. Some of these students may fall by the wayside—too weary to continue on their journey toward the life force, beaten down by the brutality of it all. As a child of Holocaust survivors, I too grew up in the shadows of horror. (p. 1)

The miracle of this book is that Feuerverger—as a child of Holocaust survivors—is able to write about the horrors she has suffered. In an edited collection called *Difficult Memories: Talk in a (Post) Holocaust Era* (Morris & Weaver, 2002), Feuerverger tells us that what saved her was her love of language. But she was drawn not to her own language but to the language of others. Feuerverger could not bear to study Yiddish but rather turned to the French language. French saved her from the devastation she endured as a child of Holocaust survivors. The study and love of language are clear in Feuerverger's writing as she takes great care with words to craft her thoughts. And perhaps it is not by accident that her name is Grace. Grace has that spirit of generosity as she shares with her readers her own struggles as a child of Holocaust survivors. Transgenerational trauma (Morris, 2001) is common among the children of victims of war and brutality. It is not easy to write through that trauma and come out on the other side with a generous spirit.

Many people become embittered and defeated. But not Grace. Grace is the life force itself as she writes through trauma in a most eloquent and graceful way. Grace tells us,

> We must come together to teach and learn about how to find an end to violence, poverty, oppression and war....The goal of this book is to bear witness to the courage of teaching and learning within a context of vulnerability....In such an atmosphere we begin to teach with true compassion. I am afraid to think of where today's children of difference, of poverty, of abuse, and of war will be if we do not offer them an education open to the rainbow of diversity and mindful of the challenges of a "humanity in ruins," in Samuel Beckett's words. (p. 5)

To bear witness is akin to giving testimony. These are spiritual acts. Becoming compassionate is also a spiritual act. Compassion is not just a word but also a way of being in the world. And there are so few people who are truly capable of being compassionate. Compassion comes out of a sense of spirituality, religiosity, and humility.

Bearing Witness to Jewish Studies

Alan Block (2007) bears witness to the fact that

> education in North America has been forever based in Greek idealist thinking, and I have spent my life in school. The texts taught as *our* heritage were really *their* heritage. The grains I harvested were not those I had planted. I planted and harvested in fields that did not belong to me. Nor were the tools I used my own. (p. 21)

Block's point is that the curriculum has excluded Jewish thought; the curriculum we inherit is mostly steeped in the Greek tradition. But it is also steeped in the Western Christian tradition. America is primarily a Christian (and Protestant) country. So our educations reflect this tradition. Block states, "I had begun searching out the silences: where and how did Jewish discourse get eliminated from the educational practices in the Western world, and more particularly in the United States" (p. 19). The elimination of Jewish thought is not unrelated to anti-Semitism. It is no accident that Jewish thought is nowhere to be found in the traditional canon that we grew up with in high school, or even in college. Svi Shapiro (1999) remarks,

> It is also a curious, if little commented on, fact that while the "postmodern" moment has meant an unparalleled acknowledgment of the salience of "difference" and the

> "other" in the constitution of our social world, within critical educational studies at least, this has not included much about Jews as either an oppressed or marginalized group. Whatever the reason…Jews who have identified themselves with a radical or critical project in education have, for the most part, been silent on their own Jewish identities and its effect on their lives and beliefs. (p. 2)

Historically, in the academy Jews were not hired, especially in departments of English and history, until after the 1930s because it was thought by mainstream academics that Jews knew little about the Western tradition. But the real reason Jews were not hired is because of anti-Semitism. As David Bleich (1999) reminds us, Lionel Trilling was the first Jewish professor of English to be hired at Columbia University in the 1930s. Bleich explains,

> The story of Trilling's entrance into the academy is, as Klingenstein details, the story of how a Jewish man entered a fraternity of Christian men. In the sixties, Jewish assimilation into the academy…was affected by the influence of feminism.…Jewish feminists, along with other American minority communities, "came out": they no longer behaved as if their being Jewish made no difference. (p. 119)

Still, not all Jewish scholars "came out." Here I am thinking of Maxine Greene. Throughout most of her work there is very little discussion of her own Jewish identity. Greene had to enter into the "fraternity of Christian men," as Bleich puts it, at Columbia, Teachers College, but she was also entering a field (philosophy of education) where women were not exactly welcomed either. Philosophy of education and philosophy in general tend to be male disciplines. So Greene had to fight on two fronts. It is truly a testament to her inner strength and wisdom that not only did she survive a sexist and mostly anti-Semitic academic culture at Columbia, but that she also became one of the most well-known educational theorists in the history of American education. Still today, educational historians tend to ignore the Jewishness of educational theorists. For example, Alan Block (2009) points out, "In J. Wesley Null's recent biography of Isaac Kandel, Null dismisses the influence of Judaism on Kandel's important work in curriculum by separating his work in Jewish education from his work in secular curriculum" (p. 9). Block also comments on the anti-Semitic atmosphere of Columbia, Teachers College in reference to Kandel. I will cite here another passage from Block's book because it highlights not only Kandel's struggles but also the struggles of many Jewish academics, not only in the United States but in Europe as well. Block states,

Indeed, there is in Null's biography even the strongest hint that Kandel's early failure to be appointed a regular faculty at Teacher's College, though other friends and "fellow students of his" ascended to professor positions, resulted from institutional Anti-Semitism, and that it was only after his work became more acceptable to Christian ears that Kandel received promotion. (p. 10)

In my 2006 book *Jewish Intellectuals and the University*, I note that this pattern of not hiring Jews or not promoting them was especially rampant in Europe. Some speculate that Walter Benjamin could not land an academic position because he was Jewish. Hannah Arendt was also a rather nomadic scholar who had little relation to the university. Freud had trouble getting promoted:

Freud (1935/1989), in his autobiography, expresses how isolated and alienated he felt as a Jewish intellectual working in an Austrian university. It is ironic that it was at the University of Vienna—and not, say, in Austrian coffee houses or just out walking the streets—that he felt most alienated. It is clear that many European universities were hotbeds of anti-Semitism. (Morris, 2006, p. 43)

But anti-Semitism is not just a thing of the past. It is alive and well in all aspects of society. Neo-Nazism is on the rise in Europe. Mara Sapon-Shevin (1999) tells us,

On the floor of my office I found a piece of paper. It read: "Shut up and get out of here or your reproductive capacity will be diminished sharply. On the back, the paper said, "Holocaust—destruction of the Jews." (p. 276)

Some of us think that anti-Semitism doesn't happen in America. Well it does and it occurs on university campuses, as Sapon-Shevin reports. It still, however, shocks that this kind of hatred is so pervasive.

Svi Shapiro's (1999) edited collection titled *Strangers in the Land: Pedagogy, Modernity, and Jewish Identity* deals with Jewish identity, issues of exclusion from the curriculum, and anti-Semitism. Alan Block has written extensively on Jewish identity in his books. Block's notable books on Jewish identity are these: *Pedagogy, Religion, and Practice: Reflections on Ethics and Teaching* (2007); *Ethics and Teaching: A Religious Perspective on Revitalizing Education* (2009); and *Talmud, Curriculum and the Practical: Joseph Schwab and the Rabbis* (2004). Shirley Steinberg (1999) has commented on her Jewish identity as she says, "Teaching has always come totally natural to me. Being a Jew has always come natural to me—I am a Jewish teacher. That may be redundant as Judaism is so deeply associated with pedagogy" (p. x). In the Jewish tradition being learned is one of the most highly valued qualities of Jewish life. Study is so ingrained in the Jewish tradition that it is not surprising that many Jews enter the academy. Roger I. Simon (1999) talks about Jewish pedagogy in relation to discussion of difference, generally speaking. Simon remarks, "What is at stake is how the explicit adhesion to the specificity of Jewish culture and sensibility can participate in a redefinition of public discussion as to how, within plural democratic communities, life might become more joyful, just and compassionate" (p. 318).

What I am trying to drive home by citing these Jewish scholars is that when talking about spirituality, scholars have to know from which tradition that spirituality springs. Jewish spirituality is very different from, say, Christian spirituality, because of the history of anti-Semitism. The history of anti-Semitism has marked Jews and has made life more difficult, especially since the Holocaust. The exclusions of Jewish thought from the curriculum, as Alan Block (2007; 2009) points out in his works, only adds insult to injury.

It has become more acceptable within the last, say, twenty years to make Jewish identity a central part of one's scholarship. Philip Wexler, David Purpel, David Bleich, Shirley Steinberg, H. Svi Shapiro, Marla Morris, Roger Simon, Grace Feuerverger, and others have contributed to the growth of this sector of the field.

Today, one of the largest problems we face in American public discourse is Islamophobia, especially since 9/11. Recently there has been public debate over the building of a Mosque near ground zero. There are many Americans who are upset by this and feel that it is inappropriate and insensitive to build a mosque so close to ground zero and some see it as suspect. All Muslims are not terrorists. Most Americans understand this, but still there are those who are blinded by their own prejudices and blame the entire Muslim world for the actions of a few. I would hope in the future that curriculum scholars write more on Islam and Islamic spirituality against the backdrop of anti-Muslim sentiment. Not much so far has been written in curriculum studies on this. However, there is a notable book on this very issue, co-edited by Joe Kincheloe and Shirley Steinberg (2004), titled *The Miseducation of the West: How Schools and the Media Distort our Understanding of the Islamic World*. Joe Kincheloe (2004b) comments,

In the Western tradition of writing about, researching, and representing Islam, Europeans have consistently positioned Muslims as the irrational, fanatic, sexually enticing, and despotic others. This portrayal, as many scholars have argued has been as much about Western anxieties, fears, and self-doubts about Islam. (p. 1)

These misrepresentations of Muslims are highly problematic to say the least. These same kinds of misrepresentations have been made about other minority groups like Jews and Blacks. The study of Muslim identity and the issues of anti-Muslim sentiment is an important sector of the field of curriculum studies for the future. Hopefully we will see the next generation of curriculum scholars take up this issue in the next ten or so years. Still, this conversation has not been widely shared or talked about in curriculum circles.

· 4 ·

COSMOPOLITAN
CURRICULUM CONCEPTS

The International Association for the Advancement of Curriculum Studies (IAACS) holds conferences globally, and the field, as William Pinar (2003a) notes, is now worldwide (p. 1). For students who are interested in the world-wideness—if you will—of curriculum studies, consult William Pinar's (2003a) *International Handbook of Curriculum Research*. This is the first book in the field that deals with curriculum studies on a worldwide scale. Pinar explains,

> This is, I believe, the first international handbook of curriculum studies. As such, it represents the first move in postulating an architecture of a worldwide field of curriculum studies. By worldwide, I do not mean uniform. As I have noted on another occasion, at this stage of formulation, curriculum studies tends to be embedded in their national and regional settings, often stipulated by national educational policies and/or reaction to them. (p. 1)

There are several issues here that I would like to tease out and think through. What does it mean to think worldwide and to think also on the national level? It must be noted that thinking internationally, though, is not new in the field of education broadly speaking. Mary Hayden, Jack Levy, and Jeff Thompson (2008) have also compiled a book on international issues in education that students might consult as well. Their text is called *The SAGE Handbook of Research in International Education*. Robert Sylvester (2008) comments,

As a discipline concerned with both theory and practice, international education may be considered wide enough to embrace both education for international understanding, as it has been known for well over a century, and education for world citizenship, which many have argued in support of for centuries. (p. 12)

Comparing these two volumes—Pinar's *International Handbook of Curriculum Research* and Hayden, Levy, and Thompson's *Research in International Education*—is an interesting study in the ways in which these two competing fields differ. Curriculum studies has become an international field of study, its scholars are interested in more than institutional structures and the practices of teachers within those institutions. Curriculum scholars, in Pinar's book, approach curriculum through various theoretical throughlines such as environmental education, postmodernism, postcolonialism, and more. I will take a closer look at how these theoretical throughlines get instantiated in various national contexts later. Conversely, Mary Hayden, Jack Levy and Jeff Thompson's book on international education is about institutional structures and teacher education. Much of the volume is about comparing schools internationally as they utilize technology or issues of classroom management. Curriculum studies, on the other hand, is a much broader field and is more interested in the various ways we approach lived experience via theoretical frameworks. The field of curriculum studies draws more on the humanities than does the field of international education or the field of comparative education. Autobiography, for example, is nowhere to be found in the Hayden et al. text. So what I am trying to suggest here is that when students study international issues and education they should know that there are a variety of perspectives available and that curriculum studies as a worldwide field, as Pinar puts it, is different from international or comparative education. I want to talk in more depth about what it is that scholars in different countries are doing with curriculum studies, as noted in Pinar's handbook, in a while. But before I do that, there are other issues that need to be sorted out and thought through. Drawing on William Pinar's (2009) book titled *The Worldliness of a Cosmopolitan Education: Passionate Lives in Public Service*, I want to flesh out a most interesting discussion on the issue of cosmopolitanism. Pinar's book on cosmopolitanism is one of the most interesting and important books on the topic in the field. Before discussing Pinar's unique contribution to the discussion of cosmopolitanism, I want to explore the broader discussion on what cosmopolitanism is. When students better understand what the majority of scholars are talking about in terms of the cosmopolitical, they will see just how unique and important Pinar's contribution to thinking the cosmopolital is. The issues raised here might spur students' interests in developing this area more.

Outline of Chapter

This chapter will be organized broadly in this way: First, it is important to think of what it means to think of the world or to think on a universal level and to think about the idea of the universal. Second, it is important to think about what it means to think on a national level and think about the idea of the national. Third, it is important to think about borders between nations and the permeability of those borders or what the idea of a border means. Fourth, it is important—as noted by many scholars in Pinar's (2003a) handbook—to think the universal and particular (or the international and national) at once. Is that even possible? Fifth, we must begin to study why people want to think the world in the first place. What has pushed us toward more international conversations?

Thinking globally is nothing new. But what is new are threats to the world such as nuclear proliferation, ecological disasters, and terrorism. These issues have forced us to begin to think about our place in the world and our responsibility toward the world, as it seems to be crumbling under the pressures of globalization (neoliberalism).

Issues of war and peace have always been issues of the universal and the particular or issues of the cosmopolital. Especially since WWI, issues of the cosmopolital have grown more intense. Most of the scholarly discussions on the cosmopolital have to do with what makes a nation a nation, how we think the world, what happens when nations collide, and how to think both nation and the world together. These are largely political concerns and abstract questions that are rather intriguing. And again, they are not new questions as philosophers have been asking these kinds of questions for a long time. But the cosmopolital has become a crucial topic of discussion, especially since 9/11; the resurgence of this literature is no accident.

After exploring these broad and abstract topics, I will turn back to the ways in which curriculum studies scholars talk about their work internationally. William Pinar's (2009) unique contribution to this discussion concerns the missing link in most books on the cosmopolital, and that is the concept of subjectivity. This should come as no surprise since anyone who has studied Pinar's work knows that subjectivity and interiority—as they relate to the larger sociopolitical scene—are major throughlines throughout his career as a curriculum scholar. Nowhere in the literature on the cosmopolitical does any scholar bring up the issue of subjectivity, except Pinar. Pinar breaks ground here. And so toward the end of this chapter I want to talk about Pinar's contribution to the field and to the larger discussion on the cosmopolitical.

Cosmopolitanism: A Problematic Term

Above I have outlined the basic structure of this chapter to help readers follow the discussion. But before I get into that outline, first what I want to do is discuss some of the problematics of the term "cosmopolitan." As I said earlier, some of the most interesting books on international issues concerning education turn on the notion of the cosmopolitan. I (2001) point out that this term—especially during the Holocaust—was used in Germany and in Russia in a negative sense to describe Jews. Ulrich Beck (2008) explains,

> Cosmopolitanism has been forgotten, that it has been transformed and debased into a pejorative concept, is to be ascribed to its involuntary association with the Holocaust and the Stalinist Gulag. In the collective symbolic system of the Nazis, "cosmopolitan" was synonymous with a death sentence. All victims of the planned mass murder were portrayed as cosmopolitans; and this death sentence was extended to the word, which in its own way succumbed to the same fate. The Nazis said "Jew" and mean "cosmopolitan"; the Stalinists said "cosmopolitan" and mean "Jew." (p. 3)

Thus, Jews were considered cosmopolitans in a negative sense by Nazis and communists. But the commonsense understanding of the term "cosmopolitan" simply means a person who is worldly wise, someone who, perhaps, reads the *New York Times*. Someone who is cosmopolitan is interested in the larger problems of the world. As the late Dennis Carlson (2003) points out, cosmopolitanism "does battle against parochialism, insularity of culture, and both close-mindedness and narrow-mindedness" (p. 8). The Nazis, for example, were both close-minded and narrow-minded as well as being hard-core nationalists. Jews—who Nazis accused of being cosmopolitan—were not seen as citizens of Germany, rather they were seen as vermin or even as parasites living off German soil, not belonging to the nation. Russians, too, have had a long history of anti-Semitism, and some still refer to Jews and Americans as cosmopolitans because many Russians see Americans—like Jews—as capitalists and, hence, cosmopolitans. Jew=American=capitalist=cosmopolitan for Russian communists (Morris, 2001). Nazi Germany is a glaring example of what is wrong with nationalism and a national spirit gone wrong. Flag, country, patriotism, nation, soil, blood, and purity are all problems of nationalism. Jews were not considered citizens and were seen as a threat to blood, country, and nation.

There are other troubles for the concept of cosmopolitanism. When people think of cosmopolitans they think of the worldly wise. But this worldly wise person is usually thought to be a white European male. The notion of the intellectual (who is cosmopolitan) has also been thought historically to be a European or Euro-American male (Morris, 2006). And, too, this male is a colonizing one. Peter Van Der Veer (2008) explains, "In gender terms the cosmopolitan is more usually conceived as a man....Cosmopolitanism is the Western engagement with the rest of the world and that engagement is a colonial one" (p. 167). The cosmopolitan male is the European white male. European colonialism has a long and horrendous history that I will explore more in the chapter on postcolonialism, but for now it is enough to say that white Euro-centric thinking is what cosmopolitanism might signify. Claudia Eppert and Hongyu Wang (2008) have commented on "the continued marginality of Eastern thought" (p. xvii) in scholarly circles. Can the cosmopolitan thinker think the East? Again the history of the word "cosmopolitan" has meant European white male or American white male intellectual. Stuart Hall (2008) remarks, "It is all very well to be a cosmopolitan if you are a white American academic" (p. 26). For those students who are interested in other ways of thinking about cosmopolitanism I would suggest reading Ifeoma Kiddoe Nwankwo's (2005) interesting and important book called *Black Cosmopolitanism: Racial Consciousness and Transnational Identity in the Nineteenth-Century Americas*. Nwankwo argues,

> Black cosmopolitanism is born of the interstices between two mutually constitutive cosmopolitanisms—a hegemonic cosmopolitanism exemplified by the material and psychological violence of imperialism and slavery (including dehumanization), and a cosmopolitanism that is rooted in a common knowledge and memory of that violence. (p. 13)

Cosmopolitanism raises serious issues of race and colonization. I want to raise these issues at the outset of this chapter to point out that the word "cosmopolitan" is not without baggage and cultural history. For blacks and for Asians— and other subaltern groups—the term "cosmopolitan" raises red flags. For peoples who have been colonized or brutalized the term raises red flags. For Jews the word "cosmopolitan" means something totally different against the background of Nazi Germany and Stalinist Russia anti-Semitism. The word "cosmopolitan" then is troubling for many.

Following Bruce Robbins (1998), perhaps scholars should rethink "cosmopolitanism" as more of a plural term. That is, Robbins suggests that there are cosmopolitanisms (p. 2). He explains,

> Like nations, cosmopolitanisms are now plural and particular. Like nations, they are both European and non-European, and they are weak and underdeveloped as well as strong and privileged. And again like the nation, cosmopolitanism is *there*—not merely an abstract ideal, like loving one's neighbor as oneself, but habits of thought and feeling that have already shaped and been shaped by particular collectivities, that are socially and geographically situated (p. 2)

So one can use the term "cosmopolitanism" in many different ways. Cosmopolitanism means many different things to many different people.

Cosmopolitanism and the Universal

Noel Gough (2003) suggests that "thinking globally" (p. 54) is no easy task. The cosmopolitan thinker thinks globally. For Gough thinking globally "remains largely unexamined and undertheorized" (p. 54) especially "within the discourses of environmental education" (p. 54). The cosmopolitan environmentalist is one who can think the world ecologically. But how does one do that exactly? Is this even possible? If you are a scientist you might understand ecological issues on a global scale. And if you can understand ecological issues as a global issue you might be considered a cosmopolitan thinker. One type of cosmopolitanism, then, is ecological cosmopolitanism. But this certainly was not the meaning that the Greeks had in mind when they talked of the cosmopolitan. Martha Nussbaum (1997) tells us,

> The meaning of the idea [cosmopolitan] for political life is made especially clear in Cicero's work *On Duties (De Officiis)*, written in 44 B.C. [E.] and based in part on the writings of the slightly earlier Greek Stoic thinker Panaetius. Cicero argues that the duty to treat humanity with respect requires us to treat aliens on our soil with honor and hospitality. (p. 60)

Nussbaum unearths the history of the words "duty" and "hospitality." These words both predate Kant and Derrida—who also use these terms to explain the meaning of cosmopolitanism. Seyla Benhabib (2008) explains, "Kant introduces the term 'Weltbuergerrecht' (cosmopolitan right) in the Third Article of 'Perpetual Peace,' with reference to the duty of hospitality" (p. 21). Likewise, Jacques Derrida (2002b) talks about the "original concept of hospitality, of the duty (*devoir*) of hospitality, and of the right (*droit*) to hospitality" (p. 5). But Derrida adds—to this ancient definition of cosmopolitan—what he calls "cities of refuge" (p. 5). Derrida asks, "What in effect is the context in which we have proposed this new ethic or this new cosmo*politics* of the cities of refuge? Is it necessary to call to mind the violence which rages on a worldwide scale?" (p. 5). What would "cities of refuge" be? Who would go there? And where would that be? And is the problem of violence part and parcel of the meaning of a cosmopolitan frame of mind? If scholars go back to the Greek meaning of the word "cosmopolitan," the words duty, hospitality, and alien are mentioned (Nussbaum). Must one then assume that the term emerged in 44 BCE because aliens or foreigners to Greek soil were not welcomed? Are aliens treated inhospitably on what Derrida calls a "worldwide scale" (p. 5)? If so, does cosmopolitanism first and foremost deal with issues of violence? Why the need to talk of hospitality at all? Some people are inhospitable to those who are not citizens. Stephen Toulmin (1992) points out,

> The Greek word "cosmopolis" calls for comment. In Classical Greece and before, people recognized that the World into which humans are born, and with which they have to deal embodies two distinct kinds of "order." There is an Order of nature.... The traditional Greek word for that first kind or order was *cosmos*...celestial events happen, not randomly, but in a natural order....The Greek word for this second order was *polis*: to say that a community...its practices and organizations had the overall coherence that qualified it...as a "political" unit. (p. 67)

So the cosmopolitical combined the celestial and earthly order. The point being that a truly cosmopolitan society would be one of harmony (p. 67). How the celestial and the political community came together in this harmonious relation was the goal of Greek life. But the universe is not a harmonious place; it is violent. Explosions in space happen all the time; the earth was created by a huge explosion, the big bang. Black holes are violent and comets and other celestial rock formations are always crashing into each other. Likewise, communities are not harmonious, but are always fighting. Nations are always at war. At any rate, part of the meaning of the cosmopolitical is about the universe itself—the cosmos—which for the Greeks, according to Stephen Toulmin, should be harmonious and the polis—the political community— should be harmonious with the universe. But this is the crux of the problem.

These two things are impossible. The universe is not harmonious and neither are political communities. So the idea of the cosmopolitical is already a problem. And then there is another meaning here too. In the Greek sense, the cosmopolitan is a person of the world (of the political community) and a person who is of the cosmos (in harmony with the universe). The cosmopolitan is a person of universal ideas.

The notion of the cosmopolitan who can think in harmony with the universe and the community is highly problematic. Kwame Anthony Appiah (2007) asks, "A Citizen of the world: how far can we take that idea?" (p. xv). Peter Van Der Veer (2008) asks, "Is cosmopolitanism a view from nowhere?" (p. 165). The cosmopolitan can think the world and the universe together as both being in sync and in harmony, according the Greeks. How is this possible? The cosmopolitan—as one who can think the world and think in universal terms—raises insurmountable problems. And these problems are partly noted by Appiah and van der Veer. The cosmopolitan mind frame is difficult because, first, one cannot think the world and, second, universals do not exist. But universal ideas like hospitality, respect, and dignity of human life are concepts that can be thought. William Pinar (2009) points out, "Hannah Arendt promoted 'worldliness' and, relatedly, 'care for the world' as 'chief' among cosmopolitan virtues" (pp. 28–29). To be worldly then means to care for the world. The Greek definition of the cosmopolitan and Kant's and Arendt's definitions did not include the nonhuman world—as Pinar points out. The cosmopolitan also cares for the nonhuman animal world as well. So we have arrived back where we began this discussion with Noel Gough (2003) and the difficulty of thinking globally and what that might mean. Again, the cosmopolitan is the person who is not narrow-minded, who can think beyond her own self-interest and her own place in the world. Narrow-mindedness is the exact opposite of cosmopolitanism. Somehow scholars must become more cosmopolitan in their thinking even if the world cannot be thought.

The cosmopolitan is the person who is well read and travels figuratively through reading. Paulo Freire (2005) talks about "reading the world by reading the word," as readers are reminded by Donaldo Macedo and Ana Maria Araujo Freire (2005, p. vii). Reading is not an elite activity, as Freire knew. He spent his lifework teaching peasants to read so that they could better understand their worlds. When you read the word you can change the world—this was Freire's message. And that is the cosmopolitan spirit. The cosmopolitan does not have to literally travel the world to have a sense of things. The cosmopolitan is the well-read, well-rounded person who tries to understand other people and tries to help others—including nonhuman animals—and tries to make the world a better place. Students have to remember, too, that when Arendt was talking about worldliness—as Pinar (2009) points out—she was talking about this against the backdrop of the Holocaust. Caring for the world, for Arendt, mean not destroying it the way the Nazis did. Destroying the world means killing the world, killing people, killing animals, and destroying the ecosphere. To destroy the world is exactly what the cosmopolitan person does not do. The cosmopolitan person tries to make the world a better place through creative activities like writing, reading, playing music, dancing, teaching, or cultivating friendships. Dennis Carlson (2003) argues,

> I approach cosmo-politics as one who believes it may be useful in helping pull together a democratic counter-hegemonic movement in American education and public life that can pose a serious challenge to the resurgent neo-liberal discourse of globalization. (p. 9)

So for Carlson, cosmopolitanism has everything to do with democracy and fighting ever-encroaching neoliberalism.

Cosmopolitanism, the Other, and Education

The cosmopolitan person—as Derrida (2002) teaches—embraces the Other and difference. This is where the idea of hospitality comes back into the conversation. The cosmopolitan person does the impossible, Derrida suggests. Paulo Freire (2005) might have called this "radical love" as Joe Kincheloe (2005, p. xii) reminds us. This is not sentimental love, but the embrace of the Other. Openness toward the Other suggests a form of hospitality that is not easy.

Can one talk about education in the context of a universal cosmopolitanism? Is there such a thing? Can education be cosmopolitan? Can a teacher be a cosmopolitan teacher? Can scholars teach in a more cosmopolitan spirit? There are some things one can take from the idea of the universal in the context of the cosmopolitan. Trying to understand the world means reading a lot and reading international texts. Studying international issues is not altogether impossible. Educators can become more international in their scope but that takes a lot of study and commitment to want to know more about the larger world outside of their own world. Traveling might not even be the answer here either because when people travel mostly they are tourists, and tourists learn little because they only stay in another country for a short while. But when scholars study international texts they are not tourists if they spend a great deal of time studying issues in other countries. But then again, there is only so much about the world that scholars can study. Knowledge is limited, always. But scholars can spend time focusing on one aspect of another part of the world. Scholars learn about this other part of the world through study and erudition. This is not an impossible task. Scholars can be cosmopolitan thinkers but this kind of thinking is always limited by what they focus on and how much time they have to do this kind of work. And this is where the problem of specialization comes in. Historians, for example, tend to specialize, say, in Eastern European politics during a particular era. So they know a lot about one specific place during one specific time. This is the nature of specialization. And it is good to specialize. But it is also necessary to welcome generalists—like curriculum theorists—into the picture. Generalists might study this part of the world and that part of the world, moving from, say, Eastern Europe, to Asia, to indigenous cultures in New Zealand, to South Africa. This is the cosmopolitan educator. But this work is difficult because you have to be sort of all over the place and the academy does not tend to honor this way of working. Dennis Carlson (2003), in talking about cosmopolitanism and education, suggests,

> Cosmopolitan progressives are border crossers in yet another sense. They increasingly identify with cultural studies, that emergent non-field that is rupturing established disciplinary boundaries in the academy, including those that have separated the curriculum reconceptualist movement, critical pedagogy, and the cultural foundations of education. (p. 26)

This citation raises many interesting questions for curriculum theorists, cultural studies scholars, and social and cultural foundation scholars of education. One of the hallmarks of the contemporary field of curriculum studies is that academic borders are permeable, as Carlson points out. Scholars work in many different fields at once. The interesting point Carlson makes is that scholars who cross disciplinary borders are working as cosmopolitan intellectuals. But is this enough? Shouldn't we also make it a point to study things on an international scale too? Shouldn't we begin to think about worldwide issues? Carlson also suggests that these are our tasks. But thinking internationally requires both specialists and generalists. This way one gets both breadth and depth. Of course scholars cannot know the world and cannot study the entire world. Certainly our work is always limited by focus and time. It is possible, for example, for an American to study European history without literally traveling to Europe. To be a cosmopolitan intellectual does not mean that you literally have to go to the places you are studying. Studying the issues at hand through reading scholarly texts and perhaps even being at a distance (place-wise) might work better for some. Distance from the event in time helps as well. When you are in the middle of something, you usually cannot get hold of it. William Pinar (2009) speaks to the issue of distance here as he suggests,

> For those of us whose profession is academic study, maintaining a critical (if variable) distance between our work and the society in which it occurs remains an obligation. Distance constitutes a prerequisite to the ongoing cultivation of disciplinary structures such as "verticality" (intellectual history) and "horizontality" (analysis of present circumstances). (p. 8)

So whether scholars study U.S. history or European history, distance is necessary to get at what they are trying to understand. Studying requires distance in that you are alone when you read and must separate yourself from the ongoings of the everyday world in order to understand that everyday world. If you are too mired in the everyday, you have no way of articulating it. Your "present circumstances" shape the way you understand "intellectual history" (Pinar, 2009, p. 8). Pinar is not saying that you escape the present world in which you live, but live more deeply in it, ironically, by getting distance from it through erudition. But there is more to being a cosmopolitan educator than studying international issues. The next section tackles some of these issues.

Cosmopolitanism: Thinking the Universal and the Particular Together

One of the most interesting conversations scholars are having currently about the issue of cosmopolitanism is attempting to think the universal and the particular together. This avoids the problem of "speaking from nowhere," as Peter van der Veer (2008) puts it. Thinking the particular means thinking in place, thinking where you are as you think about others and/or other places. William Pinar (2009) puts it this way: "'Internationalization' [or cosmopolitanism] captures the complexity of collective entities—nationally distinctive fields of curriculum studies—in disciplinary conversation with other collective entities through specific individuals" (p. 28). What Pinar suggests here is that international views on curriculum studies differ and that the field of curriculum studies is not monolithic. Nations produce different kinds of curriculum studies scholars. That the field is now international does not mean that the field is the same everywhere.

The question that arises is this: what is the connection between studying things internationally and studying things through a more cosmopolitan point of view? Are these the same things? Maybe not. Or maybe so. Is it possible to study international issues and still be a nationalist? Yes. Being a nationalist is not being cosmopolitan. On the other hand it is possible to study international issues and also have a cosmopolitan mindset. Having a cosmopolitan mindset means that you know you live in a particular place and view international issues from that place but that does not necessarily make you a nationalist. Contrarily, you might study people who live and work and teach in your own country but have a cosmopolitan outlook. Here I am thinking of William Pinar's (2009) work on Jane Addams and Laura Bragg—two Americans—who worked in a cosmopolitan fashion to change the world. Studying things cosmopolitan does not necessarily mean studying people who live outside of your own country either. Pinar suggests that scholars need to rethink the universal imperative that Kant set down when he talked about the cosmopolitan. Pinar says, "No ideal imposed from above, worldliness [a word used by Arendt] takes infinite earthy forms; it contradicts the universalism of Kant's cosmopolitanism, by remaining a particularism" (p. 35). Pinar suggests that scholars can only get at the world through their own particular perspective of it. Kant's philosophical system was about categorical imperatives that would work anywhere for anyone at any time. These categorical imperatives (for Kant) were ethical laws of behavior, international rules of behavior that if followed, all would work out. But for Pinar, there are no universal rules of behavior, no universal duties. The cosmopolitan educator, for Pinar, then, is someone who works where he works; he is in some place at some time and sees the world through his particular frame of mind. This does not mean that he is a nationalist or is parochial. No. Admitting that you live in some place in some time suggests that you see through your eyes and are grounded in a particular place. You can do international study and be cosmopolitan in outlook and also do this work through particular lenses. You might embrace universal ideas of duty, hospitality, and respect, but you embrace these universals through your own particular personhood, gender, region, psychological makeup, and so forth. Like Pinar, Bruce Robbins (1998) points out that "David Hollinger and Mitchell Cohen both describe their preferred form of cosmopolitanism as 'rooted'; Homi Bhabha qualifies his as 'vernacular'" (p. 1).

The Particularities of Place

So cosmopolitanism means that scholars study—from a particular place (from within their own national traditions)—the traditions of others. This is a view from somewhere. We are, in a way, place-bound as we study others. We grow up in a nation that has certain traditions; we grow up in the academic institutions we inherit. We are situated within the particular world in which we live. Studying the world means being situated in place and time. This means, too, that we have a particular viewpoint of the world and of our place in the world as we study others who might not live in the same place as we do.

Queering the Cosmopolitan: The Cybercosmopolitan

Is universal the same as global? Do ideas have global meanings? Or are all ideas particular and regional? How to talk about education and curriculum studies globally and regionally at once? Is internationalization the same as cosmopolitanism? What is the relation between the national and the international? Can we queer the cosmopolitan? What would that mean? Questions of the international, the national, the global, the local, the cosmopolitan are, of course, all interrelated and complicated. The meanings of these terms are changeable, sometimes interchangeable, sometimes not. In some contexts these words have had pejorative meanings and still do in some circles. Can scholars think the international at all? Amanda Anderson (1998) notes,

> The virtue of [James] Clifford's work, for Robbins, lies in its skillful dismantling of the opposition between cosmopolitan and local, its insistence on multiple cosmopolitanisms partly rooted in local cultures, partly positioned in global networks. No longer conceivable as the prerogative of the West, cosmopolitanisms manifest themselves in any instance of sustained intercultural contact and exchange. (p. 273)

The local, the global, the national, the international, the cosmopolitical, the cross-cultural, transcultural, and now "intercultural," as Anderson (p. 273) puts it, are intertwined. It is not so clear anymore what is meant by universal or particular as the particular is in the universal and the universal is in the particular and the local is in the global and the global is in the local and so forth. A more concrete example of this is what is happening in cyberspace. The Internet has made for much of this confusion. Posting something on Facebook allows your local event to go global and Facebook interfaced with Foursquare or Hootsuite makes the local even more global. You can be known now all over the world as you sit in your living room networking across the web. Cyberspace is continually on the move with Skype, Myspace, blogs, iPhones, tweeting, and so forth. It is not so clear what all of these interfaces do to us. Some argue that working in cyberspace isolates us rather than connects us globally. But still, if you post on Facebook and Google throws your image across the globe, that makes your tweeting and hooting and Myspacing, and iPhoning international, global, and local at the same time. You can now be cosmopolitan and never leave your house. Of course books provide the opportunity, too, to become more cosmopolitan by reading. But now you can travel through cyberspace and share your thoughts with the entire cybercommunity. In the literature on cosmopolitanism there is not much discussion on these new technologies as many of the writers are perhaps the generation(s) who struggle with computers and do not know what a tweet or a hoot is. Our students do, however. Talking with our students about all of this—since they were born with iPhones and tweeting and have grown up with Myspace and Foursquare— can help older generations understand the rapid pace of these changing technologies. Bruce Robbins (1998) points out,

> Like nations, worlds too are imagined [this is a reference to Benedict Anderson's idea of the "imagined community"]. For better or for worse, there is a growing consensus that cosmopolitanism sometimes works together with nationalism rather than in opposition to it. It is thus less clear what cosmopolitanism is opposed to, or what its value is supposed to be. (p. 2)

Can you be a nationalist and cosmopolitan simultaneously? The parochialism that goes along with nationalism is in contradistinction to the broader visions that cosmopolitans bring to the table. But if it weren't for nationalism, the idea of the cosmopolitan would not have emerged. These concepts are in a sort of ego-dystonic relation. David Geoffrey Smith (2003) argues,

> Globalization may especially refer to a particular kind of tension in the world, arising from what Arnove and Torres (1999) called "the glocal" (p. 14). Human self-understanding is now increasingly lived out in tension between the local and the global, between my understanding of myself as a person of this place and my emerging yet profound awareness that this place participates in a reality heavily influenced by, and implicated in, the larger picture. This calls forth from me not just a new sense of place, but also a new kind of response to the world. (p. 36)

The term "globalization" is used in the literature sometimes in a pejorative way to describe neoliberalism, whereas the term "internationalization" is not used in this pejorative way and has nothing to do with neoliberalism. In this discussion there are so many competing and confusing terms that one must be careful in the way one uses these concepts. Smith points out that his "sense of place" has now shifted and also he feels "a new kind of response to the world" (p. 36). But what is that sense of place and what is that new kind of response? If our place is partially marked by our daily intake of Facebook, iPhoning, Skyping, hooting, and tweeting, reading, writing, and teaching, what does that do to our sense of place? Does our activity in cyberspace make us lose our place, lose our footing as it were? If we have one foot in cyberspace and one foot in the world of face-to-faceness, what is our sense of place then? Carmen Luke (2001) speaks to some of these issues here:

> Moreover, whether we look at regionalization, internationalization, or globalization of education, the actual delivery and consumption of education remain situated in local sites embedded in local cultures, nation-state formulated rules and regulations, and localized subjective relations among and between staff and students. Even "virtual" degrees are consumed by subjects in a place and produced and assessed by subjects in yet another place. (p. xix)

But what is a virtual space? Classes that are offered online and fully virtual seem to displace us. If students never see the professor, do they not feel displaced? Then there are hybrid classes where students meet with professors on occasion but spend most of the time in cyberspace. What is a hybrid education all about? And the face-to-face? What will become of college campuses if there is no more face-to-face? Why have a campus at all if you never meet with your students? What is to become of the actual site of the university? Will we have places to go in the future or will we all work from our home computers? Is cybereducation a real education? Or are we just fooling ourselves into thinking that we are teaching our students anything at all? Personal interactions seem to be ever fading into the background as courses become text-based. Now a text-based course is not a bad thing, but our interactions with students change because we do not actually see them—unless we are doing Skype. Can a cybereducation be a cosmopolitan one? If students use YouTube—which can be a great learning tool—does that make them more cosmopolitan in outlook? Can we become cybercosmopolitans? Steven Vertovec and Robin Cohen (2008) comment,

Cosmopolitanism suggests something that simultaneously: (a) transcends the seemingly exhausted nation-state model; (b) is able to mediate actions and ideals oriented both to the universal and the particular, the global and the local; (c) is culturally anti-essentialist; and (d) is capable of representing variously complex repertoires of allegiance, identity and interest. In these ways, cosmopolitanism seems to offer a mode of managing cultural and political multiplicities. (p. 4)

Think about this citation against the increasingly computerized and cyber-spaced world into which we have been thrown. Cyberspace can represent the exact opposite of what Vertovec and Cohen point out above. There are terrible things out there in cyberspace. We all know the pitfalls and dangers for our children with predators and cybercriminals everywhere. We know, too, that there are many websites that teach kids how to make bombs or become part of the Aryan nation or how to join terrorist organizations. Cyberliteracy is, of course, of the utmost importance. Knowing how to navigate websites and avoid getting scammed or drawn into a cult or recruited by cyber-Nazis are things we need to teach our children to steer clear of. Cybercosmopolitanism means steering clear of these dangerous websites, critiquing them and making sure our children know how to spot cybercriminals and how to avoid them. Cyberbullying is also a problem for our kids. So a cosmopolitan education has to also teach children how to critique cybercriminality and how to avoid getting involved in bad things. So when Vertovec and Cohen talk about the cosmopolitan as being able to maneuver "various complex repertoires of allegiance" (p. 4) these allegiances are not with cyber-Nazis and cybergangs or cybercriminals. The cosmopolitan who is worldly wise knows that to educate others means to teach people how to make the world a better place, not a place of war, hatred, terrorism, and murder. Thus, a cosmopolitan education is also one of cyberliteracy and knowing the difference between what is good and what is bad, what is right and what is wrong.

The Problem with Borders: The New Cosmopolitanism

Cyberspace has created what I call the New Cosmopolitan who can travel quickly across the globe without ever leaving her living room. Cyberspace is a place without borders or nations. Yet, of course we still live in nations that have borders. But in the virtual world borders fade. People are on the move in a more concrete sense as well. Cathryn Teasley and Cameron McCarthy

(2008) comment, "The world is now witness not only to a surge in the volume of movement across borders…it is also witness to a transgression of orthodoxies and gatekeeping in conceptual spheres" (p. 1). Immigration and emigration continue on. Nations tighten borders or are unable to do so because of the sheer "surge in volume"—as Cathryn Teasley and Cameron McCarthy (p. 1) put it—of the comings and goings of people across borders.

The second point Teasley and McCarthy make is about the breaking down of tradition with the academy. The emerging academic "studies" programs (e.g., women's studies, religious studies, curriculum studies, cultural studies) signify the increasing acceptance of interdisciplinarity across disciplines in the academy. In fact, one way to think of the New Cosmopolitan intellectual is that person who dares to venture beyond the rigid boundaries of fields into other disciplines. Dennis Carlson (2003) argues that being interdisciplinary means being cosmopolitan. Here I am also thinking of what Timothy Brennan (1997) says of Edward Said. Brennan suggests,

> Whether it is in the mode of intellectual method most closely associated with Edward Said's "worldliness"—the roaming, hungry intelligence bound neither by discipline nor dogma—or the more conjunctural moments of curricular reform on behalf of studying the world's many cultures in place of narrow, job-related specializations, the ethics of cosmopolitanism are as desirable as they are embattled. (p. 15)

The boundaries between disciplines grow ever fuzzier with the ongoing emergence of studies programs that are highly interdisciplinary. This does present some problems, though, as disciplines do battle—to use Brennan's word—over turf. Disciplines still have borders because they have particular histories, but those borders are becoming ever more porous as scholars work in fields other than their own. Not only are academic disciplines losing their rigid boundaries through studies programs, borders between countries, according to Ulrich Beck (2008), continually change:

> What do we mean, then, by the "cosmopolitan outlook?" Global sense, a sense of boundarylessness. An everyday, historically alert, reflexive awareness of ambivalence in a milieu of blurring differentiations and cultural contradictions. It reveals not just the "anguish" but also the possibility of shaping one's life and social relations under conditions of cultural mixture. (p. 3)

What anguish is Beck getting at here? Why would one anguish over a "cosmopolitan outlook," to use Beck's phrase? Is this the anguish of not knowing who we are in a complex world? Is this a postmodern anguish of our multiple identities? Who anguishes over becoming ever more cosmopolitan? Maybe we are not really "boundaryless." After all, there are still nations. Etienne Balibar (1998) comments on this confusion. Balibar suggests that, indeed,

> Borders are vacillating. This does not mean that they are disappearing. Less than ever is the contemporary world a "world without borders." On the contrary, borders are being both multiplied and reduced in their localization and their function, they are being thinned out and doubled, becoming border zones, regions, or countries where one can reside and live....This means that borders are becoming the object of protest and contestation as well as of an unremitting reinforcement, notably of their function of security. (p. 220)

When we think about what has happened after 9/11 in the United States, we can better understand Balibar's position. What we are witnessing is the reinforcement of the boundaries between the United States and Mexico and the United States and Canada because of the fear of terrorists coming across the border to do us harm again. Also, the tightening of borders has much to do with an entrenched racism and nationalism.

Nationalism(s)

William Pinar (2003b), in *The Internationalization of Curriculum Studies: Selected Proceedings from the LSU Conference 2000*, remarks,

> In addition to supporting the emergence of an international field, one of my motives for this conference is to contest the sometimes unbelievable narcissism of American curriculum studies. Probably it is not a special fault of those who work in the field; it seems to come with citizenship. One way we Americans can work through that narcissism is to become more aware, in fact to regard it as part of our professional responsibility to keep track of what others interested in the concept of curriculum (or its equivalent) are doing around the world. (pp. 4–5)

Americans, generally speaking, tend to be America-centric. Part of the issue has to do not only with our own problems at home but also the way in which we see these problems getting played out in the media. Our media are clearly America-centric. The only way to build a more international perspective is to pay attention to international media via the Internet and to read scholarly materials that are more international in scope. But this takes work and it takes time and it forces us to move outside of our own American mindset—if there is such a thing—to begin thinking about what is going on outside of our own borders, both intellectually and politically. Pinar launched the International Association for the Advancement of Curriculum Studies (IAACS) with the intent of beginning conversations across borders. Pinar explains,

> At the LSU meeting in 2000, informal agreement was reached regarding future meetings: The October 2003 meeting will be held in Shanghai, the 2006 meeting in Europe (perhaps Finland), the 2009 meeting in Africa (perhaps South Africa), the 2012 meetings in South America, and in 2015, the organization returns to North America. (p. 2)

The purpose of these international meetings, partly, is to overcome American narcissism and our own tendencies toward nationalism. International conferences and handbooks are helpful to overcome our own nationalistic propensities and to begin discussions across borders. But as Noel Gough (2003) points out,

> We may not be able to speak—or think—from outside our own Eurocentrism, but we can continue to ask questions about how our specifically Western ways of "acting locally" in curriculum inquiry might be performed with other local knowledge traditions in curriculum work. By coproducing curriculum inquiry in transnational spaces, we can, I believe, help to make both the limits *and strengths* of Western epistemologies and methodologies increasingly visible. (p. 69)

We cannot step outside of our own culture (or what Gough calls Eurocentrism) when studying the cultures of others, but we can try to understand other cultures—and our own culture—by making it clear that there are still national boundaries and national ways of thinking that differ from ours. Like Pinar, Gough emphasizes that the local is always the place from which scholars begin to develop their knowledge base. Scholars can share that local knowledge on a more international scale. Still, there is always lurking behind local knowledges the narcissistic tendencies—as Pinar puts it—that foster nationalisms. Salman Rushdie (2003) asks whether

> cultures actually exist as separate, pure, defensible entities? Is not mélange, adulteration, impurity, pick 'n' mix at the heart of the idea of the modern and hasn't it been that way for most of this all-shook-up century? Doesn't the idea of pure cultures, in urgent need of being kept free from alien contamination, lead us inexorably toward apartheid, toward ethnic cleansing, toward the gas chamber? (p. 268)

Intolerance, racisms, and nationalisms of all sorts have not disappeared. In fact, since 9/11 racisms and nationalisms have only escalated. In America we have all sorts of problems, of course, racism being one of the worst. But now Americans have an added anti-Muslim issue to also deal with since 9/11. Anti-Muslim sentiment is everywhere in America and that sentiment goes along with a sort of unthinking nationalism and unthinking patriotism that is dangerous. The right wing is continually gaining momentum with the so-called Tea Party movement. The right wing in America is also particularly upset over the election of a black president. American scholars of curriculum need seriously to think about these issues of nationalisms, and one way to counter that is to do as Pinar suggests—let us have intellectual conversations with other nations across the globe to see what people are thinking outside of our own country. That is the purpose of the development of IAACS. And yet, nationalisms are stronger than international relations—especially during times of war and economic downturns. Richard Rorty (1998) comments, "Our loyalty to such larger groups (e.g., international group relations) will, however, weaken, or even vanish altogether when things get really tough....The tougher things get, the more ties of loyalty to those near at hand tighten, and the more those to everyone else slacken" (p. 45). What Rorty is saying here is that nationalism is stronger than international relations especially during, say, times of war. Take the example of the Holocaust. America goes to war to protect our national interests. The United States did not get involved in WWII until the bombing of Pearl Harbor. President Franklin Roosevelt was not really interested in saving the Jews per se (Morris, 2001). He was interested in protecting the United States from further attack and from the possibility of being invaded by enemy forces. When the U.S. military had the chance to bomb the rail lines leading to Auschwitz they did not. If they had bombed the rail lines—which they were flying over anyway—many more Jews could have been saved from the gas chambers. But again, Roosevelt was not interested in that (Morris, 2001). Americans do not seem to be interested in international politics until we are bombed. The only international politics Americans seem to be engaged in are imperialist in nature (this is what neoliberalism is all about). At any rate, nationalism is at the root of most of our problems and most countries are nationalistic. The problem is how to avoid pitfalls associated with nationalism. Benedict Anderson (2006) asks an interesting question about nationalism here as he wonders why people are willing to die for their country. Anderson states,

> Finally, it [the nation] is imagined as a *community*, because, regardless of the actual inequality and exploitation that may prevail in each, the nation is always conceived as a deep, horizontal comradeship. Ultimately it is this fraternity that makes it possible,

over the past two centuries, for so many millions of people, not so much to kill, as willingly to die for such limited imaginings. (p. 7)

And it is interesting that Anderson's thesis is that nations or the idea of a nation is imagined. We imagine we know what Americans are or what America is, but we really do not know what America is. Anderson argues,

> The birth of the imagined community of the nation can best be seen if we consider the basic structure of imagining which first flowered in Europe in the eighteenth century: the novel and the newspaper. For these forms provided the technical means for "re-presenting" the *kind* of imagined community that is the nation. (pp. 24–25)

Anderson's point is that a nation is imagined, that is, a nation is an idea and we imagine a fraternity that really does not exist. It is this imagined fraternity that makes people want to die for their country. Newspapers, today, are in trouble because the Internet is where people get their news. Journalism is not a career to go into right now with the dying of the newspaper industry. What most people know, they know from going online. How does the online experience then change how we imagine who we are as a nation? America as an idea is still an idea but people believe that they are members of a community, a nation that is real and worth dying for. America is a nation, but how we imagine what that is, is the question that Anderson raises. Gillian Brock and Harry Brighouse (2005) tell us,

> Nationalism appears to have been on the rise since the mid 1980s. The break up of the former Soviet Union, and the dissolution of the barrier between Western and Eastern Europe triggered the political advance of nationalism in Eastern Europe, as new countries emerged, defining themselves in opposition to the previously existing regimes. Simultaneously, increased immigration from the former communist countries and from Muslim countries has fuelled nationalist sentiment within Western European States themselves. (p. 1)

Nationalisms are a worldwide problem. Racism, neo-Nazism, anti-Muslim sentiment, ongoing prejudice against Gypsies and Jews are especially intense in Europe. So one must ask how we can have international conversations when there is so much hatred everywhere? How can we overcome this? Hatred far outlasts reasoned dialogue. But that does not mean we do not continue to try to have reasoned dialogue and understand other people. The problem is that Otherness is not a popular concept, anywhere. As much as academics talk about Otherness and embracing alterity, hatred in the world continues and wars rage on. Dialogue within our own country is difficult as our own political parties can agree on little. So if we cannot have a dialogue across cultures within our own country, how can we have international dialogues? The task *seems* insurmountable. But it is not impossible. This is why IAACS was launched. The international conversation must begin somewhere. IAACS is a good place to start.

Cosmopolitanism Meets the Death Wish

There is much discussion about cosmopolitanism against the backdrop of so much hatred, racism, and genocide. Can the idea of the cosmopolitan spirit also encompass the problems of living in a world that is so full of hatred? Being "worldly-wise" as Pinar (2009, p. 4) puts it, also means being realistic about how dialogue is often thwarted by nationalisms, racisms, and wars. So being well read, well rounded, and well traveled does not make the cosmopolitan. There is more. Being a tourist in the world is being blind to the cruelties of the world. Being a cosmopolitan does not mean being a tourist of the world.

Freud talked about the death wish or the death drive. He suggested that everybody has this in them. At some level everyone is self-destructive. Sometimes that self-destruction gets projected onto others and the hatred that had been turned inward gets turned toward the world: this is the root of racism, hatred, intolerance, murder, genocide. The world has a death drive. The cosmopolitan also is aware of the side of life nobody wants to talk about. One of the most impressive books on this topic is by Sharon Todd (2009), *Toward an Imperfect Education: Facing Humanity, Rethinking Cosmopolitanism*. The commonsense understanding of the cosmopolitan is the bon vivant who travels the world over, reads a lot, and knows a lot. Being cosmopolitan does mean being well rounded and well read. But if you are well read, you will begin to understand that the world we are living in is a dangerous place. These dangers are not often talked about in education classes (especially in courses on classroom management and educational methods). Classroom management and methods courses miseducate students because they make students think that (1) we live in a world that can be "managed" and (2) we can learn certain methods that will help us make things run more smoothly in the classroom. But the world is nothing like this. The world cannot be neatly managed and there are no methods for living in a world where terrorism and brutality reign. Scantron tests do not prepare our students for the messiness of this world, which can be a brutal and cruel place. This is what we learn when reading Sharon Todd's book on rethinking cosmopolitanism. To rethink this term is to rethink the commonsensical notion of the term. Todd states,

> My intent here is to show how shaky this keystone is for supporting the claims being made in cosmopolitanism's name. That is, as long as the idea of humanity disavows what is "inhuman" and imperfect about us, cosmopolitanism cannot give an adequate response to the question of violence and antagonism which plagues our lives, despite its own attestations to the contrary. (p. 3)

Todd grounds her argument in the work of Derrida, Lyotard, Irigaray, Levinas, and Arendt. All of these thinkers argue that people need to pay more attention to the brutalities of life. The idea of the cosmopolitan, then, is not just one of being well traveled. A cosmopolitan view on the world is one that integrates Freud's death drive into everything that is going on in the world. Being well read and well versed also means studying, for example, the Holocaust. This event is not something that most people want to even think about, much less study. A cosmopolitan understanding is one that attempts to understand unthinkable acts of brutality. The cosmopolitan understanding must be an international one and must—as Sharon Todd discusses in her own work—tackle xenophobia and nationalisms that foster intense hatreds. A cosmopolitan education, then, is not for the lighthearted. It is a heavy calling. This is Todd's point. Recall, Derrida (2002b) calls for "cities of refuge" (p. 5) when speaking of cosmopolitanism and the problem of (in)hospitality. Derrida when speaking of cosmopolitanism says,

> What in effect is the context in which we have proposed this new ethic or this new cosmo*politics* of the cities of refuge? Is it necessary to call to mind the violence which rages on a worldwide scale?…Is it possible to enumerate the multiplicity of menaces, of acts of censorship (*censure*) or of terrorism, of persecution and of enslavements in all their forms? (p. 5)

For Derrida, then, this " new cosmo*politics*" must grapple with what Sharon Todd refers to as the "disavow[ed]" "inhuman" (p. 3). Ulrich Beck (2008) comments that cosmopolitanism "evokes" "the most terrible histories" (p. 1). Here he is thinking of Germany. Beck says,

> Heinrich Heine…who regarded himself as an embodiment of cosmopolitanism… criticized German patriotism, which in his view involved "a narrowing of the heart, which contracts like leather in the cold, and hatred of all things foreign—a desire no longer to be a world citizen or a European but merely a narrow German." (p. 1)

It is this narrowness about which Beck speaks that troubles. We see this narrow perspective all over America and all over Europe as the rising tide of immigrants come into new countries and are forced to either leave or are persecuted. The inhuman in us—as Sharon Todd suggests—is this narrowing of perspective, pettiness, and unwillingness to even try to understand someone who is from somewhere else.

International Turmoil and Cosmopolitanism

It seems ironic that this relatively new interest in this old topic—cosmopolitanism—has risen again. One of the reasons that cosmopolitanism is something that is much talked about today is because of increasing international turmoil and the awareness of the brutalities occurring across the globe. I am wondering if people are more aware of these brutalities because of access to world news via the Internet. At any rate, Ulrich Beck (2008) suggests,

> The important fact now is that the human condition has itself become cosmopolitan. To illustrate this thesis we need only high-light the fact that the most recent avatar in the genealogy of global risks, the threat of terror, also knows no borders....The shock generated by global risks continually gives rise to worldwide political publics....Indeed, it [cosmopolitanism] has become the defining feature of a new era, the era of reflexive modernity, in which national borders and differences are dissolving and must be renegotiated in accordance with the logic of a "politics of politics." (p. 2)

I do not think that differences are dissolving but I do agree with Beck that the new interest in cosmopolitanism has grown because of global risks of terrorism. The problem of terrorism is no longer a European problem only; terrorism has now come upon our shores and this forces us to think more on an international scale than ever before. Americans have been forced to become cosmopolitan, in other words, and forced to try to understand the world around us especially because of 9/11. Not only that, even before 9/11 Americans had begun to understand these global risks, about which Beck speaks, because of nuclear accidents and nuclear proliferation. Etienne Balibar (1998) says, "The clouds of Chernobyl cannot be stopped at the border" (p. 218). Nuclear power is dangerous because of potential accidents like Chernobyl.

With the rise in terrorism, Americans worry that almost anybody can get nuclear weapons to do us harm. Think of all the ways terrorists could take over a nuclear power plant. Nuclear explosions cause damage far and wide. Terrorists are not bound by their home country; they travel—like viruses—and are all over the globe. Terrorist cells, like cancer cells, proliferate not just abroad but right here on American soil. But the ironic thing here is that the terrorists of 9/11 did not take us down with nuclear weapons but with box cutters.

Cosmopolitanism and the Environment

It is not only terrorism that worries us. Ulrich Beck (2008) also talks about environmental toxins that are destroying the planet. He talks of climate change as one clue to what is going wrong with the environment and how this climate change—or global warming—is forcing us to think in a more cosmopolitan fashion. Global warming affects the entire planet. The effects of global warming are far more destructive than we can possibly know or understand, and so we must begin to rethink ways to find new sources of energy worldwide or the planet will be no more. Beck's thesis is that people have become more cosmopolitan because of these "global risks" (p. 2). The oil spill in the Gulf is an example of such devastation. It will take generations to rebuild what has been destroyed. The destruction of wild life and the waterways (oceans or seas, or marshes, streams, lakes) affects all aspects of the world.

Cosmopolitan Clubs, Global Troubles, and Peace Education

Now, global risks, as Beck (2008) puts it, and people's responses to them (becoming more internationally aware or more cosmopolitan in outlook) are nothing new. We know that WWI heightened people's awareness of the need to think more internationally. Even before WWI, people began to develop what were called "cosmopolitan clubs" (Sylvester, 2008, p. 15). Robert Sylvester explains,

> In 1903, the original Cosmopolitan Clubs were launched (Lochner 1911, 1912) in the form of international clubs where representatives of each nation in the university would meet on the basis of brotherhood and equality. In 1907, the University Cosmopolitan Clubs…were founded with a membership of more than two thousand, including representatives from 60 countries. (p. 15)

Sylvester does not give readers much information as to why these clubs appeared when they did. But it is remarkable nonetheless that so many countries were involved in international discussions. But to what avail? WWI was right around the corner—a force in history that seemed unstoppable. The war that was supposed to end all wars did not end all wars. The purpose of the United Nations (which is sort of like a cosmopolitan club) is to engage in international debate. But the UN has little power to stop aggression. World-wide aggression seems an unstoppable force. And perhaps this is why a field called "peace education" emerged, not only in the United States but also in other countries. Takuya Kaneda (2008) tells us that Rabindranath Tagore, who lived from 1861 to 1941 (p. 176), Sri Aurobindo, who lived from 1872 to 1950 (p. 179), and Jiddu Krishnamurti, who lived from 1895 to 1986 (p. 181), engaged in "global peace education" (p. 187) Kaneda explains,

> An overview of Tagore, Sri Aurobindo, Krishnamurti and Sri Sri Ravi Shankar's educational ideas and practices reveals that all of them are inspired by Indian spiritual tradition. As dharma includes religion, spiritual pursuit, and education, all these things are inseparable for these four spiritual leaders...their final goal is *Shanti*, or peace—both inwardly and outwardly. (p. 187)

Peace education is a form of resistance against negative power, aggression, war. Most sane people want peace but there is little peace to be had. War and acts of aggression abound worldwide. Students who are interested in studying more about peace education might read David C. Smith and Terrance R. Carson's (1998) book titled *Educating for a Peaceful Future*. It is interesting that Smith and Carson talk about Maria Montessori who "suggested the historical record has shown that schools have been far more competent at educating for conflict than they have been at educating for peace" (p. ix). Competition is a form of conflict and most schooling is based on competing with fellow classmates for good grades. In fact, the competition for good grades is so fierce that in Japan, Shigeru Asanuma (2003) remarks, the suicide rate among school children is high. He also notes that these suicides are caused by bullying as well (pp. 436–437). Competition creates conflict and turmoil. Getting good grades and getting into good colleges is all about competition. Montessori points out that this only teaches conflict. There must be a better way to educate. Can we educate without instilling fear? Smith and Carson suggest that peace education is not only about teaching children to get along. Their understanding of peace education is much broader than this. Smith and Carson suggest,

> Substantively, our comprehensive definition of peace encompasses both a fundamental opposition to violence as well as an understanding of the relationships amongst the underlying causes of violence. There are seven dimensions to this broad definition

of peace education: non-violence, human rights, social justice, world mindedness, ecological balance, meaningful participation, and personal peace. (p. 26)

What is striking here is these scholars have a more ecological vision of peace education in that it includes all of these various aspects that one might not think have anything to do with peace issues. When they suggest we teach world mindedness, is this not the same thing as cosmopolitanism? World mindedness is a good definition of a cosmopolitan frame of mind. But being mindful of the world is no easy task. Cosmopolitanism and peace education certainly have things in common and both of these ideas—it seems—have sprung from a world where there is little peace.

Another way one could think of a more ecological cosmopolitanism is to think of the term in a broad sense. Here, cosmopolitanism would not only be about being well-read and well-rounded but would be much broader in scope. Cosmopolitan thinking would be in contradistinction to specialization. Generalists are more cosmopolitan because they are able to think more ecologically by way of interdisciplinarity. Thinking across disciplines is one way to get at worldwide problems. This is not to say that specialization is not needed. The academy needs specialists too. Specialists and generalists can work together on world-wide issues, not only on issues of peace but also on issues that pertain to our ecosphere.

Here, I mention the work of Isaac Kandel. According to Robert Sylvester (2008),

> Isaac Leon Kandel of Columbia University may be considered the leading researcher in International education in the twentieth century. His work during the middle five decades was matched in importance by very few other academics in the West. His views on rooting international education in the national ethic were widely demonstrated in his writings. In his seminal text on comparative education, Kandel (1933) called for the discovery of "common elements" of international understanding. (p. 19)

One common element most people can agree on is the wish for peace. The problem after that is that nobody can agree on common elements when it comes to international issues. Perhaps there are no common elements between nations but rather competing elements, which is why nobody seems to be able to get along. When one thinks about, for example, the Israeli and Palestinian conflict, common elements between these two peoples are far outweighed by disagreements over land, over issues of occupation and civil rights. Colonizing or occupying powers have little in common with the colonized. So how do we find peace in a world where people have little in common and cannot talk to each other and do not understand one another's cultures? People try to talk across cultures, and, as Gloria Anzaldúa (2002) puts it, people try to build bridges across difference but conflict reigns.

Cosmopolitan Curriculum

Thomas Popkewitz (2008) points out that cosmopolitanism is

> often traced to the Northern European and North American Enlightenments, [and] faith in cosmopolitanism is the emancipatory potential of human reason and science. The radicalism of that reason is its cultural thesis about modes of living that provide universal paths that free the individual from provincialism, the boundaries of nationalism, theological dogma, and the irrationalities of mystical faith. The freedom associated with cosmopolitanism enjoins reason and rationality (science) with notions of agency and progress that fill the future with hope. (p. xiii)

A new cosmopolitanism would be a postmodern cosmopolitanism, one that troubles many of the premises of the Enlightenment version of cosmopolitanism. For one thing, to have a cosmopolitan mindset, you do not have to be European or be from North America. Cosmopolitanism does not belong to Europeans or European Americans. Anybody from any part of the world can become more cosmopolitan in the way they see the world around them. Cosmopolitanism has little to do with emancipation. The notion of emancipation is an Enlightenment idea akin to the religious notion of redemption. Both of these concepts are highly problematic. Cosmopolitanism today (at least in a more postmodern version) would question reason and progress, scientism and the like. After the dropping of atomic bombs and the efficient killing machines of Auschwitz, people have to wonder what science and progress mean anymore. Reason and intellect are not the only paths to enlightenment. Enlightenment notions of progress have now become questionable and the notion of hope, too, has to be reconsidered. Hope is an Enlightenment concept that needs serious deconstruction. A more postmodern cosmopolitanism embraces uncertainty, ambiguity, mystery, intuition, and the ugliness of the world alongside the possibilities of human creativity, wisdom, and love. A more postmodern cosmopolitanism would be a more ecological cosmopolitanism (as students learned from Smith and Carson and from Gough). A more postmodern cosmopolitanism would embrace indigenous knowledges and other ways of knowing the world beside all things Western. For Dennis

Carlson (2003), a more postmodern cosmopolitanism is one that fosters world-wide democracy. A cosmopolitan curriculum would foster transnational conversations knowing that our understandings are limited and situated. A more postmodern cosmopolitanism would be more postcolonial and critique the problems of colonization. Claudia Eppert and Hongyu Wang (2008), in their book titled *Cross-Cultural Studies in Curriculum: Eastern Thought, Educational Insights*, have a postmodern cosmopolitan outlook. These scholars suggest that a cosmopolitan curriculum should deconstruct the European canon that has been handed down to us, but, also, scholars might begin to think more broadly, and—as Eppert and Wang suggest—"recognize the continued marginality of Eastern thought" (p. xvii). Moreover, when scholars do study Eastern thought they must, as Eppert and Wang suggest, "not romanticize" (p. xix) Eastern ideas. A more postmodern cosmopolitan curriculum is reflected in Eppert and Wang's important edited collection of essays. Eppert and Wang tell us,

> Yet, although we situate our dialogue within curriculum studies, this interdisciplinary edition discusses sage writings in Buddhism, Confucianism, Hinduism, and Taoism… and yields educational insights that invite new considerations for specific areas of scholarship, including critical pedagogy and social justice/social change education, environmental education, psychoanalysis, holistic education, character education, witness studies, professional ethics, women's and gender studies, peace education, literature and arts education, and the philosophy of education. (p. xix)

Eppert and Wang describe what I would consider to be a cosmopolitan curriculum. Clearly they have made an important contribution to the field of curriculum studies by drawing on all these different theoretical frameworks to discuss curricular issues. The unique combination of all these interesting and different ways of looking at curriculum is what makes curriculum studies so different from other branches of education. A postmodern cosmopolitan curriculum studies program, for example, would offer courses that intermix all the various things that Eppert and Wang suggest above. What is interesting here is that many of these traditions that they mention—like psychoanalysis—have their roots in European history and they use psychoanalysis (or a tradition from Europe) to discuss Eastern wisdom traditions. These scholars view the world through many cultural lenses (and mix cultural lenses) to dig deeper into curricular issues. It is worth noting that here we have a major difference between what is usually done in, say, the field of comparative education with what is done in curriculum studies. Curriculum studies is broader in scope and curriculum studies scholars dare to study outside of traditional intellectual boundaries to find out new things about the world. When students begin to study what the internationalization of curriculum means—see Pinar's (2003a) *International Handbook of Curriculum Research* and Pinar and colleagues' (2003c) *The Internationalization of Curriculum Studies: Selected Proceedings from the LSU Conference 2000*—students begin to understand that curriculum issues across the globe are studied through a variety of theoretical frameworks, which suggests that curriculum studies is not a monolithic field—and yet there are theoretical frameworks that are unique to the field of curriculum studies that students will not find, say, in comparative education or the field of international education.

William Pinar's *International Handbook*

In Pinar and colleagues' (2003a) *International Handbook of Curriculum Research* students will learn about the ways in which scholars all over the globe approach the field of curriculum studies. What is striking about the book is that scholars across the globe approach the field differently, but there are some ongoing themes that I would like to address here. Alice Casimiro Lopes and Elizabeth Fernandes de Macedo (2003) discuss developments in curriculum studies in Brazil. They state, "Hybridism is the major trait of the curriculum field in the 1990s in Brazil" (p. 200). Much of what these authors talk about is the way in which postmodernism has been incorporated into the field of curriculum studies and hybridism is one of the hallmarks of postmodernism. Lopes and de Macedo state also that cultural studies and feminist studies are important to their interpretations of curriculum studies. They explain,

> Michel Foucault, in this sense, constitutes [Tomaz Tadeau da Silva's] most significant theoretical basis. Works based on cultural studies, especially Stuart Hall, feminist studies, and, to a lesser scale, theoretical contributions by Derrida, Deleuze and Guattari are also significantly incorporated. (p. 190)

Tomaz Tadeau da Silva is one of the most important Brazilian scholars to bring postmodernism to the curriculum field in Brazil, according to Lopes and de Macedo.

Like curriculum studies scholars in Brazil, curriculum studies scholars in Australia, according to Bill Green (2003), draw on a variety of theoretical frameworks to inform work in the field. Green states:

Accordingly, a younger generation of curriculum scholars either based in Australia or with Australian connections, such as David Kirk, Terri Seddon, Bill Green, Bernadette Baker…have sought to build on earlier historically oriented work.…Ranging across both general and applied curriculum areas and topics, their work draws eclectically on post-New Sociology of Education literatures and various postmodern critical-theoretical positions and perspectives.…This work needs to be placed alongside and in specific relation to a range of innovative and exciting work also drawing on…feminism, post-colonialism, environmental activism, and cultural studies. (p. 125)

Another important Australian curriculum scholar is Noel Gough, who Green also mentions. Gough has done much interesting work in ecology, fiction, science fiction, and the uses of science fiction to teach science. He also brings to our attention the importance of indigenous ways of looking at science. Gough (2003) says, "As evidence of its marginal position in the curriculum field, I note that Pinar, Reynolds, Slattery and Taubman (1995) did not mention environmental education in chapter 14" (p. 53). This is a significant statement because today things have changed in the curriculum field and ecology and environmental education constitute an entire segment of the field of curriculum. Gough has done much to bring to our attention just how important ecology and environmental studies are to the curriculum field and today many are working in this area. Certainly, more scholars must get involved in this kind of work. The next chapter in my *Guidebook* will be an introduction to the kinds of things that scholars talk about when discussing ecological issues, and the issues that are raised are not only interesting but also of international importance, especially with all the environmental problems we face today, such as global warming.

In Japan, Tadahiko Abiko (2003) suggests that there are a variety of ways that scholars approach curriculum studies. Marxist thought has influenced Japanese curriculum theory mainly through the work of Michael Apple (p. 428). Another influence on Japanese curriculum studies is the work of John Dewey (p. 429). Here "Professors Yukitsugu Kato (Sophia University) and Shigeru Asanuma (Tokyo Gakugei Uniersity) have grouped together and are actively working on the movement [Dewey's child-centered ideas] of spreading education practices of these kinds to schools nationwide" (p. 430). Postmodernism is also an influence in Japanese curriculum studies and Abiko suggests, "Pinar and Giroux also have a relatively large impact on" this kind of thinking (p. 430).

In Botswana Sid N. Pandey and Fazlur R. Moorad (2003) tell us,

> Reconceptualized reconstructionist critical pedagogy as currently conceived through the incorporation of the ideas of social reconstructionism, the new sociology, critical theories, neo-Marxism, feminism, neopragmatism, postmodernism, and poststructuralism appears foremost in its fight against social oppression, inequities, and inequalities. (p. 165)

Students can begin to better understand that worldwide curriculum studies is approached in a variety of ways and influenced by many different theoretical frameworks not unfamiliar to American and Canadian students of curriculum studies. However, each country has its own particular history and particular problems to sort through so the historical events that shape a country also shape the ways in which these theoretical frameworks are used. This is why William Pinar (2003b) insists that even though curriculum studies is worldwide it is not uniform. Moreover, Pinar states, "Curriculum studies tends to be embedded in their [each particular country's] national and regional settings" (p. 1).

Peter Roberts (2003) discusses major trends in curriculum studies in New Zealand. Again a variety of theoretical frameworks are used to talk about particular issues. Roberts states,

> Courses examining the curriculum from sociological, philosophical feminist, and other perspectives have been sprinkled across Education departments in New Zealand universities over the years, but they have seldom formed part of a comprehensive curriculum studies program. (p. 505)

Roberts also mentions postmodernism and a host of curriculum studies scholars who have influenced New Zealand scholars. Roberts states,

> The postmodern turn in social theory has found creative expression in the diverse and sometimes conflicting voices of curriculum theorists such as William Doll, Henry Giroux, Peter McLaren, Joe Kincheloe, Shirley Steinberg, Patti Lather, and others. (p. 495)

A more detailed study of Pinar's (2003a) handbook is necessary for students to understand the ways that various countries go about doing curriculum research.

William Pinar's Worldliness of a Cosmopolitan Education

Here, in the final section of this chapter, I would like to discuss one of the most interesting and important books in the field of curriculum studies today on the issue of cosmopolitanism and the internationalization of the field of curriculum studies and that is William Pinar's (2009) book titled *The Worldliness of a Cosmopolitan Education: Passionate Lives in Public Service*. Pinar begins his book by saying, "A curriculum for cosmopolitanism juxtaposes the particular alongside the abstract, creating collages of history and literature, politics and poetry, science and art. Such a curriculum provides passages between the subjective and the social" (p. vii). Pinar's book, although political, focuses more on the connections between the inner life—or interiority—and the way in which one's subjectivity shapes one's political life. Subjectivity and interiority are hardly conversations that people in the area of cosmopolitanism are having today. Pinar tells us, "As rich and varied as the scholarly literature on cosmopolitanism is, I realized quickly that what it lacks is attention to subjectivity and its cultivation through education" (p. x). The unique aspect of Pinar's work is his ongoing interest and concern with the cultivation of the self and the impact upon the world that self might have. For Pinar, the self is always in relation to the social. Pinar's unique contribution to the area of cosmopolitanism emerges from his interest in the internationalization of the curriculum field. This book, however, takes a turn toward three biographical subjects he studies and suggests that these three individuals' (Jane Addams, Laura Bragg, and Pier Paolo Pasolini) inner lives shaped them as teachers of the world, teachers who had a cosmopolitan outlook; their classroom was the world. Pinar remarks, "Each sketch lays bare how academic study and lived experience subjectively reconstructed provide passages from private preoccupations to public service" (p. xii). Pinar's argument is that the only way to make the world your classroom is to understand yourself first. That is, understanding the self and working on the self is the only way to reach others and to teach others. Pinar states in his epilogue,

> Addams, Bragg, and Pasolini were reflective citizens; each understood the subjective project of public service as the education of the public, a concept not limited to the classroom (although each worked in classrooms), but enacted as a way of life....In our time, "the cultivation of humanity" (Nussbaum, 1997, 8) calls for the cultivation of subjectivity informed by academic study and lived experience, inspired by sexuality, spirituality and sustainability. (p. 143)

Pinar's book is the only one in the literature on cosmopolitanism that takes a serious look at the inner lives of people and the way in which their inner lives affected their political lives. For example, one of the most interesting sections in the book deals with Jane Addams's reading practices and how those reading practices influenced her work at Hull House. Pinar tells us that

Addams—while struggling through personal conflict—read Tolstoy's book *My Religion*, and Pinar says, "Addams would identify *My Religion* as 'the book that changed my life'....Addams reading Tolstoy during the depth of her own despair illustrates the 'biographic function' (Pinar 1994, 46–47) of study, the confluence of life history and intellectual interests in provoking movement in one's life" (pp. 67–68). Later, Pinar suggests, "Addams reconstructed her subjectivity through reading" (p. 69). Her reading led her to develop Hull House, which became an American landmark and an American institution where social services became available for many who otherwise would have had little opportunity to better their lives. And Hull House was an educational institution like no other in that it opened its door to the poor, to women, and to people who would never have had the opportunity to get an education. The interesting thing here is that, in some way, Pinar identifies with the struggles that Addams had in her life and the way she found her way in the world through books. Books shape us and help us find out who we are and that is what is most interesting about academic life. Scholars only learn about their own interiority through the study of others—and this is Pinar's point. Scholars must study to learn about others, yes—but to also learn about themselves and what they can do to make the world a better place. Pinar, throughout the text, emphasizes, "Worldliness implies immanence rather than transcendence" (p. ix). Thus, a citizen of the world—the cosmopolitan—is of this world, in this world, and works to better this world from her own perspective. For Pinar, then, the notion of the universal is problematic because people do not have a view that is universal. The cosmopolitan is not a universal citizen, but a particular citizen who is a person with emotions, spirit, and drive. This is the only book on cosmopolitanism that takes a personal turn, an autobiographic-biographic turn. Most of the discussions on cosmopolitanism—as I have tried to show in the earlier sections of this chapter—are abstract. But Pinar insists that scholars must "juxtapose the particular alongside the abstract" (p. xii). What is missing in most of the conversations about the cosmopolitan citizen is the particular, the person, the person who might be a filmmaker—as was Pasolini—or even a poet, such as Anne Sexton (see Salvio, 2007). A citizen of the world—the cosmopolitan—is also a person who has personal projects. And these personal projects—if made public—can work to change the world. Even the notion of the "citizen" is an abstract one. What is a "citizen?" What happens to those who are not considered citizens? They are considered nonpersons. We see this countless times as noncitizens—at least in the United States—are called aliens. It is as if these stateless people are nonhuman. Noncitizens are not treated well. So perhaps people need to rethink the word "citizen" and what this means and what it implies for those who are noncitizens. Cosmopolitanism is often about the rights of citizens or noncitizens and the language is often not filled in with much particularity. Pinar puts cosmopolitanism in another way as he suggests,

> A cosmopolitan curriculum enables students to grapple with (again borrowing from Pasolini's language) the "problem of my life and flesh." That "problem" is auto-biographical, historical and biospheric. It is a problem to be studied as it is lived through and acted upon. The worldliness of a cosmopolitan curriculum implies that general education is more than an introduction to "great works," the memorization of "essential" knowledge, or a sampling of the primary disciplinary categories…it is subjectively structured academic study of this lived-historical problem of "my life and flesh," perhaps through great works, perhaps through sampling major intellectual traditions. (pp. 8–9)

The point Pinar is making here is clear. Scholars study their intellectual traditions and study the works of others. For what purpose? To know our traditions, yes. But also, and perhaps more important, scholars study their traditions and the traditions of others to know themselves. We can only advance a field, in other words, if we know ourselves. So Pinar brings internationalization back home again—to the self. To think internationally, first, one must think through the self in order to make an impact on the world around us. We study international problems. We study the lives of others. And we study what people around the globe are doing. But mostly, we want to know what our contributions will be and the way in which our studies shape what kinds of contributions we can make to our field. Cosmopolitanism and internationalization are not just about international law and the study of crimes against humanity—although of course these issues are imperative to know. (Much of the discussions on the cosmopolitan citizen turns on international law and how to try crimes against humanity.) But there is more to the idea of the international than that. And that is what curriculum studies tries to bring home. The cosmopolitan curriculum can be so much more than the study of international tribunals. It is up to you to change culture through your own cosmopolitan projects. As Pinar suggests, scholars might all try to live "Passionate Lives in Public Service."

· 5 ·

ECOLOGICAL
CURRICULUM CONCEPTS

Introduction

This area of study is highly complex. This chapter will be organized in the following manner. First, I explore the naturalists and their decline. I move into a section on what is called human-animal studies. I examine what is called environmental education and the ways in which environmental education differs from ecojustice education and environmental justice education. Then I will move into the area of ecology. Here, I will examine the notion of home (being in place) and its opposite, homelessness (being displaced). One of the earliest books on place in curriculum studies was co-edited by Joe Kincheloe and William F. Pinar (1991), titled *Curriculum as Social Psychoanalysis: The Significance of Place*. Influenced by Kincheloe and Pinar, another generation of curriculum scholars looks at place (especially the South) in the context of autobiography (Whitlock, 2007; Casemore, 2008). Noel Gough (2008)—who writes much in the area of ecology—calls himself a "traveling textworker" (p. 73). Travel metaphors have everything to do with place. I will discuss place in the context of alterity and difference. The final section of this chapter deals with issues of psyche and ecology, or what is termed "ecopsychology." I talk about the ways in which spirituality and ecology blend together.

The Naturalists

The poetic and scientific discussions around the natural world were not always separated. Before the advent of the field of ecology naturalists combined art and science to better understand the natural world. Tom Baione (2012) points out,

> The goal of many works on natural history has been to illustrate the scientific topic at hand, but from the infancy of printing, great artists were called on to further illuminate scientific texts....In many cases, the authors themselves were talented artists. (p. x)

Thus, natural historians were both scientists and artists. Today there tends to be a wedge between the scientific study of the natural world and the poetic study of the natural world. This division occurred as the academic disciplines began to specialize in the 19th century. John Tallmadge (2011) suggests that the field of natural history (which predates the field of ecology) "emerged as both field-based observational science and a literary genre—not a hybrid, but an original synthesis" (p. 20). Today it is rare to find scientists who also consider their findings literary. But again the naturalists did not drive a wedge between science and art. Indeed, as Gage Dayton, Paul Dayton, and Harry Greene (2011) point out, many scientists who work on the environment today tend not to "acknowledge [a] debt to early naturalists" (p. 91). When most people think of naturalists they think of John James Audubon, John Muir, Rachel Carson, and, of course, Charles Darwin. But some scholars trace naturalism and natural history back to the pre-Socratics. In fact, John Anderson (2013) suggests that Thales of Miletus was the first naturalist. Anderson points out,

> Greek natural history certainly predated Aristotle, with some authors suggesting Thales of Miletus (624–540 BCE) as the real founder of modern scientific ideas. Thales rejected mystical causes for events and things and sought a rational explanation for natural phenomena. (p. 16)

Contrarily, some scholars consider Aristotle the first naturalist. Robert Huxley (2007) tells us that Aristotle was "the first great naturalist" (p. 9). Huxley explains,

> Aristotle stands out among others of his time for the scale and breadth of his study, and, more importantly, the lasting legacy of his work and its significance in the development of natural science. (p. 9)

Aristotle wrote on many philosophical topics but few know about his work on zoology. His magnum opus in this area was titled the *History of Animals*. Today there is an emerging discipline called human-animal studies, which owes a debt of gratitude to the work of Aristotle and other early naturalists, but scholars in human-animal studies rarely discuss the ancient roots of their newly found discipline. Julia Brittain (2007) tells us,

> As a natural historian, Aristotle covered many topics, but he favoured zoology, writing extensively on animal life in various works, including *Historia Animalium*, an ambitious nine-volume account of many zoological phenomena, which encompassed everything from fascinating tales of animal behavior to graphic details of physiology. (p. 24)

Why Aristotle's account of zoology is not mentioned by many scholars of ecology is rather puzzling. Writing nine books on zoology is quite an accomplishment. Clearly, Aristotle's work is of the utmost importance to study in order to understand the history of the study of the natural world. Ecology has its deepest roots in naturalism and natural history.

David Sutton (2007) explains that Pliny the Elder, a Roman natural historian who lived 23–79 CE, should be considered an early naturalist. Sutton explains,

> Pliny the Elder, or Gaius Plinius Secundus to give him his Latin name, was a Roman natural philosopher and author who is best known for his *Historia Naturalis*. This work, the title of which is usually translated as *Natural History*…was truly encyclopedic in scope, covering everything in the natural world. (p. 38)

What is interesting here is that this naturalist tried to be encyclopedic in his work. Many other natural historians, too, wanted to catalogue and order the entire natural world. Of course this is impossible but this was the goal of many natural historians. Robert Huxley (2007) tells us that Pliny the Elder wrote about "hundreds of animals, real and mythical" (p. 11). It is interesting to note that these ancient philosophers did not shy away from the mythical the way that modern scientists do today. More important, for the Roman naturalists, generally speaking, they studied plant life so as to use plants for developing medicine (Huxley, pp. 10–11).

John Anderson is one of the few scholars to examine the work of women naturalists. He writes about a Christian mystic by the name of Hildegard of Bingen who lived from 1098 to 1171 CE. Hildegard of Bingen is no stranger to theologians but she is rarely—if at all—mentioned in the literature on natural history. At any rate, Anderson tells us that Hildegard of Bingen is best known to us for her musical compositions, but she was also engaged in studies of health and medicine. She wrote an encyclopedic text, the *Physica*, which lists and partially describes nearly a thousand plants and animals. (p. 32)

It is disturbing to note that women natural historians have been erased from history because of misogyny. Most scholars know a few names of modern natural historians like Rachel Carson and Jane Goodall. In curriculum studies many know the groundbreaking work of Florence Krall and Elaine Riley-Taylor. But still not enough women are given credit for their work either in natural history or modern ecology.

Richard Ellis (2011) introduces readers to the little known natural historian named Conrad Gessner, who is considered to be the founding father of modern zoology. Ellis explains,

Conrad Gessner…was born in Zurich on March 26, 1516 and died there on December 13, 1565. His five volume *Historia animalium*…was published between 1551 and 1558, and is considered the beginning of modern zoology.…Gessner's monumental work is based on the Old Testament, Hebrew, Greek, and Latin sources, and is compiled from folklore as well as ancient and medieval texts. (p. 1)

Conrad Gessner drew upon folklore to enrich his work. Recall that Pliny the Elder drew upon myth to enrich his work. Again, today in modern science neither myth nor folklore is considered a valid scientific subject. But the ancients did not see it this way. They felt that myth and folklore could add much to their studies of natural history.

In the 17th century John Ray emerged as a noted natural historian (Huxley). Huxley explains,

The 17th century saw a move towards so-called natural classifications, which used a large number of characteristics to determine which species are related to each other. The most significant figure in this movement was the English clergyman John Ray, whose highly methodical and thorough work introduced a scientific aspect to natural history that had not been seen before. (pp. 12–13)

In his interesting commentary, Robert Huxley mentions that part of the reason naturalists like John Ray wanted to classify the natural world was so that they could make order from chaos (p. 12). But the ever-evolving natural world makes this task impossible. Species evolve and change as Charles Darwin pointed out long ago. But still there is a human tendency to rid the world of chaos in order to make sense of it. One must wonder why this is so. Perhaps modern-day chaos theorists can tell us more about this quandary. At any rate, John Anderson points out that John Ray was one of the first naturalists who attempted to order the world via taxonomy. Anderson points out, "Traditionally, the concept of taxonomy, or systematics, is credited to Linnaeus, but many people had their hand in its creation, and foremost among them was the quiet English theologian and natural historian John Ray" (p. 53). Whereas Ray is not much remembered for his contributions to natural history, Linnaeus is. Robert Huxley claims that Linnaeus was "one of the best-known of all naturalists" (p. 13). Linnaeus was known for his work on taxonomy and ordering—in a scientific manner—the natural world. Huxley suggests, "Linnaeus's great legacy was the straightforward, easily applicable and unambiguous naming system we use today" (p. 13). A question that arises here is how can nature be unambiguous? One would think that nature is terribly ambiguous. A more postmodern take on this is that nature is—in some ways—beyond comprehension because everything is always evolving and changing. Darwin understood this of course. Like Darwin, Jean-Baptiste Lamarck understood that the natural world is always evolving. Robert Huxley points out, "Lamarck is best remembered for his pre-Darwinian evolutionary theories" (p. 17). Lamarck is known for his term "invertebrate" (Huxley, p. 15). And like Darwin, Lamarck argued that the natural world evolved by itself without the intervention of God. This must have created quite a stir during his lifetime.

Judith Magee (2007) informs us that Alexander von Humboldt who lived from 1769 to 1859 is well known for his vision of the natural world as an "organic whole" (p. 224). Magee states,

> Underlying all Humboldt's study was his view of the natural world as an organic whole—a living unity of diverse and interdependent life forms rather than some mechanical structure. He developed this universal concept of nature beyond anything that was professed at the time, heralding the study of ecology and environmentalism. (p. 224)

Humboldt's work as a naturalist is credited with founding such fields as plant geography, climatology, and oceanography (Magee, p. 224). Over time one can see that naturalists were becoming increasingly more scientific and specialized. As naturalists became more scientific their work became more appreciated in university circles. But later on—as readers will see in this discussion—their work was discredited by academicians.

One of the best-known naturalists was, of course, John James Audubon who combined science and art and is most well known for his portraits of birds and his work in ornithology. Roberta Olson (2007) writes,

> Arguably one of the greatest American naturalists and water-colourists, John James Audubon had one foot in the natural sciences and the other in art, defying categorization. In both his written work, including his greatest triumph, *The Birds of America* (1827–38), he combined a naturalist's curiosity with an artist's eye and a poet's expressiveness, ensuring his uniqueness in the pantheon of natural history. (p. 233)

Audubon's paintings are instantly recognizable by both laypersons and scientists. He had no trouble drawing on both art and science to explore his subject matter. But again with the rise of scientism in the 19th century scientists frowned on drawing, art, or writing in a poetic style.

Along with Audubon, Charles Darwin's name is instantly recognizable as one of the most important naturalists of all time. As students of history know all too well, Darwin's findings are still controversial. Michael Graham (2011) points out,

> In its infancy, Natural History was inherently descriptive….Everything changed with the events leading up to and including the publication of *The Origin of Species* (Darwin 1859), after which evolutionary biology and ecology emerged as theory-driven disciplines. (p. 5)

The more specialized the sciences became during the 19th century the more they became theoretical and not merely descriptive. But Keith Thomson (2007) claims that Darwin also engaged in much description alongside theory to explore and explain the natural world. But it is crucial to recognize that Darwin's theorizing is what set him apart from other naturalists. Thomson tells us, "More than anyone else, he also extended that work into deep analysis and theory. It was never enough for him simply to observe" (p. 267). Robert Huxley (2007) points out that with the advent of Darwin and the rise of scientism, natural history "was replaced by the professional biologist and geologist, who then specialized further into geneticists, biochemists and systematists" (p. 8). When science began replacing amateur naturalists their work became discredited. And, too, the merging of art and science, poetry and scientific writing disappeared.

The Decline of Naturalists

With the rise of scientism the naturalists were left behind. One must remember that many naturalists were amateurs and not professional scientists. Academic scientists had little truck with amateurs. Sarah Rabkin (2011) writes that naturalists were "long belittled by academic scientists" (p. 110). They were belittled because academic scientists saw their work as quaint and old-fashioned (p. 110). But Rabkin argues,

> Nature study should occupy the core of any twenty-first-century school curriculum. Rachel Carson anticipated this argument in 1952 when she accepted the Burroughs Medal for her book *The Sea Around Us*. "If we have ever regarded our interest in natural history as an escape from the realities of the modern world…let us now reverse this attitude. For the mysteries of living things, and the birth and death of continents and seas, are among the great realities." (pp. 110–111)

The core of the 21st-century curriculum has little to do with the natural world and the dangers of extinction. The school curriculum today is more about getting answers right on standardized tests. These tests have little to do with the health or degradation of our planet. Robert Pyle (2011) writes that the eclipse of natural history began in midcentury (p. 163). Pyle explains,

> From midcentury on, a purge of the naturalists occurred at many universities, in favor of molecular, cellular, and mathematical biology….Even as professional, academic natural history went into eclipse, the regular presence of outdoor subjects in the public schools…withered to near nothingness…Environmental education has never managed to replace nature study. (p. 163)

To scientists natural history must seem simple minded and undertheorized. But one might argue that biology and related sciences grew out of natural history. Ecology grew out of natural history but ecologists rarely connect natural history with the field of ecology. Robert Paine (2011) writes,

> Becoming a naturalist is a road increasingly less traveled for a host of obvious reasons: dwindling habitats, species extinction, social pressures on the young, and the dangers associated with just roaming around observing and poking into the dark corners of nature. (p. 13)

Public school is certainly not about exploring nature; it is about scoring high on standardized tests. Children are indeed under much pressure to do well on these tests and in the meanwhile there is little time to appreciate nature. In many schools recess has been cut because it is thought to be a waste of time. However, recess is the time that children might explore the natural world around them.

George Schaller (2011) comments that natural history is seen by many scientists as antiquated (p. 17). A university's curriculum seldom includes natural history. Schaller laments this state of affairs. He states,

> Universities neglect courses in natural history, yet such knowledge is the cornerstone of conservation. It provides basic information, defines problems, and suggests realistic solutions. Even the rhetoric of conservation has changed. Nature has now become "natural resources," viewed all too often only in economic terms and treated as a commodity to be sold, bought or discarded. (p. 17)

Developers have little regard for nature as they think nothing of clear cutting trees, destroying wild life, and polluting the soil, leaving heavy carbon footprints on the earth. Animals are continually being displaced as developers build apartments and shopping malls where there once was a community of animals and a rich biodiverse landscape.

Gage Dayton, Paul Dayton, and Harry Greene (2011) write about what is not taught in ecology. They state,

> The "art" of describing the natural world is rarely taught in contemporary ecology, now often characterized by brief, concise reports of highly focused tests. There is much to be learned from the early naturalists about perceiving details in nature and keeping meticulous records of observations, and it is important that our educational system recover the tradition of experiencing nature firsthand. (p. 93)

Not only do students not experience nature in school or in the university they do not even experience being on campuses as many academic courses and programs have moved online. There is little reason to go outside when everything is virtual and online.

A Missing Link in the Conversation: Human-Animal Studies

One topic that I am not seeing much of in the field of curriculum studies is that of human-animal studies. One can certainly draw connections between what the naturalists were doing with what scholars do in this new field of human-animal studies. One scholar who comes to mind when talking about human-animal studies is Mark Rowlands (2009), who has written a marvelous book on animals. His book is called *The Philosopher and the Wolf: Lessons from the Wild on Love, Death, and Happiness*. Rowlands, a professor of philosophy, actually took his wolf to class. One might raise an eyebrow at this behavior and wonder whether Rowlands ever worried about the wolf attacking the students. As Marc Bekoff (2010) reminds us, wild animals, such as wolves, are—well—wild. That means that anything can happen, since these are not domesticated animals. It is remarkable that Rowlands's wolf never attacked him. The wolf, rather, was his closest companion and it is this companionship that Rowlands writes about throughout the book.

Bekoff writes about developing a "compassion footprint" (p. 3) when it comes to our animal companions. Bekoff argues that animals have emotions and feelings and if they are abused they can even develop posttraumatic stress disorder. Bekoff tells us,

> Wildlife biologists Jay Mallonee and Paul Joslin described unique changes in the behavior of Tenino, a wild female wolf, who was darted twice from a helicopter and put in captivity because she'd preyed on livestock. Tenino became hypervigilant, was easy to startle, and showed generalized fear, avoidance, and arousal. (p. 15)

These changes in Tenino's behavior are all symptoms of PTSD. Human animals (we are animals, too) suffer from this also if they have experienced trauma and/or abuse. Freud called this shell-shock. One does not have to come home from a war to be shellshocked. Being abused can make one shell-shocked. Joy A. Palmer (2003) calls for "interspecies justice" (p. 9). Bekoff calls for the end of "speciesism" (p. 25), a position that suggests that human beings are better than animals; that human beings can dominate animals and do whatever they like to them. One of the gaping holes in curriculum studies, then, is work on animals. The field of human-animal studies dovetails well with work in curriculum. However, most ecologists and environmental educators do not focus on animals but rather on the environment and the ruination of it by industry. Human-animal studies has been pushed into its own separate—and we might add ghettoized—area of inquiry. If curriculum theorists are interested in children and what nurtures them, animals are a great source of nurturance. But nobody really addresses this. In the educational literature, there is, however, a book that has a few pieces devoted to animals: *Green Frontiers: Environmental Educators Dancing Away from Mechanism*, which is co-edited by James

Gray-Donald and David Selby (2008). One piece in particular stands out by Robert S. E. Caine (2008) about his cockatiel named Woody. Caine tells us,

> Woody is a grey cockatiel with beautiful yellow feathers on his head, bright orange cheeks, and a personality more alive than most people I have met in my 39 years. Little did I know at the time, Woody was about to change my life in a momentous way. (p. 184)

Animals do change us in monumental ways—especially if they live in our homes. I would hope that the next generation of curriculum scholars take up the call to study animals, the connections people make with them, and the ways in which they can and do change our lives.

Rachel Carson

Perhaps the place to begin—when talking about ecology or environmental issues—is with Rachel Carson's (1990) groundbreaking *Silent Spring*. The fortieth anniversary of her book was recently released. When her book first came out it was dismissed by scientists. Marc Bekoff (2010) reminds us, "At first, hardcore scientists ridiculed Rachel Carson after she published *Silent Spring*, but her evidence and predictions about the horrible effects of pesticides and environmental toxins unfortunately proved to be true" (p. 9). DDT is mainly what Rachel Carson went after. In case after case she shows how toxic this pesticide is and initiated the eventual ban of DDT in the United States, although it is still manufactured for overseas markets. One wonders what pesticides are made of today and what they do to us, to our animals, and to the environment. The problem here is that, on the one hand, pesticides throw the ecosphere out of whack by killing pests, but, on the other hand, we cannot live in mosquito-infested or flea-infested areas lest we become ill. Fleas can actually kill animals; fleas are not benign.

Some people argue that taking DDT off the market has caused millions of people to die of malaria; some argue that DDT should be used only in small quantities to control malaria. There seems to be no end to the debate. But in the 1960s when DDT first came out, it was used in such great quantities that it actually killed people. One of the most poignant quotes from Carson's book is this:

> There was a strange stillness. The birds, for example—where had they gone? Many people spoke of them, puzzled and disturbed. The feeding stations in the backyards

were deserted. The few birds seen anywhere were moribund; they trembled violently and could not fly. It was a spring without voices. (p. 2)

Hence, silent spring. If you notice a lack of wildlife around your house, including bees whose colonies have collapsed, you might begin to wonder whether pesticides are the cause. Today they tell us that the pesticides are safe. I am not so sure.

Rachel Carson's book created such a firestorm because she threatened the profits of pesticide companies; that was part of the issue. There is much money to be made in pesticides. Take DDT away and profits go with it.

Environmental Education

Environmental education was born with Rachel Carson. Today environmentalists have continued the conversation that Carson began more than thirty years ago. James Gray-Donald and David Selby tell us,

> Environmental education has reached an interesting crossroads. There has never before been such media attention to hard-to-grasp issues such as climate change…the loss of biodiversity, and the health effects of human made toxins and pollutants. (p. 2)

The problems with pesticides continue. And now many realize that global warming has created new and serious problems that most of us do not understand. Global warming is also about extremes in weather patterns, not just hot weather.

EE and Social Justice

Environmental education (EE) tries to grapple with these issues from a scientific point of view. The problem with EE is that its purview tends to be too narrowly focused on the science and not on the cultural and political issues that might have something to do with environmental degradation. James Gray-Donald and David Selby remark, "Most environmental educators shy away from real engagement with social justice, peace and cultural issues" (p. 4). James Gray-Donald puts it this way:

> How inequalities of ecological, social, and economic resources are distributed amongst global citizens is a gendered, racial, and political issue of social justice and

a corresponding analysis is crucial to an effective response to the ecological crisis. Yet the dominant EE literature has made little mention of these dimensions. (p. 28)

Environmental racism is one aspect that most EE educators do not discuss. Toxic waste dumps tend to be in poor areas mostly occupied by people of color. Who suffers? People of color and the poor. Hence the term "environmental racism." Children play in toxic waste dumps. Poor schools are built on top of toxic waste sites, and school buildings in poor neighborhoods are not healthy when asbestos wraps pipes or black mold creeps in the walls.

Michiel van Eijck (2010) suggests that environmental educators would benefit from studying "critical pedagogy" (p. 188). The reason he suggests this is that many of our ecological problems are brought on by industry and greed, "urbanization and globalization" (p. 188). For the oil companies, it is always profit before people. And many see what devastation BP has caused for our friends on the Gulf Coast. The BP oil spill is responsible for the death of much wildlife. Our oceans will be forever damaged—this damage spreads. Scientists cannot completely contain toxins that are dumped in water that flows and moves and changes.

Environmental Justice

One variation on EE is what is termed "environmental justice." These scholars are trying to combine the work that is done in EE with larger social and cultural issues. Environmental justice—like critical theory—tries to show that wealthy people can escape environmental disasters because money can buy healthy school buildings or healthy playgrounds that are not built on top of toxic waste dumps. Shirley Thompson (2008) comments on these issues:

> It is the poor and marginalized of the world who bear the brunt of pollution, resource degradation and dislocation, whether as a result of a dam, toxic waste, lack of arable land, ozone depletion or global climate change, simply because they are vulnerable and lack alternatives. (p. 49)

Thompson goes on to say that "the environmental justice movement is concerned with systemic discrimination" (p. 43). Electric grids are known to cause cancer. Who lives near electric grids? Poor people. Cancer alley—as they call it in Louisiana—is located between New Orleans and Baton Rouge. Here, both the rich and the poor suffer from industrial waste and pollution.

It is known that there is a high cancer rate among people who live in these areas. Some people do not know that industrial pollutants can cause disease.

Loss of Biodiversity

Although EE has its share of problems, one thing these scholars do focus on is the ongoing ecological crisis. Joy A. Palmer (2003) says that our situation is "extremely serious" (p. 35). Palmer remarks,

> The normal rate of extinction of many of the world's biological resources has accelerated, and still are rapidly accelerating—as a result of the ongoing destruction of tropical forests and other biologically rich habitats; plus over harvesting, pollution, and inappropriate introduction of foreign plants and animals. (p. 41)

EE educators are not alone in sounding these alarms. Deep ecologists sound the alarm as well. George Sessions (1995) focuses on the terrible rate of species extinctions caused by human beings. One of the disturbing aspects Sessions points out that I have not seen in EE discussions is the role of the military in environmental degradation. Sessions remarks,

> The cost of cleaning up radioactive and toxic wastes carelessly disposed of at military bases and weapons plants has been estimated at $400 billion. Superfund toxic cleanups are so costly that political leaders are now saying that we cannot afford to clean them up totally. Overall, military activities alone are estimated to cause between 10 and 30 percent of the total environmental degradation of the Earth. (p. xvii)

Sessions ranks the military as the number one cause of environmental degradation. Think of the dropping of atomic bombs. Think of wars, explosions, missiles, tanks, landmines, air strikes. Violence not only kills people, it also devastates everything: the land, the water, the earth, the animals. This devastation cannot be contained. What happens on one side of the world affects the other side: that is the idea behind what Lorenz (1995) calls the "butterfly effect." Everything affects everything. The worst thing that scientists invented was the nuclear bomb. How can one contain a nuclear explosion? Today the problem of nuclear proliferation is very serious. The world has gone nuclear.

Gary Snyder (1990)—an advocate of deep ecology—also emphasizes that nature is violent. Deep ecology looks at this other side—what Jungians would call the shadow side—of nature as well as the beauty in nature. Snyder remarks:

> Life in the wild is not just eating berries in the sunlight. I like to imagine a "deep ecology" that would go to the dark side of nature—the ball of crunched bones in a scat, the feathers in the snow, the tale of insatiable appetite. Wild systems…can also be irrational, moldy, cruel, parasitic. (p. 118)

Deep ecology and EE have this thought in common: that all is not well with the world. Even Thomas Berry—who also advocates a deep ecology and also talks of the spirituality of nature—suggests that nature is violent. Thomas Berry (1990) notes,

> The universe, earth, life, and consciousness are all violent processes. The terms in cosmology, geology, biology, and anthropology all carry a heavy charge of tension and violence. Neither the universe as a whole nor any part of the universe is especially peaceful. (p. 216)

Human beings are part of nature and are just as violent as the universe—human beings are the universe so we share these properties. The problem is that we have made things worse by our disregard for our habitat. Michael Bonnett (2004) writes about nature in the context of the posthuman when he notes,

> At this stage in history [which he calls posthuman] it is difficult to identify an issue of greater importance for humankind than its relationship with its environment, nor one that is more fraught. It must be a unique phenomenon—on Earth at least—for a species to be contemplating the possibility of its self-extinction. (p. 1)

Does the posthuman suggest that the human will be post—perhaps compost—in the near future? Most scholars of the posthuman write about the blurring of technology, human beings, and nonhuman animals. But is it this technology that, in part, is leading to our demise?

Our Food Supply

Marc Bekoff (2010) talks about our "carbon hoofprint" (p. 119). Bekoff explains,

> People are now talking about a "carbon hoofprint" and calling livestock "living smokestacks," as ways to characterize the large amount of greenhouse gases released into the atmosphere. For example, one Swedish study found that "producing a pound of beef creates 11 times as much greenhouse gas emission as a pound of chicken and 100 times more than a pound of carrots." (p. 119)

Greenhouse gas emissions are destroying the planet; human beings are mostly responsible for this. The slaughterhouse industry has been known for its disgusting practices since Upton Sinclair's (1906/2006) novel *The Jungle*. But the new twist now is about this "carbon hoofprint" (Bekoff, p. 119) that slaughterhouses and high-density feedlots produce. Deep ecologists, EE educators, and Bekoff who is an ethologist—call for a sense of urgency (p. 2) about our current condition on this earth. But this sense of urgency is not new. Ricardo R. Fernandez (1997) tells us,

> Thirty years ago, ecologist Garrett Hardin pointed to the "tragedy of the commons" as a way to sound the alarm about the impending dangers of taking our environment for granted. The "commons" today is an even more critical issue because we live with a growing consciousness of global environmental concerns. (p. xv)

People who do not study environmental issues do not understand the situation we have gotten ourselves into. Nonhuman animals did not cause our current ecological crisis: people have. Has humankind made progress scientifically or have we become barbarians through the misuses of technology? War technology and the technology of the slaughterhouse are two of the most insidious forms of toxicity, not to mention the technologies of pesticides and the technology of computer waste. Computer dumps, cell phones, plastic all leave heavy carbon footprints because they are not biodegradable—they only degrade the earth more and spread more poisons into the earth.

At any rate, when one thinks of nature and the ecosphere, taking a walk in the woods can no longer be naïve. Here I am thinking of the American tradition of Transcendentalists (like Thoreau) who romanticized nature. Humankind can no longer afford to romanticize nature. Let me speak to this issue for a moment because many theorists comment on this in the ecological literature. Gary Snyder (1990) says, "Bioregional awareness teaches us in *specific* ways. It is not enough just to 'love nature' or want to 'be in harmony with Gaia.' Our relation to the natural world takes place in a *place*" (p. 42). So in our own places people have to be aware of what is going on and what is going wrong. The word "bioregional" suggests that people focus on their own region. For a thorough treatment of this subject students might study the work of Nathan Hensley (2011), who has written an important book titled *Curriculum Studies Gone Wild: Bioregional Education and the Scholarship of Sustainability*. Most would agree that we think where we are; others think where they are: it simply is impossible to think the world. However, we should know the implications for what we are doing in our own region against the backdrop of the larger world in which we live. Again, I come back to Lorenz's butterfly effect. Everything affects everything.

Like Snyder, William Cronon (1996b) talks about the problems of romanticizing nature:

> By the second half of the nineteenth century, the terrible awe that Wordsworth and Thoreau regarded as the appropriately pious stance to adopt in the presence of their mountaintop God was giving way to a much more comfortable, almost sentimental demeanor....The writer who best captures this late romantic sense of the domesticated sublime is undoubtedly John Muir. (p. 75)

The words I want to focus on here are these: "pious," "comfortable," "sentimental," and "domesticated." Nature should not be understood in these terms. Nature should not be domesticated because it is not domestic. To domesticate nature is to try to tame it and get the wildness out of it or to remove the violence from it. Yes, nature can be beautiful. But what many do not want to face is the violence inherent in nature and the violent ways in which people have ruined the ecosphere. Ugena Whitlock (2007) writes about these problems also as she struggles with her own nostalgia (p. 9) of place. Nostalgia is dangerous because it erases the negative. Nostalgia captures the romantic tradition. Here I am thinking of a passage from Thoreau's (2000) *Walden* where he says, "It would be well perhaps if we were to spend more of our day's nights without any obstruction between us and the celestial bodies" (p. 57). The problem is that humankind has always already obstructed relations with the ecosphere. People have obstructed relations through the misuse and abuse of nature. Thoreau wanted to drive a wedge between the woods and civilization. But there is no wedge to be drawn. There is nothing civil about the ways in which people have destroyed the earth. One of the dangers about the woods is that loggers continue to cut them down—without trees sentient beings cannot survive. But the logging trucks keep clear-cutting. Paper mills continue to spew toxins.

Ecojustice

One might wonder why I have spent so much time on the negative in the context of ecology. Perhaps readers were expecting something else. Indeed, a group of scholars do not like this negativity and sense of alarm. Here I am thinking of a book called *Cultural Studies and Environmentalism: The Confluence of*

Ecojustice, Place-Based (Science) Education, and Indigenous Knowledge Systems, which is co-edited by Deborah J. Tippins, Michael P. Mueller, Michiel van Eijck, and Jennifer D. Adams (2010). Although I agree with many of the things these authors discuss in the book—like the notion of place-based ecology and embracing indigenous knowledges—what I do not like is their Pollyanna attitude toward our current ecological disaster. In the preface to their book, these editors state,

> Therefore, ecojustice [which is not the same thing as environmental justice] recognizes the appropriateness and significance of learning from place-based experiences and indigenous knowledge systems rather than depending on some urgent "ecological crises" to advocate for school and social change. (2010b, p. v)

Michael P. Mueller and Deborah J. Tippins (2010) write in their chapter titled "Nurturing Morally Defensible Environmentalism": "When we de-emphasize the imperative of 'crises' implicitly reinforced in the vast majority of environmental scholarship about social and environmental justice, it guides us to seek greater ethics" (p. 8). I find this claim unconvincing. We are in a crisis and should acknowledge it. What does it meant to "seek greater ethics?" Again, I think the idea of ecojustice a good one on two counts: thinking in place (called "bioregional awareness") and embracing indigenous knowledges. As Noel Gough (2008) points out, Western science isn't the only science that counts as knowledge. However, I do not see how a more nurturing attitude—as the title of Mueller and Tippins's (2010) chapter indicates—and the de-emphasis of our current crisis help us to better understand our ecological crisis. How can humankind have ecojustice when the justice that is sought is blind? Here, ecojustice scholars could learn from ecofeminists and critical theorists who argue that industry (mostly invented by white men) has been one of the causes of our current disaster. Profit before people—as the critical theorists argue—is what has caused the degradation of the earth. To not acknowledge that the earth is out of balance is to argue from a naïve position. Justice means fighting against wrongs and acknowledging those wrongs. How can you have ecojustice without focusing on what is wrong? Focusing only on nurturance seems to be out of step with discussions in ecological circles.

There are other—and I might add more convincing—ways that scholars describe ecojustice. In fact, Kathryn Ross Wayne and David A. Gruenewald (2004) suggest that there is a "diversity of approaches to ecojustice…[and sometimes these approaches are] in seeming opposition" (p. 7). One position that is in opposition to Tippins et al. (2010) is the following. Peter McLaren and Donna Houston (2004) write about what they call "ecosocialism," which is an offshoot of ecojustice. They explain,

> Precisely what a dialectic of ecological and environmental justice illuminates, then is how the malign interaction between capitalism, imperialism, and ecology has created widespread environmental degradation and has developed coevally with the expansionist regimes of free markets....Moreover, it reveals how such conditions require that the most economically exploited and socially vulnerable people and places on the planet bear the burden of ecocide on their bodies. (p. 33)

McLaren and Houston make a more convincing claim here and their version of ecosocialism both sounds the alarm and puts the ecological crisis in the context of the problems of neoliberalism and the ways in which big business is at loggerheads with the concerns of ecologists.

Carol Brandt (2004) argues for an ecojustice that takes into account race, class, and gender but she also talks about the issue of sustainability. Brandt explains her position on ecojustice here:

> Sustainability, too, must be understood in a broader historical and political-economic context that is simply opposed to the demons of "industrialism." Simplistic views of sustainability obscure the history of class, gender, and ethnic issues....Chase (2002) notes that middle-class, mainstream students in environmental science classes have little knowledge of social oppression, political economy, or the history of people's movements in this or in other countries. (p. 98)

The problem with "mainstream science" is that it does not take into account the larger historical backdrop against which science is done. The cultural studies of science movement tries to rectify this narrowness of traditional science education. (For more on this see Weaver, Morris, & Appelbaum, 2001.) Studying the larger culture against which science is done raises questions about who gets to do science in the first place and what counts as science.

The most well-known ecojustice scholars (alongside C. A. Bowers) are David A. Gruenewald and Gregory A. Smith (2008). Gruenewald and Smith discuss "place-conscious education" and what is referred to as "the new localism" (p. xiii). Getting back to place is part of the ecojustice movement, but there is more here too. Gruenewald and Smith argue,

> Critical issues of race, class, gender and other aspects of culture can become abstractions unless these issues are grounded in concrete experience, experience that always takes place somewhere. Place-consciousness toward diversity and multiculturalism

means reconnecting these themes with the rooted experience of people in their total environments. (p. xxi)

These scholars also take into account "economic development that disrupt[s]" (p. xiii) people's lives in their local places and in their ecological environments. So it seems that many scholars who are doing place-based ecojustice are also concerned with issues that are larger than merely nurturing and caring for our world (Tippins et al., 2010). Of course it is important to be nurturing and caring, but this is not enough. The harder-edged place-based educators examine the ecological crisis from the larger socioeconomic, political, classed, raced, and gendered aspects of environmental issues. In many ways ecojustice dovetails with what some term "environmental justice," although again, Tippins et al. drive a wedge between environmental justice and ecojustice as two different ways of approaching ecology. Noel Gough (2008) further qualifies what he thinks place-based education should be and argues that Gruenewald and Smith's (2008) position is "too totalizing." Gough explains,

> To simply *assert* an essential relationship between place and pedagogy is too totalizing for me.…I cannot imagine "place" (as a generic abstraction) or "a place" (as a specific location) *becoming* "pedagogical" through cultural practices that enable or encourage us to attend closely to their multifarious qualities, including not only those that we might consider to be "profound"…but also their more superficial, ephemeral or obvious characteristics. (p. 72).

Gough, too, is concerned with environmental racism and sexism and the larger political and economic backdrop. He calls for an "ecocritical literacy" (p. 74) that takes all of these things into account. But more than that Gough also takes into consideration the uses of popular culture—and this is something that I have not seen in the ecological literature. Gough draws on a song by Peter Gabriel called "Shaking the Tree," about sexism, that inspired him to do ecocritical work in South Africa. I encourage students to read the full text of Gough's article titled "Ecology, Ecocriticism and Learning: How Do Places Become 'Pedagogicals'"? This article can be found in *Transnational Curriculum Inquiry* (2008, pp. 71–86).

Environmental Education and Ecojustice

Some scholars suggest that EE and ecojustice approaches have some things in common. EE is somewhat akin to an ecojustice approach as far as focusing more on the place in which you live rather than trying to think the world. Michiel van Eijck (2010) says, "Environmental education has recently moved towards more place-based approaches. Originally, environmental education dealt with rather global, abstract environmental concepts, such as those of ozone depletion, toxic waste, and global warming" (p. 187). Thinking about ozone depletion on a worldwide scale becomes difficult because the world is too vast to think. But local ecological problems are also global. Yet thinking globally is a challenge that people must take up. At any rate, EE is changing; if it is more place-based, then it might have more in common with ecojustice, at least on this count. Annette Gough—who is well known for her work on ecology and environmental education—suggests that EE is also moving in other directions, too, as she draws a distinction between these (which I will talk about in a moment) and what goes on in science education—which is different from EE. Annette Gough (cited in Tasar, 2009) points out, "I think at the other level there's probably been more critical and poststructural research happening than you'll see in science education" (p. 191). Annette Gough, then, suggests—as against some other scholars who critique EE for not being progressive enough (i.e., not drawing on critical theory or dealing with social issues)—that EE is in fact moving in these newer directions. For laypeople, all of these terms (EE, science education, ecojustice, environmental justice, ecofeminism, and deep ecology) can be confusing. Some of what goes on in deep ecology also goes on in EE, but again there are differences. Deep ecologists also emphasize the spiritual side of nature; whereas, EE—coming from the more scientific perspective—does not deal with spirituality in the context of the environment. Now, of course, again people should not fall into the trap of romanticizing ecology by waxing poetic over it. Certainly, there are divine and spiritual aspects to nature and there are beautiful things about nature as well. These things must not be forgotten in the midst of the gloomy predicament we are in. Still, it is not enough to wish for the beautiful and think of the beautiful only. Yes, Yellowstone is a beautiful place. And there are many beautiful places all over the world. But beauty is not what we are really interested in here. There is also much ugliness to contend with. Much of this ugliness human beings have caused. It is the ugliness that demands study. Otherwise, we begin to sound like the romantics and begin to forget what is at stake: our very existence.

Home and Displacement: Ecology and the Poetic

There are scholars who approach ecology from a more philosophic and poetic framework. These scholars are not science oriented but are rather interested in the larger philosophical and poetic ideas that ecology raises. The conversation here is different from the one that scientists have. Here scholars are dealing with abstract, philosophical ideas that allow us to then come back to our concrete place(s)—like home—thinking anew. David Smith (1999) in his book *Pedagon: Interdisciplinary Essays in the Human Sciences, Pedagogy, and Culture*, notes,

> The ancient Greek philosopher Plotinus put it this way: "Question: Why do you go out? Answer: In order to come in." Why would one leave home? Well, in order to come home, but in a new way, a better way. (p. 1)

David Smith is trying to get us to think about home in a Derridean way. To come home, you must leave. To leave, you must come home. This is the aporia of home. What is home anyway? Home is an ecological concept. David Smith talks about home but he also talks about agony. Smith states, "*Pedagon* is a neologism eliding two words, pedagogy and agony" (p. xiii). If home has anything to teach us, it is agony. Home is an agonizing concept. Our childhood homes haunt us. Many people, upon retirement, resettle near their childhood homes. There is sometimes a lingering nostalgia for childhood homes. This nostalgia is agonizing for some.

Like David Smith, David Jardine's (2000) book, titled *"Under the Tough Old Stars": Ecopedagogical Essays*, is a good (place) to begin talking about ecology, pedagogy, and the notion of home. Being in (place) means being at home. This book is poetic, philosophical, and lively. His prose certainly gets the attention of the reader. In fact, he speaks to issues of attention in the context of the idea of home. Jardine states,

> Ecology is therefore about returning our attention to home. It is about tending anew to where we dwell, to our nest, to the delicate and difficult reliances and debts that intertwine our fleshy lives with the fleshy life on earth; it is the moist texture that bestows our lives and makes them possible. (p. 20)

Already, one can see a different kind of conversation occurring here than in the first part of this chapter. Curriculum studies scholars who veer into the philosophic and poetic have a different way of approaching ecological issues. The way in which this passage is crafted allows different kinds of ideas to come to mind. Jardine gives his readers much to think about in this passage and allows his readers to breathe while reading. This breath opens up spaces of thought that make us think otherwise. Where do we call home? And what exactly is home? Jardine compares humans' homes with the homes of birds as he uses the metaphor of the nest to refer to home. Rachel Carson (1990) teaches that when birds go silent, something is terribly wrong. Birds are creatures that many of us usually ignore. Many take them for granted and pay them little attention. However, birds are an important part of our biodiversity; without them, other sentient creatures are in trouble. Let us take a moment and cite a passage from Marc Bekoff (2010) about birds and the way in which they actually show affection, even interspecies affection. Bekoff cites the following passage from a blog he found on the Internet.

> A local security guard recently discovered a peculiar scene where black swans can be seen feeding goldfish near the shore of a lake located in Hang Zhou, China. According to the guard, nine black swans will climb onto a raft and start feeding the goldfish with their beaks at 10 AM every morning…Locals were astonished to find such an affectionate tie existing between two creatures. (pp. 86–87)

The point Bekoff wants to make is that animals of all kinds have feelings and even interspecies feelings, so in many ways they are like humans.

Let us dwell on Jardine's (2000) point about our home being like a nest. Think these two quotes together—Jardine's and Bekoff's. What these two quotes suggest is that species are interconnected beings and there are many things that dovetail between species. Jardine uses the word "intertwine" (p. 20) to suggest that human life is enmeshed with nonhuman animal life and with the earth—which, by the way, is also a living creature. Our home is the earth, which human beings share with other creatures. Biodiversity is about the diverse nature of nature. Nature must remain diverse or things start to go wrong. Human beings have tried to get rid of this diversity by killing wolves for example (which has been going on for decades) or getting rid of pests (insects). When we kill one species, something in the biosphere goes wrong. Difference in nature is what nature is. So why do human beings have such a hard time with difference? This is why courses on multiculturalism are necessary because human beings do not like other human beings (or other species) and try to do away with difference by colonization, brutalization, or extermination. The point is that our home is a shared home. But human animals want the planet all to themselves and so they gentrify, tear down trees, encroach on animals' habitats, and wonder why bears end up knocking at their front doors. Bekoff tells his readers that a bear did end up on his front porch one day, and he suggests that he knows that even he has encroached (p. 49) on animal territory.

As Jardine reminds us, our home is shared with other creatures big and small, from bears to snakes to rats to gnats to ticks. Our home—the earth—is alive. Human beings live on the earth in buildings but these buildings are built on top of the earth, and things from under the earth eventually come into the buildings. There seems to be leakage between the earth and our buildings. There is no airtight house or apartment. This is another way we share our homes with nonhuman creatures; they just come in, and most often we do not want them in our homes. Recently in Florida, a woman went into her kitchen in the dead of night only to find an alligator there!

The Divine Nature of Nature

Let us talk about birds again for a moment. There is a holiness about the pelican. Thomas Berry (1995) writes about the divine (p. 8) nature of nature. Pelicans remind me of how old the earth is; they seem ancient and divine. Is there some relation human beings have with pelicans in our own ancientness, if you will? Interspecies relations is a topic that Elaine Riley-Taylor (2002) writes about in her book titled *Ecology, Spirituality and Education: Curriculum for Relational Knowing*. Riley-Taylor states,

> There is great potential for helping to affect a symbiotic balance between our species and the larger ecological world. However, most people remain largely inactive, with eyes closed to the potential role we could play as stewards of a planet inhabited by multitudes of life forms in an ecological balance. The word *steward* drawing from the Old English means "watchful," "awake," from the Greek, "revere," and from the Latin it means to "respect" or to "feel awe for" (p. 7)

Riley-Taylor is right when she suggests that most people pay little attention to the world, to nature and its creatures. In America, people are too busy driving back and forth on the interstate, coming and going to their jobs, worrying about this and that, so nature's creatures are the last thing on people's minds. Critics of the study of ecology suggest that ecology is a leisure activity. Who has the time to go to Walden like Thoreau? Who has the time to go to the woods and watch birds? But the point Riley-Taylor makes isn't that people

need to take time off or spend money to take care of the earth and her creatures because people can do this at home, right in the backyard. Or one can
do this work by adopting animals from rescue societies, taking care of those
creatures that need our help the most. When Riley-Taylor mentions respect
for nature's creatures, proper burials are part of that respect. People should not
let animals suffer needlessly and when they have to put them down—as the
phrase goes—it is extremely painful. Being a steward of the earth also means
being kind to animals and taking care of them through sickness and health.
Animals have no voice but they do speak to us in many other ways.

Speaking of voice, David Jardine (1998), in his book *To Dwell with a
Boundless Heart: Essays in Curriculum Theory, Hermeneutics, and the Ecological
Imagination*, says

> One of the claims of ecological understanding is that life on Earth involves a multi-
> tude of different interweaving and intersecting voices, of which the human voice is
> but one of many....Living with the richness and difficulty of this multitude of voices
> and speaking out from the midst of it is *part of the phenomenon of the integrated curric-
> ulum*. (p. 77)

Animals speak. Animals have much to teach us and they are part of our lived
experience, especially if they live in our homes. To dwell with a boundless
heart, which is the title of Jardine's book, also means to dwell with a boundless heart in relation to our animal friends. To have a boundless heart means
that we do anything that we can to help our animal friends, especially if they
are sick or hurt. Our animal friends share our homes and they are very much
integrated into the curriculum of our lives. They are part of our *curriculum
vitae* or life story.

Rebecca A. Martusewicz, John Lupinacci, and Gary Schnakenberg (2010)
write about the way in which our homes are nested (p. 12) into the larger
ecosphere. Again the metaphor of the nest emerges. Recall our discussion on
Jardine's (2000) use of the word nest and the discussion on birds and their
ability to take care of goldfish (Bekoff, 2010). Martusewicz, Lupinacci, and
Schnakenberg tell us,

> The etymology of the word ecology, which when traced back to the Greek "oikos,"
> means home or household. Thus, rather than asserting a view that positions the
> environment as outside or separate from human communities, we begin from the
> understanding that all human communities are nested and participate in complex
> communities of life—ecosystems—that we depend upon for our very lives. (p. 12)

Perhaps this citation should put things the other way around. Instead of centering the discussion on humans why not center the discussions on other creatures and "nest" ourselves back into the creature community C. A. Bowers (1995) argues that scholars need to get away from anthropocentrism and focus more on ecocentrism.

Now the problem of anthropocentrism is close to the problem of anthropomorphism—attributing human qualities to animals. Marc Bekoff comments on this quite extensively as he states,

> Critics who complain about anthropomorphism fail to notice their own anthropomorphism. The same zoo officials who accuse activists of being anthropomorphic when they call a captive elephant unhappy turn around and freely describe the same elephant as perfectly happy. Renowned philosopher Mary Midgley points out [that]... what's truly anthropomorphic is to assume that animals don't think or feel....It's important to get over this issue of anthropomorphism and move on—there's important work to be done. (p. 77)

Recall, for Bekoff the main point throughout his work is that animals have feelings and should be treated humanely. They are not objects. Some scientists argue that attributing feelings to animals is simply projecting our own human characteristics onto animals. But Bekoff shows how science is now disputing this. Bekoff argues that many scientific studies show that, in fact, animals do feel. The point is weaving into the discussion other creatures other than ourselves. People are not the center of the universe. Rather, human beings are woven in a complex thread with other creatures. And maybe people should stop being so narcissistic and start thinking about the Other in terms of other nonhuman creatures. And this Other nonhuman animal should be allowed to roam freely across the ecosphere. Animals should not be caged, or tortured, or used in experiments. The Nazis did medical experiments on Jews—tortured them and then murdered them. Cruelty to animals is no different from these Nazi so-called experiments. The only reason an animal should be put in a cage is if he is undergoing treatment for an illness and needs to be confined. Some vets recommend that you crate train your puppies. But I think this is cruel. There are other more humane ways to housetrain a dog. Dogs should never be confined to a certain part of the house; rather they should be allowed to roam freely. Allowing dogs to run free and roam in a safe space is humane.

Allowing animals to roam brings up the issue of the nomadic. Nomads roam. Here I am thinking—in a different context and in a different sense—

about what Rebecca Martusewitcz (1997) says when speaking of Yi-Fu Tuan and Jacques Derrida. She states,

> Cultural geographer Yi-Fu Tuan uses the concepts of spaces and pauses to elucidate the nomadic quality of home....As Derrida and other poststructural philosophers have taught us, any text or textual relation is characterized by a kind of indefinite supplementary movement or mobility. (p. 15)

Many human animals—namely academics—are nomads. Moving from one job to another is not uncommon in academe. The notion, then, of home for these on-the-move academics, is fluid since they are always on the move.

Homelessness and Displacement

Being at home is a luxury some human beings and animals do not have. What does it do to someone—psychologically—to be displaced? Steven Semken and Elizabeth Brandt (2010) address these issues as they state,

> Emotional and intellectual estrangement—or even the outright eviction—of people from places personally and culturally important to them is rampant in this time of anthropic sprawl, economic globalization, and cultural homogenization. Placelessness (Relph 1976) unmoors individuals, often with detrimental effects to self-identity. (p. 287)

This raises serious questions for those who focus on place-based education. How can you have place-based education in regions where people are refugees, stateless and rootless? What does place-based education mean to those who are placeless? Nothing. Perhaps being place-based is a privilege that not everyone has. Perhaps scholars should think more about education in terms of exile and mobility rather than being in place. Curriculum theorists are most concerned with people who are Othered; certainly, people who are exiled from their homes should be of our utmost concern. Think about migrant workers and their children and the way in which they are educated. What kind of an education do these children get? They get an education of mobility and displacement. What does this do to a child? Perhaps scholars should begin thinking more in terms of people who are out of place or forced out of place. Edward S. Casey (1998) writes about the worst kinds of displacement as he says,

> Still more saliently, certain devastating phenomena of this century bring with them, by aftershock as it were, a revitalized sensitivity to place. Precisely in its capacity to

eliminate all perceptible places from a given region, the prospect of nuclear annihilation heightens awareness of the unreplaceability of these places, their singular
configuration and unrepeatable history. (p. xiii)

Nuclear annihilation means that nothing is left. How to imagine this nothingness? The point is that human beings are capable of terrible things—like destroying the entire earth through nuclear war. It is not rogue nations people have to
worry about so much as it is America. Americans dropped the atomic bombs,
not rogue nations. America has more nuclear missiles than any other country
in the world. Steven Meyer (1984) tells us what Robert Oppenheimer had
to say about nuclear weapons. Meyer states, "J. Robert Oppenheimer, speaking of the United States decision to proceed with thermonuclear weapons
development, observed, 'it was so technically sweet, we had to do it'" (quoted
in Lefever, 1979, p. 21)" (p. 11). In my chapter on poststructuralism I comment on Michel Serres's decision to get out of science because of these kinds
of developments and the ethical problems with the development of nuclear
weapons. This so-called development is barbaric: it is not, in fact, a development but a catastrophic and colossal scientific mistake. When scholars write
about place, it is imperative to think through this nightmare. What does it
mean to be placeless, landless, and extinct? Is this our future? Let us not be
naïve about things. The world is a violent place. Nation against nation, people against people. War after war after war. That is life. Or should we say
death? What is a dead place? A nucleated place, which becomes a no-place.

Landscape and Place

Let us change key here and think about landscape. Put aside thoughts of nuclear war for now and let us return to our discussion on things ecological. The
land, the landscape. What do these concepts signify? Peirce F. Lewis (1979)
speaks to the issue of landscape as he states,

> The basic principle is this: *that all human landscape has cultural meaning.* It follows, as
> Mae Thielgaard Watts has remarked, that we can "read the landscape" as we might
> read a book. Our human landscape is our unwitting autobiography, reflecting our
> tastes, our values, our aspirations, and even our fears, in tangible, visible form. (p. 12)

The landscape, in other words, is another text for interpretation. And that
interpretation has everything to do with who we are and the ways in which we
perceive our world. It is interesting that Lewis makes the connection between

autobiography and landscape. Some important curriculum scholars have written on this very subject—as I have previously mentioned. (See Ugena Whitlock [2007], Brian Casemore [2008], and Marilyn N. Doerr [2004]). Of course, it was William F. Pinar who brought autobiography to the curriculum field, and he and Joe Kincheloe wrote the first book on place in 1991, *Curriculum as Social Psychoanalysis: The Significance of Place*.

Landscape is not only a text and a human construct, it is also what John Brinckerhoff Jackson (1994) calls "zones of influence" (p. viii). He explains, "The American landscape [or any other landscape] can no longer be seen as a composition of well-defined individual spaces—farms, counties, states, territories, and ecological regions—but as zones of influence" (p. viii). The question of influence could be interpreted politically. Who influences the way land will be used or not used? Who influences how these zones get interpreted? Who gets to interpret them? And if these zones are overlapping—as Brinckerhoff Jackson suggests—what does that mean? Perhaps dividing up the land is a social construct. The land cannot—literally—be divided at all because the ecosphere is all interrelated. But when you fly in an airplane and look over the land, you can see the way the land does get divided up by people who clearcut, who build baseball fields, who build neighborhoods, and so forth. Google Maps is a good way to see how the land has been divided up—and yet it is all of a piece. Blocks of trees seemingly run into buildings and buildings run into waterways. The Rocky Mountains blend into the clouds and the clouds blend into the land. You really do get a different perception of Earth if you see it from above in an airplane.

Speaking of rocky, let us think on rocks for a moment. Rocks make up the land. Rocks are everywhere. The earth is a rock. Gaston Bachelard (2002) has written one of the most important books on the earth called *Earth and Reveries of Will: An Essay on the Imagination of Matter*. His basic argument in the book is that matter—like rocks—although seemingly impenetrable, hard, and static, are in fact fluid and slippery. Bachelard says,

> Goethe felt a passionate inclination [eine leidenschaftliche neigung] toward granite and primitive rock. Granite, in his view, represented what was "deepest and highest [das Hochste und Tiefste]." His first recognition of primitive rock, or Urgestein, on a climb of Mount Brocken, was a matter of primary intuition....Elsewhere Goethe wrote of "the rocks whose power uplifts my soul and makes it strong." (p. 156)

For Freud, primary thought—perhaps like Bachelard's notion of "primary intuition" (p. 156)—emerges from dreams or the unconscious. Dreaming (of) rocks is perhaps what Bachelard means here when speaking of Goethe. The earth, for Bachelard, dreams, has an unconscious, a spirit, and a soul. Rocks are the bedrock of these dreams. Rocks—though—are not solid things; they are slippery, malleable, and always moving, changing. This is not farfetched. Think of the Grand Canyon or Bryce Canyon. These rock formations are the result of centuries of erosion by water and land shifts. The earth is always shifting.

Edward Casey (1996) comments on the Grand Canyon, saying, "The place of the Grand Canyon in my *memory* of it occupies a region of my psyche.... place is not one kind of thing: it can be psychical as well as physical...cultural and historical and social" (p. 31). Places shift as do our memories of those places. Casey argues that the site of memory is also a place or region in our minds. Those regions are always shifting, just as the brain is always changing. We think we are standing on solid ground, but in fact—as Bachelard insists in a most postmodern fashion—we are not. The ground is always unstable. The earth is on the move in mudslides, quicksand, earthquakes, tsunamis, floods, hurricanes.

Like rocks, many ecological thinkers think also about soil. Again, soil is a social construct. There is no soil-in-itself. What we think of soil—again— tells more about ourselves, our autobiography, than the soil. We don't much think of soil, unless we are gardeners. Soil is the heart of the earth: there is a lot of life in soil. Carl Jung (2005) writes,

> For it is the body, the feeling, the instincts, which connect us with the soil. If you give up the past you naturally detach from the past; you lose your roots in the soil, your connection with the totem ancestors that dwell in your soil. (p. 73)

Memory is located, for Jung, in the soil. Places evoke memory and memories—at root as it were—are made of soil. If we move from place to place—as many of us do—we take our memories with us. Does this mean that we also take the soil with us as well? Does the soil—where memories were made— come with us in our psyche? Yes, of course. Memories are made in place and place—at root—is made of soil. The deeper you dig in the soil, the more memories emerge. But what if you forget? As Jung says above, if you forget, you lose your footing, you lose your "roots in the soil" (p. 73). But again, many of us are rootless moving from place to place. But still we take our memories with us. When we begin to lose our memories as we age, our footing slips. Memory is more than just a personal memory for Jung—it is also collective and it includes ancestors (p. 73). These ancestors might not literally be our ancestors but they

might be "totem" animal ancestors. The soil is shared with nonhuman animals and our memories are also of animals, especially if we live with them in
our homes. David Abram (1996) writes about the "more-than-human" world
in his important book titled *The Spell of the Sensuous: Perception and Language
in a More-Than-Human World*. The more-than-human could mean nonhuman
animals like wolves or huskies. But also the more-than-human world means
the entire ecosphere, including the soil. Abram, too, discusses our lives in the
context of soil. Abram says,

> Thus, the living world—this ambiguous realm that we experience in anger and joy,
> grief and in love—is both the soil in which all our sciences [and other disciplines]
> are rooted and the rich humus into which their results ultimately return, whether as
> nutrients or as poisons. (p. 34)

The soil—a much overlooked and ignored part of our lives—is not overlooked
or ignored by Abram or Jung. From the soil we come and to the soil we shall
return. The soil is actually profound, yet most of us think of soil as dirt. Our
work as academics—as Abram puts it—is not done in the ivory tower but on
the soil. The metaphor of the ivory tower is troubling because it suggests that
scholars live above the soil and above the real world. The point of academe
is to figure out our world as best we can so as to make lives better. This is only
possible if we are grounded. If scholars think that they live in an ivory tower,
above it all, then they are arrogant. Arrogance does not lead to knowledge or
wisdom, it leads to ignorance.

David W. Orr (2002) comments, "The standard for ecological design
[green buildings] is neither efficiency nor productivity but health, beginning
with that of the soil and extending upward through plants, animals and people" (p. 29). When you build a building, you build it from the bottom up. The
house of the soul, if not built from below (from the soil of the unconscious),
will collapse. The structure of a green soul—like a green building—is one
that connects with "plants, animals and people" (Orr, p. 29). Orr talks about
health in the above citation in relation to green buildings. The health of the
soul, too, depends on being rooted in the soil and in connection with other
creatures that come up from the soil. H. G. Wells (1967) wrote a sci-fi book
called *A Modern Utopia*, where he said that in the future apartments will have
no dirt, no dust to clean up. Houses will be totally clear of dirt. But the irony
of dirt and dust in your house is that these things actually protect your health
by building up (like a green building) your immune system. If you lived in a
totally clean house, you would surely get sick the minute you stepped outside.

Dirt and dust (which are specks of soil) keep our immune systems healthy. So the irony is that you have to be dirty to be healthy.

To continue with this discussion on the soil, Michael P. Mueller and Deborah J. Tippins (2010) remark,

> Education begins in the womb of our mothers and before that in the soils of the Creation. It ends and begins with soils. What matters then is the regeneration of the soils in the Sacred....Education that does not offer the regeneration of the soils, and by extension, the lives of people, does much less to contribute to the moral and spiritual formation developed when living more fully within the community and environment. (p. 7)

Ultimately, then, education is about soil. *Educare* means, then, to bring forth the soil, to care about the soil. Similarly, *religio* means to tie back the spirit. A more spiritual education—the kind that Mueller and Tippins call for—is an "ecospiritual" education, much like the kind of education that Elaine Riley-Taylor (2002) calls for (p. 3).

Place/Space

Some collapse the ideas of place and space. Some drive a wedge between them. It is clear that these two concepts overlap in some ways. These concepts can be used interchangeably. Let us talk about place—generally—as a concept. Paul C. Adams, Steven Hoelscher, and Karen E. Till (2001) suggest that place has a "texture" (p. xiii).

> A place's "texture" thus calls direct attention to the paradoxical nature of place. Although we may think of texture as a superficial layer, only "skin deep," its distinctive qualities may be profound. A surface is, after all, where subject and object merge; the shape, feel, and texture of a place each provides a glimpse into the processes, structures, spaces, and histories that went into its making. (p. xiii)

These authors do use the words "place" and "space" in the same paragraph. So place and space have things in common. And that common thread might just be the texture of a place, as they point out. The notion of texture is rather complex. It is a concept that scholars do not often give much thought to. Further, these authors cited above suggest that the texture of a place makes it paradoxical because it might be both superficial and profound at once. If one does not think too deeply about a particular place, yes, it might seem superficial. However, if one thinks deeply about all places, aren't they all profound?

Place is where people—and animals—live; isn't life profoundly about place? If people are out of place—exiled—place still plays a role in exile, since exile is a sort of placeless place. But whether in exile or at home, one is always someplace, as Jane Fishman (2001) suggests in the title of her book *Everyone's Gotta Be Somewhere*. So the paradoxical nature of place is not so much about the superficial and the profound—as Adams et al. (2001) suggest—but rather it is the paradox of being in place or out of place, being at home or being in exile. Moreover, sometimes people feel that when they are home they feel that they are actually in exile; whereas, some feel that only in exile are they at home. These are the paradoxes of place. Place is not a static concept. This point is driven home by Steven Semken and Elizabeth Brandt (2010):

> Places are dynamic; [perhaps we move in and out of exiled places] just as geologic and climatic processes modify the physical landscape, population and cultural changes alter the meanings and dimensions of a place, albeit at very different rates. (p. 288)

Being stuck in place means that one cannot find the way out. This could be an intellectual place that we get stuck in. Getting stuck means that things stop. But one can find the way out of stuckness through work, study, and play. When a place seems static and dead, it is time to move on and move to another place. This is one reason why people move: they get stuck and feel dead. So people can change their place if they have the resources. Others cannot. Poor people cannot change their place, so of course they feel stuck, as if living in a dead place. Gogol (2004) wrote a book called *Dead Souls*. Dead places are where dead souls live. Michiel van Eijck (2010) says, "There are as many natural places and natural worlds and senses of place as there are different people" (p. 189). I would add, too, that many nonhuman animals have a sense of place because they are territorial.

Scholars must rethink place to begin to understand what a complex concept it is in relation to ecology and curriculum. I bring this point up because I find it interesting that, as James Gray-Donald (2008) points out, "While most EE research [which tends to be scientifically oriented] has taken note of gender, it has generally not addressed issues of race, place, and spirituality" (p. 27). Now, Gray-Donald does say that "this is changing" (p. 27) but most of the articles in EE deal with other issues besides the philosophical one of place and spirituality.

Places are engendered but there is little discussion on this in the philosophical literature about place. The home is certainly an engendered notion. The academy as a place is engendered as well. The home is associated with women and housework. The academy is associated with the male intellectual.

The bowling alley is associated with the working class. The opera is a place associated with the upper class. Place is classed, too. Now of course you can think of these places any way you like but the stereotypes are hard to change.

Helene Cixous in a YouTube post says that the word "intellectual" in the French tradition is reserved for men. She doesn't like the word "intellectual" because women historically have not been thought to be intellectuals. The place for the intellectual is the academy and if only men can be intellectuals then the academy is a place for men. Women are still marginalized within the academy since they are paid less than men and do not get the same respect or attention that male intellectuals do. William Schubert (2004), in a related discussion, talks about the place of school and the problems with thinking about school as a place to do our work. Schubert states,

> I see education sketched thickly in the context of race, politics, history, aesthetics, gender, phenomenological experience, postmodern multi-narrative, autobiography, biography, theology, global perspective, institutions, and especially place. It seems to me that this is the breadth and depth of concern that curriculum studies must embrace, not only through both school and non-school places, but because it *is* life's curriculum that educates. Should that not be where our focus ought to be fixed? (p. xxi)

Schubert's point is that our education happens in the broader *place* of life and is not confined to the schoolhouse. And his point also is that curriculum studies as a discipline works in the different *places* of history, gender, class, and so forth. All of these varying ways of approaching curriculum studies could be considered intellectual places of work.

Thought as a Place

Most discussions on ecology, though, do not take into consideration thought as a place. Most work on place is literally about a place in which we live. But there are other more ethereal ways of thinking about place. Thought is a place: it is a place scholars go to in order to work. Thinking is a place. In an article called "Ecological Consciousness and Curriculum," I (2002b) argue

> Consciousness enables us to be open to others and to the world. It is that very something that connects us to nature and to the earth. It does not make sense, therefore, to talk of consciousness as an isolated event. (p. 571)

In order to even think about ecology, first scholars have to think about what it is that allows us to think ecology in the first place. People have to be conscious and this consciousness is what connects us to the world. Developing an eco-logical consciousness could mean two things. It could mean becoming more aware of our ecological surroundings and the way in which people are en-meshed in the world. But also scholars have to think of consciousness as a place that enables thought in the first place. Consciousness is a concept that should be thought, that is, more ecologically, as always connected to our world. Now, there are people who are not consciously connected to the world—people with brain damage or severe forms of autism or dementia and so forth. There are people who suffer from psychotic breaks and one has to wonder where they go when they are in these places of psychosis.

David Orr (2004) has written a book called *Earth in Mind: On Education, Environment and the Human Prospect*. One could interpret the phrase "earth in mind" in two different ways: One is, again, developing more awareness of the earth—keeping it in mind. Or, one might interpret this title to mean that the earth is in the mind or that the mind is a sort of earth. Orr does not talk about the mind at all, ironically. He talks about the earth and keeping it in mind, that is, being more mindful of the earth, as the Buddhists might put it. Gaston Bachelard (2002) argues that the earth has a mind, a spirit, and soul. Lucy Penna (2008) says, "The Earth is a living organism and has her own form of consciousness" (p. 115). But the point I try to make in my article is that in order to be mindful of the earth, one has to be mindful of the mind because our ideas about the earth come from our mind (our consciousness), and we have to think about the place of consciousness even before we think about our place on the earth. As Penna points out the earth too has a consciousness. But there is more. What I did not write about in my article and what is not really addressed in much of the EE literature is that minds are mostly—psy-chologically speaking—unconscious. So the way in which scholars approach issues of ecology, the earth, the mind, and even consciousness has much to do with what cannot be articulated. The unconscious is a place without a center, as Jean Laplanche (1999) has argued. The unconscious—as a place—has no center; it is the most rigid place one could imagine. It is not dynamic; in fact, it is static. This is the reason people act out and engage in what is called "rep-etition compulsion." Damaged psyches are static ones. Repetition compulsion is like a broken record. We go over and over the same things all the time in our lives, never really figuring out why we are driven to destruction, why we get involved in terrible situations, why we seek out—unconsciously—bad relationships. David Orr (2004) talks about knowing how "to live well in a place" (p. 101). You can only live well in a place if you can live well in the place of your mind. I will talk more about psyche toward the end of the chapter when a field called "ecopsychology" is explored.

David Orr suggests, "Ecological literacy begins in childhood" (p. 86). But if that childhood is damaged, psyche cannot think ecologically; psyche gets split off and stuck in place. So ecological literacy might not begin to become important until adulthood when one is able to work through psychic damage. In order to think more ecologically—to think in terms of connections and associations—one has to be able to make connections and freely associate. If one cannot make connections and associate from those connections, psyche gets split off, not only from itself but also from the world. One can only become "literate" about the world—to use Orr's term—if one can be literate about the self, the psyche, the soul. Being literate means that you can articulate something. If you cannot articulate what is inside your head, you will not be able to make the connection that your head is connected to the world. So if the psyche is split off, little connection will be made with the world and there will be little "ecological literacy"—as Orr calls it—at hand.

Fusion and Alterity with the Ecosphere

Speaking of the unconscious, Stephen Aizenstat (1995) claims,

> The world unconscious is a deeper and wider dimension of the psyche than that of the personal or collective unconscious. In the realm of the world unconscious, all creatures and things of the world are understood as interrelated and interconnected. (pp. 95–96)

At a very deep—and unconscious—level sentient creatures are fused with the larger ecosphere via the unconscious. If animals have emotions and feelings (Bekoff, 2010), why shouldn't they have an unconscious element to those emotions too? Human animals are not separate and apart from nature, we are fused with it and other creatures. Our houses might seem to separate us from the outside world, but as I said earlier that idea might be an illusion. Things are always coming into our houses, including dust mites, roaches, dust, and a variety of microscopic creatures. The house is not air tight, and if it were people would probably die from suffocation. The house of the psyche is fused with the house of the world's psyche—this is the point that Aizenstat is trying to make. This fusion is what I want to address in these next few pages. Jung (2005) makes this fusion clear when he says, "Do you think that somewhere we are not nature, that we are different from nature? No, we are in Nature and think exactly like Nature" (p. 24). So if we "think exactly like nature," nature must have both a consciousness and an unconscious. World creatures and the earth are living and the living are complex thinking, conscious and unconscious beings. Everything around us is alive. If energy never dies, then nature is always changing, moving, morphing. And we change, move, and morph because, as Jung says, we are Nature and "think exactly like nature" (p. 24). Like Jung, David Orr (2002), in his book *The Nature of Design*, says,

> The environment outside us is also inside us. We are connected to more things in more ways than we can ever count or comprehend. The act of designing [buildings] begins with the awareness that we can never entirely fathom those connections. (p. 29)

Are the bones of our bodies like trees? Are leaves like our hair? The chemistry of our bodies is also found in the elements of nature. We are the stars and are made up of the same matter of the stars. This connection with the natural world is what myth teaches (Doll, 2011).

Buildings serve mostly to cut us off from the outside world—as if there are two worlds—one inside buildings and the other outside buildings. David Orr suggests that we should build green buildings so as to make us more aware of these connections between the inside and outside, that the outside is inside. On the cover of his book there is a picture of a building that is almost entirely made of glass. Glass allows us to see the outside and it is not unusual for people to feel hemmed in when working in buildings without windows. Everybody wants a room with a window. Why? Because, perhaps unconsciously, people want to feel that connection with the outside, which is always inside us too. Enclosed spaces make some people have panic attacks. Why? Because these enclosures cut us off from what and who we are. Animals go crazy in cages (Bekoff) because they are enclosed and trapped. This is why most zoos are terrible places, as Bekoff points out. Animals do not belong in zoos. Zoos are about making money, not taking care of animals.

David Jardine (1998) says that scholars have a "deep connectedness, a deep interestedness (*inter esse*—being in the middle of things)" (p. 7) in theorizing the world because scholars want to make sense of the ways in which they are "in the middle of things." Again human beings are not the center of the world; human beings are in the middle of it, as Jardine and so many other ecologists point out. But it might be an uncomfortable thought to think that symbolically people are somehow thrown into the middle of somebody else's conversation. That is what life is. The world's conversation is beyond understanding and people are thrown into the middle of it. And yes, the world is having a conversation—maybe not in words but in the way in which things are always changing. Yi-Fu Tuan (1979) speaks to these issues as he suggests,

> Buildings and topographic poems, insofar as they are artworks, clarify experience. They clarify different kinds of experience and encourage us to select different kinds of environmental clues to attend and fuse in imagination....The designed environment has a direct impact on human senses and feelings. The body reacts unreflectively to such basic architectural attributes as enclosure and exposure, verticality and horizontality. (pp. 97–98, 99)

I do not know if buildings and poems clarify experience so much as give us a certain kind of experience. I do not think that experience is ever really clarified, especially if most of it is—as Stephen Aizenstat (1995) points out—unconscious. But I do think that Tuan is right to suggest that the way we are enclosed alters our perceptions of the world. What strikes me especially in Tuan's citation above is his use of the words "verticality" and "horizontality" in the context of buildings and topography in general. Verticality and horizontality are modes of thought. Here I am reminded of William F. Pinar's (2007) book *Intellectual Advancement Through Disciplinarity: Verticality and Horizontality in Curriculum Studies*. Pinar explains,

> Like the field of intellectual history (see Pinar, 2006b, pp. 1–14), verticality documents the ideas that constitute curriculum studies. There is, of course, no one conversation, no one collective history. Moreover, disciplinary conversation is hardly held in a sound-proof [sic] room. The sounds of events outside the field—cultural shifts, political events, even institutional reorganizations—influence what we say to each other. (p. xiv)

Verticality is going deep down into the field to see what is there. But also, as Pinar points out, this verticality is not in a soundproof room—a field is not shut off from the outside. It is interesting that he uses a metaphor of a room. Again, this is a topographical metaphor much like the one that Tuan uses. A soundproof room is good in some cases though. If you are a musician and are practicing, it would be better to have a soundproof room so as not to annoy others. Or if you are in a music school where there are long hallways of practice rooms, one room next to another, soundproof rooms would be better so as not to hear your neighbor practicing. But in a discipline, the borders of that discipline leak and the outside leaks in as the inside leaks out. Curriculum studies is a rather porous discipline as it is highly interdisciplinary. Pinar's (2007) point in his book is that curriculum scholars make sure that they honor people in our field and know our field before we begin venturing out into other fields. No discipline lives in a soundproof room, as Pinar puts it. Even the most specialized of disciplines are impacted by what is going on around them. Pinar goes on to say that horizontality

> refers not only to the field's present set of intellectual circumstances....but as well to the social and political milieus which influence and, all too often, structure this set. Study of the "external" circumstances of the field must be accompanied by ongoing attention to the field's intellectual history. (p. xiv)

Pinar's thinking on curriculum studies is ecological in that the outside of the field is interrelated to the inside of the field. His point, though, is that too many scholars forget their roots and forget that the ground of curriculum studies is not treated thoroughly enough. Thinking is both vertical and horizontal—these are topographical metaphors. And these topographical metaphors are also living metaphors as a field is always changing. David Jardine (2000) comments on the living qualities of intellectual disciplines. He states,

> If we can imagine mathematics and language and science and art and social studies as living topographies, living places full of spooks and spirits and lives and voices, we find that learning to live well in such living places, learning to take good care of them, learning their ways, takes time—often a long time—often longer than the life we've been allotted. It often requires years of suffering, trying again, listening anew, speaking and thinking, changing your mind. (p. 6)

Jardine captures the livingness, if you will, of intellectual life. Disciplines are made up by people and people are living creatures. But too often, the school disciplines are treated like dead things. Dead things have no soul. The soul of the disciplines—which is a living thing—has been taken out of schooling because it is being standardized and quantified. A discipline is a living creature, as Jardine points out, and scholars should treat disciplines as such. Interestingly enough, David Jardine—like David Smith (1999) who talks about the agony (p. xiii) of teaching—talks about studying disciplines with a sense of suffering. Scholars suffer to understand but, as Jardine points out, life is too short to understand the breadth and depth of the living disciplines. The disciplines have grown too much to understand everything that goes on in them. Disciplines are not linear but rather chaotic. In fact, the livingness of the disciplines makes for a mess. This is a messy world and if disciplines are living creatures then they too are messy. Defining disciplinary borders—as

Pinar attempts to do—becomes increasingly difficult as our world becomes more and more intertwined and confused. But then again, disciplines have histories; curriculum studies is a discipline with a particular history, with particular people in that history. Scholars must honor intellectual ancestors, as Jardine (2000) puts it. Jardine speaks to this point as he says,

> "Ecopedagogy"…is an attempt to find ways in which ecologically rich images of ancestry [those who have done curriculum scholarship before us], sustainability, interrelatedness, interdependency, kinship, and topography can help revitalize our understanding of *all* the living disciplines in our care. (p. 3)

The two words that stand out in the context of the discussion here are "ancestry" and "kinship." We have a certain ancestry and particular kinship with curriculum scholars who came before us. Then, too, Jardine talks about interrelation with "*all* the living disciplines in our care" (p. 9). Jung's fascination with mandalas signifies his interest in the interrelations of all things. The mandala represents the circle of life. The mandala is an ecological symbol indeed. It is interesting that Buddhist monks come to Savannah, Georgia, on occasion and build mandalas out of sand. These are highly intricate and beautifully colored grains of sand that the monks spend hours and hours building. After they are finished, they blow the sand away as if to say, the point of the circle of life is to let go, to go back to the dust, to turn things into dust. For Buddhists the point is to acknowledge that all things will vanish and that forms are really illusory. Buddhists believe that we come from nothing and will return to nothing. "Nothingness" is the most profound idea in the Buddhist tradition. It is hard for Westerners to understand what nothingness is. But it is and it is nothing. No-thing. Life is elusive, hardly clear, and it can all blow away—like the mandalas that the Buddhist monks blow away—in a moment. The nature of life is that it does fade away. The blowing away of the sand mandalas is also a symbol of this fading away. Dying is a part of living and the wearing (Berry, 2002, p. 19) away of life is part of the circle and cycle of life. Wendell Berry speaks to this point as he suggests,

> My mind is never empty of idle at the joining of streams. Here is the work of the world going on. The creation is felt, alive and intent on its materials, in such places. In the angle of the meeting of two streams stands the steep wooded point of the ridge, like the prow of an up-turned boat—finished, as it was a thousand years ago, as it will be in a thousand years. Its becoming is only incidental to being. It will be because it is. It has no aim or end except to be. By being, it is growing and wearing into what it will be. (p. 19)

The Grand Canyon is a good example of rock erosion, or the wearing away of rock. But this erosion has created something of awe and beauty. Our own erosion—our own dying process—should not be looked on with fear and trepidation. Jung, in a YouTube post, when talking about death, says that people should look forward to the next process, for death is a process, it is the next step in the dance. Jung says that when people only focus on the past, they get stuck there. People also need to look forward to the future, even if the future includes the wearing away of our bodies. The wearing away of things—as Wendell Berry points out—is all a part of what life is about. The mandala is a symbol of a circle. Out of death comes new life. The decomposing body creates new life forms. Energy never dies.

Joy Palmer (2003) talks about the "autopoietic" nature of the Earth. Palmer states,

> The Gaia Hypothesis, closely allied to "deep" ecological thinking,…argues that Earth can be regarded as if it were a single living organism (Lovelock, 1989). All parts help to regulate and balance the planet via feedback mechanisms, thus sustaining life as we know it. In this sense, only Earth is "alive" because it is "autopoietic", that is self-renewing: it can repair its own "body" and grow by processing materials. (p. 87)

Self-renewal comes out of the dying process as well. Things die and become something else which then renews yet again into something else. This is probably where many Eastern religious traditions get the idea of reincarnation. Things do get reincarnated because decomposition leads to new forms. Decomposition is part of the self-renewal of the earth. Decomposition leads to recomposition. What troubles ecologists are materials that do not decompose—because they destroy the balance of the earth's ecosystem. Plastics do not decompose, computers, cell phones, TVs do not decompose. These things destroy the earth's balance. They are toxic to the renewal of the earth and could be the demise of the planet. The planet has a story to tell and part of that story is the way in which we are destroying the very world in which we live. The stories found in the ecosphere are many, like the wearing away of things. Aldo Leopold (1989) speaks to this point as he poetically says,

> Our lumber pile, recruited entirely from the river, is thus not only a collection of personalities, but an anthology of human strivings in upriver farms and forests. The autobiography of an old board is a kind of literature not yet taught on campuses, but any riverbank is a library where he who hammers or saws may read at will. Come high water, there is always an accession of new books. (p. 25)

The world is a text. The world, says Leopold, is full of stories. An "old board" has an "autobiography' (p. 25). A riverbank is full of stories, as Leopold points out, and is in fact an entire library of stories. The world is the largest library of all. The holdings are tremendous. But human beings have to be open to the library of the world—as it were—to hold these books of nature in our hands. The world needs—as Winnicott (2010) might put it—a holding environment. Humankind has barely given the world this holding environment. People are bent on destroying the world either through willed ignorance or indifference or even the purposeful building of "sweet" nuclear bombs—in the words of J. Oppenheimer (in Meyer, 1984, p. 11).

To say that nature is a process of fusion—that human beings are fused with the natural world and human beings are the natural world—is one way to understand ecology. But this is not all. Alterity is also part of the natural world. Biodiversity is all about alterity. William Cronon's (1996a) book titled *Uncommon Ground* points toward this biodiversity. Of course we have things in common with many creatures in nature, but wild animals are not like us. Human beings are domesticated creatures. It is nearly impossible to domesticate a wild animal. Wild animals are different from domesticated humans. And it is this difference that I want to focus on for a moment. In my (2002b) article on consciousness and ecology, I argue, "Co-consciousness arises out of differences" (p. 580). So the consciousness, of a wolf and hybrid dog emerge from their own kind of consciousness, and these kinds of consciousnesses are different from one another and from us. I note,

> The jaguar, the cat, the tree and the starfish are all wildly different from each other, even though all are webbed into the same weave of the world. And that place we (as human beings) call the world is wildly different from us as well. Even though I belong to the landscape, it can seem alien to me. Although the marshes of Georgia are home to me, they are forbidding places with alligators and snakes. (p. 579)

Human beings are nature and are in nature. People have many things in common with other creatures, but Otherness remains. Bekoff makes an important point about this issue of difference. He says that we should not "emphasize our differences as a way to establish our superiority" (p. 27). I am certainly not arguing that humans are in any way superior—all I am suggesting is that alterity and biodiversity are important to keep in mind. Yes, we fuse with nature because we are nature. But that doesn't mean that everything in nature is the same. Biodiversity means that nature is diverse. Diversity is built into the ecosystem. Every animal, every creature has his or her own way of communicating and each and every creature is necessary to sustain the ecosystem. All creatures are souls and we need to respect and treat creatures with a sense of awe. David Abram (1996) puts it this way:

> Today we participate almost exclusively with other humans and with our own human-made technologies. It is a precarious situation, given our age-old reciprocity with the many-voiced landscape. We still *need* that which is other than ourselves and our own creations. The simple premise of the book [Abram's *Spell of the Sensuous*] is that we are human only in contact, and conviviality with what is not human. (p. ix)

Abram's "many-voiced landscape" suggests that creatures have their own language that people do not share. And yet, on the other hand, Bekoff says that creatures share with us the fact that they do have feelings and emotions. Yet, a wild animal is still wild. The bones of our bodies might be hard like tree trunks, but we are not trees. Can we think fusion-in-alterity? Thinking these two competing concepts at once is what makes thinking ecologically so difficult. This world is not easy to think. Recall, I began this section talking about William Cronon's (1996c) *Uncommon Ground*. I would like to juxtapose this with what C. A. Bowers (2007) says about the notion of the commons (p. 59). Bowers states,

> By interpreting the commons to mean what is commonly shared between humans, and between humans and the non-human world, we can see that it includes the quality of air, water, plant and animal life—in effect, all that is essential to a self-renewing ecosystem. (p. 59)

Of course creatures share the atmosphere and ecosphere in which we breathe and live. We do all live on the same planet and have that in common. But the discussion has to go beyond what we have in common. We are also different from other species and this difference, too, needs to be fleshed out. It would behoove students to think Cronon's "uncommon ground" together with Bowers' concept of the commons. This is where the study of postmodern thought is useful. Derrida teaches throughout his work that the world is a place where the aporia is all. Everything is, in a sense, aporetic. Everything is a puzzle and opposites and contradictions abound in our world. Ugena Whitlock (2007), in her book *This Corner of Canaan*, also struggles with the notion of difference in the context of place. She suggests that we must not "repress difference" (p. 9) when thinking of place. Biodiversity means that difference abounds in the natural world and in order for the natural world to stay in balance, people must make certain to take care that biodiversity does not get out of whack through species extinction.

Ecopsychology and Spirituality

In this final section of this chapter, I want to talk about yet another approach to ecology called "ecopsychology," which dovetails with spirituality. Most people who do ecopsychology are Jungians. A book that I would recommend to students who are interested in this is titled *Ecopsychology: Restoring the Earth, Healing the Mind* (1995), co-edited by Theodore Roszak, Mary E. Gomes, and Allen D. Kanner. Ecopsychology is a relatively new area in ecology and one that is overlooked by EE educators. So here I want to introduce some concepts in ecopsychology. James Hillman (1995) tells us,

> What I am saying here was said far better by Hippocrates twenty-five hundred years ago in his treatise *Air, Waters, Places*. To grasp the disorders in any subject we must study carefully the environment of the disorder: the kind of water; the winds, humidity, temperatures; the food and plants; the times of day; the seasons. Treatment of the inner requires attention to the outer; or, as another early healer wrote, "The greatest part of the soul lies outside the body." As there are happy places beneficial to well-being, so there are others that seem to harbor demons, miasmas, and melancholy. (p. xxi)

The point Hillman tries to make here is that our environments can make us sick. Certainly if you live in a toxic environment, you will most certainly get sick. And this sickness is not only bodily but, as the body is the soul, it is a soul-sickness. It is hard to avoid this soul-sickness today because everything around us is polluted with toxins: pesticides, herbicides, air pollution, water pollution. If people eat meat they are eating antibiotics that the animal was fed. Or if the animals were not healthy when they were alive, people are eating sick animals and so the chance that humans get sick, too, is rather high. We really do not know what we are eating. Even vegetables can make us sick since they too are sprayed with herbicides. We ingest those, even if we wash off the vegetables before we eat them. Those toxins are still there. And we eat them. And then we wonder why so many people get cancer or come down with neurological illnesses. These illnesses also cause a soul-sickness because the body-soul is one thing, not two. If our house is built on top of a toxic waste dump, we will get sick and our soul will suffer from that illness. Hillman's other point, too, is that some places are depressing. Pittsburgh, for example, can be a depressing place to live. Sometimes at noon, the sun disappears and it seems as if it is midnight at noon. This is probably because of pollution but also Pittsburgh has a long history of soot because of the steel mills. Today most of the mills have closed, but the city is still haunted by the soot. When the mills were still in operation, the city always had a strange color about it, a strange, sort of haunted cloud hanging over it. The sun never seemed to come out. The city was so incredibly polluted. Today, things are better there. For some, though, Pittsburgh is a city of "demons, miasmas, and melancholy" (Hillman, p. xxi). As against these demons, Steven Feld and Keith H. Basso (1996) suggest that places can also bring up a feeling of yearning. Feld and Basso say,

> Senses of place: the terrain covered here includes the relation of sensation to emplacement; the experiential and expressive ways places are known, imagined, yearned for, held, remembered, voiced, lived, contested, and struggled over. (p. 11)

The point here is that places are emotional. Some people yearn to return to their childhood homes. The emotional attachment we have to places is what ecopsychology is all about. But too it is about the way in which certain places can make us ill. The soul suffers in places too. Ralph Metzner (1995) states, "Several different diagnostic metaphors have been proposed to explain the ecologically split—the pathological alienation—between human consciousness and the rest of the biosphere" (p. 55). But Metzner suggests that most psychologists do not take into account ecological issues when dealing with patients. Mostly, when you go to a psychologist, you will be asked to talk about what is going on in your head—as if the head is detached from the larger ecosphere. What is going on in your head is in relation to where you live and how you live. If you feel a sort of "pathological alienation" (Metzner, p. 55) from where you live, you need to figure out how to understand this alienation or to move from the place that makes you feel alienated. But again, the ability to move away is a class issue. You need money to move and the poor do not have this choice. So if you work in a meat-packing factory and hate your job and if you live in dire poverty, of course you will struggle with this sense of alienation. But what choices do you have if you are poor? Not many.

David M. Callejo Perez, Stephen M. Fain, and Judith J. Slater (2004) tell us, "The erosion of public spaces leads to alienation.…Using the concepts of poststructural geography…[we can examine] public spaces as psychological" (pp. 2–3). Judith J. Slater (2004) explains,

The stage, the public space, is a hegemony of class, a dictatorship held over the community, the culture, and the particular audience. It exercises power over knowledge and practices ingrained in the production of the public space, and it limits the ability of the audience to know it for what it is. (p. 42)

Slater's point is that the public space is a political space. Those in power control who can and cannot speak in the public arena. The public space is highly controlled and manipulated. When people do not have a voice in the public space and feel that they are demonized, psychological fallout is inevitable. And thus the psychological is also tied to the political. Not many neo-Marxists deal with the emotional side of living in a society that is highly classed or highly controlled. Sadistic governments produce unhappy people. But unhappy people can only take so much. This is why revolutions occur. Revolutions are highly charged emotional events. People do not revolt because they are happy. Being unhappy is an emotion and the place in which you live has much to do with your happiness or unhappiness.

Ecopsychology: The Political and the Spiritual

A critique of depth psychologists is that they are hardly political. Contrarily, most political scholars do not deal with emotions or psyche. Scholars need to read across these boundaries to get a broader picture of their world. The ecosphere is many things, it is psychological and it is political, it is a social construct, it can be spiritual, or it can be a nightmare. Many Jungians are also spiritual psychologists and so the Jungians who engage in ecopsychology are also interested in the spiritual. This interest in the spiritual comes directly from the writings of Carl Jung. Jung differed from Freud on many issues, but the spiritual aspect of depth psychology is what I call the great divide between Jungians (or today what scholars might call post-Jungians) and Freudians (or today what scholars would call post-Freudians). So ecopsychology—which is mostly a post-Jungian development—is also highly spiritual. Jung (2005) says, "Nature is not matter only, she is also spirit. Spirit seems to be the inside of things…the soul of objects" (p. 78). That objects have souls must seem completely alien to our more political scholars. That nature is spiritual might seem to political scholars a mere romanticization of a troubling issue. Nature's spirit has been wounded by toxins, pesticides, and so forth. To our more scientific colleagues, nature does not have a spirit at all. Nature just is. To give nature a spirit seems a move of anthropomorphizing her. But how else can we see the world, if not through our eyes? We cannot step out of our humanness and see the world in an objective fashion. There is no such thing as seeing the world from the outside or seeing the world as if it were—as Kant might say—a thing in itself.

Theodore Roszak (1995) suggests that ecopsychologists can work side by side with environmental activists. He suggests,

> Exploring the psychological dimensions of our planetary ecology also gives environmentalists a compassionate new role to play other than that of "grieving greenies" out to scare and shame the public. It makes them allies of the Earth in a noble and affirmative project: that of returning the troubled human soul to the harmony and joy that are the only solid basis for an environmentally sustainable standard of living. It makes them healers rather than hecklers. (p. 15)

Unlike Roszak, I think that we have plenty to be scared about. The alarm has been sounded now for at least thirty years—human beings are on the verge of extinction if we keep doing what we are doing now. Overpopulation is one of the biggest problems at hand. Rachel Carson (1990) sounded the alarm in the 1960s as readers remember from our discussion at the outset of this chapter. We might not use DDT—at least in America—but there are other pesticides that are probably just as dangerous. Nuclear proliferation, biological warfare, and taking down planes and buildings with box cutters are all scary things to think about. There is plenty to be scared about. And we should be scared. Without a sense of urgency what drives us to change? Healing the earth comes from this sense of urgency, not from a sense "harmony and joy" (Roszak, p. 15). Human beings never lived in harmony with the earth. And to think that they did, is simply to romanticize our place in the world. Human beings are the most destructive, vicious creatures on the planet. Thomas Berry (1995) states,

> While there are pathologies that wipe out whole populations of life forms and must be considered pernicious to the life process on an extensive scale, the human species has, for some thousands of years, shown itself to be a pernicious presence in the world of the living on a unique and universal scale. (p. 11)

The mess we are in is mostly our own fault. But I am not advocating a position of nihilism here. People can turn things around. But we all need to work together. Ecology, then, must be approached in a multidisciplinary fashion. Part of what I have tried to show in this chapter is just how multidisciplinary the study of ecology is already. If curriculum studies is about lived experience, what could be more important than studying our ecosphere, our world, our planet, the very earth upon which we live and work?

· 6 ·

CULTURAL STUDIES
CURRICULUM CONCEPTS

Introduction

In this chapter I discuss some of the major themes that have emerged from recent literature in the interstices of cultural studies and curriculum theory. This
chapter will focus mostly on youth cultures and the popular. Popular culture in
the context of youth is what most curriculum studies scholars focus on in this
area, although some see cultural studies more broadly as the study of cultures
generally. Some argue that limiting the focus to what is popular is too narrow.
For instance, Shirley Steinberg and Joe Kincheloe (1997) argue,

> Cultural studies has something to do with the effort to produce an interdisciplinary
> (or counterdisciplinary) way of studying...cultural practices in historical, social, and
> theoretical contexts. Refusing to equate "culture" with high culture, cultural studies
> attempts to examine the diversity of a society's artistic, institutional, and communi-
> cative expressions often ignored by the traditional social sciences, cultural studies is
> often equated with the study of popular culture. Such an equation is misleading....
> Indeed, the interests of cultural studies are much broader and include in particular
> the "rules" of academic study itself...what can and cannot be said, who speaks. (p. 5)

Part of the reason cultural studies also concerns the "rules" of who can say
what in academe is because still today in many universities writing about what

is popular is unacceptable and not thought to be scholarship. Who defines what scholarship is, is a political question. Cultural studies is suspect. For an untenured professor to write about the popular is risky. Some more conservative faculty might not think the writing scholarly enough or scholarly at all. But scholars have been writing about the popular for decades. Here I am thinking of the stunning and most difficult work of Walter Benjamin (1999). His book *The Arcades Project* is a study of the popular in European culture during the early 20th century. Students who are interested in the study of the popular should begin with *The Arcades Project*.

Benjamin had trouble with the academy as his work was not acceptable and he never landed an academic position. He was also Jewish in an anti-Semitic culture. Jewish faculty members were not welcomed in Germanic institutions. Benjamin lived on the run as he was trying to flee the Nazis but still he worked, and he wrote. He eventually committed suicide because he felt that he could not escape the Nazis.

Much of what scholars talk about today in cultural studies can be found in Benjamin's work. Although educationists might mention their indebtedness to him, they do not do much with him. I will be talking about *The Arcades Project* throughout this chapter to serve as a historical backdrop as to what it is scholars are writing about today. Most scholars associate cultural studies with the British tradition and the Birmingham school, but, as John Weaver (2009) points out, cultural studies is found in many traditions, which I will discuss later on in this chapter. One of the best overviews of cultural studies is Weaver's book *Popular Culture Primer*. I would recommend that students carefully study this book to understand the larger picture of what Weaver calls the different traditions (p. 27) of cultural studies.

Cultural studies is not considered a field in and of itself. Scholars in different fields do work in cultural studies. What makes the intersection of curriculum theory and cultural studies unique are the sorts of questions curriculum studies scholars raise. Curriculum scholars—unlike, say, English professors—are interested in questions about education, knowledge, youth, and where youth learn. One of the major points made by many curriculum studies scholars is that youth learn outside of the traditional boundaries of the school. Young people learn elsewhere. This "elsewhere" is a fascinating place. Education happens elsewhere. That is one of the major points of studying the popular because youth learn much from the popular and spend most of their lives steeped in popular culture—especially when they leave the schoolhouse doors.

Outline of the Chapter

In this chapter I will discuss the following issues in several related sections. I discuss what curriculum studies scholars write about in the context of youth cultures. Identity is a key theme here. Drawing on Shirley Steinberg and Joe Kincheloe, I use the concept "expression" (p. 5) in the context of youth cultures. That is, I explore various ways in which youth cultures express themselves via the realm of the popular. Youth cultures are raced, classed, and engendered. They are also political. I discuss these issues in the context of how youth cultures express themselves through music, graffiti, sports, and more.

I then move into a section that explores the concept of the "popular." What is popular? What are kids drawn to in popular culture? Popular culture is not an abstract concept but is grounded in the everyday lives of youth. Toward the end of the chapter I explore a variety of theoretical approaches that could be used to deconstruct the popular. Theoretical approaches have exploded over the last ten years or so and I want to take a look at what curriculum studies scholars are saying about these approaches. One of the problems in the area of popular culture is that scholars—outside of curriculum studies—tend to undertheorize the concept of the popular. If scholars are going to explore cartoons, for example, they need to understand what cartoons mean politically, historically, sociologically, psychologically, and so forth.

Youth Cultures and Identity

The notion of identity can become easily reified. However, identity should not be reified. There are as many kinds of identities as there are persons in the world. Similarly, there are many youth cultures. The idea of youth culture should not be reified either. What I would like to do here is to explore some of the main themes that curriculum studies scholars write about in the context of youth and identity. One of the major themes in the literature on youth is alienation. This is not by any means a new idea. Alienated youth has been a topic of conversation worldwide for generations. The question is, why are youth alienated? What do they feel alienated from? Why is it so hard, for example, to be a teenager? What is it about those teenage years that makes life so distasteful? Teenagehood, if you will, is rather unstable because kids are dependent upon parents—whom they might not even like—and kids have to go to school, which might seem like torture for them especially because of standardized testing. Henry Giroux

(2003) has written an excellent book on alienated youth titled *The Abandoned Generation: Democracy Beyond the Culture of Fear*. Giroux states,

> Youth are now demonized in the popular media and derided by politicians looking for quick-fix [i.e., Race to the Top] solutions to crime. In a society deeply troubled by their presence, youth prompts in the public imagination a rhetoric of fear, control and surveillance—made all the more visible with the Supreme Court upholding the widespread use of random drug testing of public school students. (p. xvii)

Since Columbine, Giroux suggests, students are treated as if they are criminals. This is the mindset of many school administrators and politicians. Since Columbine there have been many more school shootings and now shootings are also happening on college campuses. Public schools in this country—in order to protect their students and teachers—have turned into prisons. This, too, is Giroux's point. But this was also Foucault's (1979) point in *Discipline and Punish: The Birth of the Prison*. Schools have always been holding cells, ways of keeping kids off the streets. Most public schools have always been punitive in nature; things have gotten worse since Columbine. Giroux tells us,

> Schools increasingly resemble prisons, and students begin to look more like criminal suspects who need to be searched, tested, and observed under the watchful eye of administrators who appear to be less concerned with educating them than with policing their every move. (p. xvii)

When children are treated like criminals they internalize this psychologically. This only creates problems. If kids are treated like criminals and think that adults distrust them, how are they supposed to feel? Alienated.

The constant testing in the public schools does not make kids smarter or more prepared for college. Constant testing is a form of emotional torture. Constant testing is a way to punish kids. What continual testing does is make kids miserable, scared and it makes them hate reading. Alan Block (1997) says, "I think it is necessary that we acknowledge the source of dread in the child" (p. 1). That dread is school. Children associate reading with dread and with being tested, which only makes for more dread. Thus, learning is dreadful because it is associated with punishment and torment. Giroux suggests that we have abandoned youth by treating them like criminals. Like Giroux, John Weaver (2004), Julie Webber (2003), and Alan Block worry about the violence done to children through schooling. Scholars can learn much from the title of Block's book, *I'm Only Bleeding: Education as the Practice of Violence Against Children*. Block says, "I would like to discuss the violence that is practiced upon the child psychologically by the educational system" (p. 3). Schooling is a form of abuse. Giroux, recall, suggests that we have abandoned children by treating them like criminals. Abandonment is a form of abuse through neglect. Joe Kincheloe (1997) makes a similar point in discussing the 1990 film *Home Alone*. Here he suggests that this film "commodif[ies] childhood abandonment" (p. 34). Kincheloe notes,

> By the early 1990s social neglect of children had become so commonplace that it could be presented as a comedic motif without raising too many eyebrows. There was a time when childhood was accorded protected status—but that is growing obsolete, as safety nets disintegrate and child-supports crumble. (p. 34)

Social services for children might be crumbling but there has never been a time when children have been "accorded protected status." Children have been neglected and abused for decades. Today, however, it harder for parents to abuse their children because we live in a more public society. Surveillance cameras line city streets.

Child abuse comes in many forms. Outsourcing is also a form of abuse, especially when children are involved. Joe Kincheloe (2002) tells us,

> In another facet of the McDonald's-Disney alliance, the two bastions of corporate morality have recently opened a factory in Vietnam where 17-year-old girls work 10 hours a day for six cents an hour producing Disney character toys to be given away with McDonald's Happy Meals. While earning their $4.20 per 70-hour work week in February 1997, 200 young women at the plant fell ill, 25 collapsed, and three were taken to the hospital because of exposure to toxic chemicals. (p. 67)

Child slave labor is rampant around the globe. What shocks here is that both McDonald's and Disney pretend to love children when, in fact, they do not, as Kincheloe (2002) points out in the above citation. Children who eat a lot of fast food tend to become obese, sometimes even morbidly obese, develop heart problems, and sometimes even die young.

Shirley Steinberg and Joe Kincheloe (1997) point out,

> Cultural studies connected to democratic pedagogy for children involves investigations of how children's consciousnesses are produced around issues of social justice and egalitarian power relations. Thus, our analyses focus on exposing the footprints of power left by the corporate producers of kinderculture and the effects on the psyches of our children. (p. 7)

In ecology, scholars talk about being careful not to leave carbon footprints on the earth. The lighter we travel, the less we disturb the ecosphere. Here,

Steinberg and Kincheloe interestingly use the phrase "footprints of power" to describe corporate culture's negative impact on children. Stepping on people (i.e., footprints of power) means squashing them psychically. When we say that someone is a pushover we mean that he or she is easily stepped on or manipulated. Children are still at formative stages in their lives and can be permanently psychically damaged by these "footprints" of corporate power. Psychological problems are intertwined with issues of power. Sadistic behavior toward children—which is what corporate "footprints" are—can maim. The earlier the damage is done, the harder it is to undo. One of the areas in curriculum studies that needs more work is child abuse. Most of the literature on psychoanalysis in curriculum studies (which I will discuss in a later chapter) deals with defense mechanisms and issues of transference. Not many scholars in curriculum studies deal with the ways in which children become mentally ill because of child abuse.

Youth Cultures Emerge

Children respond to abuse in many ways. Youth cultures emerge for one reason or another but sometimes they emerge as a response to being treated badly. Youth talk back. Children are not merely victims—they respond, they are fighters, and they have ways to cope with a society that does not seem to have much use for them. Youth cultures often are cultures that resist these "footprints of power" that Steinberg and Kincheloe (p. 7) write about. Subcultures emerge for a reason and usually that reason concerns stress and tension. Subcultures are a creative way of coping with discrimination, alienation, abuse, being treated badly. Joe Kincheloe (1997) comments that in America there is a great amount of "hostility toward children" (p. 37). The question then becomes what do these children do psychically with that hostility? Some become numb. Numbness or depersonalization is a way to protect the psyche but it also can get in the way of experiencing life—especially emotionally. Maureen Mercury (2000) writes about numbness and what people do to overcome it. A creative way to overcome numbness is to engage in body modification. Mercury states, "Tattooing, piercing, implanting, and branding are means of jump-starting sensate functioning that has lost its capacity for feeling" (p. 22). Of course, people get tattoos for many reasons. Tattoos mark turning points. Sometimes people get tattoos to mark the death of a loved one; sometimes people get tattoos because they simply like the idea of adorning their skin with artwork. Sometimes, as Mercury points out, people feel numb so they get tattoos to overcome this numbness. Numbness protects their psyches from shattering in a world where they feel that they are not wanted. Tattoos are also a way of altering identity by saying, "This is who I am."

Some kids respond to the ongoing hostility—as Kincheloe puts it—by being full of rage. The question is, what do they do with that rage? Rage must be expressed. It can be expressed through music and other art forms. If rage is repressed, trouble is ahead. Peter and Jonathan McLaren (2004) comment on this in the context of Curry Malott and Milagros Pena's book titled *Punk Rockers' Revolution: A Pedagogy of Race, Class, and Gender*. Peter and Jonathan McLaren remark, "Combining hard data with critical sociology and personal narratives, *Punk Rocker's Revolution*…speaks to the raw emotions, the rage, and the street-spawned and knife-edged cultural insights of the punk phenomenon" (p. 123). Punk music is full of rage. It is a way of expressing what is happening to youth. Punk is not new, it has been around for a long time but there seems to be a comeback of punk in a newer version called skaterpunk, which is what Curry Malott and Milagros Pena write about in their book. Music is a creative outlet and it allows young people to express their rage. I will talk more about skaterpunk music later on, but for now it is enough to say that young people resist the ongoing hostility (Kincheloe, 1997) toward them by talking back, by singing back, or shouting back. Some punk music is about shouting. Shouting is a form of rage. Some conservative critics of punk—and other forms of loud and edgy music—say that it is the music that makes people kill. Clearly, this is not true. Most people who listen to punk do not kill people. One can express a negative emotion without literally acting it out. The point is that people need to express anger and rage so that they do not literally act it out. Without being able to express rage, people who have emotional problems are more likely to kill because they have no way to vent their anger. Anger must be expressed. If anger is repressed, problems arise. Adults must allow young people to express themselves. Julie Webber (2003) states, "Furthermore, by taking away from youth any means of expression that the public has deemed inappropriate…the adult world has also taken away this generation's facilitating environment" (p. 145). Webber draws on D. W. Winnicott's (2010) notion of a holding environment (or what she calls in the above quote a "facilitating environment") to show that if school—metaphorically—would be more like a mother holding a child in a loving fashion, perhaps we would not have violent responses (school shootings) to the violent environment of schooling itself. Webber argues, in part, that the reason kids are killing kids in school is that schools are violent places and kids are outraged at the way they are treated. Schools do not allow kids to express themselves, so they repress their rage. Repression eventually fails. Adults have created the very problem that they are trying to fix by making schools more and more like prisons. Webber's contention is that if you are treated like a criminal, you will act like one. If you are in a violent situation, you will act violently in response to being treated badly. Rage is a natural response to being treated violently. So school shootings, she suggests, should come as no surprise. John Weaver (2004) makes a similar point as he states,

> Violence is not a teen phenomenon or something provoked or nurtured by video games, movies, or music. It is spawned by adults' desires to avoid reality. Instead of trying to understand young people, we adopt zero-tolerance policies, require IDs, ship in metal detectors, and institute dress codes. All of these "actions" are just more examples of adults' lack of desire to interact with young people. (p. 29)

What does zero tolerance (as Weaver mentions in the above citation) really mean? How to deconstruct this phrase? What does the word "zero" mean? When we talk about ground zero today most Americans know that that is the site of the destruction of the World Trade Towers on 9/11. We talk about zero calories in soft drinks (which is probably is a lie). We are told to count down from ten to zero if we are having a panic attack. In a baseball game a score of zero can go on for an infinite amount of innings. But zero in the context of "zero tolerance" means none of the above. This phrase means no second chances. If a student wears baggy pants to school there is zero tolerance for that. Zero tolerance means being expelled from school. It gets worse. Henry Giroux (2010) reports there are

> zero tolerance policies in schools, which mindlessly punish poor white and students of color by criminalizing behavior as trivial as violating a dress code. Students have been assaulted by police, handcuffed…and in some cases imprisoned. (http://www.truth-out.org)

Giroux calls to our attention the hidden agenda of zero tolerance. This policy is aimed at punishing minorities and poor students. Zero tolerance is part of the Republican agenda. It is clear that Republicans do little to help the poor and minorities. Katrina is a good example of the way in which people of color and the poor were left on their own, and many died because the government did not help them.

The zero tolerance policy is like the three strikes law. If you commit three offenses you go to jail. Three strikes and you are out—just like in baseball. So punishment has become a game. Yet, corporate criminals who were responsible for the subprime mortgage scandal that caused many people to go into foreclosure were forgiven. Not many of these bankers were prosecuted. In fact, the government "bailed out" the very banking institutions that caused people to lose their homes.

Do we bail out kids? No. Kids know full well about these zero tolerance policies and know that they live in a police state. Living in a police state exacerbates their anger, as Julie Webber (2003) points out. But there are other ways to express anger.

Expressions of Youth Cultures

I began this chapter with a citation by Shirley Steinberg and Joe Kincheloe (1997) about cultural studies and what cultural studies means. Recall, one of the things they suggest is that cultural studies examines cultural forms or cultural "expressions [i.e., punk rock, graffiti, extreme sports] often ignored" (p. 7) by academics. Curriculum theorists have long been interested in what is left out of the canon and so cultural studies is a natural fit for curriculum theorists. Whatever is popular (especially when it comes to kids) is not only ignored by more conservative academics but also discounted. Some think that what is popular is not worth studying. What merit does the popular have for serious scholars? Serious scholars study serious things. But popular culture is serious business because for kids especially, this is where they live, this is where they learn, and this is where they spend most of their time. Kids can't wait to get out of school so they can listen to music, play video games, watch TV, go on the Internet, chat in cyberspace, or send text messages. All of this needs to be studied by scholars and taken seriously. If adults are to ever understand kids, we have to understand their worlds. Avoiding the study of the popular, suggesting that it has little scholarly worth, is yet another way of saying to kids, we don't care about you, we don't want to know about you, what you do is insignificant. Teachers have to have some understanding of the cultures students bring to the classroom. If teachers have little understanding of youth cultures, they cannot connect to their students. Why would students want to learn if they know that their teachers don't care about who they are and what worlds they inhabit? Therefore, the study of youth cultures is imperative to understanding who we are teaching. And isn't this, at bottom, what curriculum theory is about? Now, many conservative colleagues would argue that Facebook is a complete waste of time, that YouTube is irrelevant, that texting is not in the least educative. However, luddites cannot go back to a time before cyberspace, it is here to stay. There is educative value to be found in cyberspace but of course there is junk out there too. The same goes for books. Readers have to learn how to find good books and weed out bad books. This takes time. Not all scholarly books are good books. There is junk in scholarship just like there is junk in cyberspace. So, the study of popular culture today must entail the study of what is going on in cyberspace. Toby Daspit and John Weaver (2005) tell us,

> [Sadie] Plant is one of the first cultural studies scholars to venture into the worlds of cyberspace and information technology. Her work not only attempts to see how information technology reconfigures such issues of feminism, gender, history, psycho-analysis, and politics, but also academic writing. In *Zeros + Ones: Digital Women + The New Techno-culture*, Plant demonstrates how information technology is transforming the way we write and think about cultural studies. (p. 95)

Some undergraduate students text while professors lecture, others are on Facebook when having class discussions. Some of these students are clearly sending a message that lectures are boring and that they would rather be in cyberspace. So these students are missing out on their education because they would rather be elsewhere.

Scientists do not yet know what working on the computer or living in cyberspace does to our brains. Maybe computers can give us cancer? Or maybe our intellects are actually dulled by staying online too long and not doing our own thinking and creating. William Pinar (2012) is highly critical of technology and argues that computers do not help us become better scholars. Some argue that kids spend too much time online and not enough time reading books. Cyberspace is interfering with their capacity to read anything that takes time.

Noel Gough (2008) talks about developing ecoliteracy and similarly people also need to develop cyberliteracy as well. Scholars have to be able to teach students how to critique what they see online and how to spend good time online and not just look at junk. Cyberspace can be a dangerous place too where kids can learn how to build bombs, join cults, or become terrorists. Cyberbullying is another problem. Cyberbullying has led some kids to commit suicide. Teachers have to work to develop cyberethics and maybe even develop courses to deal with cyberethics. Kids can creatively express themselves in cyberspace through blogs, Facebook, Myspace, Twitter, and so forth. These can be exciting ways for kids to be creative and thoughtful. But these spaces have to be thought through carefully and should not be used to hurt other people.

Skateboarders and Punk

Earlier I mentioned the work of Curry Malott and Milagros Pena (2004) who have written a book on what is called "skaterpunk." Skaterpunks skateboard and listen to punk rock, hence, the term "skaterpunk." Malott calls himself a "skaterpunkhippiehiphopper" (p. 61). Malott wants to argue that there are many different kinds of punk rockers, and he admits, "Much of punk rock assists in the reproduction of patriarchal as well as homophobic ideologies" (p. 27). On the other hand, there are other kinds of punk. Malott and Pena tell us,

> Punk rock was not exclusive to straight white men. People of African descent, Latina/os, white women, lesbian women of various ethnic racial groups, and gay men have all appealed to the punk rock aesthetic....A queer punk scene in the United States... became a phenomenon in the 1980s. (p. 24)

These kinds of punk form a "grass roots resistance" (Malott & Pena, p. 26) to consumer capitalist society. Skateboarding could be considered a counterculture and it is a huge industry and can be quite interesting to watch. The really good skateboarders almost defy gravity, as they seem to fly in midair and do all sorts of stunts. Skateboards have been around for a long time and today skateboarding is a sport that has gotten quite complex.

There are left-wing skaterpunks. Malott and Pena report, "Skaterpunk-hippies would not even ride in a car, much less own one, because by supporting the automobile industry they were supporting capitalist hegemony and dominant society, and more importantly, contributing to the destruction of the earth" (p. 30). So one might call these punks "ecopunks." These skaterpunk-hippies remind me of "squatters." These are young people who find abandoned buildings to live in; they usually do not work because they see no point in having a minimum wage job. Squatters see no point in joining the rat race, so they drop out.

Natalie Porter (2007) tells us that women skateboarders are alive and well even though the skateboard community historically has been misogynist to the point where "several professional male skateboarders...made statements that females should not skate at all" (p. 124). Because women skateboarders are marginalized within the skateboarding community, Porter reports,

> For a female skateboarder to feel confident in her identity it is often necessary that she find like-minded women to share stories and encourage each other, and it was in the mid-to-late 1990s that women came together with more focus than previous attempts. An important development was the New York City–based, *Rookie* skateboards, the first female-owned skateboard-company which gathered a strong team of primarily female skateboarders in 1996. (p. 127)

Skaterpunk culture is one that many academics know little about, unless they skateboard or are punk fans or have kids who are into this sport. The reason I wanted to talk about skaterpunks here is because it is an overlooked and underexplored topic in academe. Malott and Pena's book is one of the few written on skaterpunks in the field of education. Malott is a professor of early childhood education. There are not many early childhood educators who do this kind of work. This is the kind of overlooked form of youth expression— via sports and music—to which curriculum studies scholars should pay attention. It is interesting that Natalie Porter tells us, "Just like male skateboarders, female skateboarders often celebrate and document their injuries as proof of their active participation, as well as a rejection of feminine standards that expect women to appear flawless and perfect" (p. 126). What is striking in this citation is the documentation and boasting about injuries suffered from skateboarding falls. This somehow proves that both male and female skateboarders are committed to their sport. Injuries are badges of honor in the skateboard culture.

Motorcycles

Motorcycle culture in America is not monolithic. There are many subcultures of motorcyclists. One—at least in America—is the Harley-Davidson subculture. Harley-Davidsons are usually associated with gang membership. However, all kinds of people ride Harleys today. The lure of the Harley is that it is a big and loud motorcycle.

People who ride what are called "crotch rockets" differ from the Harley crowd. Those who ride crotch rockets model themselves after professional motorcycle racers. These riders are into speed and are mostly young males. A young male and a crotch rocket is a dangerous combination. I would venture to guess that more young males get killed on crotch rockets than any other kind of motorcycle because they ride too fast and take too many risks. The third motorcycle subculture is the cruise culture. These are people who ride Suzuki, Kawasaki, or

Honda cruisers. Speed is not the issue for these riders. Cruising means taking in nature. These are the more gentle riders, the sort of ecoriders who ride to get out in nature to feel the wind. These cruisers are not terribly expensive and are not terribly loud. Harley Davidsons, on the other hand, are terribly expensive and loud. A fourth subculture would be what is called "café racers." These are riders who are nostalgic and ride motorcycles that are retro in look but technologically modern, such as Triumph Bonnevilles. Triumphs are British motorcycles made famous by the likes of Steve McQueen and Marlon Brando.

Motorcycling still remains a male-dominated sport. But women ride too, although in ads for motorcycles mostly males are featured. Motorcyclists are often thought of as thugs and bad people because of the Harley legacy. This, however, is not the case. Youth are attracted to this sport because it is exciting, dangerous, and even glamorous. Riding motorcycles is a form of expression; it can even be considered an art form. Professional motorcycle racing is quite beautiful to watch.

BMXers

Related to the motorcycle subculture is the BMX culture that attracts mostly young white males. Kyle Kusz (2003) talks about what he calls "BMXers" (p. 154). He tells us,

> BMX riding, in the 1990s "extreme" form, features riders performing daredevil spins and flips off obstacles which can launch riders as high as fifteen to twenty feet in the air, as well as execute difficult technical maneuvers and tricks in flatland competitions and on street courses....BMXers often represent their participation in BMX... as a "lifestyle." (p. 154)

Kusz also goes on to state that BMXers are usually politically "reactionary" and want to express their "unapologetic white athletic masculinity" (p. 155). What Kusz does not address are the real dangers associated with this extreme sport. There are many accounts of riders falling on their heads and becoming completely paralyzed. In fact, sports medicine doctors invented a neck brace that is to be worn while riding that is supposed to cut the risk of terrible and paralyzing injuries.

This is a beautiful—and very dangerous—sport to watch; the riders are as graceful and elegant as ballet dancers, which is ironic because ballet is not usually associated with masculinity. But the BMXers are like ballet dancers. Their performances are elegant, graceful, and almost, ironically, effeminate!

The question here is why would youth get involved in such a dangerous sport like BMX? Are they bored? Is it a crisis of masculinity? Is it the need for speed and flight? Flying too close to the sun is dangerous. The need for danger? Why? Kids think that they are invulnerable.

Extreme Sports

Extreme sports—like BMXers—are extremely dangerous. Robert Rinehart and Synthia Sydnor (2003) tell us that extreme sports include things like "in-line skating, windsurfing, sky-dancing/surfing, BMX dirt-bike racing, mountain biking, Eco-challenge, whitewater kayaking, climbing, surfing, skateboarding, extreme skiing, and snowboarding" (p. 1). Not many curriculum studies scholars have explored extreme sports as an expression of youth culture. Most of the discussions on youth culture in curriculum studies focus on rap, hip-hop, and slam poetry. But extreme sports are related to all of these other forms of expression, musical, and otherwise. Rinehart and Sydnor explain,

> Many extreme sports explode the notion of the "canon" of mainstream sport in several ways. Grassroots extreme sports participants are not institutionalized with governing bodies....Alternative athletes in some X sports wear unique street apparel, uniforms by group consensus, not imposed from outside. There are no coaches. Sometimes the apparel references urban streetwear, hip-hop, "gangsta rap" or grunge fashion. Drug-taking, alternative music…[versus] mainstream American sports [which represent]…patriotic, clean-cut…character building. (p. 6)

Extreme sports might be of interest to curriculum theorists because, as Rinehart and Sydnor point out, they "explode the notion of the 'canon' of mainstream sport" (p. 6). Curriculum theorists are interested in what lies outside of traditional canons. The sports canon—as the authors above tell us—is rather conservative. All the mainstream sports in the United States, like football, baseball, hockey, and basketball, are male terrain. Tennis and golf welcome women.

Extreme sports, unlike mainstream sports, offer kids new and different opportunities. But for women and people of color trouble abounds. Most extreme sports are the terrain of white males.

Graffiti Artists

Graffiti artists are more ethnically diverse than extreme sports participants. Again, in curriculum studies, not many people write about graffiti. Graffiti is mostly a male domain. Nancy Macdonald (2001) tells us,

> Linking the illegal and dangerous aspects of graffiti with the predominance of men and the "warrior" style meanings they attach to their activities, I examine this subculture as a site of masculine construction…male [graffiti] writers exclude female writers and, with this, their emasculating threat. (p. 8)

The danger of graffiti writing is that it is illegal and sometimes associated with gang membership.

Graffiti writing is not new. Steve Grody (2007) explains,

> Looking at the anthropological record, we find that long-buried ruins uncovered in desert regions include slanderous political writing on walls. Later, in the 1930s, photographer Helen Levitt documented children's sidewalk chalk graffiti. Graffiti on freight trains and train tracks ("hobo graffiti") has been documented as early as 1914.…And contrary to popular belief, graffiti was not born out of hip-hop culture, though the movement's influence is undeniable. (p. 11)

A major difference between extreme sports and graffiti writing is that graffiti writers come from many different ethnic backgrounds. And graffiti artists are highly political as their "tags" are mostly political statements. Here again, Steve Grody explains, "Today, Los Angeles street artists from all walks of life draw from a unique confluence of cultures—including Latino, pan-Asian, African-American, Jewish, and Christian" (p. 9). It is interesting that graffiti writers call themselves "artists" just like tattoo "artists." Many are offended by graffiti and see it as defacing property. But graffiti is a way for youth, especially, to express their rage.

Tattoo Artists

Tattoo artists work in studios (like art studios) and the term "parlor" (or "tattoo parlor") is no longer acceptable. The world of tattoos today is much like the world of graffiti writing because both are considered art forms. Still, the public perception is mostly negative. People see graffiti as defacement and people see tattoos as less than acceptable, almost an abomination, a defilement, if you will, of the body. But the subculture of tattoo artists is quite interesting as most are self-trained and extremely talented. Tattoos are very popular today; both women and men have them, some cover entire body parts with tattoos. I (2008) have written about tattoo culture in *Teaching Through the Ill Body*. I have what are called half sleeves. My tattoos took over a year, so I spent a year with tattoo artists learning about their subculture. Most of the artists were young white males. One artist in particular interested me because he was a high school dropout and was a very talented young tattoo artist. He considered himself to be a Jungian. He felt that his talents came from else-where—like the collective unconscious—and he was merely the channel for the art. At the tattoo studio where I had my half sleeves done there was a code of ethics among the artists. They would not tattoo racist, gang-related, or neo-Nazi art. Any person who arrived drunk would not be tattooed. Getting tattoos is a serious business because once you are tattooed the only way to remove the tattoo is through laser treatments. And laser treatments are very expensive. There are female tattoo artists, too, but again the males outnumber the females.

Women's Roller Derby

In Savannah, Georgia, women engage in a sport called roller derby. The particular team I will discuss is called the Savannah Derby Devils (http://www.savannahderby.com/). The Derby Devils website tells us that there is "an international re-emergence of roller derby." One learns from the homepage of the Derby Devils that "no one is paid" and the women are expected to "pitch in" for advertising and so forth. I have seen very little scholarly literature on women's roller derby; no one in curriculum studies has done work on this. Women's sports are undertheorized and underrepresented in the scholarly literature. One of the reasons that not much play, if you will, is given to women's roller derby is because the sport threatens the meaning of the feminine. This sport is hard edged and masculine. Masculine women are simply not acceptable in American culture. This is a masculine sport for women. The masculine woman threatens because queering sports in this way is not acceptable. It seems to be acceptable for women to play tennis or golf (which are considered upper-class sports), but it seems unacceptable for women to play roller derby (which is considered a lower-class sport).

Barbie does not do roller derby because it is an unacceptable sport for women in America. Barbie is, according to Shirley Steinberg (1997), "a true

American. She stands for the family values that our country holds dear. She is strictly heterosexual" (p. 211). Is there a queer Barbie? And if so, would she be a roller derby Barbie?

The Derby Devils are "devilish" because they represent a nonfamily values sport. They queer the notion of what it means to be a woman in sports. Derby Devils are certainly not "strictly heterosexual" as is Barbie. Whatever they are, they challenge the heteronormative imperative. The Derby Devils are a relatively unknown subculture. Not too many people know about them probably because they do not get much publicity. Contrarily, there is much advertisement for the local baseball team, the Sand Gnats. Baseball is a male sport; it is all about family values. Baseball is mainstream. Baseball means heteronormativity and patriotism. Derby Devils challenge all of that.

Rap and Hip-Hop

Like Derby Devils, rap and hip-hop artists challenge family values. These artists talk back to a society that is racist. Toby Daspit and John Weaver (2005) remark,

> The problem is that while Public Enemy and other rap groups are responding to the crises of our postmodern society with their hybrid mix'n, unsolicited sampl'n, and radical mess(age), academics can respond to these crises only with modernist retorts limited by the artificial disciplines and stifling methodologies they have created. (p. 90)

Rap and hip-hop are art forms that comment on racial injustice. Academics, as Daspit and Weaver point out, have trouble theorizing around rap and hip-hop artists. This trouble comes not only from "stifling methodologies" but also from not understanding these artists. Youth cultures are drawn to rap and hip-hop because these are counterculture art forms. These artists speak truth to power and are a threat to mainstream culture.

What Is the Popular?

Who defines what is popular is a political question. If scholars become too "popular" in academe, conservative colleagues no longer take them seriously. If a scholar becomes a public intellectual and appears on TV she might get criticized for being too public—which means too popular.

In academe, the popular is not thought to be a serious subject of study by conservative academics. But as I have been trying to show in this chapter, the popular is a very important area to study, especially if we are teachers and we are trying to understand who we are teaching. Most kids live in the world of the popular and can't wait to get out of school to go skateboarding, play the electric guitar, or go to a roller derby game. The study of the popular has been critiqued since Plato, and certainly Western philosophy has little to say about the popular with few exceptions.

The Popular and Walter Benjamin

One philosopher and social critic who has much to say about the popular is Walter Benjamin (1999). Again, I encourage students to study carefully his *Arcades Project*. Here one finds many interesting topics of discussion that most scholars in education ignore. Benjamin was one of the earliest scholars who wrote about the popular and took the popular seriously. Others came after him, but of the cultural studies scholars that are mentioned in the literature, he is one of the best and one of the least written about in the field of curriculum studies. Scholars might mention his name in passing but rarely delve into his texts. Here I want to talk briefly about Benjamin. Perhaps one of Benjamin's most well-known concepts is that of the "flaneur" (stroller) (p. 417). He states, "Paris [is] the promised land of the flaneur—the 'landscape built of sheer life,' as Hofmansthal once put it" (p. 417). Paris is an extraordinary city. It is here that the flaneur gets lost in the streets and takes in the smells, sounds, and life of the streets. The street walker is the flaneur. This is the person who can make something of the architecture, signage, storefronts. This is the intellectual who thinks on his or her feet, since everything takes on meaning. Life is lived on the streets; one can learn on the streets. This is Benjamin's point.

Gaslights

Benjamin (1999) poetically remarks,

> The street conducts the flaneur into a vanished time. For him, every street is precipitous. It leads downward—if not to the mythical mothers, then into a past that can be all the more spellbinding because it is not his own, not private. Nevertheless, it always remains the time of a childhood. But why that of the life he has lived? In the asphalt over which he passes, his steps awaken a surprising resonance. The gaslight that streams down on the paving stones throws an equivocal light on this double ground. (p. 416)

There is a certain romantic quality about "the gaslight that streams down" onto the streets. There are few streets in America that still have gaslights. In New Orleans—before Hurricane Katrina—there was a certain place called River Bend that was lined with gaslights. There was something very magical about that place. Gaslights have a certain aura about them.

The flaneur is akin to the street intellectual, which is similar to Gramsci's organic intellectual. But Benjamin is different from Gramsci. His writing is more in the style of bricolage. Gramsci's writing is more tightly woven and more politically oriented than Benjamin, although Benjamin was considered to be a Marxist.

Benjamin was the first important cultural studies scholar in Europe. Karen Anijar, John Weaver, and Toby Daspit (2004) comment that academics need "a people's research, and a profoundly rich public political pedagogy and pedagogical performance" (p. 15). Benjamin is a "people's" scholar and offers to us a "rich public" pedagogy. His *Arcades Project* is one of the richest cultural studies texts in the literature. The book has an overwhelming effect on the reader since Benjamin took in so much life. Everything took on life for Benjamin, including gaslights. This is what cultural studies is about—street life, the lore and lure of the street.

Department Stores

Actually, Benjamin's term "arcade" does not refer to games. Today people usually think of arcade rooms as game rooms. But in Paris in the late 19th and early 20th centuries arcades meant something totally different. Benjamin (1999) explains,

> Most of the Paris arcades come into being in the decade and a half after 1822. The first condition for the emergence is the boom in the textile trade. *Magasins de nouveautes*, the first establishment to keep large stocks of merchandise on the premises made their appearance. They are fore runners of department stores....The arcades are a center of commerce in luxury items. In fitting them out, art enters the service of the merchant. (p. 3)

Department stores are places of "rich public" "pedagogical performance," as Anijar, Weaver, and Daspit (p. 15) put it. The department store is a cultural studies object demanding study. Saks Fifth Avenue in New York City is a place where the very wealthy shop. Most Marxists would be appalled at the luxury items for sale there. But still, Saks would make for an interesting study of the upper class. Of course, there is much to critique about Saks. Old-fashioned department stores in the United States are disappearing, however. Kaufmann's and Gimbels in downtown Pittsburgh were two old-fashioned department stores that have closed. What a wonderful study these old places would have made for cultural studies scholars. Today we have shopping malls—another form of arcade and another place of public pedagogy worthy of much critique.

Strip malls have ruined the American landscape. Paris does not have strip malls. Strip malls dot the American landscape in almost every American city. The old-fashioned department stores—the kind Benjamin talks about—were quite different from strip malls or shopping malls. The strip mall and shopping mall in American culture serve to homogenize merchandise and to homogenize the American landscape. There is little beauty in a shopping mall or strip mall. These are often overlooked sites where scholars could learn much about today's youth culture.

Dolls

Another interesting topic that Benjamin (1999) writes about in *The Arcades Project* is that of dolls. Benjamin states,

> They are the true fairies of these arcades…the formerly world-famous Parisian dolls, which revolved on their musical socle and bore in their arms a doll-sized basket out of which, at the salutation of the minor chord, a lambkin poked its curious muzzle. (p. 693)

Dolls are not something that a philosopher or Marxist usually wrote about during Benjamin's lifetime. Dolls, though, tell us much about culture. The Parisian doll is quite different from, say, the Barbie Doll we find in America. Today, we have cultural studies scholars who, too, focus on dolls. One of the best treatments of dolls is by Shirley Steinberg. Steinberg writes about the politics of Barbie—which I briefly touched on earlier. Steinberg—in a Benjaminian fashion—remarks,

> I love the challenge of finding strange and wonderful factoids of trivia in little known academic nooks and crannies. However, this chapter has caused havoc in my life. Four years ago I became fascinated with the effect that Barbie had on little girls. I started to pick up Barbies, Barbie furniture, *Barbie* comics, *Barbie* books, Barbie jewelry, and Barbie toys wherever I went. I was able to even find the Benetton Barbie in Istanbul's airport. (p. 209)

The "little known academic nooks and crannies" about which Steinberg writes are places where the study of culture (popular culture especially) is of the utmost importance. Those overlooked everyday, mundane things can become richly woven tapestries of meaning. In the tradition of Benjamin, Steinberg studies dolls, albeit from a more postmodern perspective than Benjamin, as she looks at issues of race, class, and gender and the way these children's toys send political messages. There is much to critique about the Barbie industry. Dolls reflect culture and doll companies are political. Barbie is a political study. This is Steinberg's main interest.

Steinberg captures the gender, race, and class problems that Barbie raises. If girls identify with Barbie, what does this mean? Or if they dis-identify with Barbie, what does that mean? What kind of message does Barbie send? In the 1970s there was only one kind of Barbie, and she was blond and skinny. Today, things have changed. There is even a butch Barbie, as Steinberg tells us. Steinberg notes,

> There are more military Barbies than any other profession. As sergeants and majors, these booted Barbies march to the beat of a proud, patriotic America. Choosing a favorite would be hard; I guess mine is the Desert Storm Barbie. "Wearing authentic desert battle dress uniforms of camouflage material—Barbie is a medic, and she's ready for duty! Staff Sergeant Ken is ready too!" (p. 212)

Steinberg's work on Barbie is important because it points out the politics of Barbie, and how during Desert Storm doll companies jumped on the Barbie band wagon to make money from the war. The message military Barbie sends, as Steinberg points out, is one of patriotism and the glory of war. Even Barbie gets to be a soldier now. Women soldiers challenge the notion of the feminine. But even if Barbie has become a soldier, she can still be considered a woman who is, as Steinberg puts it, "strictly heterosexual" (p. 211). However, women who join the military threaten men because they step out of traditional gender roles.

Film

Another form of popular culture is film. Film is an entire area of study unto itself. Many scholars who do film studies are housed in English departments. But there are many curriculum theorists who also engage in film studies through a cultural studies lens. The difficulty of writing about film is that one is writing about what is visual and a visual text is hard to capture in words. Films slip by so quickly that they are hard to analyze. William Pinar (2009) has done much work on the filmmaker Pier Paolo Pasolini. Pinar calls him "A Most Excellent Pedagogist" (p. 99). Pinar tells us,

> Pasolini was a writer before he was a film director; his writing continued throughout his remarkable career. For example, his film *Teorema* appeared also as a book. Alberto Moravia compared Pasolini to the legendary playwright Jean Genet; others judged him to be more important than Genet. Sartre, De Lauretis, Calvino, Barthes, Deleuze, Guattari, and Foucault, among others, wrote appreciatively about Pasolini. (p. 102)

What is interesting in Pinar's work on film and his biographical portrait of Pasolini is that he is one of the few curriculum theorists to talk about film without literally tying film into teaching. That is, much work done in film in curriculum studies is about how teachers are literally portrayed in movies. Here we are thinking of Mary Dalton's (1999) book *The Hollywood Curriculum: Teachers and Teaching in the Movies*. Of course, this is important work. It is interesting to deconstruct the way teachers are portrayed in film, but there is so much more one can do in film studies if one treats the work more broadly through the lens of cultural studies. Pinar's work is not about how teachers are portrayed in film, but about how film can teach us things about the world. Pasolini, Pinar claims, was a public pedagogue. His films teach us about

> a cosmopolitan curriculum [which] enables students to grapple with (again borrowing Pasolini's language) the "problem of my life and flesh." That "problem" is autobiographical, historical and biospheric....The worldliness of a cosmopolitan curriculum implies that general education is more than an introduction to "great works," the memorization of "essential" knowledge...[but rather] it is subjectively structured academic study of this lived-historical problem of my "life and flesh." (p. 8)

So Pasolini's work is the work of a cosmopolitan educator. His films teach us about why it is important to study the biographic and autobiographic as these are always already situated in history. For Pinar, then, to study culture also means to study the self and the way in which self-formation is situated within a particular culture. Most cultural studies scholars do little with the notion of interiority. But for Pinar, interiority is crucial to understanding culture. Most cultural studies scholars use film—for example—to critique race, class, and gender issues but do little with the study of the self or interiority. Many cultural studies scholars are of the neo-Marxist bent and so they look at popular culture in order to interrogate class issues. Dennis Carlson (2002) remarks

> Critical pedagogy began to provide a discursive space for bringing cultural studies
> perspectives to bear on curriculum and pedagogy, and cultural studies recognizes no
> disciplinary boundaries....Like cultural studies more generally, critical pedagogy also
> emphasized the critical role of popular culture in the construction of everyday life and
> personal identity. (p. ix)

Carlson's point here is that critical theorists moved out of a strictly Marxist theoretical framework sometime in the 1990s and began to broaden their scope of study to include the popular. Many Marxists, that is, moved into cultural studies in the 1990s as Marxism seemed to become more and more problematic. Some of these problems are brought up also by Jennifer Logue and Cameron McCarthy (2007). These scholars state,

> In its radical ethnocentrism, cultural Marxism closed off the white working class
> from its minoritized other, orientalizing the latter, whether they were from Asia or
> the Caribbean, as metonymic attachments—the Pakis or the Jamaicans. A deadly
> consequence of this is that the working-class subject and the nature of power were
> not presented in a sufficiently complex or nuanced way. Indeed, it would be left to
> the filmic culture and the literary culture to present more complicated views of class
> power and class subjects. (p. 8)

The traditional Marxist framework is too narrow, these scholars suggest. The narrowness of traditional Marxist critique, then, becomes problematic because it cannot, for example, take into account other problems beside class.

One of the films that Logue and McCarthy mention is *Billy Elliot* (2000), which was recently made into a Broadway musical. This film and the subsequent musical deal with working-class issues but mostly with gender. Billy is a young working-class boy who wants to become a ballet dancer in a macho culture. Of course, his father is horrified because his son wants to become a ballet dancer, but toward the end of the story, he accepts Billy—at least in the Broadway version. The point here is that class cannot be separated out from issues of gender, sexuality, and race. Logue and McCarthy—in their critique of traditional Marxism—comment,

> In the cultural Marxist's elective epiphany, the third world subject would virtually
> perish (*There Ain't No Black in the Union Jack*). But this, in this disavowal, partic-
> ularism returned like a plague of innocence. Read on its own terms as a quest for
> scientificity, cultural Marxism divines class from the entrails of the social present and
> past, and ethnicity disappears. (pp. 6–7)

Not only does ethnicity vanish—in traditional Marxism—so too does gender and sexuality. A broader cultural studies framework is needed in order to incorporate into an analysis race, class, gender, sexuality, and ethnicity. It is not enough to simply study class or to study class through a Eurocentic position. However, there is value in studying Marxism and value in studying European traditions.

Certainly, there are other theoretical frameworks around which one could analyze culture. Autobiographical theory, psychoanalytic theory, poststructural theory, and literary theory—for instance—all could inform the readings of the cultural.

The Literary

Here I am thinking of the work of Susan Edgerton (1996), who was one of the first curriculum scholars to bring cultural studies into the field. Edgerton considers minority literatures as cultures. Edgerton couches her discussion of cultural studies against multiculturalism. Edgerton suggests that multiculturalism does not capture the complexity of cultures. Edgerton explains,

> Literary works of marginalized groups can provide a passage to a shifting discourse away from the conceptions of multiculturalism as something we "add on" to the curriculum, "do for" marginalized groups, or as a means to simply "change attitudes." Such a shift away is a shift toward a more fluid and thoughtful "discourse of encounters" in its abrogation of the problem of representation—representation as it concerns such entities and notions of identity, culture, and civilization—and in its problematization of cultural translation. (p. 6)

Edgerton sees the discourse of multiculturalism as problematic and wants to turn "multiculturalism into cultural studies," as the title of her book suggests. She comments that scholars need a more integrated curriculum and multiculturalism as it is currently taught is separated out from other courses and taught as an add-on course. One of the best ways at getting at the complexities of culture, Edgerton suggests, is through the study of literatures. Edgerton also makes the point that when scholars make decisions around whose literature is of most worth, they are really talking about issues concerning the canon. The canon is an issue first and foremost about culture (p. 6). Canons are cultures. The Western canon is problematic in that it excludes minorities, women, and cultures outside of the West.

What makes Edgerton's work unique is that she uses the concept of cultural studies in a broader sense than most. Pinar's (2009) work, too, is a broader form of cultural studies, especially in his study of the filmmaker Pasolini. Both Pinar and Edgerton integrate also into their work the importance of the biographic as a form of studying culture. Most cultural studies scholars, though, focus more narrowly on popular culture, not on cultures in this broad sense.

The Wax Museum, Iron Works, and Fashion

Let us think back to Walter Benjamin's (1999) *Arcades Project.* As I mentioned earlier, this work is an important historical forerunner of cultural studies. Here Benjamin studied all kinds of popular cultural phenomena like, for example, the wax museum, which Benjamin says is a "manifestation of the total work of art. The universalism of the nineteenth century has its monuments in the wax-works" (p. 531). Benjamin writes about such things as "iron construction" (p. 5) "world exhibitions" (p. 7), and even fashion. Interestingly enough, he tells us,

> Here fashion has opened the business of dialectical exchange between woman and ware—between carnal pleasure and the corpse. The clerk, death, tall and loutish, measures the century by the yard, serves as mannequin himself to save costs, and manages to single-handedly [work on]…the liquidation that in French is called *revolution*…Fashion was never anything other than the parody of the motley cadaver. (p. 63)

As one reads the above passage one sees how complicated Benjamin's analysis of fashion becomes. Benjamin's writing is very difficult to understand at times. He takes a most mundane topic like fashion, and writes about it in a highly unusual way to try to show the complexities of something around which people might not pay much attention. For Benjamin, then, cultural studies means taking the mundane and doing something with it theoretically. He talks about "wooden barricades" (p. 89), "cemeteries" (p. 99), "hashish vision" (p. 197), the "filigree of chimneys" (p. 219), and so on. Shirley Steinberg (1997) writes about doing scholarly work in the "nooks and crannies" (p. 209). Benjamin is certainly doing his work in these "nooks and crannies." Cultural studies is about finding things in "nooks and crannies" and turning those unnoticed things into theoretical discussion and thought. This is another way of thinking about cultural studies. I would not think that a chimney is a scholarly topic—as does Benjamin—perhaps because I might not have noticed that the chimney offers anything for discussion. However, a chimney is certainly a "nook and cranny," as Steinberg puts it.

Graphic Novels

The study of the popular, again, is not new but there are new forms of the popular. For example, Noel Gough (2004) captures the popular in the following passage as he says that it is important for curriculum studies students to take seriously

> a mutual interferencing and deconstruction of personal and cultural texts to read stories of personal experience within and against examples of postmodernist forms of storytelling, including metafiction, graphic novels, hypertexts, and cyberpunk science fiction, and then rewrite these stories (and/or write new stories) in ways that self-consciously display their intertextuality. (p. 91)

Gough explains that all of these forms of the popular are interrelated. They are interrelated because they represent countercultures that are either ignored or critiqued as not being scholarly enough to take seriously. But these are all serious topics to explore if we want to better understand youth culture. Our more conservative colleagues might be highly critical of graphic novels because they might think that they are less than scholarly. However, graphic novels are an important representation of literature. What do the pictures in graphic novels tell us about the written text and what does the written text have to do with images? Kids like graphic novels because they make the text come alive. Yet, some conservative academics might think graphic novels are junk and not worthy of scholarly discussion.

Cartoons

Peter Appelbaum (1999) writes about the importance of studying what he calls "Saturday Morning Magic" (p. 83) or Saturday morning children's cartoons. Scholars can learn much about popular culture by studying cartoons and the messages that they send. Appelbaum does a postmodern read on Saturday morning cartoons. He looks at "the impact of technoculture" (p. 83) and how it has affected what characters in these cartoons look like. The characters in current-day cartoons are very different, from say, the cartoons that children of the 1970s generation grew up with. The images and characters in cartoons today are technologically or computer generated. The cartoons in the 1970s differ from recent cartoons mainly because of the advances made in technology. Cartoons have much to teach us about children's cultures.

Comic Books

Cartoons and graphic novels are offshoots of comic books. It is interesting to note that John Dewey (2005), in his book *Art as Experience*, writes about the importance of comic books (p. 4) and considers them alongside other art forms. Most conservative scholars today consider comic books to be less than scholarly. John Weaver (2009) tells us, "In the late 1940s and 1950s Dr. Fredric Wertham was convinced that comic books were a major cause of juvenile crimes" (p. 35). Many people blame popular culture for crime, even today. In Michael Moore's film *Bowling for Columbine* he points out that many people blamed the rock star Marilyn Manson for the Columbine massacre because the two boys (Dylan Klebold and Eric Harris) who perpetrated this crime listened to Marilyn Manson. There is little correlation between listening to music and killing. Similarly, Wertham's worry about comic books—as Weaver points out—is without much merit.

John Weaver also points out that like Dewey, Robert Warshow (who commented about a decade after Dewey did on comic books), "is best known for his defense of comic books" (p. 35). What is there to defend about a comic book? But still there are people who think that popular culture is dangerous because of the negative effects it has on youth cultures.

Yet, there is great value in the study of comic books or any other popular cultural form because it teaches us much about who we are, politically, socially, psychologically, and even philosophically. Who develops comic books and for what purpose? Whose reflection do we see in these comics? In an interesting book by Umberto Eco (2004)—*The Mysterious Flame of Queen Loana*—the narrator of the book wakes up in the hospital one day and finds that he has lost his memory. The only things he can remember are lines from books. Eco's book is dotted throughout with cartoons, comics, photos of cigarette packages. These popular cultural objects help the narrator to remember who he is. The interesting thing about the images in the book is that they reflect a particular era in Italian history during the rise of Mussolini. Looking at a cartoon image of fascists dressed in military garb, the narrator of Eco's story wonders,

> Did I, too, march in uniform through the streets of the city? Did I want to go to Rome and become a hero? The radio at that moment was singing a heroic anthem that evoked the image of a procession of Blackshirts. (p. 183)

The cartoon images allowed the amnesiac narrator to remember who he was during the Fascist years. Cartoons and comic strips can tell us much about the politics of a particular era since they reflect history. Toward the end of the book Eco displays beautiful colorful images of the comic strip *Flash Gordon*. *Flash Gordon* was a morality tale of good versus evil. *Flash Gordon* might be a study in the way popular culture fictionalizes war. Who gets demonized and who are the heroes? At any rate, what interests me here is that Umberto Eco—who is both a scholar and popular fiction writer—makes use of cartoons, comics, and other popular cultural items to make a point about history and memory. These overlooked everyday images that are usually ignored are loaded with cultural and political meaning.

Sci-fi

Sci-fi—like *Flash Gordon*—tends to polarize gender. Much of sci-fi is quite macho and rather sexist. Suzanne Damarin (2004) notes, though, that there are traditions of sci-fi that could be considered feminist. Damarin states,

> Feminist science fiction [like the work of Ursula Le Guin who Damarin mentions earlier in her piece] can contribute to such curricula by interrupting the dominant discourses of "the natural" underlying the family values rhetoric of the radical right, a rhetoric increasingly adopted (but not co-opted) by all in the political sphere. (p. 60)

Much of sci-fi is written by men and much of it is about men's conquests over evil in outer space—like *Flash Gordon*. The sci-fi film *Star Wars* is also about good men fighting evil men. But Princess Leia—the heroine in *Star Wars*—is not a Barbie doll princess. She is a rough and tumble princess who challenges the notion of the fairy tale princess. Princess Leia fights alongside the men. Fairy tale princesses are certainly not warriors. And yet, *Star Wars* is still an Oedipal tale of men fighting men. In the sequels to the original *Star Wars* it gets even more Oedipal as we find out that Luke (a biblical name) Skywalker's father is actually Darth Vader (the evil character whom he tries to kill). Sons killing fathers is what the Oedipal complex is all about. Luke falls in love with Princess Leia—but is stunned when he finds out that Leia is his sister. Incest in *Star Wars* comes as a surprise. Even though *Star Wars* is an entertaining Hollywood film, it takes on some serious issues that are not found in most sci-fi films.

Fantasy

Matthew Weinstein (1998) comments on sci-fi and fantasy in the context of doing educational research. He states, "My merging of these genres is facilitated by the fact that SF & F and ethnography are not entirely distinct literatures" (p. 5). Fantasy is a particular genre of writing that is very close to sci-fi. Fantasy is make-believe. Anything can happen in fantasy. Fantasy is otherworldly. Fantasy is not based on science but on myth.

Weinstein claims that ethnography—as a form of educational research—is much like fiction writing in the way the ethnographer puts materials together. Ethnographers invent, use imagination, and decide what to leave out of their findings. Fiction writers invent, use imagination, and decide what to leave out of their imagined worlds.

A psychoanalytic take on ethnography in its relation to fantasy turns on the ethnographer's unconscious fantasies that come into play while doing research. When doing research ethnographers transfer old psychological issues into their research without realizing it. This is called "transference." Freud writes about the positive transference of falling in love. Freud suggests that patients who fall in love with therapists are merely fantasizing about who the therapist might be. The strictly Freudian analyst never reveals anything about himself or herself. The analyst, then, serves as a mirror for the patient. The patient can also begin to hate the analyst and this is called "negative transference." This hate is transferred from an old hate—usually of a bad parent—onto the analyst. And then there is what Freud called "generalized transference," which happens outside of the analytic situation. We take our pasts with us and transfer—unconsciously—love and hate onto others. As scholars, we continually project these fantasies onto texts and read into things what we want to. Freud claimed that most of our lives are made up of fantasies. One might wonder, then, if the literary genre of fantasy comes from our unconscious. Fantasy as a literary genre is the world of make-believe. So too are unconscious fantasies of love and hate.

Video Games

Another place that fantasies are enacted are through video games. One of the most well-known writers on video games is James Paul Gee (2007). Kids who play video games identify with the characters in the video game. The draw toward video games is the visual pleasure that one gets from looking at cyber-images and colorful fantasy worlds. This is a place that kids can go to escape the mundane world of school—which for them is mostly torment. James Paul Gee is a defender of the use of video games, much like Robert Warshow—as John Weaver reminds us—was a "defender" (p. 35) of comic books back in the 1940s. Gee argues,

> Good video games reverse a lot of our cherished beliefs. They show that pleasure and emotional involvement are central to thinking and learning. They show that language has its true home in action, the world, and dialogue, not in dictionaries and texts alone. (p. 2)

Language and images are always already intertwined. Language brings up images and images bring up language. Visual images are a draw for young people. They grow up in a very visual culture. There is much money in game design and many young adults are now going to college to learn how to design these games. However, Gee points out that it is

> violence that dominates the public discussion of video games, despite the fact that the best selling video game of all, The Sims, is not violent and that a great many non-violent games are made each year. (pp. 2–3)

Comic books, punk rock, and video games all get excoriated. Some argue that school shootings are caused by kids playing too many violent video games. But isn't that argument simplistic? It is easier to dismiss popular culture than to look at the deeper and broader cultural issues that might cause violence. Gee tells us, "When I wrote *What Video Games Have to Teach Us About Learning and Literacy* (2003) I took a lot of heat for not discussing the violence issue" (p. 5). Perhaps Gee should have addressed the issue of violence and video games because there are violent video games out there and lots of kids enjoy playing them. One has to wonder why kids are drawn to violent games and how those games affect them psychologically. Henry Giroux (2008) is a fierce critic of violent video games. Giroux reports that many of these games are made by the military or at least funded by the military. Giroux states,

> The military has found numerous ways to take advantage of the intersection between popular culture and the new electronic technologies. Even as such technologies are being used to recruit and train military personnel, they are also tapping into the realm of popular culture with its celebration of video games, computer technology, the internet....Video games such as *Doom* have a long history of using violent graphics and shooting techniques that appeal to the most hypermodes of masculinity. (p. 47)

Giroux points out that the military has undermined, in many ways, the video game subculture. In fact, Giroux reports, "The US Army purchased and now maintains its own video game production studio" (p. 47). When one thinks of the word "studio," one thinks of an art studio or a recording studio.

But these military "studios" have nothing to do with art, but everything to do with learning the "art" of killing.

Sociopaths kill for the sport of it. Sociopaths can learn how to kill by playing violent video games that teach how to kill. But not all kids are sociopaths and not all kids who play violent video games kill. But again the question is, why are some kids drawn to violence? The military uses video games to teach soldiers how to kill. Unmanned drones that fly over Iraq are controlled by soldiers who sit in an office somewhere in the United States. When they want to kill someone, they press a button on their computer. There is no visceral experience of killing. It is all clean. The soldier goes home to his family at night and eats dinner, watches the evening news, and goes back to work the next day, sitting in his office pressing buttons to kill people who are thousands of miles away. Killing has become virtual, but it is not only that. It is real. The drones send back pictures that look like a video game. So war—today—is not only like a video game, it is a video game.

Theoretical Positions

In this final section of the chapter, I want to explore a variety of theoretical perspectives used by scholars to analyze cultural studies. A rigorous analysis of cultural studies makes for a rigorous cultural studies. It is simply not enough to talk about cartoons by describing them. Scholars need to analyze them politically, socially, historically, psychoanalytically, and so forth.

I want to go back to the problem of violence and connect it to thinking through cultural studies in a more international fashion. Norman K. Denzin (2007) argues that "the old cultural studies narratives, both methodological and interpretive, are exhausted" (p. xii). Denzin argues that since 9/11, cultural studies must change. Denzin states, "We need a new language and a new way of representing life under violent, global postmodernism" (p. xii). Denzin also states, "A cultural studies that matters must speak from the historical present" (p. xi). Yes, the present is important. But the past is also important. So although I agree with Denzin that scholars must speak from the now, they must also think through issues historically.

Studying popular culture since 9/11 might seem trivial to some. But if scholars study popular culture against the larger historical backdrop—especially since 9/11—then the work is not trivial. So first and foremost, popular culture must be studied in a historical context. History can serve as a theoretical framework for cultural studies.

Another theoretical framework that studies popular culture historically and also studies violence—both literal violence and symbolic violence (i.e., through psychic colonization)—is postcolonialism. Postcolonialism deals with the symbolic and literal violence of colonization on an international scale. John Willinsky (1998) studies postcolonialism in the context of education and how Western education has worked to colonize and erase indigenous cultures. He does not do too much with popular culture per se, but his book would be a good companion piece to books that deal with popular culture in both Western traditions and indigenous traditions. Likewise, Greg Dimitriadis and Cameron McCarthy (2001) collapse cultural studies with postcolonialism in their book titled *Reading & Teaching the Postcolonial: From Baldwin to Basquiat and Beyond*. These scholars develop what they call "postcolonial aesthetic formulations" (p. 3). Dimitriadis and McCarthy explain,

> We have sought to focus attention on a number of exemplars: The critical work of C. L. R. James and James Baldwin; the paintings of Arnaldo Roche-Rabell of Puerto Rico; Gordon Bennett, an Australian artist; the Haitian-American artist Jean-Michel Basquiat; and Wilson Harris of Guyana; and African American novelist and Nobel laureate Toni Morrison. We look, as well, at the circulation of popular "world musics" around the globe. (p. 3)

The point of Dimitriadis and McCarthy's book is to show how artists develop under colonial situations. The questions raised by the book concern the ways in which colonized peoples express their rage through art. One of the interesting things to note here too is that—as Dimitriadis and McCarthy tell us—Basquiat began as a graffiti artist! Museums today take his paintings seriously. Today Basquiat is considered a serious artist.

What is striking about the collapse of cultural studies and postcolonialism is that it raises important questions about both popular culture and the historical backdrop in which it is produced. Most scholars of postcolonialism do not address issues of popular culture and most scholars of cultural studies do not address issues of postcolonialism. So this interesting hybridity (of cultural studies and postcolonialism) brings up many important questions that otherwise would not be raised.

There are other theoretical frameworks scholars use to analyze cultural studies. Cameron McCarthy and his fellow co-editors, Aisha S. Durham, Laura C. Engel, Alice A. Filmer, Michael D. Giardina, and Miguel A. Malagreca

(2007) tell us in their collection, *Globalizing Cultural Studies: Ethnographic Interventions in Theory, Method, and Policy,* the

> contributors draw on a wide variety of disciplines and subdisciplines—queer theory, hip-hop feminist theory, critical race theory, cultural studies, postcolonial theory, anthropology, sociology, linguistics, psychoanalysis, media studies, and literary criticism—for their interventions into globalizing cultural studies. (p. xxi)

This is an excellent collection of essays that shows that cultural studies can be analyzed in many different ways. All of these interesting theoretical frameworks raise different kinds of questions for cultural studies in its intersection with education. What I do not see in the passage above, however, is any mention of curriculum theory. Why is this not thought to be a possible "intervention into globalizing cultural studies" (p. xxi)? The main point of my chapter here is to explore the intersection between curriculum studies and cultural studies. One of the reasons I have focused mostly on youth cultures is because I think curriculum studies is most concerned with the way in which popular culture affects youth. Of course, there are exceptions to this. William Pinar's (2009) work on Pasolini is about popular film and the work of the public intellectual or the cosmopolitan intellectual in relation to curriculum theory. Susan Edgerton's (1996) work is about exploring minority literatures and issues of canon formation as these relate to cultural studies and curriculum theory. Neither Pinar nor Edgerton interrogates youth cultures. But both work to broaden the way one might think of cultural studies and its intersection with curriculum theory. Dennis Carlson's (2002) work *Leaving Safe Harbors* is another example of thinking through cultural studies in a broader fashion as it intersects with education. He, too, deals with issues of canon formation but, unlike Edgerton, Carlson is interested in rereading works from the Western tradition in order to show us ways to "leave safe harbors" and begin raising questions about what the Western tradition means. Carlson argues,

> In both philosophy and popular culture it is possible to find basic democratic narratives of education and public life, and ones that suggest a radical new vision of what education and public life could be. At the same time, it should go without saying, but unfortunately cannot, that both philosophical and popular cultural "texts" are, for the most part, deeply Eurocentric, classist, and patriarchal. (p. 4)

An important question that Carlson raises is this: when scholars study popular culture should they not also study it alongside the traditional Western canon? This does not mean that we do not critique the Western traditional canon. Carlson's point is that the Western canon and popular texts spring from the same foundations. Popular culture cannot and should not be studied in a vacuum or students will not understand what it is that they are studying. Most of the work done in cultural studies, however, looks exclusively at the popular and ignores what is considered "high" culture. I do not think "high" culture—or the Western traditional canon should be ignored. It too must be studied and critiqued. This is why Carlson's book is especially important. The crucial problematic for the study of popular culture is the Western tradition. For Dennis Carlson the tradition he looks at is the Western philosophical tradition—which is highly problematic. But if scholars do not study the problematic—of the West or of white privilege (which is part of the problem of the Western canon)—they leave out half of the picture. This is the same argument that Cameron McCarthy (1998) makes when he writes about studying the "metropole and the periphery" (p. 4) in his book *The Uses of Culture*. Angela McRobbie (2005) suggests, "I would always want to preface a course on contemporary cultural theory with a number of lectures on Marx, and then on Adorno, Benjamin, Althusser, Gramsci, Laclau and Mouffe, and Stuart Hall" (p. 3). McRobbie's point is that students cannot understand cultural studies without understanding the traditions from which cultural studies spring. Cameron McCarthy is highly critical of Marxism in its Eurocentrism and narrowness of focus. But McRobbie is right to say that still scholars need to study Marxism with all of its problems in order to understand how cultural studies came about. Many scholars who come out of critical theory or critical pedagogy have made that turn into cultural studies. Critical theory is a natural fit for cultural studies, since much of what is analyzed is political in nature. Having a solid foundation in political theory would be a good idea before launching into an analysis of popular culture. The political philosopher who is left out of McRobbie's list above is Hannah Arendt (1979). She is perhaps one of the most important and perhaps overlooked political philosophers of the 20th century. One reason she might be overlooked is that she is a woman. Cameron McCarthy would add to this list Paul Gilroy. McCarthy points out,

> Very little attention has been paid in the sociological, historical, communications, and emergent cultural studies literatures to the circulation of black intellectual ideas and activism....[Paul] Gilroy's coupling of the topics of black popular cosmopolitanism with the issue of diasporic intellectual formation brings into sharp view the remorseless process of cultural porosity. (p. 127)

McCarthy's point is important and scholars must remember that study must include the intellectual traditions of all kinds of people. Again, here is where cultural studies dovetails multiculturalism.

When most people think of cultural studies they tend to only associate it with the Birmingham Center in Great Britain. But John Weaver (2009) points out that there are, in fact, many traditions of cultural studies and he also suggests, "Many scholars associated with the Birmingham school, such as Stuart Hall, Angela McRobbie, and Paul Willis, dismiss the idea that the Centre for Contemporary Cultural Studies invented the term or was the first 'to do' cultural studies" (p. 39). The Birmingham school—and especially Paul Willis—is best known for the study of "British lads" or working-class (white) British boys. There is more to cultural studies than British lads. Today cultural studies has broadened, to say the least. Susan Edgerton's (1996) groundbreaking book *Translating the Curriculum: Multiculturalism into Cultural Studies* has little to do with British lads, but more to do with a feminist and poststructural analysis of minority literatures. Edgerton's work is quite different from the kind of work that the Birmingham Center produced. There are many approaches scholars might take when analyzing curriculum theory in the interstices of cultural studies.

· 7 ·

POSTCOLONIAL
CURRICULUM CONCEPTS

Introduction

Postcolonialism, in the interstices of curriculum theory, is a crucial area of study for students interested in issues of colonialism, racism, and the ways in which education has been complicit with colonial aspirations. After studying postcolonialism students might begin to wonder about issues around the canon and tradition. The ideas of canon formation and tradition are political. Whose knowledge is of most worth? Out of what tradition is our knowledge born? What does this tradition mean? Whose tradition do students inherit and why? These are political questions.

Outline of Chapter

Postcolonialism is (post). But what exactly does this (post) mean? This is where the discussion on the postcolonial will begin. I will engage in a discussion of (mis)education and the colonial. I will examine the ways in which colonial peoples have resisted colonialism. I will explore the psychological problems that colonial rule causes. Toward the latter part of this chapter I will discuss what is called "anticolonial education." Anticolonial education offers a critique of the notion of the postcolonial and approaches problems of colonialism in different ways.

The (Post)colonial

A topic of discussion among scholars of the postcolonial is whether the colonial is really (post) at all. What is "post" about the colonial? One of the most important scholars of the postcolonial, Edward Said (1994b), raises this question in his well-known book *Orientalism*. Said states, "Twenty-five years after its publication, *Orientalism* once again raises the question of whether modern imperialism ever ended, or whether it has continued in the Orient since Napoleon's entry into Egypt two centuries ago" (pp. xxi–xxii). The implication here is that colonization is not over, it is not actually "post." Both postcolonial scholars and scholars who do what is called "anticolonial theory" agree that colonialism is ongoing.

Colonization

There are many ways to colonize people. The British, the French, and the Americans are often cited as colonizers who have forced their way into other countries and—in one way or another—have put in place imperial governments. Ideology plays a role in colonialism whereby the dominating culture's ideas get embedded in the colonized country.

Psychological colonization occurs when one country colonizes another—whether through brute force or through the force of ideas (or ideology). Subjugated peoples become psychologically colonized. Psychological colonization of children who come from abusive homes is not uncommon. Abusive mothers colonize their children psychologically and the psychological scars from child abuse almost never go away.

Freud suggests we retain memories even if they are unconscious. So even during what is called the "preverbal period" (when children cannot yet speak), if the mother is abusive, the child will introject that abuse; the memories of that abuse stay in the psyche of the child forever, even if the child cannot remember consciously what happened. The unconscious is the storehouse for what people cannot remember and negative introjections remain in the unconscious. Eventually these repressed memories come to the surface of consciousness sometimes through nightmares. The "return of the repressed" is the phrase Freud used for failed repression. When the repressed returns it returns in bizarre forms. Acting out what cannot be remembered is called "repetition compulsion." When we compulsively repeat an unconscious memory of terrible events that happened to us as children we usually engage in destructive behavior of which we are not conscious. This is called "acting out." We act out what we cannot remember. It is as if we keep trying to work through something but we cannot remember what it is we are doing or why.

These same psychological issues affect subjugated peoples long after the colonizers have gone; this is one of the reasons many postcolonial scholars—like Said—ask whether colonialism is ever over. One of the best writers on the psychological wounds left by colonialism is Frantz Fanon, who I will discuss later on. I suggest that students begin studying Fanon (1963) by reading his well-known book *The Wretched of the Earth*. Fanon was a psychiatrist and knew much about psychoanalysis and colonization as he experienced both issues firsthand and witnessed the psychological fallout of colonization among psychiatric patients.

Is the Colonial (Post)?

Is the colonial (post)? And if not, why do scholars insist on calling this area of study postcolonial? One of the most important books in curriculum studies on the postcolonial is by John Willinsky (1998). In his book *Learning to Divide the World: Education at Empire's End*, he raises the question about the (post) in the context of the colonial and in the context of education. Willinsky remarks,

> Given the enormity of imperialism's educational project and its relatively recent demise, it seems only reasonable to expect that this project would live on, for many of us, as an unconscious aspect of our education. After all, the great colonial empires came to a reluctant end only during the years when I and the rest of the postwar generation were being schooled. It may take generations to realize what lies buried in this body of knowledge as a way of knowing the world. (p. 3)

Willinsky suggests that colonialism is over and yet it lives on in the way in which people are educated—especially in the West. Much of Willinsky's remarkable book deals with issues of tradition and canon formation. The educational tradition that most of us in the West have inherited is the European tradition. Willinsky's major thesis is that many of us are unconscious of our own knowledge formation; therefore, many of us do not question the tradition into which we are thrown. After studying his book, students might begin to wonder about the uses and abuses of the Western tradition and the politics behind Western education.

Anti-essentialist Pedagogy

Edward Said (1994b) has written much about the problem between the Palestinians and the Israelis. The Israelis clearly have colonized the Palestinians. One of the problems that emerges from being (mis)educated about these conflicts is that many tend to essentialize peoples: not all Israelis are right-wing and not all Palestinians are religious fundamentalists. However, the Israeli government is hard to the right. One of the reasons they are hard to the right is the fear of being annihilated. Students who know their history know that many of the older Israelis are Holocaust survivors and students know how fierce anti-Semitism is, not only in the Middle East but also all over the globe. Since 9/11 anti-Arab sentiment has grown as well. Some Americans—especially those who are (mis)educated about the Arab world, which is quite complicated—think that all Arabs are terrorists. Of course they are not, but this is a common misperception. This is a terrible problem in the United States right now and it would behoove us to better educate our children about the complicated Arab world.

Scholars must engage in anti-essentialist pedagogy. Not all Arabs are alike and not all Israelis are alike. Joe Kincheloe and Shirley Steinberg (2004) are the first scholars in curriculum studies to write about the mistreatment of Arab people in the United States and the ways in which our children continue to be (mis)educated about Arab people. This issue has not been researched by many in the field of curriculum studies.

What Is (Post) about the (Post)colonial?

Most scholars think that the colonial is not over—on any level. Here I am reminded of the work of both Gayatri Spivak and Stuart Hall. John Willinsky reports that Spivak "insists on using the term 'neocolonial,' which does not betray the continuation of colonialism the way that the term 'postcolonialism' does" (p. 3). Obviously, for Spivak colonialism has never been over; rather, it takes on new (neo) forms. As long as people are steeped in the Enlightenment tradition—the European tradition (as most academic disciplines are)—scholars will continue to perpetuate a symbolic form of colonialism through ideology.

Postcolonialism is an offshoot of postmodernism (or poststructuralism as these two concepts can be used interchangeably) and shares some of the same problems with postmodernism. Many postmoderns are steeped in the tradition of European thought. Derrida is a good case in point. Derrida's work is mostly based on male European texts. So even some of the postmoderns are still, in some way, modern. Is modernism really (post) after all? If scholars are still steeped in Enlightenment thought as well as the European tradition, then modernism is still here. We are—whether we like it or not—children of the Enlightenment.

The (post)modern era reflects where we are historically; the postmodern is (post) in that scientists have discovered how to smash the atom and build weapons of mass destruction. This is what separates us from our modernist ancestors. They too had wars. But they did not have weapons of mass destruction, which have thrown the entire world into a state of continual chaos. Nuclear proliferation is what sets us apart from our modernist ancestors. The thought of nuclear proliferation undermines any sense of stability people might have about living in this world. Derrida, Lacan, Zizek, Deleuze, Guattari, and Serres attempt to write about a postnuclear age where everything is unstable. These thinkers are trying—through their difficult and dense language—to reflect an historical era that is almost beyond understanding. Like the dropping of the atom bombs, 9/11 shattered America. 9/11 is another example of living in a (post)modern era. During the modern era, people did not fly airplanes into buildings. People who live in New York City and survived this horrific attack remember all too well how the world can crumble in a moment. Enlightenment ideas like scientific progress and rationality make little sense against the backdrop of 9/11. And yet scholars still cling to many modernist notions without even realizing it. Thus the idea of the (post), both in the context of postmodernism and postcolonialism, is fraught. One might argue that the (post)modern era has arrived with the advent of the dropping of the atom bombs and the advent of 9/11, yet many still cling to modernist ideas and draw on Eurocentric Enlightenment texts.

Yatta Kanu (2006), in her important edited collection titled *Curriculum as Cultural Practice: Postcolonial Imaginations*, raises the ongoing concern that the colonial is not, in fact, "post" by drawing on the work of Stuart Hall. Kanu states,

> An overview of the field suggests that colonialism has been identified both as physical conquest and control of territories, as well as control of the mind of the conquered and subordinated in an imperative to "civilize" the Other and keep the Other in a

perpetual state of psychological subordination. Although physical occupation and control of territories may end, the processes of colonial cultural production and psychologization persist, a situation that provokes Stuart Hall's (1996) oft-quoted concern: "When was the postcolonial?" (p. 9)

Perhaps the question should be thought of this way: when *is* the colonial "post," if at all?

(Mis)education and Colonialism

One of the ways to colonize people is by (mis)educating them. Most of us have been (mis)educated during our formative years. When students attend college perhaps (mis)education is questioned by some professors, but certainly not by all. Many of the academic disciplines are still steeped in the European tradition, not that there is anything wrong with studying the European tradition. But there tends to be little critique of this tradition still, plus there are many other traditions students need to study as well. European philosophy, for example, is not the only kind of philosophy, but most traditional departments of philosophy still teach only European texts. George J. Sefa Dei (2011a; 2011b) argues that indigenous philosophies are important to study, but in the academy indigenous ways of knowing are often ignored. There are other ways of doing philosophy and these other ways need to be taken seriously. Until students study indigenous knowledges they are being (mis)educated.

Colonized peoples' cultures are erased by colonizing powers. (Mis)education begins with the erasure of cultures. Time after time, country after country, in school after school, people report that colonizing countries have forced them to abandon their own culture only to learn the culture of the colonizing country. This is (mis)education. Edward Said (2001) says,

> The school I went to in Egypt before I came to this country was called Victoria College—it was modeled on a British public school. When you enrolled in the school, they gave you a handbook which contained a little statement, "English is the language of the school." If you got caught speaking Arabic, which was the native language, you would be punished. (p. 263)

Language and identity are inextricably intertwined, so by erasing language, part of one's identity is also erased. In the postcolonial literature one reads countless examples of what Said describes in many different countries across the globe. Thus, the first way to (mis)educate people is to take away their language and erase part of their identity. What happens to that part of one's identity that gets erased? What does it mean to speak and write in the language of the colonizer? These are open and complicated questions.

What is striking in Said's citation above in particular is the word "punishment." Punishing someone for speaking and writing in her native tongue is a way of saying that who you are is wrong. If you cannot speak your native tongue, what happens to your sense of self? Mouloud Feraoun (2000), a native Algerian, says during the French occupation:

> When I say that I am French, I give myself a label that each French person refuses me. I speak French, and I got my education in a French school. I have learned as much as the average Frenchman. What am I then, dear God? Is it possible that as long as there are labels, there is not one for me? Which one is mine? Can somebody tell me what I am! (pp. 65–66)

Clearly, Feraoun is pained by his conflicted identity. This is a powerful passage that speaks to the situation that many colonized peoples suffer. What is striking in the above citation is Feraoun's question: "What am I?" It is the "what" that is especially troubling. Are we not all human beings? Under colonial rule, subjugated peoples are often thought to be subhuman, like vermin. Jews were thought of as vermin during the Holocaust. They were considered noncitizens, not considered German; they were considered worthy only of extermination (Pinar, 2012).

Studies on the Holocaust usually are not considered part of the postcolonial literature, but many of the things that scholars write about in the postcolonial literature dovetail with what scholars of the Holocaust discuss. One could couch the discussion of German occupation of European countries as another form of colonialism. Germans did colonize many other countries, but for whatever reason Holocaust literature is treated as separate and apart from the literature on the postcolonial.

Like European Jewry during the Holocaust, Linda Tuhiwai Smith (2007) comments that both Maori women and Australian Aboriginal women have been thought to be nonhuman under colonial rule. Smith tells us,

> Across the Pacific, Maori women writers Patricia Johnston and Leonie Pihama make reference to Joseph Banks's description of young Maori women who were as "skittish as unbroken fillies." Similarly, Aborigine women talk about a history of being hunted, raped and then killed like animals. (p. 9)

An excellent film students might watch that deals with Australian Aboriginal women is *Rabbit-Proof Fence* (2002). In this film, Australian Aboriginal women are treated like animals, hunted like animals, and children are stolen from their mothers. The children are forced to attend British schools and live apart from their families. But the children in this film, which is based on a true story, run away several times from these British camps—they run along what is called the "rabbit-proof fence"—and find their way back to their mothers. In the film, the British imperialist—who oversees the girls at the camp—wants to "breed" the Aboriginal children with white men so as to lighten their skin over generations and eventually to turn them into white people. These generations of children who were stolen from their mothers and put in camps to learn English and become more like the British are often referred to as the stolen generation. Only recently—in an historical sense—have these practices been put to a stop.

Memory, History, and Colonial Domination

When one is forced to learn the language of the colonizer, Albert Memmi (1967), a native Tunisian, says,

> The memory which is assigned him is certainly not that of his people. The history which is taught him is not his own. He knows who Colbert or Cromwell was, but he learns nothing about Khaznadar; he knows about Joan of Arc, but not about El Kahena. (p. 105)

Memmi's key terms in this passage are "memory" and "history." Whose memory do we inherit? Whose history? For what purpose? Inheriting a Eurocentric canon is political. Inheriting this canon is also inheriting the memory and history of Europe. Native Tunisians—like Memmi— inherit a memory and history of Europe, while the colonizers erase the memory and history of native Tunisians. To inherit—through schooling—only a Eurocentric canon is a way not only to erase native identities but also to dominate others as Edward Said (1994a) puts it: "Neither imperialism nor colonialism is a simple act of accumulation and acquisition. Both are supported and perhaps even impelled by impressive ideological formations that include…forms of knowledge affiliated with domination" (p. 9). To force school children to learn a Eurocentric canon to the exclusion of their own cultural traditions is a way to dominate subjugated peoples. Knowledge formation—as Said tells us above—is partly about dominating others if it is used in a way that erases indigenous cultures and identities. Knowledge formation is political. The way we learn about the world is the way we understand it. If children are taught from an early age only about someone else's culture, how do they get their own culture back as adults? These problems create conflicted identities. Colonizing a child's mind through a particular kind of knowledge formation (the knowledge base of the colonizer) is troubling. Knowledge formation forms our identity. Interestingly enough, Spencer Segalla (2009) points out,

> The political and economic inequities of colonialism produced resistance throughout the European empires, and Morocco's French schools for Muslims, rather than functioning as centers of cultural hegemony and political collaboration, became focal points of contestation. The prominent and disproportionate role that graduates of the colonial schools played in anticolonial political movements highlights the frictions produced by colonial schools. (p. 8)

It is important to note that subjugated peoples are not just victims. Resistance to colonization is always possible.

Fighting Back, Colonization, and Abuse

Like subjugated peoples that have been abused but rebel against colonial powers, most child abuse survivors also fight back. Derrick Jensen (2000) was raped by his father repeatedly as a child and so too were his siblings. Today Jensen is a well-known activist and writer. He uses his writings to work through his traumatized childhood and in the process helps others. Colonizing children through abuse—whether sexual or emotional—is similar to colonizing peoples through the power of empire. Jensen writes,

> My family is a microcosm of the culture. What is writ large in the destruction of the biosphere was writ small in the destruction of our household. This is one way the destructiveness propagates itself—the sins of the fathers (and mothers) visiting themselves unto the children for seven generations, or seven times seven generations. The death of my childhood may have been traumatic, but in a nation in which 565,000 children are killed or injured by their parents or guardians each year, my childhood does not qualify as remarkably abnormal. (p. 61)

Colonization begins, as Jensen points out, within the patriarchal family structure. This patriarchal structure then is writ large in culture. Empires have historically been patriarchal. Patriarchy means power. Colonization is the abuse of entire cultures. There is not much in the postcolonial literature that ties together child abuse and the abuse of nations through colonizing powers. But there are connections between both of these problems. Frantz Fanon (1963) is the most well-known writer on the psychological fallout from colonization but he does not address issues of childhood or child abuse or make any links between child abuse and colonized countries. There are, however, two important curriculum scholars—Gaile Cannella and Radhika Viruru (2004)—who have made connections between postcolonialism and the ways in which schools colonize children through violent practices. Cannella and Viruru remark,

> Today, modernist science fully accepts the surveillance of children in hospitals, homes, schools, and many other settings. This continued belief in surveillance is based on the position of inferiority in which children have been placed, at the lowest level of the patriarchal hierarchy. (p. 109)

When Cannella and Viruru talk about the intersections of childhood and postcolonialism and the violent practices of surveillance, their largest concern is the way in which children are colonized by adults who consider them inferior. Radhika Viruru (2001), in her book *Early Childhood Education: Postcolonial Perspectives from India*, also speaks to this issue of inferiority in the context of growing up in India. Viruru states,

> Even when I began this study I would not have described myself as a postcolonial anything. To me, and to many people of my generation, colonization was something that was over and done with and had no influence on our lives. This was despite the fact that I went to an English medium school in India run by Catholic missionaries, whose syllabus was based upon the English O and A levels. Although we grew up in a free society, we were still dealing with the aftermath of centuries of systematic plundering and looting. Probably the biggest issue that we faced was a widespread feeling of intellectual inferiority. Our own ancient culture was something that we valued and learned…but in most official places like colleges and schools Western thought was given a higher place. (p. 15)

What is striking about Viruru's passage is that she writes that she did not realize how colonization had affected her until she wrote her book. She suggests that many people thought that colonization was over in India. But then she thinks again and wonders about her education and why it was that she was studying English and why it was that in school the Western tradition was valued and her tradition ignored. This is what led Viruru to suggest a "widespread feeling of intellectual inferiority" (p. 15). We tend not to question what they teach us in elementary or high school—when we are children—because perhaps we are still too young to realize what it is that we are being taught. As we get older, though, questions begin to arise. Perhaps it is through study that we begin to uncover the hidden curriculum of schooling. What do we know when we are kids? We know what they tell us. This kind of schooling (i.e., colonial schooling) is a form of abuse. Children's identities—especially if they are minorities or colonized peoples—are molded in such a way that their own cultures and traditions are made invisible. It is this invisibility that leads to problems. Indeed, feelings of inferiority are a psychological disaster. Writing through that inferiority—as Viruru did—is a way to work through it. Scholarship can serve as a coping mechanism. Freud suggested that if one has a problem the best way to cope with it is to write it out, or talk it out. Writing can be a cathartic experience. It does not erase the problem at hand, but it does allow for expression of the problem. It is the expression that leads to catharsis.

The worst kind of child abuse is sexual and emotional. The violent practice of surveillance in school settings is harmful, yes, but a parent sexually or emotionally abusing a child is much worse. But, too, the reason parents think that they can abuse their children is because they think children are inferior to adults—as Cannella and Viruru point out. But there is more to it than this. Children who come from abusive families are abused for many reasons we do not understand. It is unconscionable that a parent would strike or sexually abuse a child. As Jensen (2000) points out, however, this abuse is rampant. The number of victims of childhood abuse in America is underreported. Victims are afraid to report abuse because they are afraid of further retaliation.

Native American scholar Vine Deloria Jr. (2007) reminds us of the violence that was done to Native American children for decades. Deloria tells us,

> Indian children were kidnapped and taken thousands of miles away to government boarding schools. Once there, they were whipped if they used their native languages or made any reference to their former mode of life. All religious ceremonies were banned on Indian reservations. Priceless objects of art were destroyed on the advice of the missionaries and bureaucrats because these were thought to be manifestations of the old pagan way of life. It was a time of forced obliteration of native culture. (p. 109)

Native American traditions are obliterated from the curriculum in most public schools. Children seldom learn about what the white man did to the Natives on American soil. Children are still taught in many public schools that Columbus "discovered" America. White people not only colonized the Native Americans but also murdered them by the millions. Today the scars of this horrific genocide are still with us. But again, how many American school children learn about these brutalities? American history textbooks still "obliterate"—as Deloria puts it—the American past. History is rewritten, or unwritten, by textbook companies that want to make profits by being nonoffensive. The Native American genocide, for the most part, then, gets written out of history—still. Like Native Americans, African Americans were also colonized, brutalized, lynched, and murdered (Pinar, 2001). Colonization does not just happen in faraway countries, it happens right here on American soil.

Global Colonialism

The study of colonization must be global. I turn to the study of other countries so that students can get a sense of how pervasive colonial practices have been worldwide. Patience Elabor-Idemudia (2008) discusses the colonization of Nigeria and what it was like for a child to grow up in this atmosphere. Elabor-Idemudia tells us,

> Under the colonial administration of Nigeria, new forms of production were introduced and new systems of power relations were imposed. New patterns of inequality were established involving people of different backgrounds, languages, and beliefs. At age six, children of my cohort were required by the newly imposed colonial policies to go to Western-style schools to acquire "formal" knowledge through education. At the school we were forced to give up the knowledge of folkways that we had acquired at our homes. (pp. 106–107)

Folklore, or lore of the folk, is as valuable as any other kind of knowledge. People who have suffered colonization and have had their folklore taken away suffer disaster both emotionally and intellectually. Colonizers destroy not only countries but also people's way of living (folkways). The British, French, and American imperialists historically have always wanted their subjects to assimilate into the dominant culture and yet, even if colonized people submerge themselves in the British, French or American culture, they still are not thought to be human enough, or smart enough, or "good enough"—as D. W. Winnicott (2010) might put it. Subjugated peoples around the globe historically have always been treated as second-class (non)citizens. Njoki Nathani Wane (2008) comments,

> Like most Kenyans, I was not taught about my culture or about the things my parents learned from their parents in school; yet I *was* taught about the American Revolution, Niagara Falls, and the Second World War. As a graduate student in Canada, I realized that my formal education had somehow divorced me from my roots, and that what I had was a partial education. (p. 55)

What Wane had was not a partial education but rather a (mis)education. Like Radhika Viruru (2001), Njoki Nathani Wane suggests that it was not until later in life that she became aware that she was not educated in the way that she should have been. There was something missing in her education—hence she was (mis)educated. It was not until graduate school that Wane understood what had happened to her. Again, we do not realize—as children—what happens to us through our schooling. We do not have the intellectual tools to be able to critique what comes before us. The curriculum is what it is and we accept it. Children do what their teachers tell them to do. They have little power to do otherwise.

Ladislaus Semali (1999) tells the story of his childhood in Tanzania and what happened to him when the British came and wrecked his schooling. He states,

> Then, I went to school, a colonial school, and this harmony [of his native tradition] was broken. The language of my education was no longer the language of my culture. I first went to Iwa Primary School. Our language of education was now Kiswahili. My struggle began at a very early age constantly trying to find parallels in my culture with what was being taught in the classroom. In school we followed the British colonial syllabus....We read stories and sang songs about having tea in an English garden. (p. 9)

This example brings to light the absurdity of colonial schooling. Teaching kids from Tanzania about "having tea in an English garden" is completely irrelevant to their own lived experience and traditions. What is even more absurd is that Semali tells us that the children had to *memorize* these songs and stories about having tea in an English garden.

R. Sambuli Mosha (2008), who grew up in Tanzania, reports similarly,

> In High School (1962–65) most of my history classes were about West European history, a few on American history, and almost none on early African, Asian, or South American histories. In English literature we knew Shakespeare's works like the back of our hands and little or nothing about African literature. (p. 172)

To colonize minds through education makes one wonder about the uses and abuses of education. Teaching people only about other people's cultures is a good way to destroy minds. Edward Said (2001) suggests that he had a remedy for this problem, however. Said tells us,

> Before I left for the US, I had a colonial education and I felt out of place. There was something that didn't correspond between what I felt to be myself and that kind of education. So I always felt that two educations were going on—the conventional

education at school and the self-education taking place to satisfy the other self that was excluded. (p. 282)

When Said became an adult, he tried to fix his (mis)education through self-education, to make up for the lack he experienced as a child. To become self-educated—as Said points out—is one way out of this problem of growing up in a colonial school system. But when do students learn that they need to become self-educated? Probably not until graduate school or even later. Schools do not teach children how to think; they teach them what to think. Becoming self-educated takes a lifetime of discipline and struggle. To do intellectual work on your own takes a lot of effort and even pain. It is painful to learn about the ways in which schooling has not been adequate. It is even more painful for those who were colonized as children to learn about the violent practices of exclusion through colonial schooling. For many, it is not until they leave school that they are able to get a good education. That good education comes from being self-taught, mostly. The beauty about making study your profession (by becoming a professor) is that you have the chance to figure out—through study and through scholarship—what went wrong with your education as a child. William Pinar (2012) comments much on subjectivity and the need for study and scholarship. The more that was taken away from children educationally the more they want to know. Of course the wounds of colonization never go away, but students can through study figure out ways of coping with those wounds and finding out about themselves through study and scholarship. Yet still, as John Willinsky (1998) points out, the effects of colonial educations "live on" in an "unconscious aspect of our education" (p. 3). It takes a lifetime to undo what has been done in the name of education. Studying the postcolonial helps to better understand the ways in which many are colonized through schooling.

Canon Formation

Canon formation is an issue taken up by postcolonial scholars. Taiaiake Alfred (2004) remarks,

> Universities are, to turn an old anti-imperial phrase, "the heart of whiteness." They accomplish the acceptance and normalization of Western ideas, the glorification of Western societies as the highest form of human organization, and promote the emulation of North American culture to the next generation of citizens (and to Indigenous students as well unless there is some critical intervention). (p. 96)

The study of postcolonial literature is the "critical intervention" needed, according to Alfred. Studying postcolonial scholarship helps us to better understand ways to undo the white privilege of the university curriculum. But it is not enough to offer courses in postcolonialism. Postcolonial thought should be integrated throughout the curriculum. However, (mis)education is hard to undo because it gets so ingrained that it is hard to break out of what Homi Bhabha (1994) calls "fixity" (p. 96). Bhabha says,

> An important feature of colonial discourse [the history of Western philosophy, for example] is its dependence on the concept of "fixity" in the ideological construction of otherness. Fixity, as the sign of cultural/historical/racial difference in the discourse of colonialism, is a paradoxical mode of representation: it connotes rigidity and an unchanging order as well as disorder, degeneracy and daemonic repetition. (p. 66)

Edward Said (1994b) speaks to these issues. Said suggests,

> It is as if, having once settled in the Orient as a local suitable for incarnating the infinite in a finite shape, Europe could not stop the practice; the Orient and the Oriental, Arab, Islamic, Chinese, or whatever, became repetitious pseudo-incarnations of some great original (Christ, Europe, the West) they were supposed to be imitating. (p. 62)

"Christ, Europe, the West"—as Said puts it— sums up education in the university. But the problem is not that the Western tradition isn't worth studying—clearly it is. The problem is what about non-Western traditions, indigenous traditions?

Dipesh Chakrabarty (2000) suggests, "European thought…is both indispensable and inadequate in helping us think through the various life practices that constitute the political and historical in India" (p. 6). European thought is also both "indispensable and inadequate" in thinking through lived experience in North America or anywhere in the world. European thought is only part of the picture. There are other canons of knowledge that scholars need to study. The study of indigenous knowledges, for instance, should be integrated into the curriculum. However, professors should not introduce other canons and throw out the European one. The practice of throwing away the old and introducing the new only begins once again an exclusionary canon. Paul Gilroy (2005) suggests that scholars should think of knowledges as "tangled." Gilroy tells us,

Repudiation of those dualistic pairings—black/white, settler/native, colonizer/colonized [I would add the Western canon versus indigenous knowledges] has become an urgent political and moral task. Like the related work of repairing the damage they have so evidently done, it can be accomplished via a concept of *relation*. This idea refers historians and critics of racism to the complex, tangled, profane and sometimes inconvenient forms of interdependency. (p. 42)

Perhaps knowledge formation is not so clear-cut as to say that there is the West and everything else. Rather, as Gilroy suggests, thought is woven and interrelated across traditions: the notion of the canon is messy. Similarly, Derrida (1995a) suggests that one cannot easily separate speech from writing (which is what the history of Western philosophy attempted to do, according to Derrida). Rather, Derrida suggests that speech is already in writing and writing in speech.

Since at least as far back as Plato, the Western tradition has attempted to clarify what is not clear. Up until the advent of postmodernism, the history of Western philosophy attempted to put into neat and tidy categories what is not neat and tidy. The postmoderns, however, have turned all of this upside-down. Likewise, scholars should begin to think of canon formations not as neat and tidy, but as messy and, as Paul Gilroy suggests, "tangled" (p. 42). Thus, scholars need to study things in this tangled fashion. Jonathan Langdon (2009) suggests similarly, "There is an overly simplistic understanding of cultural knowledge production—an understanding that positions Indigenous communities as if they exist in some isolated context without any cross-fertilization of ideas from other cultures" (p. 5).

Thus, colonial knowledge is not separate and apart from the knowledge of the colonized. Both knowledge(s) intertwine and both should be studied as interconnected knowledges. This point is also made by Philip Leonard (2005) who states, "A more compelling approach would be one which recognizes the heterogeneous character of both the subaltern and the colonized, and which admits to the constitutive inter-dependence of both" (p. 107).

Another way to think about this is on a more psychological level. Earlier I made a connection between victims of child abuse and colonized peoples. Let us take the discussion further here. A child who is abused by her mother, say, introjects that abuse and might later project it out onto others. Introjection and projection are always going on in our psyches simultaneously. A child transfers her early experiences onto later situations, usually repeating them without remembering. The mother imago is always embedded in the psyche and the more the mother is abusive the deeper she gets embedded in the psyche.

The same psychological problems arise for colonized peoples. The deeper the colonization, the deeper the internalization of the colonizer into the psyche of the colonized peoples. The earlier the damage is done psychologically and the longer it goes on, the harder it is to undo or "untangle" (to use this term in a different way from Paul Gilroy, 2005). Likewise, the colonized person who was tortured by the colonizer introjects that torture, which becomes difficult to forget. That is why many colonized peoples who have been victims of torture suffer from posttraumatic stress disorder. So too do victims of child abuse. The memories of colonization or abuse never go away. Thus, colonizer and colonized are tied by a sort of twisted symbiosis. However, it is in the twistedness, if you will, that knowledge production happens.

Cameron McCarthy (1998), in the context of knowledge formation, suggests that there is a "heterogeneous basis of all knowledge" (p. 19). The heterogeneous basis of knowledge is not merely a problem of epistemology, it is also a psychological problem. In terms of studying the postcolonial, McCarthy suggests that his book *The Uses of Culture*

> argues against the current tendencies to oppose Western culture against the cultures of the non-West, the first world against the third world, and so forth. Drawing on the work of postcolonial authors such as Homi Bhabha, Stuart Hall, and Edward Said, we argue that any single overmastering or ruling identity at the core of the curriculum—whether it be African or Asian or European or Latin American—is in fact a confinement. (p. 19)

The notion of a core curriculum therefore is highly problematic. What does "core" mean? Who decides what is "core?" There is no core to knowledge, McCarthy points out. Knowledge is highly complex and messy. There should be no centrism in the curriculum—this is McCarthy's point. Greg Dimitriadis and Cameron McCarthy (2001) argue that scholars need to question "center-periphery relations" (p. 3). The center and periphery are in a complex relation since one blurs with the other. As against Descartes, knowledge is porous, not clear and distinct. The boundaries of knowledge blur continuously, always changing. Just as a human being has no core identity (according to the postmoderns), so too with knowledge formation; there is no core knowledge. Studying a variety of traditions is important in order to situate our own knowledge production.

Disciplines as Complicit

John Willinsky (1998) argues that all disciplines are complicit with coloniza-tion. Willinsky notes,

> By the time the age of empire was over, no branch of learning was left untouched. New academic disciplines of anthropology and orientalism were born and the old ones of geography, philology, and anatomy were recast in the ordering of the new world. Colonial rule gave rise to a new class of knowledge workers in universities, government offices, industry, and professions devoted to colonial conquest by classi-fication and organization. (pp. 25–26)

Through education, or (mis)education, the world is "divided up" as the title of Willinsky's *Learning to Divide the World: Education at Empire's End* suggests. This division is about which knowledges are considered civilized and which ones are considered savage. The disciplines inherited in the academy are problematic if they still do not question their origins, purposes, and histories. Willinsky specifically examines

> five of the academic disciplines that have become staples of the school curriculum: history, geography, science, language and literature. [He explores]…traces of the co-lonial imagination that form part of how we have learned to divide the world. (p. 19)

Questions scholars might ask at this point are these: Whose history, and for what purpose? Whose geography, and for what purpose? Whose science, and for what purpose? Whose language and literature, and for what purpose? Will-insky asks: "An education for whom?" (p. 101). Let us think about history for a moment. Who writes history? The conquerors. Think of geography. Who gets to map the world? The powerful. Whose science do we study? The white man's. Whose languages do we honor? The languages of empire. The gist of these questions comes down to this: those who have the power decide what is to be studied. Academic disciplines were created by the powerful (mostly white men of colonizing countries). Linda Tuhiwai Smith (2007) claims,

> From the vantage point of the colonized, a position from which I write, and choose to privilege, the term "research" is inextricably linked to European imperialism and colonialism. The word itself, "research," is probably one of the dirtiest words in the indigenous world's vocabulary. (p. 1)

When reading Smith's passage, anthropology is brought to mind. Original-ly this discipline was about studying the exotic, native, "savage," Other.

Ethnographers—even today—have to be careful not to treat their participants as objects for study or to use participants to further their career. Studying indigenous peoples is highly problematic for ethnographers because the world is divided in terms of "us" (privileged academics) and "them" (indigenous, uneducated peoples). Here I am especially thinking of indigenous forms of science or medicine that do not conform to Western models. Academics tend not to take seriously other forms of science and medicine. Also I am thinking of Native Americans who are suspicious of white people who "study" them. Daniel Heath Justice (2004) remarks,

> Perhaps the biggest concern I have about Native literary studies is the fact that there are still too many scholars—mostly non-Indians, but some of our own too—who approach the work as though Indians aren't really even a part of the work at all or, if present, exist only as antiquated museum pieces who should just look exotic and keep quiet. (p. 105)

Exoticizing the Other is highly problematic when studying indigenous cultures. This is why the discipline of anthropology is so problematic because for decades this is what anthropologists did. Today, anthropology has changed for the better, but still there is always the problem of voyeurism and appropriation. The ethnographer comes from a place of privilege; the nonacademic who has been a victim of colonization or whose family has been victimized for generations by colonization is being "studied" for the ethnographer's academic gain. But there are also counterexamples to this problem. James D. Le Sueur (2005), writing about the French and Algerian War, suggests that some intellectuals—although responsible for the occupation of Algeria—grew to hate the occupation and fought against it. Le Sueur comments,

> During the French-Algerian War intellectuals (on right and left) intervened in the public debates on decolonization, and they were frequently targeted by the state, military, police and other intellectuals, vigilante groups, and even the fascistic terrorism of the OAS for their real or perceived role as intellectuals. (pp. 4–5)

The point here is that not all academics, not all intellectuals, are complicit with imperialism. In fact, many intellectuals, as suggested by Le Sueur, have fought against imperialism and argued strongly for the freedom of the colonized. There are some ethnographers today who do careful study of other cultures without exploiting them for their own gain. Nicholas Ng-A-Fook (2007), for example, did a careful study of the Houma Indians in Louisiana. He clearly did not do this study for his own academic gain. Students might consult his important book if they are interested in Native American culture (see *An Indigenous Curriculum of Place: The United Houma Nation's Contentious Relationship with Louisiana's Educational Institutions*).

The Case of Albert Camus

There are intellectuals whose motives are not so clear. Here I want to explore the case of Albert Camus. In the postcolonial literature on the French-Algerian War, Camus's name comes up quite frequently. James D. Le Sueur suggests, "A comprehensive study of the French-Algerian War neglecting the question of Camus would be suspicious" (p. 98). While Camus spouted liberty and freedom for peoples around the world, he was against the decolonization of Algeria. Richard Keller (2007) comments, "Emily Apter's work on Albert Camus, for example, highlights the 'nullification of Arab characters' in his works: Algerian Arabs are either absent or appear as underdeveloped set decoration" (p. 9). Likewise, in German, non-Jewish fiction after the Holocaust, Jews do not appear in German novels. If they do appear, they are faceless or in the background somewhere (Morris, 2001). This facelessness or absence—both in the case of Camus's fiction and in the case of German non-Jewish fiction after the Holocaust—suggests that the Other (either the Arab or the Jew) gets Othered by their disappearance in these texts. Now, Camus's case is rather alarming because he thought that the Arabs were incapable of governing themselves, as if they were savages or children. He felt that the Arab Algerians were better off under French colonization. In other words, like a tyrannical parent, he felt that it was for their own good that the Arabs were under French colonial rule. The irony about Camus—and he was much excoriated for his position on the Arab Algerians—is that, according to Le Sueur (2005), "Many of his disagreeable predictions about Algeria's future came true. He was especially adept in predicting how the FLN's penchant for authoritarianism would threaten Algerian society" (p. 99). To flesh this problem out Le Sueur tells us,

> His [Camus's] contradictory transition from outspoken commentator on questions of violence and liberty during his Resistance days to quintessential reticent intellectual concerning the Algerian question raised eyebrows and exacted heavy personal and professional costs. Simone de Beauvoir was only one of the hundreds of intellectuals who condemned Camus as a hypocrite. (p. 100)

Camus' position was basically freedom for everybody else in the world, except the Arab Algerians.

The relationship between colonizers and the colonized fosters (on the part of the colonized) nationalist and sometimes even extremist tactics in order to resist the violence of the colonizers. This is what happened in Algeria. Extremisms are sometimes born out of oppression. Authoritarian rule does not emerge out of nowhere. Something in people makes them want to rule with an iron fist. Perhaps it is the lust for power. But historians do report time and time again how oppressed people can become oppressors themselves. This is a point that Frantz Fanon (1963) makes in his book *The Wretched of the Earth*. Fanon remarks, "The native is an oppressed person whose permanent dream is to become the persecutor" (p. 53). There is (sometimes) something sadomasochistic about the relation between the colonizer and the colonized. The masochist wants to become the sadist perhaps as a form of revenge (Pinar, 2001).

Ecological Colonialism

The problem with colonization is that it does not go away. Those who are colonized are psychologically maimed; generations of people suffer the consequences of colonization, especially through being (mis)educated. The signs of colonization linger on for generations.

Another way that colonization manifests itself, as Edward Said (1994a) tells us, is

> through what Alfred Crosby calls "ecological imperialism," the reshaping of the physical environment, or administrative, architectural, and institutional feats such as the building of colonial cities (Algiers, Delhi, Saigon); at home, the emergence of new imperial elites, cultures, and subcultures (schools of imperial "hands," Institutes, departments, sciences.) (p. 109)

The remnants of colonialism remain, especially in architecture and monuments. For example, if one visits St. Petersburg, Russia, one will notice two things. The center of the city looks like Paris with its beautiful buildings. However, upon leaving the center of the city one will see Soviet-style housing projects that are reminiscent of the housing projects in the United States: every building is exactly the same. The Soviet-style housing projects eerily remain. But most tourists do not venture beyond the center of the city of St. Petersburg and so they get the wrong impression. There seems to be two Russias: the Parisian city of St. Petersburg and the Soviet remains of the housing projects. Today most Russians are poor and live in difficult situations. The newly "democratized" Russia is highly problematic because of the dire poverty in which people have to live.

There is much corruption since the mafia runs rampant and many government officials are ex-KGB, so one has to wonder about the continuities between the Soviet Union and today's democratic Russia.

The second point in this discussion is about monuments and colonialism. In Savannah, Georgia, Confederate monuments abound. Without much comment, most white people see no reason why these monuments should be torn down. The Confederate monuments are symbols of slavery, and slavery is a brutal a form of colonization. The South has yet to work through its Confederate past. Contrast the American South to postwar Germany. Monuments to Hitler do not exist and it is illegal to fly a Nazi flag. While Germany has worked through its Nazi past, the American South has not.

Colonial remnants remain also in Calcutta, as scholars learn from Dipesh Chakrabarty (2000) who tells us,

> "Europe" was not a word that ever bothered me in my middle-class Bengali childhood or youth as I was growing up in postcolonial Calcutta. The legacy of Europe—or British colonial rule, for that matter is how Europe came into our lives—was everywhere: in traffic rules, in grown-ups' regrets that Indians had no civic sense, in the games soccer and cricket, in my school uniform. (p. ix)

The traces of colonialism are found everywhere, even in the street. Recall Walter Benjamin's (1999) *Arcades Project*. He teaches that one can learn much from everyday signs, posters, billboards, department stores, and so forth. Although Benjamin was not concerned with colonialism, he did understand that people could learn much about a culture just from walking down the street. As Dipesh Chakrabarty shows in the above citation, even traffic rules smack of colonialism in Calcutta.

Returning to the idea of "ecological imperialism" (a term coined by Alfred Crosby), some postcolonial scholars flesh out the notion of space. For instance, Kate Darian-Smith, Liz Gunner, and Sarah Nuttall (1996) suggest,

> The notion of space as a multidimensional entity with social and cultural as well as territorial dimensions has been a prime concern in recent scholarship in the fields of post-colonial literature and history, and social and cultural geography. Space has been linked to concepts of power, as in the writing of Michel Foucault, and there is a growing body of historical and literary criticism which deals with the peculiarities of colonial space. (p. 2)

Spaces are political entities carved out by the powerful. Only the powerful can build buildings, monuments, and cities. If spaces are built by colonial powers, they will reflect those colonial powers. A disturbing aspect about the United States, for example, is that the president lives in the White House—a colonial space for "white" people. In the South—especially in Georgia and South Carolina—many places are still called plantations. The space of the plantation brings up a hideously brutal past. But most Southerners are not troubled by this.

Kate Darian-Smith, Liz Gunner, and Sarah Nuttall remark on a book by Paul Carter called *The Road to Botany Bay*. They tell us that Carter suggests,

> The imperial landscape of Australia was created through the European naming and mapping of its geographical features by white explorers, administrators and settlers. The act of naming, and the names themselves, either blatantly ignored or subverted and incorporated pre-existing Aboriginal names and histories of the land. (p. 5)

Changing names of streets tell stories. Naming, as the above authors point out, is not benign.

Resistance to Colonialism

One of the most important points that scholars make about colonialism is that the colonized are not just victims. Throughout the postcolonial literature one finds many examples of colonized peoples' resistance to their colonizers. There has been much controversy in the Holocaust literature since the 1960s about this notion of resistance. And again, the Holocaust is typically not treated as part of the postcolonial literature—but it certainly could be. The well-known phrase "led like sheep to slaughter" referred to European Jews not fighting back against the Germans and their collaborators. But many argue that this was not the way things happened. Jews did fight back when they could. One example of this is the Warsaw Ghetto Uprising that was a focal point in the film *The Pianist* (2002). But as the saying goes, you can't fight tanks with potatoes. One of the reasons Israelis have become so militant—at least this is the image that Americans seem to see the most—is because of this long-standing idea that Jewish men are not fighters and that they were "led like sheep to slaughter" (Morris, 2001). Jewish men have long been thought to be effeminate (Pinar, 2012). But now all of that has changed—especially in Israel. Again this image of the macho Jewish man is a reaction to the idea that Jewish men are weak, effeminate, and cannot stand up to the enemy. Did the Jews resist or not? Of course they did. But tanks outnumbered Jewish firepower. Jewish women resisted in whatever way they could as well. People wonder: why didn't they just leave? But where were they to go? Almost every European country was collaborating with the Nazis and anywhere Jews went in Europe they were sure to be turned back or turned over to the Nazis. Some of the only safe places to go were Great Britain, the United States, China, and South Africa. But tightening immigration laws made it more and more difficult for Jews to escape.

In the postcolonial literature much is made of the notion of resistance. It is again important to take note that people are not merely victims. They do fight back. Here I will cite some of the examples in the postcolonial literature of resistance.

Spencer Segalla (2009) discusses Moroccan resistance to French colonization in the context of schooling. Segalla states,

> The beliefs, experiences, and desires of the colonizers would not alone determine the shape of colonial education in Morocco, of course. Moroccan resistance to French agendas was ever present, forcing colonial authorities to repeatedly recraft the imperial educational agenda. (p. 28)

Segalla does not say exactly what the "recrafting" of the educational system entailed but one might imagine that the French did not like this. Despite the recrafting, however, Segalla does tell us, "Moroccan resistance occurred within the context of widespread accommodation and overt acceptance of French rule" (p. 28). Perhaps there are always two things going on simultaneously under colonization: resistance and assimilation. But still in the postcolonial literature, assimilation under colonial rule is conflicted and identities of colonized peoples are affected by this ongoing conflict. For example, those colonized by the French are at once French and not French. Those colonized by the British are at once British and not British. As Cameron McCarthy (1998)—who grew up in Barbados, which was colonized by the British—tells us,

> I speak with at least two voices. The first is as an intellectual whose formative and perhaps most decisive education occurred in a third world country, the postcolony of Barbados. I am, for better or worse, a child of the empire—an "English rustic in black skin." My other voice is that of an Afro-Caribbean immigrant intellectual displaced to the putative center of the industrial world. (p. 15)

McCarthy captures this doubled identity; he is at once British and not; he is also what he calls Afro-Caribbean and yet also British, but not quite British, and so on. McCarthy tells us that his education was British and yet he is not British but yet influenced by British education.

Edward Said (2001) talks about resistance to colonial power via what he calls a "counter-will" (p. 188). Said tells us that this "counter-will" is "the will of other people to resist imperialism's will. I discovered this in my own experience, amongst people in my own community (like the Palestinian community) and elsewhere in the Third World, in Ireland, and so on" (p. 188). Somewhere between a will and a "counter-will" identities are born. One could say that under colonial rule, identity is shaped *against* something. I am not this! The "this-I-am-not," shapes the "I am."

Still it gets more complex. A child is born of a mother and father. Clearly, the child is part of these two people. But the child who is a victim of child abuse—which I have been arguing is a form of colonization—wishes to disavow the abusive parent. However, the abusive parent always remains somewhere in the psyche of the abused child. No matter how hard the child tries to rid herself of the abusive parent psychologically, the abuser remains buried in the psyche.

The colonizers, too, remain buried in the psyches of colonized peoples, no matter how much they develop what Said calls a "counter-will" (p. 188). You can "will" away abuse but it doesn't magically go away. The will is a conscious move to oust the colonizer from the psyche. But the psyche is driven mostly by the unconscious and there is no will in the unconscious. The unconscious has a mind of its own. If the abuse—or colonization—is not worked through psychologically, repression fails. When repression fails, posttraumatic stress disorder is likely to emerge. People have little control over this. Many people who have suffered under colonial rule suffer from a lifetime of posttraumatic stress, just as abused children do later in life.

Frantz Fanon (1965), in his book *A Dying Colonialism*, tells us how native Algerians used the radio as a force for resistance against the French colonizers. Native Algerians relayed messages through what was called "The Voice of Fighting Algeria" (p. 84). According to Fanon this was one of the most important ways that the native Algerians countered the French colonizers. Fanon comments,

> The radio set was no longer a part of the occupier's arsenal of cultural oppression. In making of the radio a primary means of resisting the increasingly overwhelming psychological and military pressures of the occupant, Algerian society made an autonomous decision to embrace a new technique and thus tune itself in on the new signaling systems brought into being by the Revolution. (p. 84)

Obviously, the radio played a major part in the success in the Algerian war since the French eventually retreated and finally pulled up and left Algeria for good. James D. Le Sueur (2005) tells us that this war was "one of the bloodiest wars of independence of the twentieth century" and claims that "four hundred thousand people had perished" (p. 1). Clearly, the French did not want to give up Algeria; they did not relinquish Algeria easily. Le Sueur tells us that French historians "have until recently shied away from the French-Algerian war" (p. 4). Either the French were embarrassed at this disgraceful part of their past, or they were humiliated by defeat. It is also interesting to note that in my study of the Holocaust (2001), the French took a long time to admit complicity in the Vichy Regime. Like the disaster in Algeria, many years passed before French historians began to grapple with French complicity. Entire countries can go into a state of denial about embarrassing aspects of their histories. Le Sueur comments on the "gap in [French] historiography" in the context of the French-Algerian War and finds it a "conspicuous absence" (p. 4). In the United States, one might say the same about the Civil War and the South's unwillingness—still—to grapple with slavery and brutality. High school history texts, clearly, are not doing a good job—at least in the South—of educating young people about what happened. Often students arrive at college knowing little about the South and slavery. Raising issues of race to Southern white students is always a challenge. The Confederate flag—for many rural Southern white students—represents rebellion. Many of these students do not make the connection between the Confederate flag and the atrocities and brutalities for which it stands. These students are being undereducated in high school and (mis)educated about the South: they have not studied slavery in any depth; they know little about the history of the South; they know little about lynching or Jim Crow (Pinar, 2001). Similarly, in Germany school students often complain that they do not want to hear about the Holocaust again. German non-Jewish students complain now that they are the "victims" of the Holocaust because they have to keep studying it (Morris, 2001). An embarrassing past is not something that people want to hear about, so they misremember and rewrite the past of their country. Former East German historians often rewrote their embarrassing history and turned the blame on the former West Germans, calling them fascists. Austrians too rewrote the past and many said, ""It wasn't our fault, we were 'invaded.'" Yet a disproportionately large number of Austrians were high-ranking officials in the Nazi Party (Morris, 2001). Andrea Merkel, Chancellor of Germany, has remarked that multicultural Germany is not working. The Turks are now the new Jews: the Germans have directed their hatreds towards these foreigners. Merkel implies that Germany should be a single culture (read "pure").

Kate Darian-Smith, Liz Gunner, and Sarah Nuttall (1996) tell us that in South Africa during apartheid, "Black locations and townships such as Soweto became places that sustained distinctive African cultural identities, and were the sites of vigorous resistance to the apartheid state" (p. 14). Despite a colonized South Africa, the authors here suggest that native Africans could hold onto their "distinctive African cultural identities" (p. 14). The decolonization of South Africa is historically relatively recent. Many American students know little about this history. American students in general are not educated about global issues or international issues unless these issues have something directly to do with free trade or making money.

There are certainly parallels between South African apartheid and slavery in the Southern part of the United States. These parallels bring up our own embarrassing and disgraceful past in the United States. Americans know little about apartheid perhaps because apartheid reminds us too much of white peoples' complicity in slavery. Like black Americans, South Africans suffered lynchings, police brutality, torture, murder, and segregation. An important book that students might consult about South Africa is by Alan Wieder (2003), titled *Voices from Cape Town Classrooms: Oral Histories of Teachers Who Fought Apartheid*. The brutality these teachers suffered—who resisted and fought against apartheid—is shocking. Wieder tells us,

> The people I worked with in South Africa all testified. They spoke of the atrocities and hardships that apartheid brought teachers. Neville Alexander and Sedick Isaacs spent twelve and thirteen years respectively in Robben Island prison; many other teachers were detained for short periods; most were spied on and harassed in their jobs. All of the people I worked with suffered the treatment of their students who challenged the government because students were beaten, arrested, and sometimes killed. (p. 2)

The brutalities of apartheid are little known in the United States. Killing students because they protest shocks. Think of Tiananmen Square. Many American students, however, never heard of Tiananmen Square or apartheid. Perhaps in different parts of the country students are better educated, but in the rural South students seem to know little about history or international issues. Does the South historically lag behind the North in education? Perhaps.

Yatta Kanu (2006) tells us,

> In the former European colonies in Africa, for example, repudiation took the form of nationalist movements that eventually led to independence for these countries. Independence, however, has been followed by the march of neo-colonialism in the guise of modernization and development through globalization and transnationalism. This reinvention of imperialism implies that schools and school curriculum cannot separate themselves from the task of neo-colonialism (p. 16)

Kanu argues that colonialism now takes on new forms (neocolonialism) and she suggests that colonialism has been reinvented (p. 16). Similarly, after Algeria gained its independence from the French, James D. Le Sueur (2005) reports, "Algeria was sliding into what would regrettably become the firm thirty-year grip of the Front de Liberation Nationale's (FLN) authoritarian leadership" (p. 1). Decolonization brings with it, then, its own problems. One wonders if any of these former colonies became truly liberated. It seems that many of them became recolonized in other ways. This is certainly an aspect of colonization that psychoanalysts might attribute to transgenerational trauma. This is repetition compulsion acted out by entire nations. Repetition compulsion is unconscious, so the new forms of colonization are perhaps unconscious results of having been colonized and not being able to work through colonization. Does one ever work through being colonized? Maybe not. All countries, however, have different histories. Reina Lewis (2005) makes this clear in the following passage as she states, "French history is divided into epochs that do not match English history; postcolonial history challenges the colonialist demarcations of imperial history; women's history challenges the masculinist exclusions of her-story" (p. 7). There are many histories, not one overarching postcolonial history. The French, the British, and the Americans colonized countries but in vastly different ways. Each of these countries has a distinct history.

Part of the problem with studying postcolonialism in a comparative manner, which is what I have done here, is the incorrect assumption that all these countries suffered the same and that colonialism is much the same everywhere. This is wrong-headed. Linda Tuhiwai Smith (2007) also points out that even

> the term "indigenous" is problematic in that it appears to collectivize many distinct populations whose experiences under imperialism have been vastly different. Other collective terms also refer to "First Peoples" or "Native Peoples", "First Nations" or "People of the Land," "Aboriginals" or "Fourth World Peoples." (p. 6)

All of these terms are potentially problematic because, within each of these groups of people, difference abounds. Across these groups of people difference abounds. Terms such as "indigenous"—as Smith suggests—essentialize entire groups of people. Postcolonial scholars sometimes use the terms "indigenous knowledges" or "indigenous peoples" without much comment or critique. Indigenous peoples can mean many different things to many different people. All indigenous people are not the same.

Feminist Critiques

On another front, some feminists are highly critical of the discussion of Orientalism, especially in the work of Edward Said. Meyda Yegenoglu (1999) argues that Said left women out of his discussion on Orientalism. Yegenoglu states,

> With a few exceptions, questions of sexual difference in the discourse of Orientalism are either ignored or, if recognized, understood as an issue which belongs to a different field, namely gender or feminist studies. My decision to explore this question came with an awareness that the critiques of Orientalism and colonial discourse manifest a persistent reluctance to examine the unique nature of the articulation of cultural and sexual difference in the case of Orientalism. (p. 1)

This is a critique also made by Nina Asher (2003). More specifically, what is lacking in debates on Orientalism—for scholars like Edward Said (1994a, 1994b), Albert Memmi (1967), Frantz Fanon (1963), Mouloud Feraoun (2000), and Aime Cesaire (2000)—is discussion about women, either as victims of colonization or as perpetrators of it. It is important to make a clear distinction between women perpetrators of colonialism and women who were or are victims of it. These are two entirely different kinds of experiences, neither of which are brought up by any of the male scholars I mention above. Reina Lewis (2005) remarks on "the role of white European women as cultural agents" of imperialism (p. 2). Contrarily, the film *Rabbit-Proof Fence* deals with experiences of women and young girls during the British colonial travesty in Australia. This film is a powerful, emotionally charged, shocking study of the way in which girls were stolen from their mothers. The fierce struggles of the girls—who continually elude capture and manage to escape the British colonizers by running away (along the rabbit-proof fence)—are a testament to the strength and determination of these girls to return home to their mothers. These Aboriginal girls put up fierce resistance to their colonizers. Women and men experience resistance to colonization differently because they are treated differently by their colonizers. The Aboriginal girls were treated differently by the British because the British saw them as breeders. The British wanted to "save" the Aboriginals from themselves and turn them into white people through interbreeding the girls with British men.

Reina Lewis argues that in the context of postcolonial literature, if gender is treated at all, it is "uneven, preliminary and tends to be ahistorical" (p. 1). So here is an area of study that needs much work. I encourage students to go deeper into this area in future studies. This is a weakness of the postcolonial literature.

Psychic Wounds of Colonialism

Colonialism leaves psychic wounds for generations. Those living in a (post) colonial society suffer the remnants of colonialism. Although the colonizers might be long gone, the psychic scars are there to stay. Likewise, children who suffer from sexual or emotional abuse might repress this abuse or move on. But one thing is certain: although the physical scars might be gone the psychic scars remain. Pierre Orelus (2007) remarks, "My contention is that the material disaster that came along with colonization is not as profound as the psychological scar it has caused 'postcolonial' subjects" (p. xi). The profundity of the psychological scar is generational. Transgenerational trauma almost never goes away. This is uncannily like what victims of child abuse suffer. While child abuse might damage one person—namely, the child—colonial abuse damages entire countries. Cameron McCarthy (1998) notes, "The postcolonial soul can know no peace" (p. 4). Being a victim of a colonial society means having your identity stripped. What part of the self is left after that? Or does the self evaporate? It can. But for most, the ego is strong enough that the self continues on. When McCarthy suggests that there is "no peace" for victims of colonization one must ask what kind of life remains? What is left? A wounded psyche is left to go on, or not.

Edward Said (2000) writes about the postcolonial subject and exile. One can read this in two ways: a colonial subject might flee his native country to escape the horrors of colonialism, or a colonial subject becomes exiled from himself psychologically. This psychological exile I would call "detachment." When a person feels distance from herself or feels that she is not there (in her mind), this is a way to actually protect the self from deteriorating. The problem with any defense mechanism is that a person becomes so used to being detached, say, under colonial rule, that after the colonizers are long gone the detachment actually works against the person. The detachment is no longer needed when the psyche is not under constant attack or surveillance, but it keeps working and causes the psyche to become arrested. When you no longer need to be detached but still are, you are not living a full life because you are not fully present in the world. It is as if you are exiled from yourself and cannot get back. Being literally exiled from one's country is another thing, of course, but still the psyche can act in this dysfunctional way even if living in another country away from the horrors of colonization. It is to these horrors that Said speaks. He claims,

> I have argued that exile can produce rancor and regret, as well as a sharpened vision. What has been left behind may either be mourned, or it can be used to provide a different set of lenses. Since almost by definition exile and memory go together, it is what one remembers of the past and how one remembers it that determines how one sees the future. (p. xxxv)

In order to "provide a different set of lenses" you must "mourn" your loss. Mourning and seeing the future differently are not incompatible but rather are inextricably connected. It isn't as if mourning is a bad thing and shouldn't be done. In fact, Freud teaches that in order to work through melancholia—which petrifies the self—one must mourn one's loss and let go of the lost object. Without mourning, there is no going on. A new vision—as Said points out in the above passage—is not possible unless one mourns one's loss. Regret, as Said points out, comes when one gets stuck in melancholia. To regret is to be stuck. To be in a state of melancholia is to be psychically stuck. The only way to work through regret is to mourn the loss at hand. Regret is not helpful if it makes you psychically arrested. However, one can use regret in other ways if one mourns loss. A mourned regret can be used to find this new vision that Said talks about above. When Said talks of memory I think of two kinds of memory: one kind is what Freud called memory work and the other is nostalgia. Nostalgia is being stuck in a past that never was. Memory work is quite different. Memory work is work. Memory work is closer to the work of the historian: a historian works on a subject because she wants to find things out. So, too, the memory worker. She tries to remember to find things out. Of course, memory is quite complicated. Memory and history are not the same things, as historians follow certain methods and rules while memory workers do not follow academic rules or methods. But the fact is that historians have memories and if they write about a recent past they also work out of their memories. This muddies the water.

Memory and Exile

Said's point is that memory and exile are of a piece. One might long to go home. But then what is home? Where does one go when in exile? Where is home? There is no home for the exiled. The new home is not home and the old home is no longer welcoming. So the exiled lives in a state of limbo. Hannah Arendt (1979) writes about being stateless. She escaped the Nazis and fled Germany. Walter Benjamin was on the run. What is it like to live on the run? Benjamin was prolific despite being on the run. Maybe it was the pressure of being on the run that made him feel compelled to write. This is what Said is getting at when he says that being exiled gives you a different kind of vision. There is urgency in Said's writing, as there is in Arendt's and Benjamin's writings. When one is complacent the urgency to get things done is not there. Not that being exiled is a good thing. The point here is that when you know your time on this earth might be cut short, you know you have no time to waste. The sense of urgency changes you.

Mummification

Albert Memmi (1967) discusses the "mummification of the colonized society" (p. 98). The feeling of being psychically dead to oneself is a defense mechanism. In much of the psychoanalytic literature the concepts of numbing or desensitization are used to describe what happens when one is traumatized. Mummification—as Memmi puts it—is the concept that postcolonial scholars use to describe the end results of trauma. To be without feelings is a terrible way to live, indeed. During the Holocaust, many reported that after a while they numbed out to the whole experience. Numbing is a defense mechanism when the psyche overloads. But when the Holocaust was over the numbing continued for many. This again becomes the problem. What saved you from psychic deterioration (numbing) can later create problems (after the colonizers are long gone) and can actually harm the psyche. To become a permanent mummy—to use Memmi's word—is a way to live without being alive. This is what war and colonization can do to people. Memmi says that victims of colonization suffer "an internal catastrophe" (p. 99).

Psychic Fallout

One of the best writers on the psychic fallout of colonialism is Frantz Fanon (1963) in *The Wretched of the Earth*. Fanon was a psychiatrist and so he could articulate this "internal catastrophe" about which Memmi (1967, p. 99) speaks. Both Memmi and Fanon agree that a strange thing occurs between the colonized and the colonizer. As was mentioned earlier, the colonized bond with the colonizer and, in some ways, want to be like the colonizer. Why would this be? Psychiatrists do not fully understand this. Why would a victim of torture want to be like the torturer? Why would a victim of torture fall in love with the torturer? Sado-masochism is a complex that emerges in these colonized-colonizer situations. The reason I add a hyphen between the sadistic and the masochistic is because there is a relation between the two (sado-masochist). In some instances the masochist wants to trade places with the sadist. This is why after colonized peoples are liberated they sometimes become colonizers themselves. Likewise, some victims of child abuse later become abusers themselves. If a country does not mourn its colonization, the danger of falling into dictatorship (which is sadistic) is likely. If a child does not seek help and work through the abuse she suffered at the hands of a parent, the likelihood that she turns around and does the same thing to her own children is probable.

Toward the end of Fanon's book he lists a number of psychological problems that he sees with patients who were victims of colonialism. Many of these same psychological problems are also common with victims of child abuse. Fanon lists things like "reactionary psychoses" (p. 252), insomnia, anxiety, and "suicidal obsessions" (p. 253), psychic blocking (p. 262), depersonalization (p. 252), and the utter inability to speak (p. 252). Fanon tells us of one individual who

> could not speak anymore, and asked us for a pencil. Wrote: "I have lost my voice, my whole life is ebbing away." This living depersonalization [or what is sometimes termed dissociation] gave us reason to believe that the illness had reached a serious stage of development. (p. 262)

Most of the literature on postcolonialism ignores the psychological fallout of being colonized. With the exception of Frantz Fanon and Albert Memmi and a few others, little is done with the psychological problems that result from being colonized. This is an area of study that students can take up and develop more in the future. The problematic here, though, is that in order to work in this area students must have a solid grasp of psychological literature or psychoanalytic literature, and they must have a solid grounding in post-colonial literature. It might be overly ambitious to combine the two (say, psychoanalysis and postcolonialism) unless you are a psychologist or psychiatrist—as was Fanon—or a psychoanalyst. It is not an impossible task, but a difficult one.

One of the startling things about studying postcolonialism is the way in which education has historically been complicit in colonizing people. So postcolonialism and curriculum studies seem a natural fit. Studying postcolonialism makes us more suspicious of our own (mis)education. Students in the United States have grown up in the European or Euro-American tradition, and the curriculum has reflected this from the time students start grade school on through and into college. Now again, I am not arguing that the Western tradition should be thrown out. It should be critiqued. Scholars should also study marginalized traditions. I do not mean to set up clear binaries. I have discussed already the complications of relations between colonized and colonizer. However, still it is important to keep in mind that perpetrators are different from victims. In my (2001) book on the Holocaust I discuss President Ronald Reagan's visit to a cemetery in Germany where German soldiers were buried. He made the statement that everybody was a victim of the Holocaust (meaning the German soldiers, the Nazis, the people who were complicit). Hartmann (1986) says of the incident: "Reagan: F in history, a French newspaper declared" (p. 11). Perpetrators and victims are not the same and to say that Nazis were victims of history is not only ridiculous but also disgusting. Colonizers are not victims of history.

Anticolonial Education

Anticolonial education is another way to approach the problems of colonialism. Anticolonialism offers critiques of the notion of the postcolonial. Arlo Kempf (2010) argues,

> The term anticolonialism brings to mind different things for different people. For some it is the African struggles for independence against European colonialism in the 1950s, 1960s, and 1970s. Others conflate it with terms such as neocolonialism

and postcolonialism…although anticolonialism draws on certain postcolonial and neocolonial works, it is by no means synonymous with these approaches. (p. 14)

As Kempf points out, some ideas of the postcolonial, neocolonial, and anti-colonial overlap. But anticolonial scholars want to drive a wedge between the postcolonial and the anticolonial. However, there are many similarities between postcolonialism and anticolonialism. Some of the themes I discuss here will be familiar as I touched on them in the context of the postcolonial. The overarching point of contention is that scholars of anticolonialism are uncomfortable with poststructuralism and postcolonialism is an offshoot of poststructuralism. Leila Angod (2006) contends,

> By doing away with "post" [in the notion of postcolonialism] as it applies to co-lonialism, anti-colonialism forges links between past and present bodies, histories, challenges and resistances, thus violently rejecting the former's tacit insinuation that colonialism is in any way over. (p. 164)

The "post" in the postcolonial does suggest in some ways that colonialism is over. But recall postcolonial scholars do debate this term and problematize it the way that anticolonial scholars do. Still, anticolonial scholars do not like the signifier postcolonialism because of this problem. George J. Sefa Dei (2010) remarks that in thinking about the colonization of African peoples, the only approach to understanding this colonization and the only approach to undoing it is through anti-colonial theory. Dei states,

> Any critical teaching and learning about Africa and its peoples must necessarily be "anti-colonial." Pan-African social thought is anti-colonial to the extent that it seeks to subvert the continued intellectual, economic, cultural, spiritual, and political subjugation and marginalization of Africa, its issues, and concerns in contemporary geo-politics. (p. 54)

The underlying assumption here is that African peoples are still colonized and still suffer from colonization. Anticolonialism not only critiques colonialism but also "seeks to subvert" it. This is a theory in action since it works toward social change. Anticolonial scholars such as Dei argue that postcolonial scholarship has little to do with actual social change.

Dei mentions spiritual subjugation of African peoples. In the postcolonial literature there is hardly any mention of the spiritual. But for Dei the spiritual matters. African peoples have been colonized through missionaries and these missionaries want to erase religious traditions and assimilate African peoples into Christianity. Assimilation is a way to undermine African ways of understanding their world spiritually.

Jonathan Langdon and Blane Harvey (2010) contend that Dei wants to drive a wedge between the postcolonial and the anticolonial, especially when it comes to the material realities of suffering from colonialism. Langdon and Harvey comment,

> Dei (2006) has detailed the importance in moving from postcolonial to anticolonial theory. For Dei, this move involves embedding the discursive and identity consciousness of postcolonial theory in a recognition of the profound material consequences of the continuation of colonial domination. Yet, this does not mean undermining the importance of the discursive approach. (p. 221)

The charge against postcolonialism is that it does not deal with on-the-ground suffering, that it does not deal with the everyday lives of people living in colonial conditions. Anticolonial scholars like Dei argue again that postcolonialism is too theoretical, not practical; that it does not deal with the practicalities of living under colonial conditions. But the important point made by Langdon and Harvey is that Dei does not wholly discount the "discursive approach" to colonialism. Dei wants to make certain that the way in which scholars discuss colonialism be both discursive and material, but that postcolonial scholars leave out discussions of the detrimental material conditions people suffer under colonization. Dei drives this point home as he states,

> In fact, Benita Parry (1995) and Ahmad (1995) have both criticized the discursive analysis of postcolonial theorists for their heavy reliance on textuality and idealism at the expense of deep historical enquiry and materialist interpretations. In offering a bridge between these stances, contemporary anti-colonial thought argues that colonial constructions affect knowledge production with profound material consequences. (p. 13)

Again, the charges against the postcolonial are the same charges some scholars make against poststructuralism. Scholars who do not like poststructuralism often say that it is too text based or focuses too much on discursive formations while neglecting discussion about real people. Anticolonial theory has more in common with Marxist theory or with what is called "critical theory" in that it deals with issues on the ground and seeks to change things. Philip S. S. Howard (2006) agrees with Dei on these points. Howard remarks,

> Anticolonial discourse takes issue, quite pointedly, with the manner in which postcolonial theory tames the political bite of resistance discourses. It attempts to grasp the complexity, of subject positions at the expense of the ability to articulate an

unambiguous political rejection of colonial power relations. Further, the overemphasis on the discursive belies the urgency of the tragic material effects lived by the oppressed. (p. 46)

Howard argues that the language of postcolonialism does a disservice to the oppressed and to real people who suffer under colonialism. The language of postcolonial scholarship, in a word, obfuscates these struggles. Postcolonial language, in other words, is not sharp enough and waters down or tames the realities of the struggles of the oppressed.

Anticolonial scholars argue that scholarship must begin from below, from the struggles of colonized peoples, and thus there is an emphasis on studying and embracing indigenous knowledges. The language of the struggle must come from indigenous peoples. Temitope Adefarakan (2011) claims that postmodern theorists tend to essentialize the notion of indigenous. Adefarakan argues,

> There is a need for a shift in how notions of Indigeneity are taken up so that they are not imagined as singular, in the way that those who often work from exclusively Eurocentric or postmodern [or postcolonial] perspectives do. (p. 34)

However, as I discussed earlier in the chapter, some postcolonial scholars do take issue with the problem of essentialism when it comes to the notion of indigeneity. Not all postcolonial scholars essentialize this term and make sure to point out that there are different kinds of indigenous peoples and indigenous knowledges.

Another point made here by Adefarakan is that African peoples are often left out of the conversation when it comes to indigenous peoples. Scholars must be cautious, thus, not to leave African peoples out of this conversation. Recall, that Arlo Kempf (2010) argued that anticolonial thought emerged from African colonization. In speaking of indigenous knowledges and indigenous peoples, George J. Sefa Dei (2011a) contends that scholars must "recognize and acknowledge Indigenous knowledges as legitimate knowings in their own right, and not necessarily in competition with other sources or forms of knowledge" (p. 2). Dei suggests that scholars approach the problem of knowledges as multiple (p. 2) and nonhierarchical (p. 3). But the academy is clearly steeped in Eurocentrism. Dei (2011b) further remarks, "Postmodern, post-structural, and postcolonial theories as modes of thought have dominated the (Western) academy" (p. 22). Dei would like to see the academy integrate anticolonial discourse and the discourse of indigenous knowledges into the curriculum, and this he claims would be a highly "political and intellectual exercise in decolonization" (p. 22). But most universities in the West—at least in their core curriculum—offer only courses steeped in Eurocentric ways of knowing. Some Eurocentric ways of knowing are also racist ways of knowing. Leila Angod (2006) claims that even postcolonial scholarship erases the concept of race. Angod states that "in terms of the colourline, the otherness machine [of postcolonialism] is implicated in the disappearance of coloured bodies into the abyss" (p. 163).

Anticolonial scholars argue that postcolonialism is not political enough. This is the same complaint that some scholars have against poststructuralism. But I argue that both Derrida and Foucault are political poststructural scholars. At any rate, anticolonial scholars argue that the postcolonial scholars are not political *enough*. Leila Angod claims that postcolonial theory is "too apolitical" (p. 160). Philip S. S. Howard (2006) argues that postcolonial theory offers little more than "political paralysis" (p. 46).

As against postcolonialism, anticolonial theorizing is political, these scholars claim. George J. Sefa Dei (2011a) argues that scholars must engage in a "particular politics of decolonizing dominant knowledge" (p. 2). Dei (2011b) also suggests, "Creating a space in the academy to discuss indigenous knowledges in the first place constitutes a political act" (p. 24). Contrarily, I argued in earlier parts of this chapter that postcolonial scholars also engage in "decolonizing dominant knowledge" and they also discuss the importance of embracing indigenous knowledges. So there seems to be some overlap of what it is that postcolonial scholars and anticolonial scholars do.

Both postcolonial scholars and anticolonial scholars have something to offer. It is suggested here that scholars study these two schools of thought alongside each other to see where overlaps and differences occur. It is clear that anticolonial scholars want to see change happen in real-world politics. They seem confident that this can be done through anticolonial education. George J. Sefa Dei (2010) argues,

> Anti-colonial theory also moves beyond critique to new visions of society (See Dei and Kempf 2006; Kempf 2009). Education has a key role to play in this task. Education must provide learners with the tools to understand and transform society. (p. 34)

Anticolonial scholars seem certain that with the right education, people can and will change the world for the better.

· 8 ·

POSTSTRUCTURAL
CURRICULUM CONCEPTS

Introduction

This chapter will serve as an introduction to poststructuralism in the interstices of curriculum theory. I offer some introductory remarks to help students make their way through the labyrinthine literatures of poststructural writers. The major poststructural writers who have influenced not only curriculum theorists but also scholars across the disciplines are these: Jacques Derrida, Michel Foucault, Judith Butler, Gilles Deleuze, Felix Guattari, Michel Serres, Bruno Latour, Donna Haraway, Emmanuel Levinas, Helene Cixous, Julia Kristeva, and Slavoj Zizek. As Michael Peters (1996) points out,

> Poststructuralist thought has its origins in Alexandre Kojeve's and Jean Hyppolite's existentialist readings of G. W. F. Hegel and is foreshadowed in the structuralism of Jacques Lacan, Roman Jakobson, Claude Levi-Strauss and others. Here the master discipline is linguistics (following Ferdinand de Saussure) in both its structuralist and poststructural modes in its seemingly endless developments and theoretical refinements of analysis: semiotics, schizoanalysis, deconstructionism and discourse analysis. (p. 1)

Poststructuralism, generally speaking, is about discourse, language, uncertainty, the suspicion of the notion of progress. It is also about power, politics, ethics, notions of responsibility, and the crisis of representation (Derrida, 1995a; Foucault 1972). For some, like Judith Butler (1990), poststructuralism is about the notion of gender performativity. For others, like Michel Serres (2000), it is about nonlinear notions of time and multiplicities. Deleuze and Guattari (2000) introduce notions of deterritorialization, transversality, desiring machines, and schizoanalysis. For Donna Haraway (1997), it is about the posthuman. For Zizek (2009), it is about gaps and discontinuities. For Derrida (1995a), it is about the aporia and undecidables. James Williams (2005) tells us that poststructuralism is

> a thorough disruption of our secure sense of meaning and reference in language, of our understanding of our senses in the arts, of our understanding of identity, of our sense of history and its role in the present, and of our understanding of language as something free of the work of the unconscious. (p. 3)

The main point in the above citation is that for poststructuralists our understanding of reality is no longer secure. The uncertainty of thought—in all these various manifestations—will be demonstrated in this chapter by exploring the works of the major poststructural thinkers and the ways in which curriculum theorists have been influenced by these thinkers.

Pinar, Reynolds, Slattery, and Taubman (1995) define poststructuralism this way. They state,

> In *Modern French Philosophy*, Vincent Descombes (1980) locates the emergence of poststructuralism in France in the 1960s as a response to the intellectual scene in Paris. In its very name poststructuralism reveals its ties to structuralism, and indeed poststructuralism is a response to those theories which purported to discover invariant structures in society, the human psyche, consciousness, history, and culture. Poststructuralism, then, is both an assault on structuralism and also an outgrowth of it. (p. 452)

As the above writers point out our knowledges, our consciousness, culture, and the notion of history are unhinged. Reality is not what it seems. Further, there is no longer a Kantian thing-in-itself. The signifier and the signified do not exactly correspond; there are no Cartesian clear and distinct ideas.

Like poststructuralism, postmodern thought shares many of these same ideas. For Jean-Francois Lyotard, postmodernism problematizes what is called the "grand metanarrative." Lyotard (1993) explains,

> I will use the term *modern* to designate any science that legitimates itself with reference to a metadiscourse of this kind making an explicit appeal to some grand

narrative, such as the dialectics of Spirit, the hermeneutics of meaning, the emancipation of the rational working subject, or the creation of wealth. (p. xxiii)

For Foucault (1979) change is produced by what he calls "micro-physics" of power (p. 160). There are no grand stories of emancipation in Foucault's *Discipline and Punish*. However, in other places— for example in his *History of Sexuality Volume 1* (1990)—Foucault seems to be ambivalent about notions of liberation, as Fredric Jameson (1993) reminds us (p. xix).

Pinar et al. (1995) describe postmodernism through the work of William E. Doll Jr. (1993) in remarking,

> In William E. Doll's (1993a) *A Post-Modern Perspective on Curriculum* we can see the emergence of a curriculum theory which incorporates...critiques of linear time, of reality as finally representable, of modernism, and of techno-rationality....We can also see the postmodern emphasis on flux, randomness, multiple interpretations, variancy, indeterminacy, and fluid relationships. (p. 503)

Postmodern scholars—like William Doll Jr. and Patrick Slattery (2006)— raise many of the same ideas of poststructural scholars. In fact, Patti Lather says that she "use[s] the terms interchangeably" (cited in Pinar et al., 1995, p. 504). Michael Peters (1996) argues, "'Postmodernism' and 'poststructuralism' are now so commonly conflated" (p. 19). Yet he draws a distinction between the two. Peters states,

> In general, I regard the term "postmodernism" as a broad cultural and aesthetic phenomenon with its original home in the American and European avant-gardes, in poetics and literary criticism and architecture....By contrast the genealogy of the term "poststructuralism," at least in its initial and developing formations, is clearly a distinctively French phenomenon, tied to innovations in structural linguistics. (p. 19)

I do not drive a wedge between postmodern thought and poststructural thought but rather collapse the two since so many similarities are evident in each. Like Patti Lather, it seems to me that postmodernism and poststructuralism are interchangeable. For the purposes of organization, however, I will refer to the thinkers I discuss here as poststructuralists.

General Overview of Chapter

Curriculum theorists have carved out at least four areas of thought in relation to poststructuralism: chaos and complexity theory, posthumanism, postformalism, and poststructural ethics and politics. Michel Foucault, Jacques Derrida, and Emmanuel Levinas are three major figures upon whom curriculum theorists have drawn recently. Throughout this chapter I will introduce the work of curriculum theorists and show how they draw on a variety of poststructural thinkers.

A Notion of Thought: Poststructuralism

In this first section, I begin with what poststructural thinkers think about the notion of thought. What is a thought? Where do thoughts come from? Emmanuel Levinas (1985) remarks that thought

> probably begins through traumatisms or gropings to which one does not even know how to give a verbal form: a separation, a violent scene, a sudden consciousness of the monotony of time. It is from the reading of books—not necessarily philosophical—that these initial shocks become questions and problems, giving one to think. (p. 21)

What strikes me in this passage is that for Levinas, thought (poststructural thought) comes about through a struggle. Thought does not come easily: one almost has to be shocked into thought. These thoughts come slowly as a groping for Levinas. Groping in the dark implies that the many paths toward thought are uncertain ones: to grope is to be uncertain. For Levinas, further, thought comes from the study of other people's work: scholars only come to thought through the thinking of others. Levinas was a Holocaust survivor so he feels, perhaps, that traumas like the Holocaust give rise to thought. What kind of thought emerges from trauma? This as an open question for now but I will come back to this toward the end of this chapter. Thought for Levinas comes through intellectual work, which is slow, since one "gropes." To build ideas takes time and hard work.

In contradistinction to Levinas, Gilles Deleuze and Felix Guattari (1994) suggest that the "problem of thought" is not its slowness but its speed. Deleuze and Guattari tell us,

> From Epicurus to Spinoza…from Spinoza to Michaux the problem of thought is infinite speed. But this speed requires a milieu that moves infinitely in itself—the plane, the void, the horizon. Both elasticity of the concept and fluidity of the milieu are needed. Both are needed to make up "the slow beings" that we are. (p. 36)

The thing about thought for Deleuze and Guattari, then, is being able to capture its speed. Writing on computers, rather than writing with a pen or typewriter, helps to capture the speed of thought. The mind is incredibly complex and quick and the pen cannot keep up with the pace of thought. The irony in the above passage is that Deleuze and Guattari say also that people are "slow beings." So perhaps thought is both fast and slow. Scholars slow down thoughts when crafting paragraphs that serve to separate ideas and help make sense of things. Readers would never be able to follow if ideas are not developed. And it takes time to develop ideas. But thought in the mind differs from thought on the page. In our minds many thoughts are going on at the same time and they are fast and they are slow simultaneously. Moreover, Freud suggests that there is always an undercurrent of thought that cannot be accessed: the unconscious. So, too, there are thoughts that are not even available to the thinker.

How Do Scholars Come to a Thought?

How do scholars come to a thought at all? Eva Krugly-Smolska (2001) draws on the work of Gaston Bachelard who argues that thought comes only through obstacles (p. 45). Krugly-Smolska says of Bachelard,

> While the understanding of an obstacle as a hindrance is very much in evidence in his work, there is also a positive aspect to it, in that obstacles can be the driving force for the evolution of scientific thought. (p. 45)

Bachelard was a philosopher of science. But he was a poetic philosopher, not one usually associated with the Western tradition of philosophy because his work is considered too soft. The Jungians have embraced Bachelard because his work speaks to their own. Bachelard takes the basic scientific elements like earth, air, fire, and water and writes poetically about them. In many ways, he is like the pre-Socratics who also worked on the basic elements, like water, fire, air, and so forth.

The point here, again, is about how one comes to a thought. Bachelard is closer to Levinas on this issue as both suggest that coming to a thought means slowness, blockage, and in the case of Levinas (1985) groping (p. 21) and for Bachelard obstacles. There is a certain abyss when one engages thought. Things are always getting in the way of thought, as Bachelard might put it, and these obstacles actually open up pathways to thought. One cannot get stuck in the obstacle, however, but rather one must use it to build ideas. Frustration is probably the greatest friend a scholar can have. Without frustration and the climb over the abyss one is stuck in the everyday.

In order to come to thought, scholars need a new language; that is what theory offers. But a new language is only acquired, as Levinas puts it, through reading books and studying the work of others. Thought is never singular. No one lives in a vacuum. Our thoughts come from our studies, our experiences, and the larger sociopolitical and historical backdrop into which we are thrown. But thought is never easy. It comes quickly, slowly, or not at all. Heidegger (1962) suggested in *Being and Time* that thought comes in the clearing. Think of the forest and how dense the trees in a forest are. That density is like the mind. To get to the clearing in the forest (of the mind) one must work hard; many wrong steps will be taken. One day an opening emerges. This opening is the clearing. Patti Lather's (2007) book *Getting Lost*—which I will discuss later—deals with the ways in which thought gets lost or the ways in which one loses one's way while trying to think through something that is unthinkable such as AIDS. For Lather poststructural philosophy helped her to understand that there is little certainty in the world of AIDS. Life is uncertain and at every turn death hovers.

For Judith Butler (1990) thought is always already engendered. Butler argues that gender is performed. She states,

> In this sense, gender is not a noun, but neither is it a set of free-floating attributes, for we have seen that the substantive effects of gender is performativity produced and compelled by the regulatory practices of gender coherence. Hence, within the inherited discourse of the metaphysics of substance, gender proves to be performative. (pp. 24–25)

Thus, for Butler thought must be engendered and gender is a performance. There is nothing static about the notion of gender since it is a social construction, always on the move. Thoughts do not emerge from disembodied people; they emerge from engendered people, raced people, and classed people as well.

The Unthinkable

Poststructural thought engages with that which is unthinkable, such as AIDS; it is, as Levinas (1985) might have put it, a traumatism (p. 21) that is beyond the thinkable. Yet scholars still must try to think what is unthinkable: that is the conundrum Lather faced as she thought through a book she wrote on women living with AIDS.

Madness and Thought

Gilles Deleuze, in a book by Felix Guattari called *Chaosophy: Texts and Interviews 1972–1977*, says that thought entails two things: "a breaking through, and a collapse" (2009, p. 65). Deleuze notes: "I'm reminded of a letter of Van Gogh. 'It's a question,' he wrote, 'of breaking through a wall'" (p. 65). To think is to break through something. Deleuze suggests that having a thought is akin to being mad. Deleuze talks about thought in the context of the madness of Artaud, Nietzsche, Van Gogh, and others. Deleuze and Guattari (2000), in their book *Anti-Oedipus: Capitalism and Schizophrenia*, were quite interested in exploring issues of insanity and the problems of the psychiatric treatment of the mentally ill. Foucault (1988), too, was interested in where psychiatry went wrong in his book *Madness and Civilization*. When Van Gogh says that thought comes by "breaking through a wall," Deleuze tells us, and then by a "collapse" (p. 65), it makes one think differently about how one comes to thought.

Thought Unsure of Itself

The difference between a modern conception of thought and a poststructural one is that the moderns thought that they were sure of what they were doing. The history of Western philosophy up to about WWI turned on epistemological questions like: How do we know what we know? The philosophical tradition in the West is based on notions of certainty or solving a problem. Poststructural philosophy, on the other hand, is not so sure of itself. Foucault thought that Western philosophy was asking the wrong question to begin with.

For Foucault, one comes to a thought by studying things historically. History is thought for Foucault, and history is anything but linear (e.g., see his books *The Order of Things: An Archaeology of the Human Sciences* [1994] and *The Archaeology of Knowledge & the Discourse on Language* [1972]).

Brent Davis and Poststructural Thought

Curriculum theorist Brent Davis (1996) has some interesting ideas on what I would consider to be poststructural thought. Davis remarks:

Our mathematical knowledge, like our language, our literature, and our art, is neither "out there" nor "in here," but exists and consists in our acting. As such the character of our knowledge changes with every action, as do the characters of the agent and of the world. (p. 79)

Drawing on the work of Varela, Thompson, and Rosch (p. 11), Davis calls his work "enactivism." Here, our actions are our thoughts and our thoughts get acted out as they get thought out. Hannah Arendt (1979) said something similar to this when she suggested thought and action go hand in hand. You cannot act without thought and your thoughts change your actions. Our theory gets acted out in the world and can serve to change the world. As Marx said, the point of writing is to change the world. And one could also connect this to discussions of theory/praxis. Scholars need theory in order to teach. Doctors need theories in order to practice. Poststructural theory, however, is not sure of itself; it hesitates before the world and turns ideas in ways that differ from modernist philosophy. Brent Davis (1996) puts it this way:

An important upshot of this move from "the world as given" [as was thought by modernist philosophers] to "the world as unfolding through a choreography of action" is that the modern Cartesian desire to know the world *as it is* is thoroughly frustrated. The universe is constantly evolving, forever eluding any attempt to fix and know it. (p. 13)

The world "as it is" is always mediated through culture. So the ways in which people interpret the world are shaped by culture. There is so little that people really understand. This is the gist of poststructural thought.

Gaps, Chaos, and Weariness

In this section I would like to paint a collage of poststructural ideas to show that they serve to undo our certainties about anything. This will be a study of concepts. These concepts make up part of the poststructural landscape. Here I discuss some of the major concepts that poststructural thinkers explore. Here, too, I will begin to introduce some curriculum theorists who draw on these concepts. As I discuss these concepts, try to think of them together, as a collage or portrait.

So let us begin with the concept "gap." Slavoj Zizek (2009) says that the world is like a "gap [that is]...irreducible and insurmountable, a gap which posits a limit to the field of reality" (p. 10). When trying to explain the world, or reality, one cannot because there is a gap between what is seen and how one articulates what is seen. But there is more to it than this for Zizek, who adds the concept "parallax" to gap. He states that there is

> the occurrence of an insurmountable *parallax gap*, the confrontation of two closely linked perspectives between which no neutral common ground is possible….The notion of the parallax gap provides the key which enables us to discern its subversive core. (p. 4)

So the "parallax gap" is the gap between my way of interpreting the world and your way of interpreting the world and the complete and utter disagreement between us. Your language, the way you re-present things, is completely incompatible with the way that I might interpret the world and re-present things. There is, as Zizek says, no common ground between us. The parallax gap is the noncommunication between us. Thus, we do not really ever talk to each other and we never really agree on anything because there is no such thing as a common perspective. So when we think about the notion of the commons, or something that is commonplace, or the common school, the parallax gap problematizes these ideas. There is no meeting place for two people to come to an agreement. In other words, we do not understand each other, ever. This could also be called, as Levinas (1985) might put it, "absolute alterity." This position is the complete reversal of what is called "liberal humanism," where it is thought that human beings are alike and can understand each other because we share a common culture. Conversely, Zizek is suggesting that people do not have a common culture. One can think of this problem generationally. Consider a book called *The Gutenberg Elegies*, by Sven Birkerts (2006), who states,

> In the Fall of 1992 I taught a course called "The American Short Story" to undergraduates at a local college. I assembled a set of readings that I thought would appeal to the tastes of the average undergraduate…We would begin with Washington Irving, then move on quickly to Hawthorne, Poe, James, and Jewett.…But then came Henry James's "Brooksmith" and I was completely derailed.…My students could barely muster the energy for a thumbs-up or-down.…I asked: Was it the difficulty with the language.…Was it vocabulary, sentence length, syntax? "Yeah, sort of," said one student, "but it was more just the whole thing." (pp. 17–18)

As Zizek puts it there is a parallax gap between generations and professors such as Birkerts cannot understand why students don't like "the whole thing." This is more than simply a generation gap, it is a parallax gap. The older we get as professors, the younger the students seem to get. And the younger they get, the more the gap widens. Professors and students talk completely different languages and live in completely different universes. There is no bridging the gap between us. So what professors teach, students don't get. They do not see the relevance of reading the books we grew up with. As professors try to relate to the younger generation, they text in class, answer their cell phones, and surf the Internet while we teach. This is the complaint that Birkerts makes in his book. William Pinar (2012) is skeptical of all things cyberspace. Tweeting, Facebook, email, and texting keep these youngsters entertained but only serve to get in the way of students' education. There is a parallax gap here. So what to do? How to bridge this gap? According to Zizek, this is impossible. The parallax gap is a disturbing phenomenon in the classroom. But it is even more than this. These gaps, Zizek points out, are insurmountable (p. 10).

Brent Davis (1996) writes about gaps: "Consonant with this effort, the text is incomplete. It has gaps, discontinuities, inconsistencies, and loose ends. It lacks the structure and conclusive certainty of a deductive (and seductive) logical argument" (pp. xxvii–xxviii). The mark of a poststructural text is that the writer admits that he—and in this case Davis—has incomplete thoughts and even inconsistencies in thought. That people are contradictory beings is a poststructural admission.

Discontinuities

Speaking of gaps and discontinuities, Michel Foucault (1972) has written one of the most important books on the notion of discontinuities in the poststructural literature. In *The Archaeology of Knowledge & the Discourse on Language*, Foucault points out,

> The problem is no longer one of tradition, of tracing a line, but one of division, of limits; it is no longer one of lasting foundations, but one of transformations that serve as new foundations, the rebuilding of foundations. What one is seeing, then, is the emergence of a whole field of questions....How is one to specify the different concepts that enable us to conceive of discontinuity (threshold, rupture, break, mutation, transformation)? (p. 5)

Again, for Foucault it is through the study of history that students learn about discontinuity. History is not one grand metanarrative with a plot structure. It is the simultaneity of many experiences happening in different ways and people perceiving history in different ways. History is not one story. There are multiple histories. The study of history allows us to open up a "whole field of questions" (p. 5) that were not apparent before. Studying the ways in which history gets represented shows that there are gaps and discontinuities in perspectives. Foucault suggests that the study of history is about interpretation and that our interpretations serve as breaks and ruptures (p. 5). Our knowledge is not linear; it is constantly mutating with newer findings. Knowledge is in no way static, it is always on the move: it is always changing just as the world changes. For the poststructuralist there is no foundation for knowledge, but only new ways of looking at things that are built on old ways of seeing. The new comes out of the old and transforms the old. This is what archaeologists do. They keep digging and building, but with each artifact, old knowledge cracks and breaks open to new things. Furthermore, the study of artifacts has little to do with "facts" but rather with interpretations. When archaeologists go on digs and find things buried in the ground, they offer to us interpretations of these artifacts and put together stories based on what artifacts they find. But as time marches on and more artifacts are found the stories continue to shift and change. This is what knowledge is. Perhaps Zizek's parallax gap will help us to understand the shifting nature of the contradictions of knowledge. To know is to unknow; to learn is to unlearn: there is little in the way of Truth. The poststructural world is not the world of Plato. Poststructural philosophy is not the quest for Truth. Poststructuralists are not searching for the eternals, or unchanging truths. Poststructuralists are not on a quest for indubitable things, as was Descartes. Nothing is indubitable. There are no categorical imperatives as Kant believed. Our actions are not driven by categorical imperatives. There are no rules to follow, no guidelines for our actions. This is in an unstable time, even more unstable than when Foucault was alive. It is this very instability, however, that propels thought.

Leaving Behind

But how to understand? Both Jacques Derrida and Gilles Deleuze agree on this point: scholars must leave complacency behind in order to try to think things otherwise. Let us start with this question: What does leaving mean? Jacques Derrida (2004) takes the notion of leaving literally when he tells us,

> I am tempted to call my states of travel *commotions*....To travel [and he means this literally] is to give oneself over to commotion: to the unsettling that, as a result, affects one's being down to the bone, puts everything up for grabs. (p. 36)

Derrida, then, comes to new thoughts through travel. As he suggests, traveling puts one into a state of commotion that allows thought to be generated. The work of thinking, as Derrida notes, is the work of being unsettled.

Leaving and Learning

Like Derrida, Deleuze says students must leave in order to learn. But for Deleuze leaving isn't that easy or straightforward. This is his concept of "lines of flight." Deleuze (2009) tells us, "In every social system, there have always been lines of flight [which is a form of leaving], and then also a rigidification to block off escape" (pp. 46–47). A line of flight is a new way of thinking, but new ways of thinking—especially in the academy—are blocked by conservatism or even fascism. Felix Guattari (2009), in his book *Chaosophy: Texts and Interviews 1972–1977*, has a chapter titled "Everybody Wants to Be a Fascist." Guattari suggests that there is a fascist (propensity) in all of us. That is called the superego in Freudian terms. The sadistic superego is the fascist of the psyche. As Claire Colebrook (2008) reminds us, "In his preface to *Anti-Oedipus* Foucault points out that the task of Deleuze and Guattari's work is to guard against the 'micro-fascisms' in us all" (p. 36). Fascists are the ones who "block" the "lines of flight" about which Deleuze (pp. 46–47) speaks. Or, let us put it another way. (Here I am reminded of the work of Melanie Klein [1946/1984] and her work on envy.) People who are envious try to block the other's creativity, action, living. Envious people can be fascists in the Deleuzian sense. Envious people do not like to see others succeed, so they try to cut off their line of flight, as Deleuze would put it.

Curriculum theorist Kaustuv Roy (2003), in his book *Teachers in Nomadic Spaces: Deleuze and Curriculum*, suggests that scholars have to be nomads—travelers—to get anything done, intellectually. Roy explains that for Deleuze,

> The notion of "deterritorialization" [is]…a movement by which we *leave the territory*, or move away from spaces regulated by dominated systems of signification that keep us confined within old patterns, in order to make new connections. (p. 21)

Deterritorialization is a major concept for Deleuze. As Roy points out, this concept suggests that people find a way out of oppressive situations by leaving or getting out of the way. But how to leave? Scholars are thrown into a controlled culture, a controlled academy, where only certain things count as scholarship. The "spaces regulated by dominated systems" (as pointed out by Roy) are nearly impossible to break open or escape. The purpose of a university is to conserve tradition. The scholar who tries to do new things or to break open new territories will soon find that he or she will be subject to fascistic crackdowns. This is why Derrida (2005), in a book called *Rogues: Two Essays on Reason*, talks of a "democracy-to-come" (p. 11) because democracies are in process but not yet there. And this is why Derrida talks about a "university without condition" (p. 11), because universities are not democratic.

Deleuze and Guattari (2000) write about schizophrenia and suggest that the schizophrenic "scrambles all the codes" (p. 15). Thought becomes possible only when the codes are scrambled. Inna Semetsky, in her book, *Nomadic Education: Variations on a Theme by Deleuze and Guattari* (2008), remarks, "*Transcoding* is one Deleuzian neologism used to underline an element of creativity, of invention" (p. xi). Perhaps professors can find some freedom of expression in scrambling codes or in what Derrida (1986) calls "graphic disorder" (p. 3). Speaking in code and in graphic disorder is a way to elude the authorities. Subjugated peoples have always spoken in code to elude their colonizers.

Is the schoolhouse a place of colonization? Kaustuv Roy (2003) seems to think so. Roy notes,

> The inability to *think* difference in most institutional settings makes such attempts at transformation crucial. This is especially so in colonized spaces of which the urban school setting is a prime example. Deleuzian concepts place us in a transformational matrix, a space of potential difference through which passes, from time to time, a spike of lightning that is the active realization of the transformative power of life. (n.p.)

By "scrambling all the codes" (Deleuze & Guattari, 2000, p. 15) scholars might be able to—as Roy points out—find those "spaces of potential difference...and spike[s] of lightning" that allow us to "transform" our thinking and our lives.

Time Scrambled

Scrambled codes and graphic disorders are interesting because they also reflect the notion of time. Time is a scrambled code (Deleuze & Guattari) and a Derridean graphic disorder. But Michel Serres (1995 writes,

> Time does not always flow according to a line...nor according to a plan but rather, according to an extraordinary complex mixture, as though it reflected stopping points,

ruptures, deep wells, chimneys of thunderous acceleration, rending gaps—all sown at random, at least in a visible disorder. (p. 57)

Time is about gaps, but there is more to it than that. For Serres, time is not a straight line, it is all disorder. If it both stops and moves ahead in "thunderous acceleration," then one cannot get a sense of what time is. It is confusing. Notice, too, that Serres says that time has no plan. One cannot straightjacket a thought and one cannot plan a curriculum without the possibility of break-downs, ruptures, as Serres put it, or stoppage. On the other hand, sometimes when things go well, one experiences this sense of "thunderous acceleration," as Serres (p. 57) notes, when thoughts come seamlessly and effortlessly. But these experiences are rare. All classroom experiences differ because the sense of time teachers have in the classroom differs depending on what they are talking about, the possible disruptions, not only of students, but of our own thoughts, and the psychological baggage carried into the classroom. For those students who are trying to pay attention, to attend to the meaning of what teachers are trying to teach, there is always a delay in their understanding—if they ever understand at all. Derrida (1991) speaks to this point as he suggests,

> The structure of delay (*Nachtraglichkeit*) in effect forbids that one can make of tem-poralization [or time] a simply dialectical complication of the living present as an originary and unceasing synthesis—a synthesis constantly directed back on itself, gathering in on itself. (p. 73)

There is always a delay in the temporalization of knowledge or of under-standing for both the teacher and student. The students experience a delay of temporalization in digesting the material at hand. They might not get it immediately—if at all.

Seeking Passage: Rebecca Martusewicz

To synthesize is to put together disparate parts of things, to "seek passages," as Rebecca Martusewicz (2001) puts it. Martusewicz tells us that Michel Serres helped her to find her way through labyrinthine ideas and to "seek passage"— to make sense of disparate concepts. She states,

> The work of Michel Serres has been inspirational to me, not only for its breadth and depth but also for the courage Serres has for navigating difficult passages be-tween seemingly unrelated and unrelatable terms or bodies of knowledge. For Serres, the natural sciences, mathematics, literature, mythology, and philosophy have been

islands of thought that when linked inform us of the political and cultural landscape that is human life. (p. 9)

Seeking passage, as Martusewicz puts it—drawing on Serres—does not necessarily mean synthesizing in neat and tidy ways knowledges that are seemingly unrelatable. It takes time to understand a writer like Serres and, as Derrida says, there is always a delay in understanding. The codes are always scrambled, as Deleuze and Guttari (2000) remind us. Scrambling codes is subversive yes, but perhaps that is what scholars are doing when trying to attempt to "seek passage." Professors are always jetlagged, as it were, in our thinking and in our teaching.

Patti Lather: Getting Lost

When talking of poststructuralism, Patti Lather (2007), in her book *Getting Lost: Feminist Efforts Toward a Double(d) Science*, works out of a Derridean and Deleuzian framework as she argues,

> Here, one might begin to think of a "new" new ethnography or a (post) ethnography, deferred and diffused across disciplines and working in borders and wrestling with urgent questions in moving into postfoundational practices. In postfoundational thought…one epistemologically situates oneself as curious and unknowing. This is a methodology of "getting lost." (p. 9).

The field of ethnography is not past, or dead, but has moved—at least for Lather—in the poststructural frame of delayed meaning and unknowables. Ethnographers cannot get at the Truth, they cannot represent what they see with any certainty and they know that representation is perspectival and socially constructed. Lather also means that when doing an ethnography the ethnographer cannot be so sure that what she writes will be understood either by her participants or by her readers. If the poststructural ethnographer enters the scene of ethnography in a state of curiosity and unknowing, the project at hand will raise more questions. The issues of what Lather calls the "postfoundational" can also be traced back to pragmatist philosophy.

Cleo Cherryholmes on Pragmatism and Poststructuralism

Cleo Cherryholmes (1999), in his book *Reading Pragmatism*, argues that pragmatism could be considered a form of poststructural thought as pragmatism is inductive. It anticipates where we might go from where we are. The properties of inductive argument lead pragmatists to reject essentialism, representationalism, and foundationalism. These characteristics of pragmatism, as I read them, describe a poststructural way of looking at the world. (p. 9)

Like Cherryholmes, Morris Dickstein (1999) suggests that Dewey returned to "jostle Derrida, Lacan and Foucault" (p. 17). What he means by this is that the renewed interest in pragmatism—or what is called neopragmatism—coincides with the interest in poststructuralism. Dewey—as well as some of the other pragmatists like William James—talked of antifoundational thinking and of the uncertainties of the nature of thought itself.

The Problem with Method: William Doll Jr.

Lather (2007) speaks of (post) ethnography as a sort of methodology (p. 9). This concept of methodology troubles. Derrida's deconstruction, as he points out, is not a method. In Hans-Georg Gadamer's (1975) book *Truth and Method*, he contends that there is no truth in method. William Doll (1998) has written over the course of his career about his own suspicion about this "blessed rage for order" (see David Tracy, 1996) and method and traces these concepts of control back to Peter Ramus in the 16th century. Ramus, says Doll, "provided a map of all knowledge…and this map was carefully and definitively ordered" (p. 304). The fallout of this blessed rage for method and order, Doll says, haunts us in "curriculum methods courses" (p. 304). How can curriculum have a method? What methods do professors offer to students in a (post) 9/11 world? 9/11 is not dead, not post, but ever with us as Americans are constantly living out the memory of the Twin Towers crashing to the ground. The media showed these "graphic disorder[s]"—as Derrida (1986, p. 3) might put it—over and over again as if to instill in us a permanent nationwide post-traumatic stress (graphic) disorder. Michel Foucault (1994) likewise writes about *The Order of Things* and the methods used by academics to try to put things in order, to flatten out history, and make history seem like a seamless sameness. But ordering things, ordering disciplines, for example, is—in actuality—arbitrary. Method and logic hide the fact that anything can be put in any order. The ordering of the disciplines could have been completely different than they are today. Academic disciplines grew out of chaos and chance, not order and method. The upshot of this discussion is that scholars have to be careful when using the concept of method, especially in a poststructural context. Method harkens back to logic, order, and control in a world that is illogical, out of control, and out of order. Lather (2007) talks about "getting lost" but I do not think getting lost needs a method or has a method or is even an epistemology.

William Reynolds and Julie Webber on Dis/Positions

William Reynolds and Julie Webber (2004), in their edited collection titled *Expanding Curriculum Theory: Dis/Positions and Lines of Flight*, speak to the problem of method in the context of curriculum theorizing. In a Deleuzian fashion they argue

> The curriculum theory field is used as an example of the type of thinking that can dis/position in general. This line of flight research is connected by its shared concern for viewing educational phenomena from alternative perspectives that are not method driven, but instead draw from the insights of a disposition that seeks to disentangle research from its traditional dependence on formalities. (p. 10)

Two things to comment on here: First, Reynolds and Webber argue that doing curriculum theory has little to do with method; second, that scholars should "dis" the positions formally taken previously in the curriculum field. In other words, what these authors suggest through the use of nomadic thinking—as they draw on Deleuze—is that curriculum theorists should be freed up from positioning themselves inside of a category, but rather work in a more no-madic way to go wherever their thinking takes them. To "dis" the positions is to try to move beyond formalities of theoretical frameworks and think more in terms of Deleuzian lines of flight. However, scholars do take positions and do have theoretical frameworks that remain rather consistent throughout their academic careers. But staying within a particular theoretical framework does not mean being method driven. Reynolds and Webber, in fact, do take a position—Deleuzian poststructuralism—to "dis" the positions. So have they dissed the positions? I am not so sure. In essence they are still working inside of a position, or within a particular theoretical framework: to be completely (un)framed is impossible. Scholars all have a framework around which they work, otherwise scholarship would be chaotic. In order for readers to under-stand us, scholars must work inside of a frame—even in poststructuralism, which tries to dis-frameworks. Poststructuralism is still a frame, even as it tries to rid itself of its frame—especially in the Deleuzian tradition. Wen-Song Hwu (2004), commenting on the work of Jacques Daignault, who also works in a Deleuzian manner, suggests that "Daignault did not propose that we should stop defining but, on the contrary, to *multiply* the definitions, to invite a plu-ral spelling" (p. 183). The curriculum field has worked in multiples as it has expanded, as Reynolds and Webber point out, by adding new frames and com-bining frames. That is, scholars cross over theoretical frameworks and work in several areas at once. Postcolonialism, psychoanalysis, and poststructuralism can be used simultaneously to broaden the conversation, for example. This is what Daignault might think of as "invite[ing] a plural spelling" (Hwu, p. 183).

Perhaps interdisciplinarity is the movement of the Deleuzian nomad about which Reynolds and Webber speak. Some more conservative critics might argue that this kind of scholarship is too all over the place (the nomadic wandering from topic to topic). Still, there is a framework out of which no-madic wanderings spring. When Reynolds and Webber talk about loosening up the formalities of curriculum scholarship, maybe this is what they mean. Finding a so-called research agenda means—traditionally—that the schol-ar writes about one idea for the remainder of her career. But for curriculum theorists research agendas shift and are indeed more nomadic than in other disciplines because that is the nature of our work. So in this way, our work has loosened formalities because of the interdisciplinary nature of it and also because many of us work inside of several theoretical frames simultaneously. Recall what Deleuze (2009) says in the context of the work of Van Gogh. He states: "I'm reminded of a letter of Van Gogh. 'It's a question,' he wrote, of breaking through a wall'" (p. 65). Breaking through a wall suggests breaking down the boundaries between theoretical frameworks to work through sev-eral simultaneously. Still, scholars tend to work in one major area and spin that area through different frames. This is where the concept of epistemology becomes problematic because curriculum theorists—who are drawn toward poststructuralism—are not interested in this problem. Perhaps philosophers of education still wonder about the question of how we know what we know (epistemology), but curriculum theorists' work is much broader than that. As Foucault teaches, epistemology as the topic of philosophy since Plato has led us astray. Epistemology leads us in the wrong direction. To raise the question of epistemology is to raise the wrong question. Rather, for Foucault, studying ideas and the formation of the disciplines teach that we do not know how we know and that ideas and the formation of academic disciplines are arbitrary. Knowledge, ideas, and academic disciplines are tenuous. Interdisciplinarity is about "getting lost," as Patti Lather (2007) put it. And Deleuze and Guattari (2000) suggest again that one should "scramble all the codes" (p. 15) because this reflects more closely what life is like, it is a scramble. Getting scrambled means letting go of ego control and, in a more psychoanalytic way, allowing what is unconscious to speak. There is no order in the unconscious—this was Freud's message. Freely associating is unlocking the ego and letting go of internal censorship and ultimately means getting lost in thought. If the unconscious drives thought, thought is, at bottom, about disorder and scramble. Unconscious thought goes wherever it pleases. As Derrida (1986) might put it, the unconscious is a form of "graphic disorder" (p. 3). Also Derrida (1991) suggests that alterity is the heart of the unconscious. He states,

> The alterity of the "unconscious" makes us concerned not with horizons of modified—past or future—presents, but with a "past" that has never been present, and which never will be, whose future to come will never be a production or a reproduction in the form of presence. (p. 73)

The Past and Digressions

The past is about time. What one remembers about the past is not what actually transpired. One does not remember things literally. Our memories are subject to alterity, to alterations and to fictionalizing, filling in the blanks, changing things to fit the present, or erasing parts of the past that are unbearable. The past is not a "presence," that is, something that can be described as real, as solid, as true. The past, Derrida (1991) says, is like a trace (p. 73). A trace is hazy and fades. Our past(s) fade. Childhood is but a trace. Not that the past does not exist, but it is only a trace in our memory because most of it gets forgotten and gets buried deeply in the unconscious. Much of it one can never retrieve—especially if one suffers from "graphic disorder"—as Derrida puts it—or posttraumatic stress disorder.

This sense of graphic disorder is also related to what Deleuze and Guattari (1994) think of the discipline of philosophy in general. They state: "From this point of view, philosophy can be seen as being in a perpetual state of digression or digressiveness" (p. 23). One could also say this about the history of curriculum theory. Studying this field is like being in a "perpetual state of digression" (Deleuze & Guattari, p. 23). As one works to theorize concepts and theorize the various sectors of the field it seems that the discussion is a constant "becoming"—to use the notion of Deleuze and Guattari. This becoming digresses from one sector to the next, with overlaps, holes, intersections, gaps, and repetitions. The unconscious, the trace, power, and control are concepts that are found in several sectors of the field so that the discussion digresses in various directions as the concepts of curriculum get fleshed out. One segment of the field digresses into another it seems. Digression is the way in which the unconscious drives the mind. Freely associating means digressing, going hither and yon, without censorship. So scholars are continually disgressing, repeating, overlapping, and creating holes and gaps. Exclusions or gaps might be unconscious. Hence, the project is never finished. There are always gaps in texts.

Chaotic Time

Books are written in a sort of chaotic time. Jacques Daignault (2008) says,

> On several remarkable pages inspired by a book by D. H. Lawrence Deleuze and Guattari portray creators as the courageous beings who risk their lives by stealing a piece of chaos from Time....We are, however, too slow and too fragile to inhabit the more turbulent and chaotic zones where problematic Ideas reside. Still, how do we gain access? (p. 49)

Perhaps scholars are not "too slow and too fragile" to get into chaotic and turbulent zones (which is terminology that is used by chaos theory). Perhaps scholars just do not want to feel that chaos and turbulence because it is uncomfortable. But letting ourselves feel the chaos and turbulence allows for new avenues of thought to emerge. Recall, Derrida says he needs commotion to think. Commotion is a form of turbulence that allows for new thought.

Isolation

Mostly, what one needs in order to write and think through difficult ideas—like the ones I am exploring in poststructuralism—is isolation. Michel Serres (1995) speaks to this point when he says,

> New ideas come from the desert, from hermits, from those who live in retreat and are not plunged into the sound and fury of repetitive discussion. All the money that is scandalously wasted nowadays on colloquia should be spent on building retreat houses, with vows of reserve and silence. (pp. 81–82)

I agree with Serres that our money would be better spent, and our time would be better spent, going to writers' retreats, like artists do. Our time would be better spent in a cabin in the woods to write. Atul Gawande (2002) says,

> The anthropologist Lawrence Cohen describes conferences and conventions not so much as scholarly goings-on but as carnivals—colossal events where academic proceedings are overshadowed by professional politics, ritual enactments of disciplinary boundaries, sexual liminality, tourism and trade, personal and national rivalries, the care and feeding of professional kinship. (p. 84)

Sometimes conferences interfere with doing scholarship. Scholarship is a private activity that needs to be guarded. Isolation is a must. Working in a university, too, makes it hard to find the time to be alone and write.

Poststructuralism Is Digression

The digressions I take in this chapter are part of the poststructural project: the most interesting things are explored when one thinks sideways rather than linearly. Digressions are the stuff of writing and this is something that Derrida (2000a) was adamant about. He talks about digressions in the context of the art of citation and what happens when scholars cite other texts. Citing always creates digressions because the citation takes a concept and moves it into another context and then the text changes meaning because it is now out of context. That is the way digressions work. Derrida explains:

> Every sign, linguistic or nonlinguistic, spoken or written…in a small or large unit, can be *cited*, put between citation marks; in so doing it can break with every given context [this break constitutes a digression], engendering an infinity of new contexts [which constitutes still more digressions] in a manner which is absolutely illimitable.…There are only contexts without any center or absolute anchor. (p. 12).

The work of scholarship, then, is putting things always out of context and digressing always away from a center or anchor. Thus, the work of scholarship is unstable and open to millions of micro-moves and alterations depending upon where the thought of the writer goes.

The Center Will Not Hold

This discussion reminds me of a book by Elyn R. Saks (2007) titled *The Center Cannot Hold: My Journey Through Madness*. This is a fascinating study of the way in which a scholar tries to hold together her psyche through studying philosophy, law, and psychiatry while she experiences episodes of psychosis. Psychotic breaks erode the feeling that there is a center or core to the self. Saks talks about watching her psyche deteriorate. This, too, was a fascination for Deleuze and Guattari, who wrote much about schizophrenia, especially in *Anti-Oedipus: Capitalism and Schizophrenia* (2000). Students learn from studying schizophrenia—or what Deleuze and Guattari call "schizoanalysis"—that the center (or ego) that most of us take for granted can disappear easily if we fall into psychosis. Now, I am not saying that one is psychotic when doing scholarship, but the process of doing scholarship, trying to hold together and structure concepts that slip out of context because every time we cite and digress, every time we interpret—as Derrida (2000a) teaches—we are moving farther and farther away from a center point. There is no center to a text that uses citations, so scholarship, although it is highly structured, has a bit of psychosis in it since we continually move away from the text to change the context of that text in order to form other texts, which yet again have other contexts.

It is interesting to note that Elyn Saks tells us that she was drawn to the study of philosophy because it helped her structure her thought, even though she was always fighting off her descents into psychosis. She remarks that philosophy is not unlike psychosis because it is highly abstract and difficult to understand. Poststructural philosophy resembles psychosis more so than does the philosophy of the moderns. Just think about Derrida's play with language. The play with language is almost maddening at times because it is so difficult to follow. Zizek, too, is very difficult to understand; sometimes one begins to wonder if his work doesn't resemble psychosis. Again, I am not saying that poststructural thought is madness, but at times it can resemble the thought patterns described by psychotics. This is the chaos and turbulence about which Jacques Daignault (2008) writes. Chaos and turbulence of thought—whether in philosophy, scholarship in general, or in psychosis—is a place that we do not want to go to. Nobody likes to feel that they are living in a chaotic state. But it is into this chaos that scholars must travel—the poststructuralists suggest—in order to get anywhere. Thought is by no means logical and the more logical one tries to make it the more illogical it becomes. Thought is by no means linear and people who try to make a straight line out of that which is curved or bent have a hard time getting to new spaces intellectually. Straight lines are straightjackets of thought. Modernist philosophy, especially that of Descartes, is problematic in this sense because Descartes tried to make everything a straight line. Indubitable principles or Kant's categorical imperatives are straight lines that do not get us very far and do not make much sense in our postmodern era where planes are crashing into skyscrapers and people are dying from AIDS and oil spills are ruining our coastlines. Cartesian and Kantian thought no longer makes sense in a world that is mostly violent and unpredictable. Nuclear proliferation was not something either of these modernist philosophers experienced. But history shows that people always find ways to torture other people (for more on this see Foucault's 1979 book *Discipline and Punish*) even if they don't have nuclear weapons. The world has always been a violent and unpredictable place. But the smashing of the atom made everything worse.

The Crisis of Representation

Foucault (1972) made much of what is now referred to as the "crisis of representation." That is, while looking at something, one has a hard time describing what one sees. Terry Tempest Williams (2001) writes about a recurring dream she has that describes the way a crisis of representation works in the unconscious. She tells us,

> Over dessert, I shared a recurring dream of mine. I told my father that for years as long as I could remember, I saw a flash of light in the night of the desert—that this image had so permeated my being that I could not venture south without seeing it again, on the horizon, illuminating buttes and mesas. (pp. 282–283)

The recurring dream Williams experienced could be a form of posttraumatic stress as the unconscious tries to send messages that the psyche cannot unpack. These dreams she experienced were actually memories of nuclear explosions that occurred in Utah between the years 1951 and 1962. The memories of nuclear testing were so hideous to her that she couldn't remember them as being real, but Williams's unconscious kept pushing them up to the surface. Here is a case of a crisis of representation. When you see something—especially when it is as traumatic as a nuclear explosion—you cannot, as Foucault (1994) puts it "say what you see" (p. 9). Patti Lather (2007)—in the context of trying to understand and write about working with women with AIDS—suggests, too, that writing about such a traumatic event creates a crisis of representation. Lather says, "The text becomes a site of the failures of representation and where textual experiments are not so much about solving the crisis of representation as about troubling the very claims to represent" (p. 37).

Thinking about the World Differently

In order to get us to think differently about the world and our place in it, Derrida (1992a) suggests that scholars study the Greek term *mochlos*. Derrida explains,

> Then we might say that the difficulty [of thinking otherwise] will consist, as always, in determining the best lever, what the Greeks would call the best *mochlos*. A *mochlos* could be a wooden beam, a lever for displacing a boat, a wedge for opening or closing a door, something, in short, to lean on for forcing or displacing. When one asks how to be oriented in history, morality or politics, the most serious discords and decisions have less often to do with ends...than with levers. (p. 31)

To displace a thought, to displace a trend or pattern, is to move between things using a wedge or lever. To displace something is to move a field along, but this movement, according to Derrida, comes in small spaces or small steps by wedges between ideas or levers that move things this way or that, up or down. However, this is a very different concept than the one that chaos theorists use when they talk about "level jumping" (Davis & Sumara, 2006). Level jumping suggests that large steps are taken in order for things (organic or inorganic) to change. Davis and Sumara explain level-jumping within the context of chaos theory:

> Complexity thinking [or chaos theory] prompts level-jumping between and among different layers of organization, any of which might be properly identified as complex and all of which influence (both enabling and constraining) one another. Complexity thinking also orients attentions toward other dynamic, complicated, and implicated levels, including the neurological, the experiential, the contextual, material, the symbolic, the cultural, and the ecological. Each of these levels/phenomena can be understood as enfolded. (p. 26)

So the enfolding of everything demands level-jumping, which implies that rather large moves are needed to enfold things. Changing phenomena—as the world is woven together in both chaotic and orderly patterns—demands jumping through levels. To jump, or to leap, is a very different kind of metaphor than the one that Derrida uses to talk about change, that is, *mochlos*. Recall, mochlos is like a wedge or lever that displaces things. It is in the small spaces that things move or change, for Derrida. In contradistinction, in complexity and chaos theory, jumping implies rather large shifts across multiple planes for change to occur. So for a field to change—that is, curriculum theory—Davis and Sumara might say (within the frame of chaos and complexity theory) that the reconceptualization shifted by level-jumping, by a large paradigm shift. The move from Ralph Tyler's rationale to William Pinar's notion of currere required not a lever or wedge—as Derrida might have put it—but a level-jump. The reconceptualization, as Pinar saw it, was more like a level-jump than a wedge between doorways. There are huge differences between the pre-reconceptualization and the reconceptualization. The (post) reconceptualization, however, is more like Derrida's notion of mochlos. The changes that have occurred in the field since, say, 1996 have been in increments. There are more segments that have been added to the field and more people crossing over into different theoretical frameworks, but those moves are more like levers or wedges, not level-jumping. Again, small shifts have occurred and new dimensions have been added, but once the reconceptualization was put into place the basic concepts of curriculum theory have remained.

Chaos and Complexity Theory: The Sciences and the Humanities

Chaos and complexity theory is a branch of poststructuralism that is based more in the sciences than in the humanities. Poststructuralists Michel Serres, Gaston Bachelard, Bruno Latour, and Donna Haraway have a science-based outlook on the world. But Serres and Bachelard—who were both philosophers of science—were also steeped in the humanities, so their work crosses over fields. Chaos and complexity theory draws little on the humanities for many but some straddle both the sciences and the humanities. Dennis Sumara, for instance, has worked both in chaos and complexity theory, as well as in the humanities, in literary studies, and in literacy. Others, too, have been working in chaos theory while straddling the sciences and the arts. M. Jayne Fleener (2002) straddles the sciences and the arts in her book *Curriculum Dynamics: Recreating Heart*. What is interesting about Fleener's work is that, like Serres, she crosses over disciplines to discuss chaos. She talks about spirituality, the humanities, as well as the sciences to make her points. She contends that chaos theory can be read as a way to recreate heart (p. 3). Fleener states,

> "Recreating heart" can be read in a variety of ways. Recreating heart is my vision of putting the heart back into schooling. Gandhi's notion of *Satygahraha* captures part of this meaning. *Satygahraha* is a plan of action for personal and social transformation. It connects meaning, truth, and spirit by emphasizing the "soul" work of transforming society. (p. 3)

Like Brent Davis's (1996) enactivism, Fleener argues that doing chaos theory in connection with spirituality allows us to change the world for the better and to change schooling for the better by giving it back its heart. Unlike Davis (1996) and Davis and Sumara (2006), Fleener's book works around the "interplay among religion, education, spirituality, and science…from the perspective of relational logic" (p. 5).

Another interesting book on chaos theory is co-edited by William Doll, M. Jayne Fleener, Donna Trueit, and John St. Julien (2005) titled *Chaos, Complexity, Curriculum and Culture: A Conversation*. This book is a good reader for students interested in the intersections of chaos theory and curriculum studies. In the introduction to this collection, Fleener (2005) explains,

> There is no consensus, nor should there be, on how to describe or define New Science [which includes chaos theory]. Typically, scholarship that refers to "New Science" includes the techniques and explorations of complex adaptive systems theory, the theory of dissipative structures, or chaos theory. Incorporated into the latter are chaos mathematics and dynamical systems theories. (p. 2)

The New Sciences are part of the poststructural paradigm. They are poststructural because they have moved beyond modernist frameworks. Unlike string theory or M-theory, Davis and Sumara point out that "complexity thinking makes no claim to be a 'theory of everything'" (p. 35). String theory or M-theory tries to explain everything in the universe.

M. Jayne Fleener, Mary Aswell Doll, and Noel Gough

Fleener (2005) integrates the humanities into the science of chaos and uses Vico as an example of an earlier theorist who also crossed over disciplines. Like Fleener, Mary Aswell Doll (2011), in her book *The More of Myth: A Pedagogy of Diversion*, has taken an interest in new science but mostly ties it back and relates it to mythology. Doll states

> The mystery of science, the mystery of myth: both fields are full of dynamic forces, energizing thought as reimagined matter. Myth matters. Its root stems from the Indo-European stem *my* found in myth, mystery, muttering, and mother (Doty, 2000, pp. 5–7). The searched-for T.O.E. (theory of everything) known as M-theory also has roots: membrane, murky, mystery, magic, mother, matrix, and monstrous (Greene, 2003, DVD). (p. 118)

That science has much in common with myth is a position Doll takes and is not unlike the position that Noel Gough (2001) takes about science being a fiction. Gough argues that the lines between science and fiction are not so clear. Gough states,

> Similarly, "science" and "fiction" do not exist in separate domains but are cultur-
> ally connected. This is not simply a matter of science and literature finding com-
> mon meeting places in SF and other forms of popular media….As Katherine Hayles
> (1984) demonstrates, "literature is as much an influence on scientific models as the
> models are on literature" (p. 10), insofar as there is a two-way traffic in metaphors,
> analogies and images between them. (p. 254)

Science is both fiction (Gough) and myth (Doll). Now, a conservative scientist would not be happy with either of these positions. Science—for a conservative scientist—has little to do with fiction or with myth.

But Michel Serres thinks differently. Serres (1995) grew discontented
with science (which I will talk about more later on) although his work is based
mostly on information theory. He embraces the humanities in the context of
his scientific background. Coming out of a science background, Serres draws
both on the sciences and humanities but his work is more playful than the
work of most chaos theorists. Michel Serres—especially in his book *Genesis*—
plays with language.

Understanding Curriculum Studies from a Poststructuralist Perspective

In this brief digression let us think about understanding our own discipline of
curriculum studies from a poststructural perspective. Many curriculum scholars
work in several areas at once (straddling the social sciences and the humanities
mostly) as I suggested earlier. Derrida (2002b) says of this that "whether one
wants it or not, one is always working in the mobility between several positions,
stations, places, between which a shuttle is needed" (p. 12). Like Reynolds and
Webber (2004) in their book *Expanding Curriculum Theory: Dis/positions*, Derrida argues, "For me negotiation [which is like a dis/position] is the impossibility
of establishing oneself anywhere" (p. 12). But clearly Derrida is a poststructuralist. What happens when a scholar in a particular discipline establishes himself nowhere? Well, then there would be no field at all. That is the trouble
with being a nomad, as Deleuze would put it. Curriculum theorists grapple with
this problem all the time. Part of the canon project suggested by William Pinar
(2010) is to ensure that curriculum theory remains a field and doesn't become a
no-field. For a field to remain a field, for a discipline to stay intact as a discipline,
there have to be continuities as well as discontinuities in the work at hand.
A field is built on its history and the people who make up that history. Clearly,
curriculum scholars have a history and continue that history in the way in which

curriculum concepts get fleshed out. Of course, the canon is always changing, but curriculum theory is a distinct field of study, constantly on the move, but still it is a field of study different from, say, philosophy of education. Curriculum theory is a discipline. There are major concepts and themes in curriculum theory. Curriculum theory has a canon. Some might argue that curriculum has multiple canons. However, multiple canons are not straight lines; multiple canons are not straightforward. Within a canon there is much disagreement over concepts. The vast array of work being done in curriculum studies today is difficult to conceptualize as one thing, because it is not one thing. Curriculum studies scholars write about many things, and these many things sometimes are at loggerheads. This is the nature of academic fields. Michel Foucault (1972) talks about disciplines as archaeologies. In a dig, and in the interpretation of that dig, archaeologists are hardly in agreement as to what the artifacts mean. Let us cite Foucault here in this context:

> By taking contradictions as objects [artifacts found in an archaeological dig] archaeological analysis does not try to discover in their place a common form of theme, it tries to determine the extent and form of the gap that separates them. In relation to a history of ideas [here the history of curriculum studies] that attempts to melt contradictions in the semi-nocturnal unity of an overall figure, or which attempts to transmute them into a general, abstract, uniform principle of interpretation or explanation, archaeology describes the different *spaces of dissension*. (p. 152)

In recent discussions over the canon of curriculum studies, there has been much dissensus as to the use of the concept of a canon, especially at the American Association for the Advancement of Curriculum Studies (AAACS) conference in 2009. William Pinar's canon project has created dissensus in the field because people do not want to be put into categories, and curriculum scholars feel that the concept canon is conservative. But without a canon of curriculum scholarship where are we? Who are we? The question that we must ask is who are we as curriculum scholars? Again, we need to remember our curriculum history, and a history creates a canon. But within this canon there is much bickering and rancor. That is the nature of academe. Nobody can agree on who is and isn't in the canon. The problem is what gets excluded and what gets included. This is an ever-changing field and trying to write about something that is ever changing is impossible. Is there such a thing as a poststructural discipline? If a discipline is thought of as an ever-changing thing, then yes, curriculum studies can be thought of as poststructural. All the competing segments of the field are on the move; nothing is static. But these changing segments are hard to understand because they are changing all the time. The changes almost seem chaotic and yet simultaneously they seem orderly. Atul Gawande (2002) says of the medical field that when attending a conference,

> the discussions were sparsely attended and mostly went over my head: it is impossible nowadays to have a working understanding of even the basic terminology in all of the fields under consideration. But as I sat there listening to the scientists talking among themselves, I caught a glimpse of where the edges of knowledge were. (p. 82)

Like the medical field, curriculum studies is so vast and so complex that it, too, is hard to see "where the edges of knowledge" are. These edges are often in contradistinction, and at loggerheads, and much of the work is hard to understand.

Our capacity to understand the field of curriculum studies in its entirety is limited by our own backgrounds and specialties. Our knowledge will always be uneven or as Zizek (2009) puts it "asymmet[rical]" (p. 29). One can only know so much and grasp so much; this is the difficulty with trying to understand a field as complex as curriculum studies. While reading the passage below think of the vastly complex field of curriculum studies. Zizek says,

> Every field of "reality" (every "world") [here one might think of the worlds of curriculum studies] is always-already enframed, seen through an invisible frame. The parallax is not symmetrical, composed of two incompatible perspectives on the same X: there is an irreducible asymmetry between the two perspectives, a minimal reflexive twist. We do not have two perspectives, have a perspective and what eludes it, and the other perspective fills in the void of what we could not see from the first perspective. (p. 29)

Think about your own knowledge about the recent work in the curriculum field. You have your perspective and then what eludes you. Other peoples' knowledges elude. There are certain segments of the field that you will understand better than others and some segments of the field will elude you. Zizek is right in saying that scholars have one perspective and they work from that. Scholars are always, in a way, blinded both by what they understand and what they do not understand because there is always more to learn. It is our professional responsibility as scholars of curriculum to try to grasp the field in its entirety. That is an impossible task but it is one of our responsibilities as scholars to try to learn what we cannot, to go beyond the knowledge that we already have. If we are to do our students a service as curriculum scholars, we have to keep studying this field—all of it—not just what we already know. Studying poststructuralism might make readers venture into unknown lands; it is not easy to go into places where one feels lost. But as Patti Lather (2007) puts it, "getting lost" is where we should be. Hongyu Wang (2004), in her book *The Call From the Stranger on a Journey Home: Curriculum in a Third Space*, suggests that when scholars come to a roadblock in knowledge that they should not work by "erasing conflicts" (p. 16). Scholars should rather try to work through conflicts, not so that problems are resolved but to understand that the conflicts should be grappled with. Michel Foucault (1983) says that in scholarship

> you can't find the solution of a problem [the non-understanding of a complex idea] in the solution of another problem raised at another moment by other people. You see, what I want to do is not the history of solutions. (p. 231)

Foucault suggests knowledge is not about finding solutions to problems. That is what the scientific method was all about. There are problems of knowledge that are unsolvable partly because of our own limitations as scholars and partly because the problems of knowledge are also about the problems of describing a world that is beyond our understanding. Scholars will always be, as Hongyu Wang puts it, "The Stranger[s]," as the title of her book suggests. But in contradistinction to her title, I would like to say that this stranger can never be on a "journey home"—again as the title of her book suggests—because scholars are never at home in their knowledge as it keeps changing. Thus, scholars are always stranded in the middle, grappling with a world that is far beyond the capacity to get it. What our knowledge of curriculum studies does, is that it produces, as Patti Lather points out, "bafflement rather than solutions" (p. viii). If anything, what students learn from the poststructuralists is that we do not get it, nor will we ever get it and so we are constantly on edge in a world where there are no answers. Part of the problem, too, has to do with what Deleuze and Guattari (2000) point out about schizoid thought. Schizoid thinking is sort of all over the place. Thinking through schizoid thought helps us understand why knowledge is an impossible quest. Deleuze and Guattari comment,

> There is a schizophrenic experience of intensive quantities in their pure state, to a point that is almost unbearable—a celibate misery and glory experienced to the fullest, like a cry suspended between life and death, an intense feeling of transition, states of naked intensity stripped of all shape and form. (p. 18)

Intensities of Understanding Curriculum Studies

I want to focus on the concept of intensities. The mind can only handle so much intensity. How much can one's mind interiorize? The scholar must attempt to tune into such intensities, to all of the shifting and changing states of a field in constant flux. But this is almost too much to bear. (Here again think of the complex nature of the field of curriculum studies.) The nuances in scholarly fields are too great and too overwhelming to psychologically take in. To understand a field such as curriculum studies—especially through a poststructural lens—can feel like insanity. Insanity is intensity and studying curriculum is intense. The poststructuralists I have been discussing all agree that people cannot agree on anything. Everything is in flux, continually changing, and everybody is in disagreement over everything. There is just too much to learn or handle. These realizations are intense indeed. In her brilliant autobiography, Elyn Saks (2007) writes about her experience of these schizophrenic intensities around which Deleuze and Guattari (2000) speak. Saks says,

> Now consider this: the regulator that funnels certain information to you [perhaps your ego which serves to keep you intact and in touch with reality] and filters out other information suddenly shuts off. Immediately, every sight, every thought, feeling, memory, and idea presents itself to you with an equally strong and demanding *intensity* [emphasis mine]. You're receiving a dozen different messages in a dozen different media. (p. 229)

Cognitive scientists argue that the function of the brain is to throw out more stuff than take in. Most of us throw out this stuff without being conscious of it. Freud might call this our censor. The censor of the mind gets rid of what we cannot take in. But when there is no barrier, when the ego dissolves, and when everything around you gets introjected, the mind cannot handle it all. These are the intensities that Saks is talking about. When the ego is not intact and there are no defense mechanisms in place—as they have seemingly vanished—everything comes in at once. This is, for the schizophrenic, overwhelming. Can you imagine not being able to filter every little thing going on around you? William James said that if you remembered everything you would go crazy. So there is a point at which forgetting becomes necessary to keep one's sanity. Forgetting serves its purpose, too, especially if one lives through trauma. Sometimes it is better to forget. But then the forgetting can catch up with you as the unconscious boils over in recurrent nightmares.

I digress here on these issues of intensities and the introjection of every-thing because understanding curriculum is about trying to figure out what counts as knowledge and what it is that scholars need to throw out. So Herbert Spencer's old question of what knowledge is of most worth is a psychological one. Knowledge is not just political, it is also psychological. How much can one take in? How much can one know? What does it mean to be thorough in scholarship? Writing a text like this one is like diving into a sea of intensity where one has to know when to stop and what to try to understand.

Bernadette Baker and Poststructural Historiography

Bernadette Baker (2001), in her book titled *In Perpetual Motion: Theories of Power, Educational History, and the Child,* argues that history is "in perpetual motion" as the title of her book suggests. How to capture that which is always on the move? Baker points out that history—as the marking of time—seems to be all over the place and in fact multiple (see Deleuze & Guattari, 2000, and Serres, 2000, on multiplicities). As Serres (1995) points out time flows and yet it doesn't; it is contradictory and percolates; it is nonlinear. However, when writing a historiography the scholar has to gather up her work in a way that is not all over the place, otherwise readers will not be able to follow the text. That means when the historiography is done it falls into place for the reader and has a linear feel to it. Yet history is not linear. How else to write history? If the history that one is writing is all over the place, then the work is little more than word salad and the jumble of a schizophrenic. Baker puts it this way:

> To that end, this history cannot claim in regard to time an overwhelming nonlinear-ity and then tell the story that it tells. Its story is not outside a conception of linear time. Serres does not *wholly* discard the conception of linear time, but, like Foucault, challenges its meaning and unlike Foucault, provides an array of metaphors for thinking it otherwise that run from motion, to space, to sound…[in referring to her own book Baker says] this history of the child, power, and education cannot sustain appeals to nonlinear time or explanations without implicit forms of dependence on the imagination of time as linear. (pp. 37–38).

Baker's book is a Foucauldian interpretation of the history of childhood and education. It is clear that Baker struggles with the poststructural notion of the nonlinear and she speaks to these points. Baker suggests that ulti-mately one has to write a historiography that seemingly has a timeline and logic to it. What is ironic about Baker's book is that while she attempts a poststructural interpretation of history, what she actually does is trace the history of Western philosophy in a most traditional fashion by taking readers through Locke, Rousseau, Herbart, G. Stanley Hall, and then as an aside tries to think through Foucauldian issues. Baker's work is quite brilliant and her thoroughness is daunting. But the question is whether she really is doing a Foucauldian interpretation of the child or not. Much of her book deals with the history of Western philosophy, which is about the history of white, mostly European, men. In what way is that poststructural? This raises a question not just for Baker but also for the poststructuralists themselves. If one reads Foucault, Derrida, Latour, Lyotard, women are hardly, if ever, quoted. Although Foucault (2003) mentions what he calls "counterhistory" (p. 73) and "subjugate[d]" (p. 68) peoples, his sources are mostly white men. Although Derrida writes against phallocentrism, he does not cite women. So I could launch the criticism of sexism against mostly all of the poststructuralists. Those working on posthumanism—like Donna Haraway (1997), who is also a critic of the male-dominated discipline of science—suggest that the discourse has to change to include women and subjugated peoples.

Weariness

There is a strain in much poststructural thinking that turns toward what Levinas (2001) calls weariness. Many writers who draw on poststructuralism overlook this strain in poststructural thought. Levinas—a Holocaust survivor—knows about weariness from his own experience, and his writings, although highly abstract, reflect his experience as a Holocaust survivor; sometimes he writes as if totally worn down by the world. Levinas says,

> There exists a weariness which is a weariness of everything and of everyone, and above all a weariness of oneself. What weariness then is not a particular form of life—our surroundings, because they are dull and ordinary, our circle of friends, because they are vulgar and cruel; the weariness concerns existence itself. Instead of forgetting itself in the essential levity of a smile, where existence is effected innocently, and where, gratuitous and graceful, its expansion is like vanishing, in weariness existence is like the reminder of a commitment to exist, with all the seriousness and harshness of an unrevokable contract. One has to do something, one has to aspire and undertake. (pp. 11–12)

What strikes me in Levinas's quote is the idea that despite the weariness of existence, as he calls it, "one has to do something" (p. 12). This something that one must do, for Levinas is driven by the ethicality of relations. I will talk more about this later on, but for now it is important to note that there is a side of poststructuralism that seems tired in the face of a troubled world and yet the work continues. This is the Beckettian side of poststructuralism. For Levinas, doing something means writing about the ethical. He was driven to write about the ethical, perhaps, because he was a Holocaust survivor.

Poststructuralism in a Painful World

Levinas (2001) was devoted to a life of writing and the life of ethical relations; he found a way to go on despite his "weariness of existence" (p. 11). Levinas (1987), in his book *Time & the Other*, writes about suffering. Again, this is an overlooked aspect of poststructural writing. What I am trying to drive home here with these examples is that poststructuralists take on the world in a se-rious way and talk about the concrete aspects of living in a painful and brutal world. Levinas (1987) says,

> In suffering there is an absence of all refuge. It is the fact of being directly exposed to being. It is made up of the impossibility of fleeing or retreating. The whole acuity of suffering lies in this impossibility of retreat....But in suffering there is, at the same time as the call to an impossible nothingness, the proximity of death. (p. 69)

What is striking here is Levinas's use of the word "refuge." He suggests that in suffering there is no refuge. There is no place to hide, no place to turn.

Like Levinas, Michel Serres (1995) writes about suffering and serious-ness. He is a philosopher of science and knows quite well about the unethical practices of scientists, especially physicists and mathematicians during WWII. Serres's greatest concern was the smashing of the atom and the fallout, if you will, of that scientific discovery. His disgust with the scientific community led him to finally get out of science altogether and move into philosophy and literature. Serres says, "I had been in the sciences. I had abandoned them" (p. 15). Serres goes on to tell us,

> I belong to the generation that questions scientism. At the time one could not work in physics without having been deafened by the universal noise of Hiroshima. Now, traditional epistemology still was not asking any questions on the relation between science and violence. Everything was taking place as if the scientific Ivory Tower were inhabited by good children—naïve—hard-working and meticulous, of good conscience and devoid of any political or military horizons. But weren't they the contemporaries of The Manhattan Project, which prepared the bomb? (p. 16)

Serres was so distraught over the turn in physics (toward smashing atoms) and the ethical fallout of that, that he was driven right out of his profession because he could not live with the consequences of what scientists were doing. He remarks, "Even before the war certain physicists had abandoned science out of *wariness* [emphasis mine] of collaborating with what later became the atomic bomb" (p. 16). To be wary is akin to the weariness about which Levinas speaks. But to be wary is to be suspicious. If students do not know this historical background, they might not understand what Serres is doing. He is poetic and playful with words, yes, but he is also deadly serious about his work. Serres says, "I ask my readers to hear the explosion of this problem in every page of my books. Hiroshima remains the sole object of my philosophy" (p. 15). Again, one wouldn't necessarily know this unless one read the context around which Serres writes.

What students also learn from Serres's conversation with Bruno Latour is that he was influenced by the writings of Simone Weil. He calls Weil the "Philosopher of Violence" (p. 18). Serres is one of the few poststructuralists who cannot be accused of sexism in his work as he says that Weil was a major influence in his thinking. Serres remarks, "Weil's *Gravity and Grace* appeared on my table. It is largely because of this book that I resigned from the Naval Academy and that I left the sciences for philosophy...she was the only philosopher who really influenced me" (p. 18). Weil is certainly not considered a philosopher by most contemporary (male) philosophers; she is not given a consideration, not even a thought. Philosophers, for the most part, draw on male philosophers. Many would not consider Weil's book *Gravity and Grace* as philosophy, but perhaps theology or spirituality. George Panichas (1977) says that Weil wrote on

> religion, politics, sociology, anthropology, philosophy, economics, aesthetics, and education....Her life instances a spiritual collision with the demonic. Her testimony stands as a refusal to accede to it. Indeed, there is no other religious thinker who is more pertinent to our time. When one considers the exigencies of the historical era into which she was "thrown," the barbarity and brutality that it occasioned, the explosive cruelty and ugly hatreds, that it engendered; when one thinks, in short, of the terrible and terrifying conditions...Simone Weil remains for us an astonishing example...for she provides a prophetic wisdom. (pp. xv–xvi)

Weil lived through the horrors of WWII and wrote much about spirituality in the context of living during a time of unthinkable violence. Hence, if one is to understand the writings of Michel Serres, one has to also study the writings of Weil. Students need to read writers in the context of their influences. In-fluences shape writing.

Like Michel Serres, there are some curriculum theorists who have com-mented on the dangers of scientific discovery and the unethical nature of some scientific work. Davis and Appelbaum (2002) comment,

> Physics was privileged by the regime from the beginning as useful, and most phys-icists were offered high status and job security as long as they did not oppose the regime....Physicists readily demonstrated how physics could be used to "prove" Nazi ideology, for example through reinterpretations of Heisenberg and Bohr....Biologists offered evidence as to the various means by which a body could be starved, gassed, or poisoned. Chemists and chemical engineers responded with new technologies to administer this control over life and death. (pp. 173–174)

Science curriculum avoids the history of this complicity. The point that Da-vis and Appelbaum make is that students should study science, history, and the culture in which science is done to get a better understanding of what it is that they are studying. But science teaching is usually ahistorical and pre-tends that science happens outside of culture. That is why many in curriculum studies are suggesting that we look again at the science curriculum and argue for what is called the cultural studies of science (for more on this see Weaver, 2001; Blades, 1997, 2001). David Blades, in his book *Procedures of Power and Curriculum Change: Foucault and the Quest for Possibilities in Science Education* (1997) worries, like Serres, Davis, and Appelbaum, that somewhere science took a wrong turn. Blades says, "Growing up in the fifties, sixties, and early seventies the promise of science and technology seemed contradictory: How could we reconcile the development of antibiotics, television, and transis-tors with DDT, nuclear weapons, and napalm?" (p. 1). Doing what Foucault (2003) calls a "counterhistory" (p. 72), Blades helps us to better understand that science and technology have been complicit in the horrors of the 20th century. But again, students in various science classes are hardly ever taught this counterhistory until they reach college, if then, or if at all. Foucault says of counterhistory that it "has to disinter something that has been hidden, and which has been hidden not only because it has been neglected but because it has been wickedly misrepresented" (p. 72). Foucault notes, "History is the discourse of power" (p. 68). Historians have the power to unwrite history, to rewrite history, or to leave out pieces of history that are embarrassing.

Roxanne Lapidus (1995) remarks that Michel Serres is one of the few philosophers to point out that "technology contains shadowy areas of archaic violence" (p. 205). Curriculum theorist Brent Davis (1996) comments on the shadowy side of mathematics. Davis tells us that mathematics

> has also been identified as a key contributor to a plethora of modern crises. An enabler of scientific "advances," of military technologies, or normalizing statistical reductions, mathematics has been associated with the establishment and maintenance of power imbalance; contributing to wide-scale destruction of the planet; and disenfranchising and depersonalizing the citizenry of Western cultures...all in the name of "progress." (p. xxii)

The notion of progress is one that disturbs many of the poststructuralists. Progress—in the context of science, mathematics, biology, chemistry, and physics—has led us where? To the atomic bomb and other horrors. In the context of cosmopolitanism, Sharon Todd (2009) comments, "As long as the idea of humanity disavows what is 'inhuman' and imperfect about us, cosmopolitanism cannot give an adequate response to the question of violence" (p. 3). Education, then, Todd argues should be about studying the inhuman and man's inhumanity to man. This, too, was the purpose of William Pinar's (2001) book on lynching and violence in America. Too much of the history of education ignores these questions. The epistemological question of how we know what we know has been overshadowed by horrors such as slavery, lynchings, the Holocaust, 9/11, natural disasters, and manmade catastrophes like the BP oil spill. Sandra Gilbert (2006) writes about the so-called Great War, and she suggests that it was the Great War that introduced the uses and abuses of technology that resulted in an even more efficient killing machine during the Holocaust. Gilbert states that during WWI,

> With its trenches surrounded by barbed wire; its ceaselessly rattling machine guns, bursting shells, and constantly roaring cannons; its swarms of trains, ambulances, even double-decker buses, and even too with its newly swooping planes; its stammering radios [was the]...Springboard to what 1918 would ultimately lead the world into: a second war where death was still more scientifically and industrially delivered in the murderous cities of Auschwitz and Bergen-Belsen as well as (very differently) to the cities of London, Dresden, Berlin, Tokyo, and Hiroshima. (pp. 149–150)

Wars make for weariness, as Levinas points out. I argue that there is a tiredness, a weariness, an anguished side to poststructuralism. This is a point that many commentators leave out of their discussions. Poststructuralism is about many things of course; I mentioned its turn toward chaos and complexity theory, deconstruction, language, and so forth. But the driving force behind the poststructural turn is this war weariness that many of these European writers grew up with. My take on poststructuralism is this: that the turn against modernism came with the advent of the Great War, then WWII, the Holocaust, and the Algerian War. These were the major issues of the day for Levinas, Derrida, Foucault, and Serres especially. Poststructuralism was born with an explosion, was born in the trenches of WWI even. American pragmatism might have been about antifoundational thinking (which is also the hallmark of poststructuralism) but American pragmatism had little influence on European poststructural thought. There are certainly some things in common about American pragmatism and European poststructural thought (as Cleo Cherryholmes [1999] and Morris Dickstein [1999] point out). But these philosophical movements are entirely separate. They both have different histories and evolved from different countries.

Think of the work of Derrida against the historical backdrop I mention above. Like Levinas (2001), Derrida (2002b) speaks of a certain fatigue in living and writing. It is hard to imagine that someone as prolific as Derrida felt fatigue, but obviously he did. Derrida says, "Thus, when I think negotiation, I think of this fatigue, of this without-rest, this enervating mobility preventing one from ever stopping" (p. 13). Derrida was born in Algiers and knew all too well about the Algerian War, French colonization, anti-Semitism, and racism. Like Levinas, these experiences—although again, he does not write much about them—had to have taken a toll on Derrida.

To negotiate a position—as Derrida says—means that one is never quite sure about anything; continual negotiation is the way in which Derrida did his work. He was "without rest" as he was constantly writing. Some say that he was driven by the ethical; some say he was driven by politics. But there is more to Derrida than politics and ethics. He wrote about everything from animals, to death, to painting, to the university, to Freud, Marx, and the uses of language. He was prolific, without-rest, always working, always writing. He was driven. He remarks that this without-rest was enervating, and he felt fatigued. People who are driven, as he was, must feel, at some point, tired and worn out. Derrida wrote right up until his death. There is a certain tiredness about thinking about the end of life; the philosopher's stone is about *The Gift of Death*, as the title of Derrida's (1995b) book suggests. The gift of death is the thought that one must leave a mark, leave an archive. Without death, we would get nothing done. Time marches on. Derrida, in the last few years of his life, knew that he was dying but that did not stop him from writing. As Levinas put it, people must do something in this life that is meaningful and ethical. For both Levinas and Derrida that something was writing and leaving behind an archive. Without the archive, without the writing, nothing remains except memories. Derrida (1978) talks about writing in terms of anguish (p. 9). Derrida remarks,

> Writing is the anguish of the Hebraic *ruah*, experienced in solitude by human responsibility; experienced by Jeremiah subjected to God's dictation ("Take thee a roll of a book, and write therein all the words that I have spoken unto thee"). (p. 9)

Note the words "responsibility" and "solitude" here. This is what makes writing a sort of anguish. One has a responsibility to talk about what is wrong with the world. It is obvious that Derrida felt driven and even anguished by this responsibility. It is interesting that he draws on the prophet Jeremiah to talk about anguish and responsibility. Some of the prophets in the Hebrew Scriptures today would be considered schizophrenic—especially Ezekiel. Many schizophrenics think that they are God or that God speaks to them (Morris, 2006). Perhaps Derrida felt a certain burden to write, as did the Hebrew prophets. When they were "called" to do the work of God, many of them at first refused. But the anguish and responsibility—to do God's work—was overwhelming. To feel called to do the work of philosophy is, too, overwhelming. To feel one is called to write brings on a certain fatigue, as Derrida puts it. Derrida identified with Jeremiah, perhaps, because he felt it was his ethical responsibility to write. Writing brings on a certain anguish he says because one must continue without rest. There is a certain seriousness of Derrida's work that commentators overlook. Derrida was a man of conscience. He took on many serious topics and took his work seriously. The anguish Derrida felt is better understood against war weariness that he experienced growing up in Algiers.

The Posthuman

Brent Davis and Dennis Sumara (2006) talk about the notion of "interobjectivity" (p. 34). They use this term in the context of complexity theory. They explain, "Complexity thinking posits that truth is not strictly a matter of intersubjectivity—coherences among humans—but of interobjectivity—conversations between a dynamic humanity within a dynamic more-than human world" (p. 34). This "more-than-human world" about which Davis and Sumara speak could be interpreted in two ways. First, I am reminded of ecologist David Abram's (1996) book *The Spell of the Sensuous: Perception and Language in a*

More-than-Human World. Here Abram discusses the meshing of humans and nature. He argues that humans are not separate and apart from nature. Rather, human and nature are not two things but one. The more-than-human, for Abram, has to do with the ecosphere into which we are thrown. Abram argues,

> Direct sensuous reality, in all its more-than-human mystery, remains the touchstone for an experiential world now inundated with electronically-generated vistas and engineered pleasures; only in regular contact with the tangible ground and sky can we learn how to orient and to navigate in the multiple dimensions that now claim us. (p. x)

Abram suggests that technology gets in the way of experiencing the sensuousness of the world. But there is no way to avoid technology today as it has become so much a part of our everyday experience.

As against Abram, posthumanism is about the connections between human, machine, and animal. Now, Abram argues that the more-than-human world is not about human-made things like "electronically-generated vistas" (p. x). But scholars of posthumanism would argue that the more-than-human world is also about electronically generated vistas in the intermix between human, animal, and machine. This is the posthuman. Donna Haraway (1997) describes the posthuman when she says, "I have tried to queer the self-evidence of witnessing, of experience, of conventionally upheld and invested perceptions of clear distinctions between living and dead, machine and organisms, human and nonhuman self and other" (p. 267). Let us focus on Haraway's comment about the living and the dead. Hardly any posthuman writers comment on this. Think of the word "posthumous." There is a post in the human; posthuman means also human life in its relation to death. What is the relation between the living and the dead? From a biological standpoint, a decayed body becomes food for thought, food for some other creatures, or ashes. Leaving carbon footprints, or not leaving them. The posthuman is akin to the posthumous.

Another angle that posthumanists do not take is the psychological. I argue that there is a psychological dimension to the posthuman. Think of the concept of the "crypt" coined by Nicholas Abraham and Maria Torok (1994). They explain,

> Inexpressible mourning erects a secret tomb inside the subject. Reconstituted from the memories of words, scenes, and affects, the object correlative of the loss is buried alive in the crypt as a full-fledged person, complete with its own topography. The crypt also includes the actual or supposed traumas that made introjection impracticable. A whole world of unconscious fantasy is created, one that leads its own separate and concealed existence. (p. 130)

Freud suggests that when one cannot mourn the dead properly melancholia overwhelms. A melancholic, in other words, has never been able to get over the death of someone. Abraham and Torok take and extend that idea. When an abusive parent dies, the child may not mourn properly because of the ambivalent love-hate relation that was carried on in life. Thus, the abusive parent gets psychologically buried in a metaphorical crypt. While in the crypt, that dead parent takes on a life of its own to continually haunt the child even into adulthood. The dead parent haunts like a ghost. The dead parent is no longer there, but is there in the continual haunting. This is what I consider posthuman from a psychoanalytic perspective. The posthuman is the haunting of the dead parent who gets buried inside what Abraham and Torok call an "intrapsychic tomb" (p. 130). From a psychoanalytic perspective, the posthuman could also be the memories we carry around with us of the dead person. This is not at all what most scholars write about when thinking the posthuman, however.

N. Katherine Hayles (1999) has written perhaps one of the most important books on the posthuman called *How We Became Posthuman: Virtual Bodies in Cybernetics, Literature, and Informatics*. Hayles describes the posthuman as:

> a cybernetic circuit that splices your will, desire, and perception into a distributed cognitive system in which represented bodies are joined with enacted bodies through mutating and flexible machine interfaces. As you gaze at the flickering signifiers scrolling down the computer screens, no matter what identifications you assign to the embodied entities that you cannot see, you have already become posthuman. (p. xiv)

Today people are more connected to machines than ever. We email, we teach online courses, we use Skype in dissertation committee hearings, we write papers on computers, we submit book proposals online, we talk on cell phones or in chat rooms, or engage with Facebook and Twitter. Some are skeptical about the posthuman condition; some argue that computers do not make for better scholars (Pinar, 2012). John Weaver (2004) argues that luddites need to begin to think differently though. Weaver suggests, "For curriculum theorists, educating the post-human generation means abandoning the technophobic tradition that stems from the Frankfurt School tradition in critical theory, in which technology is seen as a means of control and oppression" (p. 31). The posthuman condition, if you will, runs counter to not only the Frankfurt school critique but also to the critiques by many of the poststructuralists, who worry that technology has gotten us into a lot of trouble. Recall, the previous discussion of technology in the context of the Great War, the Holocaust, and the Algerian War. Serres, Derrida, and Levinas were suspicious of too much reliance on technology and how technology is used to kill, not to help. Some technophobia is necessary—no matter from which tradition it springs (whether from the Frankfurt school or the poststructural School). I think that one should always be wary of machines and try to make use of them only if they are useful in a good and productive way. One should never be complicit with building killing machines or supporting killing machines. Computers— as writing machines—are a great benefit to those of us who need to quickly capture our thinking. Writing with a pen (which could be considered a form of technology too) slows down thinking.

Whether we like it or not, we all—according to Katherine Hayles—have become posthuman. Does the posthuman mean dis-embodiment? In online classes professors never see students; all they see is text on a machine. Does the computer erase bodies, race, class, and genders? By working on comput- ers have we have become part machine? Scholars and students are connect- ed to computers so much that one wonders if we are becoming-computer, as Deleuze and Guattari might put it. Deleuze and Guattari (2000) talk about "desiring-machines" (p. 3). Are people becoming these desiring-machines? Schizophrenics talk about themselves as machines (Morris, 2006). Descartes said that cats were machines. And surgeons use robot arms to operate, so are they machines too?

Were cats already posthuman during Descartes' days? Are surgeons real- ly robots? Can a machine actually desire? Or is the whole conversation about machines a throwback to Artificial Intelligence (AI) in the 1950s? Are MRI machines smarter than doctors? Who counts, then, the doctor or the machine?

Perhaps the posthuman discussion should focus more on the ways that objects like computers change humans. Is this what Katherine Hayles (1999) and Donna Haraway (1997) suggest? Are musicians posthuman? (This is an- other avenue of thought left out of most conversations on the posthuman.) A musician thinks of herself as tied to her instrument, connected in a sen- suous way to her instrument. The hands are an extension of the keyboard. An instrument, like a piano or a cello, is a machine. In order to make the machine work, you have to know how to play it and connect to it. And these connections come about through touch and listening and much practice and patience. Not just anybody can be a cello machine. But again, this is not what posthuman conversations are usually about.

Students should consult John Weaver's (2010) book on the posthuman called *Educating the Posthuman: Biosciences, Fiction, and Curriculum Studies.*

What is interesting in Weaver's work on the posthuman is his idea that the posthuman isn't only about machines and our interactions with them, but also with the ways in which fiction has prepared for the coming of the post-human world. Weaver's work is what Michel Serres (2000) calls for in his *The Troubadour of Knowledge*, as he straddles the humanities and the sciences. A troubadour is someone who can cross disciplines. Weaver crosses disciplines. He states that the posthuman

> is about the merging of biotechnologies (pharmaceuticals, cosmetic surgery, germline engineering, and stem cell research) as they converge with/in our bodies and reshape our identities as human beings. It's about how certain forms of literature [i.e., fiction] (*Frankenstein, A Scanner Darkly, The Picture of Dorian Gray, Stoner, Harry Potter and Order of the Phoenix, and A Mercy*) have prophesized our present condition and have forever altered our mind's imagination. (pp. 1–2)

Weaver adds to the discussion the ways in which fiction has always been pre-paring the way for the posthuman. The posthuman could also be about body modifications such as tattoos, scarification, or piercing. For Weaver, things like cosmetic surgery could be considered posthuman. Machines (surgeon's knives) can alter the way we look. I want to add to this discussion sex change operations. This, too, is a form of cosmetic surgery. Transsexuals feel that they are born in the wrong body and need an alteration of sorts to feel better. Is a transsexual posthuman? I would say yes.

Sander Gilman (1998) in his book *Creating Beauty to Cure the Soul: Race and Psychology in the Shaping of Aesthetic Surgery* says that "philosophers ask whether one can even speak of aesthetic surgery as medicine in the sense that it attempts to cure anything" (p. xi). The question here is whether aesthetic surgery can be considered medicine. This is a very interesting question. Does a sex change operation cure someone of something? Does it cure their soul, as the title of Sander Gilman's book suggests? If surgery doesn't serve to cure an illness, is it even ethical? Weaver says that the posthuman "is experienced through a radical transformation of our aesthetic sensibilities" (p. 14). So then the question becomes, what counts as aesthetic? Is a sex change operation aesthetic? Is cosmetic surgery aesthetic? Is our relation to computers an aes-thetic one?

Another way to think the posthuman is to remember that human beings are animals. We are human-animals. But most people do not like to think of themselves as animal. I argue that to think the human and the animal together is posthuman. Derrida's (2008) book called *The Animal That Therefore I Am* has the same premise. In Foucault's (1988) book *Madness and Civilization: A History of Insanity in the Age of Reason*, he tells us that it was once thought that only people who were considered insane were considered animals. Foucault comments,

> Unchained animality [which is what the insane exhibit] could be mastered only by *discipline* and *brutalizing*. The theme of the animal-madman was effectively realized in the eighteenth century, in occasional attempts to impose a certain *pedagogy* [emphasis mine] on the insane. (p. 75)

The posthuman is about our own animality. It isn't that we are merged with animals but that we are animals. And we are in relation to nonhuman animals as well as machines.

Power and the Politics of Representation

I contend that power and the politics of representation are poststructural concerns. Michael Peters and Peter Trifonas (2005), in the context of Derrida's work, point out that for Derrida,

> He is suspicious of the view that language represents the world, at least in any straightforward way. But "representation" is also important to him as a political principle indicating the ethical and political stakes in presenting an argument or characterizing a people, a text, an image, or one's relation to another thinker—the so-called politics of representation. (p. 5)

Derrida teaches, then, that when writing about someone or something, that writing is never neutral, it is always political. To represent something is a complicated affair. It is indeed political. Derrida knows, as Michael Peters and Peter Trifonas in the above quote mention, representation is highly perspectival, and the way in which a scholar represents a particular history reflects the scholar's perspective and interpretation as well as the actual event at hand. Even though words, as Derrida suggests, do not represent events exactly as they happened, words can capture gists and patterns that are filtered through interpretation and culture. This does not mean, however, that anything goes and that any representation will do. We try to honor the event or the words of the scholar upon whom we draw and we try to get it right; that is, we try to understand things the best way we can, knowing that we can never get behind a text or understand fully what the words of another mean.

Power and the Use of Foucault

Poststructuralism is not merely about the play with language. It is also about power, representation, and cultural construction. Michel Foucault—who some would consider a poststructuralist—writes about these topics.

Who has the power to say who is and is not intelligent? Who decides who is intelligent? What does that mean? That is a political question. Who decides what a child is and how that child gets represented in history is also a question of power. The concept of intelligence and the concept of the child are both culturally constructed. Both of these discourses (around intelligence and the notion of the child) serve to control, contain, and normalize. Much of the impetus for this work has sprung from Michel Foucault's (1979) book *Discipline and Punish: The Birth of the Prison*. What I would like to do here is to discuss Foucault's book as the backdrop to the work of educationists Joe Kincheloe (2004c), Nancy Lesko (2001), and Bernadette Baker (2001).

In curriculum theory, many draw on Foucault's *Discipline and Punish* because much of what he discusses deals directly with what is going on in public schools today. Foucault, in the context of prisoners (and here you could replace the prisoner with the school student), says,

> A whole set of assessing, diagnostic, prognostic, normative judgments concerning the criminal [or school student] have become lodged in the framework of penal judgment [schools have become like prisons and students are treated like criminals, see the work of Henry Giroux (2003) also]. (p. 19)

To assess is to judge and to judge is to regulate and control. Schools and universities have become places where students are judged and assessed by the use of rubrics that reduce education to standardized "facts." If a student's knowledge doesn't fit into a rubric, that knowledge does not count as knowledge. Even graduate programs of education are now being assessed by the use of rubrics that supposedly sum up what students learn. This summing up dumbs down the entire idea of education. Accrediting agencies like National Council for Accreditation of Teacher Education (NCATE) dumb down what it means to be an educated person by reducing knowledge to rubrics and assessing students' abilities by putting them into boxes. This is a way to judge the capacity of students' learning and to make value judgments of programs. Foucault uses the word "normality" several times in his book in the context of prisoners as he says that the court system uses "judgments of normality" (p. 20) and uses "assessment[s] of normality" (p. 21). The point is to normalize criminals, tame them. The point for school students, too, is to normalize them, tame them and assess "normality" through accrediting agencies like NCATE. NCATE serves to normalize students.

Foucault talks about what he calls a "micro-physics of power" (p. 29) that is used to control prisoners. Here, too, school students and teachers struggle under a "micro-physics of power" (p. 29) since what gets taught is dictated by the state. Accrediting agencies also serve as organizations of power. Foucault tells us, "At the beginning of the seventeenth century, Wallhausen spoke of 'strict discipline' as an art of correct training" (p. 171). When students attend colleges of education, they attend teacher "training" programs. Pre-service teachers enter teacher "training" programs where they are closely monitored and "disciplined." Often, faculty must write up students who do not have the proper "dispositions" and report these students to a manager of the training program. Then these students are strictly disciplined and if they do not change their behaviors (or dispositions) they are kicked out of the training program. Foucault mentions that already in the early European history of the school

> the same movement was to be found in the reorganization of elementary teaching: the details of surveillance were specified and it was integrated into the teaching relationship. The development of the parish schools, the increase in the number of their pupils, the absence of methods for regulating simultaneously the activity of a whole class, and the disorder and confusion that followed from this made it necessary to work out a system of supervision. In order to help the teacher, Batencour selected from among the best pupils a whole series of "officers—intendants, observers, monitors." (p. 175)

This passage is eerily familiar to those of us who teach in teacher education programs and even now in doctoral programs. NCATE puts professors under constant surveillance as all data from courses and programs are closely monitored and judged. NCATE and program managers serve as the current day "intendants, observers, monitors" about which Foucault (1979) writes. But these "intendants, observers [and] monitors" do not help professors, but rather discipline them if they step out of line and dare to teach something that is not dictated by state mandates. Syllabi are scrutinized; student spies report professors who teach materials that might be too far to the left or report teachers who might discuss politics in class. As Foucault puts it, this strict surveillance and monitoring is an old European tradition that has made its way to the United States and other countries around the world. Standardizing curriculum nationwide, or even worldwide, is on the table for discussion at national conferences. To think that people would want everyone in the world to think alike is Orwellian to say the least. Foucault talks about "methods relating to the army, the school and the hospital" that produce "docile" "bod[ies]" (p. 136). The purpose of standardizing, monitoring, assessing, and data collecting of student work produces not only docile bodies of students but also forces professors to become docile as well. Not only this, in many public schools, and even in some universities, cameras in classrooms and in hallways work to ensure that everyone is behaving correctly. Teachers are watched, supervised, monitored, controlled, manipulated. Foucault says that the

> work-shop, the school, the army were subject to a whole micro-penalty of time (lateness, absences, interruptions of tasks), of activity (inattention, negligence, lack of zeal), of behaviour (impoliteness, disobedience), of speech (idle chatter, insolence) of the body ("incorrect" attitudes, irregular gestures, lack of cleanliness)....It was a question of making the slightest departures from correct behavior [that was] subject to punishment. (p. 178)

How eerily relevant this passage is to our own experiences in teacher education programs. Preservice teachers are watched, monitored, and reported on, subject to rubrics, dispositions. They are observed for the way they speak, dress, act, the clothes they wear, the attitudes they have. As Foucault puts it "the slightest departure from correct behavior" means getting kicked out of the teacher education program. NCATE has ensured that professors have now become like prison guards and preservice teachers are under the strictest surveillance possible to make sure that they are normalized and controlled. Why colleges of education agree to go along with the dictates of NCATE has much to do with funding issues and prestige. To be accredited by NCATE is like receiving a badge of honor. But many professors who have to work under these strictures know that these are impossible conditions and immoral ones at that.

What is interesting about Foucault, is that his historical approach to the topics at hand teaches that these restrictions on what teachers and students can and cannot do in the classroom are not new. Europe has a long history of control and surveillance of teachers. We have inherited a European system that is antiquated and even scandalous. Some colleges of education are saying no to NCATE. But state schools get told what to do by state officials and professors have little control over the assessment industry—which by the way is an industry. Certainly there are other ways of assessing student progress that allow for more freedom.

Foucault's work on power has changed the way scholars of education talk about what is going on in schools and colleges of education today. Thomas Popkewitz and Marie Brennan (1998) point out,

> Translations of Foucault have provided entrée for English speakers to an intellectual tradition that has emerged forcefully in the past two decades to challenge the hegemony of Marxist theories about issues of power and politics of social change. Until then, explicitly Marxist projects had been the main—at times even the only—means for considering power and politics within and across social settings. (p. 4)

Traditional Marxists discuss power in terms of the proletariat and the ruling classes. For Foucault power is more complex. And power is not only negative. It must be remembered that Foucault also says that power produces as well. He explains:

> We must cease once and for all to describe the effects of power in negative terms: it "excludes," it "represses," it "censors," it "abstracts," it "masks," it "conceals." In fact, power produces; it produces reality; it produces domains of objects and rituals of truth. The individual and the knowledge that may be gained of him belong to this production. (p. 194)

Still, most educationists use Foucault's work to describe the negative forces of power, especially in the context of schooling. Knowledge production, for Foucault, is a form of power. Here Foucault does not mean that knowledge is power (in the commonsense understanding of this phrase). Rather knowledge that is gained through our studies gives us the power to represent the world in a certain way. This is what Foucault means by the power of representation. Sometimes this power is negative and sometimes it is generative, so scholars have to be cautious when reading the work of others to be on the lookout for what kind of knowledge gets generated. There are right-wing representations of knowledge and there are left-wing representations. There are representations of knowledge that pretend neutrality or objectivity and these tend to hide racisms, sexisms, homophobias, nationalisms, and the rest. The way in which knowledge is represented is always political and driven by some form of power, either a productive form or a negative form. But then again, representations of knowledge are not so clear cut; they are complicated. When scholars pretend that they are objective and neutral we should engage in a hermeneutics of suspicion. Michel Serres (1995) is suspicious of this kind of hermeneutics and thinks that it is, in a way, unethical and even violent. Michel Serres dislikes this way of interpreting texts as he says, "These philosophies [or ways of reading texts] took up a position like spying" (p. 133). If we take up a hermeneutics of suspicion, "philosophy [or any discipline for that matter that interprets texts] becomes like a police state" (p. 133). Further Serres argues that suspicious readings "come down to strategies of war" (p. 134). I think Serres is wrong on this point; reading suspiciously does not necessarily mean spying or reading in a warlike fashion. We have to be ever cautious of a scholar's position. It is imperative to understand a scholar's political position and try to understand the historical context around which he or she writes.

Joe Kincheloe, Nancy Lesko, and Bernadette Baker

So now I turn to a discussion of the work of educationists Joe Kincheloe, Nancy Lesko, and Bernadette Baker. Think about their scholarship in the context of Foucault. Much of what they are doing could be considered Foucauldian.

Joe Kincheloe's (2004c) edited collection titled *Multiple Intelligences Reconsidered* is a critique of Howard Gardner's (1983) book *Frames of Mind: The Theory of Multiple Intelligences*. Kincheloe invited various authors to deconstruct, chapter-by-chapter, Gardner's book. Gardner argues in his book that there are basically eight kinds of intelligence, and he suggests that maybe even there is a ninth one. Gardner was trying to expand the intelligences "measured" on SATs and GREs. These tests measure reading and writing and mathematical skills. Gardner tries to expand what counted as intelligence to suggest that there are more than two kinds of intelligences (reading and math); in fact there are at least eight ways of being intelligent. I applaud him for breaking through the simplistic psychometric mind frame of thinking that only reading comprehension and mathematic skill count as knowledge. However, the problem is that he reduces the mind to eight things (for more on the eight ways consult Kincheloe's text). Many of the authors in Kincheloe's book were critical of this for again reducing intelligence to a number. Neurologists know that the mind is much more complex than Gardner allows.

Kincheloe calls himself a postformalist. Postformalism moves beyond Piaget's formal categories and hierarchies of development. Postformalists suggest that children should not be reduced to stages of development because all children develop differently at different rates and in different ways in different countries (for more on this see Cannella & Viruru, 2004). Postformalism is a version of poststructuralism because it argues for complexity over simples.

Kincheloe (2004c) uses postformalism to critique Howard Gardner. Let me explain.

First, let us deconstruct the term "intelligence." What does Gardner mean by this? How one defines intelligence is political. What counts as intelligent? Who counts as being intelligent? What is intelligence testing really about? All of these kinds of questions are raised throughout Kincheloe's edited collection. It is one thing to say that people are intelligent in different ways, but it is another thing to say that there are only eight ways that people are intelligent. Now, if a child does not exhibit intelligence in one of the eight ways suggested by Gardner, then the child must be arrested intellectually. So now we are back to the same problem that we had with Piaget. If a child does not develop according to the correct stages of development that means that the child is not normal. Intelligence cannot be reduced to either stages of development (Piaget) or to a number (Gardner) whether it is two or eight. Kincheloe argues, "While Gardner's notion of linguistic intelligence at first glance appears to value a more equitable classroom, it tacitly privileges the language of the dominant culture" (p. 6). The language of the dominant culture in America is English. So any student whose first language is not English falls outside of Gardner's frames of intelligence. Kincheloe goes on to say,

> Outside of an abbreviated reference to African drumming, African Americans and Africans in general and Latinos living in the United States and Latin American peoples in general, are absent in Gardner's work. In his examples of genius he stays quite close to those who test high on IQ tests. (p. 10)

But what do IQ tests really measure? Do they really measure whether or not you are smart? Or do they simply tell us that kids can take a test and answer the right questions? Who is making up the questions for these kinds of tests, and what kind of power game is being played here? Whose knowledge is being represented and for what purpose? Kincheloe helps clarify when he says,

> Throughout his [Gardner's] work…[he justifies] tacitly assuming that there are "proper" ways of producing truth (the scientific method of Descartes, Newton, and Bacon) and that some cultures have higher claims to truth, beauty, and morality than others (white Europe vis-à-vis Africa and African America). (p. 12)

Gardner's real point in his book is that only white European Americans are intelligent while everybody else is intellectually arrested. Here is where Foucault comes in. Kincheloe points out that for Gardner "multiple intelligences are value-free, objective constructs of science" (p. 12). Foucault taught that claims to knowledge are politically driven. There is no such thing as neutral and objective knowledge. Everything about knowledge is about power and politics. Again, Gardner suggests that intelligent people are white and of European descent. Is that objective and value free? No, that is called Eurocentrism and some might even call it racism. Kincheloe goes on to say,

> MI is a child of Cartesian psychology that fails to recognize its own genealogy. Gardner uses the intelligences to pass along the proven verities, the perennial truths of Western music, art, history, literature, language, math and science. (p. 13)

Recall Foucault (2003) as he suggested that history—and in this case the history of the Western tradition—must be scrutinized because it is about power. Where are Foucault's "subjugated knowledges" here? All of the world is not the West. There are other traditions rich in history, music, art, and literature. But Gardner seems to value only the white Eurocentric tradition. Foucault says, "History is the discourse of power, the discourses of the obligations power uses to subjugate" (p. 68). Thus, Gardner's "frames of mind" are clearly Western and serve to erase and subjugate the knowledges of others who do not fit into his frames of reference. Kincheloe (2004c) is calling for what Foucault terms a "counterhistory" (p. 73) of subjugated knowledges. Foucault explains,

> When I say "subjugated knowledges" I am also referring to a whole series of knowledges that have been disqualified as nonconceptual knowledges, as insufficiently elaborated knowledge: naïve knowledges, hierarchically inferior knowledges, knowledges that are below the required level of erudition or scientificity. (p. 7)

In essence, Kincheloe's take on Gardner's MI theory is that it is Eurocentric, racist, classist and sexist. To be intelligent for Gardner is to know the Western tradition. Whose cultural knowledge counts? And why? These are politically driven questions. Knowing the European tradition is fine and it is a fine tradition. But there are other traditions beside the European one and these other traditions should be taken seriously and seriously studied by scholars. This is partly what postcolonial scholarship is about as well. Colonized peoples learn the culture of the colonizers while their own traditions, for the most part, are erased, put down, denigrated. Colonized peoples are subjected to the culture of the colonizer.

Kathleen Berry (2004) says,

> Very limited, if any, criticism is directed at how intelligence theories like MI are in fact a classification system that reproduces the thought and knowledge of Western

civilization (excluding knowledge and values of women, nonwhite races, non-Christian, local, and premodern ways of knowing). (pp. 236–237)

Berry concurs with Kincheloe as she suggests that underneath Gardner's eight ways to knowledge are really eight ways of relearning the Great Books Tradition. The Great Books Tradition conserves the tradition of European white males. And one could consider the Great Books Tradition to also include not just books but European music, art, dance, and so forth. Classical forms of dance, classical forms of music and art are deemed "classical" only because the powerful deem them so. What is considered nonclassical? What is a classic and what kind of politics is behind what is considered classic? Again, what is considered classical are white European male writings, music, art, dance, painting, and so forth. However, there are other ways of knowing the world.

Posthistory: The Power and Politics of Representation of Histories of Children: Nancy Lesko and Bernadette Baker

Nancy Lesko

Nancy Lesko and Bernadette Baker engage in what Foucault (2003) calls "counterhistory" (p. 73). Recall, that Foucault (1979) insists that power is also productive, "power produces" (p. 194), it generates new knowledges, and this is what both Lesko and Baker are doing in their work.

So let us begin by looking at Lesko's (2001) work. Lesko states early on that the social construction of adolescence must be seen against the backdrop of "a technology of whiteness, of masculinity, and of domination" (p. 11). Children who, therefore, were not white and not masculine (which includes both boys and girls), were historically perceived as less-than-human. The technology of whiteness—about which Lesko speaks—is a way to normalize children. One hears the echoes again of Foucault (1979) who talks both about students and soldiers in 18th century France in the same context. Foucault suggests that students and soldiers have to "conform to the same model...so they might all be like one another" (p. 182). Foucault goes on to say that both students and soldiers are subject to a kind of "discipline" that (the school and the military) "compares, differentiates, hierarchizes, homogenizes, excludes. In short, [these institutions, the school and the military] serve to 'normalize'" (p. 183). Curriculum studies scholars have written much about the problem of normalization. For

Lesko that problem turns on "the technology of whiteness"; for Kincheloe that problem turns on the normalization of knowledge. To normalize is also a psychological technology, if you will, because children who study the Great Books Tradition internalize (or introject) what Lesko calls a "technology of whiteness" (p. 11). Children internalize the idea that the only knowledge that counts is the knowledge of the Western white European male tradition. Normalization, as a technology of the psyche, is also an important issue for Foucault (1988) in his book *Madness and Civilization* as he states that "the asylum [and one could also think of the school] reduces differences, represses vice, eliminates irregularities" (p. 258). One can think of Lesko's "technology of whiteness" (p. 11) in the context of Foucault's idea that disciplinary institutions like the insane asylum and the school serve to "eliminate irregularities." Lesko also was influenced in her thinking by Donna Haraway. One can see in Haraway (1989) what the technology of whiteness meant in the context of early 20th-century American history. In Haraway's book *Primate Visions* she discusses this craze of masculinity in the context of the Natural History Museum in New York City. The purpose of the museum was not really to exhibit natural species in order to teach people about the wild. No, the underlying agenda of the history of this museum was about preserving, not species, but masculinity. The museum was built, in part, to preserve the idea of nature as something to be conquered and tamed by manly men. A manly man like Teddy Roosevelt—whose statue is outside of the museum—is that very symbol of manhood conquering beastlyhood, if you will. The conservation and preservation of manhood are, at root, what the natural history museum was all about as Haraway tells us,

> To enter the Theodore Roosevelt Memorial, the visitor must pass by a James Earle Fraser equestrian statue of Teddy majestically mounted as a father and protector between two "primitive" men, an American Indian and an African, both standing, dressed as "savages." (p. 27)

American school children growing up during the days of Teddy Roosevelt were especially subjected to the craze of masculinity, racism, and the "technology of whiteness" (Lesko). Roosevelt represented this technology of whiteness, but even more than that, he represented the American call to conquer, to use Lesko's word here, to "colonize" the other. Lesko states, "This perspective on adolescence was framed, in part, through colonial relations and through sciences such as anthropology that originated in colonial settings with their racism and sexism" (p. 11). Similarly, Haraway—in the context of the biological sciences—says, "Literally and figuratively, primate studies were a colonial affair" (p. 19). To colonize primates meant that scientists like Yerkes, says Haraway, imposed his own view of how primates should be, rather than how they really were. Haraway goes on to explain that for Yerkes, "not accidentally, the primate story echoed primal themes in monotheistic religion, for there sex, power, and fatherhood are not strangers either" (p. 63). The way Yerkes saw primates, says Haraway, was like the way he saw people, especially those who were not white or manly. Primates were thought of not only as beasts but as Haraway puts it: "It takes little imagination to substitute the words *child, slave, patient,* or *woman* for *chimpanzee* in a rationally managed household" (p. 63). Haraway's take on Yerkes is not unlike Lesko's view that adolescent children who were not white and not masculine were thought of as beasts, savages, weak, unmanly, womanish, or even queer. Lesko states,

> The equation of children and primitive [read primate], of children and colonized savage, [think of the so-called savages standing next to Teddy Roosevelt's statue outside the Natural History Museum] was operative in overt colonialist discourse but also in child-rearing manuals, children's literature…racial science. (p. 34)

White male children had to live up to the image of the Rough Riders and Teddy Roosevelt, especially during the fin-de-siècle. The closing of the American frontier when all was thought to be conquered had men in a panic (Pinar, 2012). The white masculine child had to be manly and strong. Lesko says that interestingly enough

> homosexuality and effeminacy were added to the repertoire of men's anxieties, and gay-bashing was legitimated by appeals to nation, normalcy, and masculine upholding of purity. Elizabeth Young-Bruehl notes that adolescents and homosexuals shared the limelight as two newly defined populations in the turn-of-the-century United States. Both of these populations were tropes that in one sense promoted the importance of normalized bourgeois selves. (p. 39)

Lesko mentions gay bashing in the context of the early 20th century and its "legitimation." Gay bashing is nothing new.

Nancy Lesko uncovers some disturbing history as she studies the work of G. Stanley Hall who "wears the mantel of the 'father of adolescence' and was inspired mostly by The German Youth Movement" (p. 51). Lesko tells us,

> Although the German Youth Movement officially maintained an apolitical stance, its politics and activities contained elements of anti-Semitism, sexism, racial superiority, homophobia, and right-wing nationalism. Attitudes that intensified within later youth organizations, most notably, Hitler Youth. (p. 52)

G. Stanley Hall's ideas, Lesko suggests, were not unlike the ones advocated by the German Youth Movement. Hall was interested in "scouting, outdoor education, bountiful physical experience, and visits to farms" (p. 59). Hitler, too, was interested in the Volk (the people) getting get back to nature and living more simply. Hitler was threatened by the rise of industrialism—and yet he used industrial powers to build killing machines. The idea of the Volk is reactionary and parochial. The Volk—for Hitler—also represented all the things that Lesko mentions above: purity, anti-Semitism, homophobia, nationalism, and so forth. Purity for the Germans meant Ayran. Purity for G. Stanley Hall meant white. To be a real man means going out into nature and conquering it like Teddy Roosevelt. Thus, outdoor education was a way to ensure manhood, manliness. Play really meant the preparation of war. Scouting is like soldiering. Both wear uniforms and take oaths. Lesko mentions playgrounds and suggests that the agenda of the playground is not innocent. Playgrounds are places where boys learn to become men by playing games (as a preparation for war games). It is disturbing to note that in Hitler's *Mein Kampf* he suggests that German youth take up boxing so as to make themselves more manly (Morris, 2001). Boxing is a violent game and also a preparation for war. Hitting someone in the head is a prelude to shooting someone in the head. The Nazis found more efficient ways of killing people, though, by gassing them to death; they could easily kill at least two thousand people at a time without having to get their hands dirty (Morris). The gas chambers were efficient killing machines. Today, the military has learned how to make efficient killing machines as drones are controlled from offices in the United States by military officers who simply press a button to kill people in far away places like Afghanistan. The military officer never gets his hands dirty. He is engaging in a war without actually seeing blood. This couldn't be more different from the Great War where soldiers in the trenches lived with blood and guts splattered everywhere. Sandra Gilbert (2006) comments, "As many writers on the First World War have noted, trench warfare also frequently forced combatants to confront the unmediated 'primacy of death': soldiers sharing muddy holes with rats and cadavers" (p. 157).

Both Lesko (p. 49) and Haraway (p. 55) talk about the crisis of masculinity at the turn of the century and the "technology of whiteness." They both talk about the fear of "race suicide." For Lesko, the normalization of the adolescent had to do with the preservation of the white race. One way to ensure the preservation of the white race was to teach books only written by white men. Adults also feared that white boys—especially teenagers—were out of control, were "promiscuous…and regularly invoked discussions about the threats to nation and empire, the erosion of Anglo Protestant values and morals…and fears of racial suicide" (p. 49). Now, this phrase "race suicide" is rather curious and violent. How do you commit race suicide?

One has to remember that during the fin-de-siècle in America the eugenics movement was very popular. Eugenics was all about racial purity and getting rid of contaminants. Donna Haraway (1989) reminds us that many well-known American figures were "leaders of movements for eugenics" (p. 56). Haraway, in the context of the discussion of the Natural History Museum, tells us,

> Theodore Roosevelt's father was one of the incorporators of the museum in 1868. His son, Kermit, was a trustee during the building of African Hall. Others in that cohort of trustees were J. P. Morgan, William K. Vanderbilt, Henry W. Sage, H. F. Osborn, Daniel Pomeroy, E. Roland Harriman, Childs Frick, John D. Rockefeller III, and Madison Grant. (p. 56)

Eugenics, purity, manliness, nature and the great outdoors, taxidermy—as the real proof of man conquering beast—Haraway tells us, were all part of the agenda of the Natural History Museum. Lekso (2001) and Haraway both argue that these institutions (the Natural History Museum and the public school) were about making sure that boys became real men, masculine men, and learned to conquer primitives (read people of color, women, and children). Public schools, like the Natural History Museum, were to teach the lessons of white, pure, Anglo-Saxon culture where boys would become virile men, learning to conquer the world and colonize the Other. The lessons taught to high school students were lessons of whiteness and Eurocentric culture. No race mixing. Girls were taught that they should remain invisible and were taught that they were not intelligent or worthy of college. Girls were meant to marry, and if they did not marry then they were thought to be less-than-human spinsters. But schooling was not about girls or about people of color; schooling was not for girls or people of color. Schooling was for boys and schooling was meant to turn boys into men. Rough Riders. Lesko's book is truly a counterhistory, as Foucault put it, and truly *produces new knowledges* in the context of the broader cultural history against which the concept of the adolescence emerged.

Bernadette Baker

Like Lesko, Bernadette Baker (2001) offers a counterhistory of the child. Baker, *In Perpetual Motion*, tries to unsettle the concept of the child as a static category through a Foucauldian lens. Baker uses the phrase "thought-in motion" (p. xiii) to point out that thinking about the concept of the child is to undo any static definition people might have of children. What the child is, she suggests is unpredictable (p. xiii). She calls her work a "Historical Choreography" (p. 1) and suggests that thinking of the child is like thinking of a dance. To dance is to be in perpetual motion as the title of her book suggests. So if the concept of the child is in perpetual motion, one cannot think of the child as a static concept. Historicity teaches us, according to Baker, that the concept of the child changes over time. It is Foucault who has taught us about the changeableness of concepts and the "slipperiness" (p. 23), as Baker puts it, of terms through the study of history. Baker suggests that the ways in which scholars have talked about the concept of the child have to do with power—as Foucault suggests. Historiography is about power, as students know from our previous discussions of Foucault. The gist of Baker's text turns on the following passage as she states,

> The known child is active, mobilizing notice-abilities and shifting as a point of reference in the midst of what becomes knowable. Thus there is a ghost in the contested subject, child, which floats into the reading of documents. The ghost is that which is familiar, already recognized, unable to be discarded or suspended. (p. 28)

The concept of the child, then, for Baker is always on the move, always changing. It is not clear, after studying the concept of the child historically, what that concept really means. Baker tells us early on in her book,

> To that end, it is better to understand this work, not as a history of what children did, ate, played, wore, prayed, or learnt, but a history of what has been done with "the child." Through the writings of John Locke, Jean-Jacques Rousseau, Johann Herbert, and G. Stanley Hall the shifting conceptualization of the child, power, and strategies for education-rearing will be traced. (p. 3)

Baker seems more interested not in the literal child, but in the concept of the child, the representation of the child and the ways in which that representation has shifted across history. The child is not static, nor is it a thing. The child is a concept. And the concept of the child is a symbol for larger cultural issues.

Baker (1998) writes about "childhood-as-rescue in Child-Study, the first educational movement directed toward reforming U.S. public schools" (p. 118). Baker is suspicious of the rescue fantasy of children. The rescue fantasy turns again on Foucault's idea of normalization that I discussed earlier. Advocates of the child-study movement as well (like developmental psychology) wanted to rescue children from falling outside of normal development. But what are normal children? Who is normal? Baker's (2001) book is a particular kind of history of the child, and she wants to make sure that readers know that histories of the *concept* of the child change according to who is doing the writing. This was also Foucault's point. So if students want to read an interesting Foucauldian history of the concept of the child, Baker's (2001) book is crucial.

Foucault, Derrida, and Levinas

In this final section of this chapter, I want to first explore that I call the "other Foucault." Here I draw on Lawrence Grossberg's (2003) idea that there are, what he calls "different Foucaults" (p. 26). Most curriculum scholars draw on Foucault's (1979) *Discipline and Punish*. That book ties into many concerns scholars have about the institutions of public schooling and the university. But there are other important ideas Foucault discusses that tend to be overlooked by curriculum theorists. Briefly I want to talk about some of these ideas. Finally, I move onto commentaries by curriculum theorists on the works of Derrida and Levinas.

The Other Foucault

In Hubert Dreyfus and Paul Rabinow's (1983) book titled *Michel Foucault: Beyond Structuralism and Hermeneutics*, there is a question-and-answer section in which Foucault talks about many things that tend to get overlooked in his work. First, he talks about the Stoics in the context of the issue of normalization. Foucault (1983) states:

> I don't think one can find any normalization in, for instance, the Stoic ethics. The reason is, I think, that the principal aim, the principal target of this kind of ethics was an aesthetic one....The reason for making this choice was the will to live a beautiful life, and to leave to others, memories of a beautiful existence. I don't think that we can say that this kind of ethics was an attempt to normalize the population. (p. 230)

What strikes me in this citation is that Foucault talks about the problem of normalization in the context of ethics. This is interesting because many critics of poststructuralism think that poststructuralism has nothing to do with ethics. An ethic of normalization can be traced throughout the history of the concept of the child—as students learned from Baker (2001); an ethic of normalization can be traced throughout the history of psychiatry and ego psychology as students learn from Foucault (1988) in his study of madness. The issue of normalization has been taken up especially by queer theorists (e.g., see William Pinar's, 1998 edited collection on *Queer Theory in Education*). But the Stoics, says, Foucault, were not interested in normalizing people. To live a "beautiful life" as Foucault (1983) puts it—according to the Stoics—was a "personal choice" (p. 230). That personal choice could not be normalized because it was up to the individual to decide what a beautiful life meant. Today, scholars do not often talk about ethics in the context of the beautiful. So what does it mean to go back to the Stoics and think about ethics in the context of living a beautiful life? Perhaps this notion—of a beautiful life is—antiquated, quaint even. Living the beautiful life is about living aesthetically, as Foucault puts it. But what does that mean in today's crass consumerist society?

Foucault returns not only to the Stoics, but he also returns to the writings of Plato to ask interesting questions that often go unasked today. Foucault (1983) says that in Plato's text *Alcibiades* one comes across "the notion of *epimeleia heautou*, 'care of the self,' about the role of reading and writing in constituting the self" (p. 231). Foucault returns to Plato to explore the ways in which reading and writing—the scholar's vocation—can change the self. To take "care of the self," then, according to Plato is to read and write. But ironically, Socrates never wrote anything. In Plato's dialogues, Socrates is given voice through the mouthpiece of Plato, if you will. Plato reconstructed what Socrates taught through his dialogues. According to Derrida (1976), Plato valued speech over writing, because when the speaker speaks he is present and his presence makes his speaking more real. Writing is worth less—for Plato—because the speaker is not there to defend his writing and thus the writing leaves only a trace (to use Derrida's term) behind of what the speaker meant. So writing, according to Derrida, for Plato took a backseat to speaking. For Plato what really "constitutes the self" is not so much writing as it is speaking. In Derrida's (1976) book *Of Grammatology* he argues that the history of Western philosophy has been about the primacy of speech over writing. The history of Western philosophy, Derrida says, functions to

> confine writing to a secondary and instrumental function: translator of a full speech that was fully *present* (present to itself, to its signified, to the other, the very condition of the theme of presence in general), technics in the service of language, *spokesman* interpreter of an originary speech itself shielded from interpretation. (p. 8)

Again, according to Derrida, for Plato, what counted (about taking care of the self) was not writing, but speaking. Foucault, however, does not make this point. For Foucault, he reads Plato—especially in the text *Alcibiades*—as suggesting that a cared for and cared about self means developing good reading and writing practices. But then what to make of Socrates? He never wrote anything. How did Socrates constitute his self if he did not write?

Foucault (1983) continues this discussion of care of the self in another context as he talks about the Greek *epimeleia heautou* (p. 243) Here he argues that this "is a very powerful word in Greek which means working on or being concerned with something" (p. 243). What does it mean to work on something, or to be concerned about something? This is an ethical question. That question implies not only an ethic but also suggests taking care of the self. You cannot take care of yourself if you have nothing to work on, if you have no work, if you have no projects. Working on something—like a piece of writing or, say, composing a piece of music, means you are taking care of yourself. Many Americans work at a job that they don't like and they work at making money. Making money and working at a job you don't like is not taking care of the self. If your only concern is with money, you are not taking care of yourself. Foucault mentions this issue with money when he talks about money in connection with anti-intellectualism. Foucault (2003), in a lecture he gave in 1976, says:

> While it is true that in recent years we have often encountered, at least at the superficial level, a whole thematics: "life, not knowledge," "the real, not erudition," "money, not books," it appears to me that beneath this whole thematic, through it and even within it, we have seen what might be called the insurrection of "subjugated knowledges." (p. 7)

In America—the anti-intellectual culture that it is (see Richard Hofstader's (1965) *Anti-Intellectualism in American life*)—there are intellectual subcultures. These intellectual subcultures produce subjugated knowledges. Thus there are people who value Othered knowledges even in such an anti-intellectual climate, as Foucault points out.

Foucault (2003) also speaks about the role of the scholar. He says,

> Well, whatever meaning it was intended to have when it was founded long ago, the College de France now functions essentially as a sort of research institute: we are paid to do research. And I believe that, ultimately, the activity of teaching would be meaningless unless we gave it, or at least meant it, this meaning. (p. 1)

Working at an institution that prides itself on "teaching first" means that scholarship is secondary to teaching. But as Foucault points out, one cannot be a good teacher unless one does research. Even if an institution prides itself on teaching, professors must do scholarship, do research and write. But many professors in these institutions—where teaching is considered more important than publishing—publish nothing and stop reading, especially after they get tenure. Contrarily, in research institutions, at least in the United States, it seems that the teaching is secondary to research. This, too, is a flawed way of looking at scholarship and teaching. Both teaching and scholarship should be important. The scholarship should inform the teaching and the scholar should take care to care about his or her teaching, even if the university in which he or she is housed does not. In research universities, tenure is based mostly on scholarship, not on teaching. But ultimately, as Foucault points out, the scholarly life should be based on the intersection of research and teaching.

Foucault (1988) talks about a certain "mania for study; the life of the library" (p. 217). He suggests that this mania for study can lead to certain madness. Derrida (1995a) says, "A madness must watch over thinking" (p. 339). There is something mad about the life of the scholar—both Foucault and Derrida suggest. There is a never-ending quest to read, study, write. The scholar has to be a little mad to have a "mania for study," as Foucault puts it. But he also argues that this, too, can be dangerous. The scholar is two steps away from falling off the edge of the earth. Freud once said that psychoanalysis was an impossible profession—well the profession of the scholar, too, is impossible. There are some similarities between the schizophrenic and the scholar gone mad. Salomon Resnik (2001), says,

> Minkowski (1972) quotes Anglade, who compares the schizophrenic to a book in which the page numbering has gone haywire—all the pages are there, but they are dreadfully mixed up. If I may be permitted to continue the metaphor, I would add that the binding is often defective, and some of the pages tend to drop out. (p. 181)

Think about the scholar in the context of the above quote. The scholar writes books and those books are composed in the mind and sometimes the page numbers, ideas, thoughts, concepts, bindings go missing when the scholar reaches a blockage, or cannot follow her own train of thought. The writing of scholarly texts can go wrong if the scholar is not careful to take care of the self. Recall, Derrida (1995a) says "a madness must watch over thinking" (p. 339), meaning that the madness of the lost pages, the broken binding, the mess of it all, makes for interesting work. In fact, poststructural scholarship is not unlike what Resnik talks about when drawing on Anglade who suggests that for the schizophrenic "the pages are there, but they are dreadfully mixed up" (p. 181). Deleuze and Guattari's work is akin to the minds of madmen. The same with Zizek. But in the madness you can find a certain richness of thought. The world is not in order, it is not logical. Nothing makes much sense. But the scholar's task is to try to put things in order—as Foucault (1994) points out in his book *The Order of Things*—so as to try to make sense of things. But what students learn from Foucault is that the "order of things" is quite arbitrary. Derrida suggests that scholars always have to sit on the edge of a precipice to push thinking, to push the boundaries of thought, otherwise all we are doing is commenting on what everyone else has already said. Deleuze and Guattari (1994) write about "a threshold of indiscernibility" (p. 19). One of the reasons people are troubled by poststructural thought is that they cannot handle the indiscernibility of it, they want a reasoned, rational, logically argued philosophy. These are children of the Enlightenment. But those of us who can handle the not-knowing of life, find poststructural thinking interesting because in many ways it mirrors the world.

Jacques Derrida

One of the things that strikes me about the commentaries on Derrida by curriculum theorists is their focus on the political. This is what I will be exploring in this section. As students move through some of Derrida's work, I will introduce some of the most important Derrida scholars in curriculum studies.

Derrida (1988) suggests that there is a political aspect to reading and interpreting texts. The act of reading is political. On studying Nietzsche, Derrida remarks,

> In the terms of this context, the gesture consists in hearing, while we speak and as acutely as possible, Nietzsche's voice. But this does not mean that one simply receives it. To hear and understand it, one must also produce it, because like his voice, Nietzsche's signature awaits its own form, its own event. This event is entrusted to us.

Politically and historically…it is we who have been entrusted with the responsibility of the signature of the other's text which we have inherited. (p. 51)

When we read texts that are handed down to us—the texts that we inherit like Nietzsche's—it is our responsibility to not only read him and try to understand him but also to produce something from his work. Scholars are entrusted to the political act of reading and making Nietzsche's writing our own through our signature. What we do with a text, then, the way in which we make that text our own to produce something new is a political act; scholars must take responsibility for the way they make the text their own. Nietzsche comes alive again through the seriousness with which scholars interpret his texts. Thus, the act of reading is also an act of writing. For Derrida, these two acts are inseparable and political. It is not enough to read Nietzsche; scholars also must bring him to life again by writing about him and doing something with his texts. Derrida says, "It is the ear of the other that signs" (p. 51). This means that texts only come to life as others read them and write about them. As scholars it is our responsibility to bring texts to life and write about them, comment on them, and make them come alive once again. Derrida (2002c) remarks, "The context [of a text] is not only or always a discursive context. One politics is always being played against another" (p. 135). Texts are political. Reading and writing about texts is also political.

One of the most careful and thoughtful interpreters of Derrida in curriculum studies is Denise Egea-Kuehne. I would recommend to readers her co-edited book with Gert Biesta (2001) called *Derrida & Education*. This is one of the best collections of essays on Derrida and his impact on education. Some other excellent collections of essays on the intersections of education and Derrida are *Deconstructing Derrida: Tasks for the New Humanities*, co-edited by Peter Trifonas and Michael Peters (2005); *Derrida, Deconstruction, and the Politics of Pedagogy*, co-edited by Michael Peters and Gert Biesta (2009); and *Derrida, Deconstruction and Education: Ethics of Pedagogy and Research*, co-edited by Peter Trifonas and Michael Peters (2004). Peter Trifonas (2002) has written an important book on Derrida called *The Ethics of Writing: Derrida, Deconstruction, and Pedagogy*.

Denise Egea-Kuehne (2004) tells us, "Indeed, in his 2002 interview with France 3, Derrida insisted that philosophy is more necessary than ever to respond to the most urgent questions raised by today's sociopolitical context, questions of politics, ethics, and especially rights and law" (p. 25). Most of the commentary on Derrida by educationists is about his political writing. Most people consider Derrida to be a deconstructionist (which I see as a form of poststructuralism). Perhaps twenty years ago deconstruction was not thought to be political, but was thought of as an a-political way of interpreting texts. But today, many point out that interpretation—and certainly Derrida's insistence on the political aspects of interpretation—is what is key about Derrida. This might be surprising to our friends who do critical theory. But Derrida is not doing yet another kind of Marxism (although he has written on the importance of Marx). His form of political writing is unique. For example, in his book titled *The Other Heading: Reflections on Today's Europe*, Derrida (1992b) says, "The condition of possibility of this thing called responsibility is a certain *experience and experiment of the possibility of the impossible: the testing of the aporia* from which one may invent the only *possible invention, the impossible invention*" (p. 41). Now, Marxists might be uncomfortable with Derrida's writing because it is in no way straightforward. There is a lot of wordplay here and the text is rather confusing on a first read. But what Derrida is trying to do—like many other poststructuralists—is to show through wordplay how complicated reality is. The world is not transparent and neither is language. Derrida pushes us to rethink concepts by wordplay and by the careful use of words and the sheer love of language. Language is anything but transparent and the way in which Derrida uses it, much of the time through contradictions, forces readers to think again about concepts and their complex meanings. In the passage cited above, what Derrida is trying to say is that ethics, responsibility, and politics begin in unknowing—the aporia is that unknowing—it is that unresolved puzzle, the contradiction that has no resolution. That is what life is about, puzzles without answers. This is the heart of Derrida's thought. This is what makes Marxists nervous when reading him. They seem to be uncomfortable with Derrida's puzzles and suggest that there is nothing concrete about Derrida's wordplay and questioning. But they are wrong. Critics of Derrida should give him another try and try to better understand that his word puzzles are not only abstractions but they are also concrete and have real, material consequences. To say that it is our responsibility to begin from an unknown and to keep the puzzle or aporia alive is to say that politics is also a puzzle, to be political is to be complicated. Derrida is interested in what is impossible (p. 41). This is a political problem. To be political in a confusing world is impossible but necessary. It is impossible to understand, for example, the sheer act of violence in blowing up the World Trade Center. How could any human being do that? Political scholars understand that the United States has been, in many ways, what Derrida (2005) would call a "rogue" nation—through the exploitation and colonization of other peoples. But still, even if Americans are not liked—which they are not—blowing up the World Trade Center by flying airplanes into skyscrapers is unconscionable. There is no answer to this puzzle. This is what troubles Derrida. Derrida (2005) addresses violence in the form of torture in his book *Rogues: Two Essays on Reason*. He states, "There is always a wheel [*roue*] in torture. Torture always puts to work an encircling violence and an insistent repetition, a relentlessness, turn, and return of a circle" (p. 8). Think of waterboarding as a form of torture that was sanctioned by the Bush administration. This kind of brutality made the United States, under Bush, a rogue nation. What Derrida is suggesting above about the wheel of torture is that historically there has always been torture and torture comes back again and again like the spinning of a wheel. There is a sadistic element in torture. William Pinar (2001) makes this point in his book on lynching. Pinar suggests that there was a sexual (sadistic) element to lynching. Here again is the puzzle, the aporia about which Derrida speaks. Torture is not rational. But then again we do not live in a rational world, and that is Derrida's point. Torture and the discussion of it is a political issue. When Derrida discusses torture he is not merely involved in wordplay, he is deadly serious about this terrible problem that comes back and back and back again throughout history, like the spinning of a wheel.

Derrida (2002c) also talks about what he calls a "politics of memory" (p. 63). Memory and history are linked. We must remember our history. This is Derrida's point. Remembering our history is political. The danger of not remembering history is forgetting that torture, for example, is a historical event that recurs time and time again. It is our responsibility as scholars to grapple with that which is terrible, unthinkable. That is exactly what Derrida does in his work.

Memory, as Derrida says, is not just a personal thing, it is a political act and it is also a public responsibility. Interestingly enough, Derrida writes about the responsibility of memory in the context of education as he says,

> A politics of memory is necessary, perhaps, doubtless, but it is also necessary, in the name of the politics of memory, to educate....It is also necessary to educate or awaken "whomever" to vigilance with regard to the politics of memory. (p. 63)

Curriculum theorists in particular have embraced Derrida because of his interest in education. He comments on educational issues throughout his work. He is interested in the politics of education and the responsibility we have as educators to be vigilant in the way we educate others. To be educated means to grapple with the terrible, to grapple with the world in all of its violence. To awaken people, for Derrida, means that teachers need to make sure people understand that the world is violent; that racism and other hostilities are alive and well. Derrida (2000b) suggests that people become more cognizant about the politics of hospitality (p. 25). Here he is not being frivolous, and he certainly is not talking about the industry of hoteliers and hospitality in the context of vacations. To be hospitable means that one must not engage in hostilities toward the other. Derrida says,

> To put it in different terms, absolute hospitality requires that I open my home and that I give not only to the foreigner…but to the absolute, unknown, anonymous other, and that I *give place* to them. (p. 25)

The notion of the absolute other is also one that Levinas takes up throughout most of his writing. But how to welcome the absolute other into our home? Perhaps, as Derrida points out, it is another impossible task. Who is invited? Who decides? Who is not invited and why? How far does hospitality go? In the end hospitality is not something we can grant to everyone. Derrida is not a radical relativist. He is quite critical of what is going on, for example, in Europe today. He says in his book *The Other Heading,*

> Signs are coming to us from everywhere in Europe, where, precisely in the name of identity, be it cultural or not, the worst violences, those that we recognize all too well without yet having thought them through, the crimes of xenophobia, racism, anti-Semitism, religious or nationalist fanaticism, are being unleashed. (1992b, p. 6)

Scholars who critique deconstruction as some kind of silliness, do not read Derrida closely, if at all, and completely skip over passages like the one above or do not bother to find out that Derrida is concerned with issues of violence, politics, racism, and the rest. Discussions of racism are not only of concern to scholars of multiculturalism or postcolonialism, Derrida, too, is concerned with issues of racism and violence. One has to remember that Derrida grew up during the Holocaust and the Algerian War and that when he was a child he was forbidden to attend school because he was Jewish. He is very aware of the problems of anti-Semitism because he was a victim of that as a child. He does not write much about his Jewish background—there is some discussion of it here and there—but he does mention his childhood experiences with anti-Semitism and how they shaped him and how they made him aware of the problems of hatred, violence, and prejudice. The Algerian War, one of the most brutal wars of our time, also shaped Derrida's ideas on the problem of colonization and violence. He is much concerned with the idea of democracy and speaks about democracy throughout his work. He suggests, however, that we haven't yet achieved a democracy; it is, as he puts it, "to come," it is still in process. He even talks about what he calls "CyberDemocracy" (2005, p. 18). Is there cyberdemocracy, Derrida asks? No. Clearly, even the Internet is censored. Cyberdemocracy is to come.

Michael Peters and Peter Trifonas (2005) comment, "For Derrida the right to education and the question of the Humanities is articulated as the problem of protecting the right to a free expression of subjectivity and the alterity of human being" (p. 7). Freedom of speech is not guaranteed in our educational institutions and this is what bothers Derrida. Certainly, alterity is not prized either. In America, conformity is everything, and playing the game in the academy of not stepping out of line and being liked and likeable means hiding one's difference or alterity, as Derrida puts it.

Denise Egea-Kuehne and Gert Biesta (2001) remark, "The idea that responsibility, ethics and politics play a central role in Derrida's work goes against a widely held and often reiterated belief that deconstruction is concerned with anything but these issues" (p. 2). Again, people who do not read Derrida hold these misconceptions about his work. Michael Peters and Gert Biesta (2009) tell us more about this debate as they say,

> Surprisingly, the Left has castigated him for his *lack* of politics. We have never been able to understand the claim made periodically over the last thirty years, particularly by members of the liberal and Marxist Left and by the likes of Jürgen Habermas, Thomas McCarthy, and Richard Rorty, that Jacques Derrida is not "political," or that deconstruction is agnostic, politically speaking. In our view, Derrida is not only a political philosopher but perhaps even the most political of all contemporary philosophers. (p. 6)

Yes, Derrida is political. Two other texts by Derrida that concern politics are these: *Politics of Friendship* and *Ethics, Institutions, and the Right to Philosophy*, which is translated and edited by Peter Trifonas.

As I said earlier I would not reduce Derrida to being only a political philosopher because this is not his only focus or only concern. He writes on all kinds of topics, from painting and the arts, to television and popular culture, from language and reading, to animals. When I think of a political philosopher, Hannah Arendt (1979) is the first scholar who comes to mind. She devoted her life to political philosophy. Not so for Derrida. His work is much broader than Arendt's. However, curriculum scholars drive home the point that Derrida must be reread in order to understand that much of his work is devoted to politics. Peter Trifonas (2000) says, "The ethical and political efficacy of deconstruction continues to be vehemently questioned, argued, and vastly undertheorized" (p. 5). The curriculum scholars I mention in this section are working to theorize Derrida's writings on politics. Derrida's ideas on politics are not only "vastly undertheorized" by, say, literary critics or even other philosophers but also completely ignored altogether by many educationists outside of curriculum studies. Michael Peters (2004) points out that "much of the hostility [against Derrida] is defensive and held by those who have not read Derrida" (p. ix). Philosophers who are academy trained do not read or teach Derrida because what he does in his work is unlike what has been done traditionally in the field of philosophy. The academy is slow to accept new ways of thinking and the discipline of philosophy tends to be conservative. The study of Western philosophy is also partly the study of the Great Books Tradition. Progressive English professors and curriculum theorists and some philosophers of education have embraced Derrida's work. Derrida is a good fit for curriculum theorists because he presses the boundaries of thought and challenges the notion that philosophy has to be written in a particular style. To theorize curriculum is to think differently about academic work, and Derrida helps us to think differently about what counts as academic thought and scholarship. Derrida is probably not taught in many philosophy departments today. This probably also applies to the other poststructuralists because they, too, are thought to be illegitimate, not really doing philosophy. Poststructuralism, although it has been around now for at least thirty years, is still an unacceptable mode of philosophy for many traditional philosophers.

Emmanuel Levinas

Some might wonder why I include Levinas in this chapter. Many read him as a modernist. For me, Levinas is a poststructuralist mainly because of his concept of alterity. For Levinas there is no system of ethics. For him ethics is a way of relating to others. Remember that modernists like Bentham, Mill, and Kant had systems of ethics because they thought everybody could follow the same rules. However, the Holocaust was the major event that changed all of that. Levinas was a Holocaust survivor. His work comes out of that experience. Systems and rules for doing the right thing fell away during the horrors of the Holocaust. Even psychoanalysts who survived concentration camps felt that their training in understanding the human psyche was of little use (Morris, 2001). How so many people could do so many horrible things to innocent people, including children, remains a question. Where did ethics go then, where were the rules to life then? Even many churches hung Nazi flags (Morris). It is against this backdrop that Levinas wrote. Girt Biesta (2009) comments,

> The central insight of Levinas's writing is that Western philosophy has been unable to recognize the alterity of the other because it understands the relationship between man and world (including other men) primarily as an *epistemological* relationship, a relationship where an isolated, self-present mind or ego attempts to get accurate knowledge of the external world. Levinas refers to this gesture of Western philosophy, in which the ego or subject is the origin of all knowledge and meaning, as *egology*. The main implication of the epistemological preoccupation of modern philosophy is that the other can appear only as an object of knowledge. (p. 28)

To think of the other as "an object of knowledge" reduces a human being to a knowledge machine. Recall, Foucault believed that Western philosophers all along were asking the wrong question, that of epistemology. How we know what we know—as the main concern of modern philosophy—erases questions of culture. But more to the point, modern philosophy misses the main problem of the human being and for Levinas that question is ethical: how do we relate to one another? What is this relation about and why should we care about relationship? Human relating was Levinas's main concern and probably again this issue might have come out of his experience as a Holocaust survivor. Surviving the Holocaust had to shape his thinking in some way. Here I want to mention the most important book in curriculum studies that deals with the work of Levinas for students who are interested in reading excellent commentary on his work as it relates to education. The book I will be drawing on here is edited by Denise Egea-Kuehne (2008) and titled *Levinas and Education: At the Intersection of Faith and Reason*. Although as of yet there is not much scholarship in the field of curriculum studies outside of this excellent collection of essays, this collection is the beginning of an important conversation we need to be having on the work of Levinas. Perhaps the next generation will continue to take up Levinas's work and use it in its own way to grapple with educational issues.

Sharon Todd (2008) understands Levinas's "starting point for finding the meaning in ethics does not lie in definitions of what a subject ought to do, but how a subject becomes an expression of an ethical relation" (p. 170). Bentham, Mill, and Kant—considered the most important writers on ethics in modern philosophy—wrote "definitions of what a subject ought to do," as Sharon Todd suggests. For Levinas, though, he was not interested in "oughts" but, as Todd puts it, in the expression of a relation. This is an interesting turn of phrase in the context of Levinas. To express a relation is to complicate things. How I express myself to an Other is what matters for Levinas. This expression must be ethical in that I accept the absolute alterity of the Other and do not reduce the Other to the same. Not only this, as Denise Egea-Kuehne puts it, Levinas "establishes that humanity cannot be reduced to two individuals, because there is always *un tiers*, a third party—the reality of society—who disrupts, upsets the simplicity of this one-on-one encounter" (p. 33). The one-on-one encounter, as Freud well knew, was not in fact simple. There is much complexity in the relation between self and other. Levinas complicates what is already complicated by adding a third thing—the world. And the world gets in the way, or disrupts the conversation between the self and the Other, as Egea-Kuehne puts it. The world that disrupted Levinas's life was again the Holocaust. That was the horror of disruption. The self and Other are set against the backdrop of a world that is sometimes awful and violent. So how to express, to use Sharon Todd's (2008) word, a relation then? Levinas (1985) comments,

> One of the fundamental themes of *Totality and Infinity* is about which we have not yet spoken is that the intersubjective relation is a non-symmetrical relation. In this sense, I am responsible for the Other without waiting for reciprocity, were I to die for it. Reciprocity is *his* affair. (p. 98)

It takes an ethically mature person to engage in this kind of "non-symmetrical relation," as Levinas puts it. Most of us do things for people expecting something in return. When they do not do something for us in return, we tend to be disappointed or even insulted. But Levinas insists that reciprocity is not what we are after here. To expect something from someone else is ethically immature. But it seems that we do always want something from someone. Levinas says that this should not be our concern; rather we should focus on our own relation to the Other and responsibility for the Other. Now this relation to the Other again is one of accepting the absolute alterity of the Other. The Other is not the same. We should, then, not try to make the Other be like us. Achieving freedom means accepting the Other as Other. Levinas does not think that the ethical relation to the Other is about love. Levinas says,

I distrust the compromised word "love," but the responsibility for the Other, being-for-the-other, seemed to me, as early as that time, to stop the anonymous and sense-less rumbling of being. It is in the form of such a relation that the deliverance from the "there is" appeared to me. (p. 52)

Love seems perhaps too sentimental a word for Levinas. No, for him it is responsibility that carries the weight of the relationship. This "rumbling of being" is the absolute solitude that we find ourselves in when we experience existence in its naked form. We live our own lives—yes, in the company of others—but we die our own deaths. That is the naked reality of life. Being—that is, naked existence—is a difficult thought to comprehend. Responsibility for the Other and the acceptance of her total and utter difference and the acceptance of the non-reciprocalness of the relation are difficult to put into action. We want others to be like us; we want to believe that such a thing as love exists, and we do not usually think in terms of the responsibility to accept the Other in all her differences. If relations turn on responsibility and not on love, what kind of relations those would be?

Another interesting notion for Levinas (1985) turns on the problematics of vision in the context of ethicality. Although he speaks of the notion of "the face," he says, "I have just refused the notion of vision to describe the authentic relation with the Other; it is discourse and, more exactly, response or responsibility which is this authentic relation" (p. 88). So the notion of the face is not a literal one, it is a trope or metaphor for interrelation. Relating to someone is not about literally seeing her; it is about communicating with her. Perhaps the literalness of seeing someone gets in the way of our relating to her. If you are blind, seeing the other is not part of your relation at all. Derrida (1988) also raises questions around vision in his book *The Ear of the Other*. Derrida says, "It is the ear of the other that signs" (p. 51). Listening to someone is far more difficult than one might expect. There are different ways of communicating and listening.

Paul Standish (2008) tells us, "John Llewelyn…explores the possibility of an ecological reading of Levinas that extends the relation to the Other to animals and other living things" (p. 60). It is interesting to think of using Levinas to discuss human (animal) relations with nonhuman animals. Nonhuman animals are Other to us but we are Other to nonhuman animals as well. And yet we are both animals. Scholars might think of engaging in more conversations about Levinas in the context of human-animal relations. This might be work for the next generation of curriculum scholars.

· 9 ·

PSYCHOANALYTIC CURRICULUM CONCEPTS

Introduction

Psychoanalytically oriented curriculum theorists draw on a wide range of psychoanalytic theory to inform their work. Curriculum studies scholars draw on psychoanalytic theorists such as Sigmund Freud, Melanie Klein, Anna Freud, D. W. Winnicott, Julia Kristeva, Jacques Lacan, Carl Jung, and Wilfred Bion to name a few. In the first part of this chapter I will examine some key ideas of Sigmund Freud, Melanie Klein, and Anna Freud. This brief overview of these theorists will help students understand basic psychoanalytic concepts.

In the second part of this chapter, I will examine the connections between education and psychoanalysis. Educationist and psychoanalyst Deborah Britzman has written significant work on the strained relations between education and psychoanalysis. Hence, I will focus on Britzman's work to better understand the complex relations between education and psychoanalysis.

In the third part of this chapter I will unpack the work of curriculum theorists who draw on psychoanalysis to inform their work. Here I will discuss the work of William F. Pinar, Wendy Atwell-Vasey, Sharon Todd, Alice Pitt, Alan Block, Tamara Bibby, Peter Taubman, Paula Salvio, Madeleine Grumet, Jonathan Silin, Mary Aswell Doll, and Marla Morris.

Sigmund Freud

Sigmund Freud is the father of psychoanalysis. Through the use of primary and secondary texts I will explore some key concepts for Freud. Freud's work is difficult and at times his writing is quite obscure. Students who want to understand psychoanalysis must read Freud. Freud is the most important and foundational figure in the history of psychoanalysis. In one way or another, all psychoanalysts have been influenced by Freud. Peter Gay (1989b) claims,

> Sigmund Freud—along with Karl Marx, Charles Darwin, and Albert Einstein—is among that small handful of supreme makers of the twentieth-century mind whose works should be our prized possession. Yet, voluminous, diverse, and at times technical, Freud's writings have not been as widely read as they deserve to be...he was a great stylist and equally great scientist. (p. xi)

Part of the reason Freud's writings have not been widely read is perhaps because of their difficulty. Reading Freud closely one finds that he changes some of his positions over the course of his life. Clearly Freud captures the complexity of the mind. The mind is not a static thing for Freud, but always changing. He knew this from a neurological standpoint since he was an MD and neurologist. Sander Gilman (1988) points out, "Psychoanalysis originated not in the psychiatric clinic but in the laboratories of neurology in Vienna and Paris. Its point of origin was not nineteenth-century psychiatry but rather nineteenth-century neurology" (pp. 15–16). Ironically, his writings do not read like neurological texts, but rather they are poetic, literary. And because of his style, some wonder whether he was really doing science after all. One might say that Freud was a literary scientist.

Stephen Mitchell (1988) remarks,

> The theory of instinctual drive is the conceptual framework which houses all of Freud's ideas: theoretical postulates, clinical insights, technical recommendations. Freud characterized the drive theory as part of his "metapsychology"—which suggests that it is the most abstract level of his theorizing, the furthest from clinical experience. (p. 1)

Deborah Britzman (2011) explains Freud's theory of drives and shows how over time Freud changed his position. Britzman writes, "At the time of the metapsychology, Freud had two drives in mind—the sexual drive and the self-preservation drive. With this early view, sexuality is greatly dispersed, polymorphous, and perverse"(p. 108). Britzman explains that in 1920, in Freud's later work, he "would change this to the postulates of Eros and Thanatos" (p. 109). Eros is the life drive and Thanatos is the death drive. Like Freud, Melanie Klein (1948/1993) would discuss "the struggle between the life and death instincts" (p. 32). Anna Freud, too, wrote about drives. Rose Edgcumbe (2000) reports,

> Anna Freud's loyalty to Sigmund Freud's drive and structural theories, in which instinctual drives are seen as the motivating force for all human behavior, meant that when writing or speaking theoretically she formulated all her ideas about relationships in terms of drive theory and ego functioning. (p. 3)

The idea of the death drive became controversial, especially among object relations theorists. Later I will discuss object relations but for now it should be pointed out that all psychoanalysts did not agree with Sigmund Freud on this point. Peter Rudnytsky (2002) tells us, "[The] achievement of the object relations school has been precisely to clear away the detritus of Freud's instinct theory—a relic of nineteenth-century psychophysics" (p. 10). Deborah Britzman reminds us that Freud suggested, "The drives are mythology" (p. 109). The drives are not found in the brain but are metaphors. Taken too literally, drive theory becomes problematic. Still, many object relations theorists had little use for the concepts of instincts or drives.

Another theory that Freud would change is what he called the "seduction theory." Peter Gay (1989a) explains, "First he had to jettison the 'seduction theory' he had championed for some time. It held that *every* neurosis results from premature sexual activity, mainly child molestation, in childhood" (p. xiii). Gay claims that Freud's mistake was that he suggested that all forms of neuroses were caused by child molestation. Clearly, neurosis has multiple causes. It is important to note that—as Gay tells us—"Freud never claimed that sexual abuse does not exist" (p. xiii). Of course Freud was well aware that children are in vulnerable situations, especially when they grow up in homes where, say, incest, occurs.

Freud would also change his theory of the mind from what he called the "topographic model" to the "structural model." Freud (1952) explains,

> The subdivision of the unconscious is part of an attempt to picture the apparatus of the mind as being built up of a number of *functional* systems whose interrelations may be expressed in spatial terms, without, of course, to the actual anatomy of the brain. (I have described this as the topographical method of approach.) (pp. 34–35)

Greenberg and Mitchell (1983) explain that there are "three psychic systems delineated in this model—the unconscious (Ucs.), preconscious (Pcs.), and conscious (CS.)" (p. 69). This topographical model was introduced in 1900 and was replaced in 1923 by what Freud called the structural model of id, ego, and superego. Juliet Mitchell (1998) reports,

> In the 1920s Freud argued that the neonate is born with what is to become the id, the ego and the super-ego undifferentiated. The ego and the super-ego (in that order) are carved—never totally, never forever—out of the id. The id…is the repository of ideational representatives of human drives. (p. 17)

Again, these terms "id," "ego," and "superego" are metaphors; they are not literally found in the brain.

On a close reading of Freud's texts one finds a multitude of descriptors that work to explain the complications of the id, ego, and superego. In *The Question of Lay Analysis* Freud (1978) explains,

> Everything that happens in the id is and remains unconscious, and that processes in the ego, and they alone, *can* become conscious. But not all of them are, nor always, nor necessarily; and large portions of the ego can remain permanently unconscious. (p. 19)

In *Beyond the Pleasure Principle*, Freud (1961a)—even though drawing on the topographical model of mind—states, "It is certain that much of the ego is itself unconscious" (p. 20). In Freud's (1959) book *Inhibitions, Symptoms and Anxiety*, he claims, "In many situations the two [the ego and the super-ego] are merged; and as a rule we can only distinguish one from the other when there is a tension or conflict between them" (p. 17). In *An Outline of Psycho-Analysis*, Freud (1969) states, "The new super-ego now has an opportunity for a sort of *after-education* of the neurotic; it can correct mistakes for which his parents were responsible in educating him" (p. 53).

Deborah Britzman (2003) will make much of Freud's phrase "after-education." I will explore in detail Britzman's work later on. What is striking about this phrase "after-education" is that obviously Freud believes that the super-ego is not always punitive. The super-ego can also serve as teacher. His suggestion is that parents do not always get it right when raising a child. When the child becomes an adult she has to undo miseducation and start all over again. But this task is not so simple. The internalization of the parents never fully disappears. There is always already a remainder of the internalized parents and that remainder might not go away—ever. This is the case especially when children are abused by their parents.

The ego serves different functions according to Freud. In the following passage one begins to understand how complex the ego is. Freud (1969) writes,

> No such purpose as that of keeping itself alive or of protecting itself from dangers by means of anxiety can be attributed to the id. That is the task of the ego, whose business it also is to discover the most favorable and least perilous method of obtaining satisfaction, taking the external world into account (p. 17)

In *Inhibitions, Symptoms and Anxiety*, Freud (1959) states that "the ego is the seat of anxiety" (p. 12). In *The Ego and the Id*, Freud (1960a) claims that the ego "exercises the censorship on dreams" (p. 8). In *The Question of Lay Analysis*, Freud (1978) says, "The ego is an organization characterized by a very remarkable trend towards unification, towards synthesis" (p. 18). Being ego-syntonic means that the ego is capable of integrating all kinds of experience. It is not difficult to integrate good experiences but it is difficult to integrate bad experiences, like the death of a parent. Freud (1978) also writes, "For us the ego is really superficial and the id something deeper.... The ego lies between reality and the id" (p. 17). Freud (1978) tells us, "In the id there are no conflicts, contradictions and antitheses persist side by side in it unconcernedly, and are often adjusted by the formation of compromises" (p. 17). The id is the unconscious, and if most of the ego and superego remain mostly unconscious, one wonders how people get along in life at all. After all, if we are led around by the unconscious, how do we know what we are doing, or saying for that matter? In *The Psychopathology of Everyday Life*, Freud (1960b) writes about various parapraxes—as he called them—like forgetting names, words, slips of the tongue, and bungled actions. Freud suggests that, for example, a bungled action, as he calls it, is no accident. Something in the id or unconscious is behind these mix-ups. And for Freud, the only way to make the unconscious conscious is through psychoanalytic treatment. In this treatment the patient is to say whatever comes to her mind (this is called "free association"), but this is extremely difficult to do because the ego acts as a censor and blocks our understanding of conflicts. Deborah Britzman tells us that Freud

> admitted his method of free association was hardly original. The method was derived, he said, from a book he received in his youth written by one Ludwig Borne and carrying the title *The Art of Becoming an Original Writer in Three Days*. The advice was to write everything down in one's head. (p. 14)

Some fiction writers might call this method "stream of consciousness." But again it is extremely difficult to do this because the ego serves as a censor, especially for uncomfortable or troubling thoughts.

Another concept, namely the id, was not original to Freud. Louis Breger (2000) points out,

> Freud borrowed this idea from Georg Groddeck, a German physician and psychotherapist, whose *Book of the It* he had read in manuscript form just before writing *The Ego and the Id*. As he described elsewhere, the unconscious id is a "seething cauldron" of instincts. (p. 272)

Groddeck's "It" is a mystical term. Freud's "id," rather, is a scientific term. Freud would have no truck with mysticism. This was part of the reason Freud broke his friendship with Carl Jung—he was too mystical and his theories broke away from Freud's. Freud believed that his work was science.

Another idea that is not original to Freud is the unconscious. Peter Gay (1998) claims,

> Freud did not discover the unconscious, by the Age of the Enlightenment, some perceptive students of human nature had recognized the existence of unconscious mentation. One of Freud's favorite eighteenth-century German wits, Georg Christoph Lichtenberg, had commended the study of dreams as the avenue to otherwise inaccessible self-knowledge. Goethe and Schiller, whom Freud could quote by the hour, had sought the roots of poetic creation in the unconscious. (pp. 127–128)

There is no doubt that scholars are influenced by others. Freud's ideas emerged in a certain time and place and he read scholars who influenced his ideas. Nobody lives in a vacuum. Scholars are influenced by other scholars, and by poets, novelists, artists, and so forth. It is interesting to note that Freud's science was actually built on mythology.

The Oedipus complex comes from Greek mythology. Mythology, according to Mary Aswell Doll (2011), was the first science. Freud's science was built on myth. But again, this does not mean that his work is unimportant. The Oedipus complex is one of the most important ideas for Freud. Many of our psychological problems stem from this complex, which some dub the "family romance." Jean Laplanche and J.-B. Pontalis (1973) define the Oedipus complex as follows:

> In its so-called *positive* form, the complex appears as in the story of *Oedipus Rex*: a desire for the death of the rival—the parent of the same sex—and a sexual desire for the parent of the opposite sex. In its *negative* form, we find the reverse picture: love

for the parent of the same sex, and jealous hatred for the parent of the opposite sex. (pp. 282–283).

For Freud, the Oedipus complex occurs when children are three to five years of age (Britzman, 2011). It is remarkable that children have such intense emotions at such an early age. Desire, jealous hatred, the death wish are all emotions that one might attribute to teenagers but not to toddlers. The Oedipus complex, for Melanie Klein, occurred even earlier, during the first year of life (Petot, 1990). That children experience, say, jealous hatred shatters the notion of the innocence of childhood. Peter Rudnytsky (2002) tells us "Freud embarked on a quest to find a *Kernkomplex*—a core or nuclear complex—of the neuroses" (p. 6). The Oedipus complex is that "core or nuclear complex." Love and hatred of parents are, at bottom, the root of most of our psychological problems. Even long after parents die, children still get caught up in the Oedipal drama but now with new authority figures. And this is what Freud called "transference." People tend to transfer old feelings onto new people without realizing what they are doing. Freud (1952), in *An Autobiographical Study*, remarks that only in psychoanalytic therapy can the patient understand old psychic conflicts through transference. Freud (1952) says,

> The transference is made conscious to the patient by the analyst, and it is resolved by convincing him that in his transference-attitude he is *re-experiencing* emotional relations which had their origin in his earliest object-attachments during the repressed period of his childhood. (p. 47)

For Freud, love and hate play a role in the transference of the patient. The psychoanalyst, too, is subject to what Freud called "countertransference," the love and hatred of the patient. Freud felt that if the psychoanalyst experiences countertransference she was not analyzed well enough. Psychoanalysts must go through analysis before they engage with patients. For the analyst the point is not to act out love and hate but to try to understand why the patient invokes these feelings in the analyst.

Dreams

A patient who undergoes psychoanalysis discusses her dreams. Dreams are of great importance for Freud. Freud's (2010) *The Interpretation of Dreams* and Freud's (1980) book *On Dreams* are crucial texts, for they teach much about the workings of the unconscious. Freud (2010) tells us, "All dreams are fulfillments of wishes" (p. 171). Freud remarks that his "patients invariably contradict my assertion" (p. 171). Greenberg and Mitchell (1983) point out "wishes are behind all psychic activity" (p. 29). This claim is rather curious. However, Freud (1980) suggests, "The wishful fantasies revealed in analysis in night dreams often turn out to be repetitions or modified versions of scenes from infancy" (p. 50). Since most people cannot remember infancy dreams serve to remind, to work something out, to send messages. But these messages are not so clear. Deborah Britzman (2011) remarks,

> In a footnote to *The Interpretation of Dreams*, added in 1925, Freud cautioned analysts on their desire to interpret the dream's latent meaning and even advised them to question their motives in holding to the idea that dreams can be interpreted and put to rest. (p. 85)

Freud suggests that there are both latent and manifest content in dreams. The manifest content is the plot of the dream, the storyline of the dream, while the latent content is what the dreamer makes of the dream. Freely associated, the dream interpretation takes curious shifts and turns that seem to make little sense. And yet there is some sense to be made although it is unclear what that sense is. For Freud, then, the important part of the dream is the latent content and the freely associated work around the images of the dream. And yet, as Britzman points out in the above citation, Freud admitted that dreams hide meaning and freely associated lines of thought are never really clear. To think that one can easily interpret a dream is too literal a thought. Dreams are anything but literal. In *An Autobiographical Study*, Freud (1952) explains,

> The *manifest* dream was no more than a distorted, abbreviated, and misunderstood translation, and usually a translation into visual images. These *latent dream-thoughts* contained the meaning of the dream, while its manifest content was simply a make-believe, a façade, which could serve as a starting-point for the associations but not for the interpretation. (p. 48)

Another reason that it is difficult to get the meaning from a dream is that dreams are highly censored by the ego (Freud, 1952). They are products of distortion and are disguised (Freud, p. 48). Thus, it seems that dreams can teach us things but for the most part they are confusing and misunderstood. Still, freely associating around the dream might help to put together parts of the puzzle that is the mind. Freud (1961c) says in *Five Lectures on Psycho-Analysis*, "The interpretation of dreams is in fact the royal road to a knowledge of the unconscious" (p. 33). But the road to the unconscious is not what it seems. In fact, Freud (2010), in *The Interpretation of Dreams*, says, "Our scientific consideration of dreams starts off from the assumption that they are products of our own mental activity. Nevertheless the finished dream strikes us as something alien to us" (p. 77). There is something strange about dreams; there is something unsettling in the psyche. We are not who we think we are. This alien feeling we experience in dreams makes us Other to ourselves. Carl Jung would take this notion further with his idea of the collective unconscious. Here, the psyche is impersonal and has within it contents from culture passed down from generation to generation. The images experienced in a dream might be found in ancient texts. There is, in other words, always already a cultural aspect of dreams. The dreams do not come out of nowhere but relate to a forgotten past. For Freud, however, the dream relates to a forgotten childhood.

Freud (1966a) claims that there is a connection between dreams and neurosis. In fact, he states that "the study of dreams is not only the best preparation for the study of neurosis, but dreams are themselves a neurotic symptom" (p. 102). But what this neurotic symptom is, is not so clear. Deborah Britzman (2011) comments, "Dreams carry on their machinations through procedures of condensation, substitution, reversal into their opposites, consideration of representations, and displacement" (pp. 4–5). Interpreting dreams is akin to putting a puzzle together but some of the pieces get lost or misplaced. This puzzle, however, is never fully put together as things get in the way of completing the work of the puzzle. Dream work, as Freud puts it, is this puzzle.

What might puzzle readers of Freud is that, on the one hand, he suggests that dreams are neurotic symptoms, but on the other hand, he also claims that dreams are psychotic. Freud (1969), in his book *An Outline of Psycho-Analysis*, states,

> A dream, then, is a psychosis, with all the absurdities, delusions and illusions of a psychosis. A psychosis of short duration, no doubt, [is] harmless even entrusted with a useful function, introduced with the subject's consent and terminated by an act of his will. None the less it is a psychosis. (p. 49)

What Freud attempts to say here is that all of us have a bit of psychosis within. Dreams are psychotic and according to Freud they are also neurotic. But isn't neurosis different from psychosis? How do these two things square? Perhaps the line between neurosis and psychosis is not so clear. Is it possible that someone could be both neurotic and psychotic?

In Freud's (2010) *The Interpretation of Dreams*, he tells us, "We shall be in agreement with every authority on the subject in asserting that dreams *hallucinate*—they replace thought by hallucinations" (p. 79). Thus, dreams are neurotic, psychotic, and hallucinatory. Of course, hallucinations are psychotic. Hence, it becomes difficult to interpret dreams. Mitchell and Black (1995) say that because of all of these complications the dreamer gets thrown off track (p. 9). Freud (1980), in his book *On Dreams*, tells us, "From the point of view of analysis, however, a dream that resembles a disordered heap of disconnected fragments is just as valuable as one that has been beautifully polished and provided with a surface" (p. 49). Freud (1980) also values trivialities in relation to dreams. What seems unimportant can actually be extremely important in understanding the patient's psychic life. When a patient freely associates from what is trivial, other things come up that were not intended or expected. Sometimes amid the trivia one finds profundity. In analysis, too, it is what we do not say or think to say (perhaps because we think the idea unimportant) that becomes key to what is going on psychically. At the end of the day, the analyst does not interpret the dream. Laura Marcus (1999) tells us, "It is the dreamer himself, Freud asserts, who should tell us what his dream means" (p. 21). Most often, though, dreamers do not know what their dreams mean. The analyst, by asking questions, attempts to help the dreamer understand the dream or make sense of the dream. But deeply repressed material is not easy to get at. To make what is unconscious conscious is all part of what Freud called the dream work. It is, indeed, work to uncover the hidden meanings of dreams. Freud (1952), in *An Autobiographical Study*, remarks,

> I have given the name of *dream-work* to the process which, with the cooperation of the censorship, converts latent thoughts into the manifest content of the dream. It consists of a peculiar way of treating the preconscious material of thought, so that its component parts become *condensed*, its mental emphasis becomes *displaced*, and the whole of it is translated into visual images or *dramatized*, and filled out by a deceptive *secondary elaboration*. (p. 50)

Dreams are distorted, displaced, and confusing. Dreams point to the complications of psyche and how difficult it is to know thyself. Dreams, then, are the heart of psychoanalysis. Dreams are the key to a center that will not hold. Dreams shatter the notion of a core self. And at the end of the day, we really do not understand, after all, what dreams are or what they mean.

Object Relations and Melanie Klein

Melanie Klein (1948/1993) is considered the mother of object relations theory. While Klein draws on some of Freud's concepts, her work veers in a different direction. Klein was one of the first psychoanalysts to work with children, along with Anna Freud. Here too, Klein's work differs from Anna Freud. Klein's theoretical work poses difficulties for readers. Klein startles. Here, I will unpack some of Klein's work to help understand better how curriculum theorists draw on her theories to inform their work.

David Scharff (2005) tells us,

> The notion of "object relations" originated with Freud's discussion of the fate of the sexual instinct, libido, seeking an object or person by which to be gratified. However, a psychology of object relations that put the individual's need to relate to others at the center of human development first achieved prominence in the work of Ronald Fairbairn and Melanie Klein, who thought that the efforts of each infant to relate to the mother constituted the first and most important tendency in the baby. Winnicott's work, which began slightly later, soon became a central part of this legacy. (p. 3)

Klein's writings deal mostly with the unconscious relations between the baby and the mother. For Klein, psychological problems for the child begin with unconscious phantasies of the mother. Sometimes these phantasies have little to do with the real mother or the actual mother. Conversely, for Winnicott, the actual or real mother—who is a bad mother—causes psychological problems. Winnicott felt that a child has problems because the mother or the environment causes them.

For Klein, psychological problems for the child begin in the pre-Oedipal phase. Jean-Michel Petot (1990) points out that for Klein an "'early' Oedipus complex [occurs] at the end of the first year of life" (p. xi). For Anna Freud the Oedipal complex arrives later when the child is between three and five years of age (Holder, 2005). Lyndsey Stonebridge and John Phillips (1998) argue,

> The differences between Sigmund Freud and Melanie Klein often focus on the theoretical role of time. For Freud a symptom is always the return of a past that was created by repression (the return of the repressed). Klein on the contrary is apparently more interested in the perpetual present of infantile experience. Significantly, of course, the foundation of Klein's theory is in the pre-Oedipal child, who, in Freudian terms at least, is a child without memory, a child who has not acquired a history. (p. 7)

Children, early in life, develop psychological problems and these problems could predate the arrival of this early Oedipal conflict. If the child cannot yet speak, how do we know that psychological problems arrive early in the child's life? Klein's theories come from her work with very young children. She observed disturbing behaviors in young children. Julia Segal (1992) points out that for Klein, young children have rich—and sometimes disturbing—phantasies about the mother. These phantasies of the mother are often negative. Segal tells us that for Klein

> children relate to the whole world through the unconscious fantasies. Nothing is seen simply as it is: some kind of unconscious fantasy is attached to every perception: structuring, colouring and adding significance to it. Following Strachey, Klein used the word "phantasy" for unconscious fantasies to distinguish them from conscious fantasies. (p. 29)

The question that some might ask is how Klein knew what went on in the minds of young children who did not yet speak? Again, Klein's speculations about young children came from her observations from working with children. These early phantasies structure the psyche in such a way as to make for grave psychic problems when the child gets older. Meira Likierman (2001) explains,

> Klein also showed how the severe mental illnesses of schizophrenic and manic-depressive psychosis were subject to predictable unconscious patterns which could be traced back to early anxiety situations and their impact on the partially formed, fragile psychic apparatus of the infant. (p. 12)

Klein contends that paranoid schizophrenia and manic-depressive psychosis first emerge in the early years of the infant. Full-blown schizophrenia usually presents in young adult life, say, around twenty years old. But for Klein schizophrenia and other mental illnesses have deep roots in early childhood.

Klein (1940/1975) teaches that there are two phases (p. 2) of mental illness that occur in infancy. Klein states,

> The early period (first described as the "persecutory phase") I later termed "paranoid position", and held that it precedes the depressive position. If persecutory fears are very strong, and for this reason (among others) the infant cannot work through the paranoid-schizoid position, the working through of the depressive position is in turn impeded. (p. 2)

What is striking about the paranoid-schizoid position and the depressive position is that Klein argues that these phases occur in "the first few months of life" (p. 32). Thus, these phases present during the preverbal stage of life. If the infant does not yet speak how does Klein come to these conclusions? How do we know what goes on in the mind of an infant? Klein argues, "The root cause of persecutory fear in the paranoid individual, is, I believe, the fear of annihilation of the ego—ultimately by the death instinct" (p. 33). The fear of annihilation begins early on in the life of the infant and reemerges (what Freud would call the return of the repressed) in adulthood. Because of this fear of annihilation, the infant becomes destructive (p. 2). Klein puts it this way:

> From the beginning the destructive impulse is turned against the object and is first expressed in phantasied oral-sadistic attacks on the mother's breast, which soon develop into onslaughts on her body by all sadistic means. The persecutory fears arising from the infant's oral-sadistic impulses to rob the mother's body of its good contents, and from the anal-sadistic impulses to put his excrements into her. (p. 2)

For Klein the child is not innocent but paranoid. It seems quite clear that Klein believes that the paranoid-schizoid and the depressive position begin early on. These are two serious forms of mental illness. Again, for Klein these negative phantasies begin early on and they have little to do with the real mother.

Klein draws upon the notion of envy in relation to the phantasized mother. Klein (1940/1975) states,

> My work has taught me that the first object to be envied is the feeding breast, for the infant feels that it possesses everything he desires and has an unlimited flow of milk, and love which the breast keeps for its own gratification. This feeling adds to his sense of grievance and hate. (p. 183)

Envy is related to "persecutory anxiety" (p. 187). If the infant can work through persecutory anxiety she develops "a strong capacity for love and gratitude" (p. 187). But before she develops this capacity she must work through the depressive position and begin the process of guilt and reparation. Klein claims, "The reparative tendency can, therefore, be considered as a consequence of the sense of guilt" (p. 36). In other words, the infant who once believed that the mother (or bad breast) wanted to annihilate the infant, now feels badly or guilty that she felt such negativity and wants to make amends.

Klein claims that the line between the paranoid-schizoid position and the depressive position is not clear (p. 16). Klein says, "Some fluctuations between the paranoid-schizoid and the depressive positions always occur" (p. 16). Klein also puts it this way: "However, persecutory and depressive anxieties, though conceptually distinct from one another, are clinically often mixed" (p. 45). And Klein restates this idea again as she declares, "But even during the next stage, the depressive position…persecutory anxiety persists" (p. 37).

Lyndsey Stonebridge and John Phillips (1998) suggest that, for Klein, both the paranoid-schizoid position and the depressive position do not go away during childhood but rather persist into adult life:

> But the relationship between the adult and child is perhaps what is most difficult to read in Klein's writings. One of the controversial issues is the question of how much the infantile mechanisms, represented by paranoid anxiety and depressive guilt, remain in operation during adult life. The Kleinian answer is disturbing. The adult is never free of the infantile processes. (p. 6)

These archaic problems haunt. The older the psychic problem the harder it is to undo. The question becomes what can a mother do for the child so as to prevent illness. Recall that for the infant the mother is a phantasized mother, not the real mother. For Klein, schizophrenia and depressive psychosis have little to do with the real mother. Likierman (2001) states that Klein analyzed young children and developed many of her theories by observing and

> taking detailed note of the verbal and symbolic expressions of her patients, Klein chronicled the many states of instinctual turmoil, sadistic cruelty and acute anxiety....The data opened the door into the child's inner life and led Klein to conclude that young children suffer from extremes—their cruelty is uncontrollably sadistic. (Likierman, 2001, p. 9)

The first question that comes to mind here is whether young children can be psychoanalyzed. Klein believes that the mind of a child is not that different from the mind of an adult. The child can develop transference with the analyst. Emotionally the child is no different from the adult. Klein felt that children have the capacity to understand what analysis is about. These beliefs opened the floodgates of criticism, especially by Anna Freud who did not think that children could be psychoanalyzed. I will explore these ideas in more detail when I discuss the work of Anna Freud.

Klein states that anxiety plays a large role in the development of illness. Klein writes that the "primary cause of anxiety is the fear of annihilation, of death, arising from the working of the death instinct within" (p. 57). Klein states that there are "two main forms of anxiety—persecutory and depressive anxiety—but I pointed out that the distinction between these two forms of anxiety is not by any means clear-cut" (p. 34). To clarify here, persecutory anxiety is related to the paranoid-schizoid position and depressive anxiety is related to the depressive position. Thus anxiety plays a large role in the development of infants. Adults who suffer from anxiety probably—as Klein might point out—experienced anxiety in infancy. Anxiety, for Klein, is an archaic problem. Julia Kristeva (2001) remarks, "Klein believed that the child, from the very beginnings of life, is consumed with anxiety" (p. 61). Deborah Britzman (2003) writes, "For Melanie Klein, the analysis of unconscious anxiety must and can be readily encountered as the basis of analytic work" (p. 63). The problem here is how to make unconscious anxiety conscious? Through psychoanalysis.

Eli Zaretsky (1998) states, "Melanie Klein is probably the most important figure in the history of psychoanalysis after Sigmund Freud, yet her contributions are not widely understood" (p. 33). Part of the reason why Klein is "not widely understood" is that her writings are highly difficult to unpack. Further, Klein's theories of the preverbal period are hard to understand. Lyndsey Stonebridge and John Phillips (1998) state, "For some readers and analysts, it seems, Melanie Klein has always been hard to swallow" (p. 1). Stonebridge and Phillips also state, "At the centre of Kleinian theory is the necessarily unmasterable and endlessly disruptive work of negativity, anxiety, alterity" (p. 6). Klein's work shocks. She seems to imply that infants can be vicious, envious, and violent. Julia Kristeva (2001) claims, "Without Klein's innovation, the clinical practice that focuses on children as well on psychosis and autism, a practice dominated by such names as W. R. Bion, D. W. Winnicott, and Frances Tustin would never have come to pass" (p. 11). Klein was certainly an innovator. She was a maverick indeed. Klein started a new school of thought and had followers even in the early days of her career (Kurzweil, 1998). Some of her early followers, according to Kurzweil, were "Joan Riviere, Susan Issacs, Eva Rosenfeld, Paula Heimann" (p. 139). Julia Kristeva considers Klein to be "the founding mother of child analysis" (p. 5), although Hermine Hug-Hellmuth was one of the first to do child analysis (Kurzweil). But Hug-Hellmuth did not found a school of thought as did Klein.

Ego Psychology and Anna Freud

Anna Freud's theories are at loggerheads with the theories of Melanie Klein. If students want to read an in-depth book about the contrasts of Anna Freud and Melanie Klein, I suggest that they start with Deborah Britzman's (2003) *After-Education: Anna Freud, Melanie Klein, and Psychoanalytic Histories of Learning*. Here I will draw on Britzman's text as well as other commentators to explain Anna Freud's work. I will also draw on some primary texts of Anna Freud as well.

Anna Freud was involved in child analysis like Melanie Klein. However, Anna Freud took a different direction than Melanie Klein. Recall that Klein argued that psychic life is built up through phantasies. Anna Freud, as Deborah Britzman (2003) points out, "eschewed neither phantasies nor the interpretation of child dreams. In opposition to Klein, she felt that phantasies kept the child back, while a love for the world outside would become the resource for the child's freedom" (p. 61). Thus, external reality and the real world were more important for Anna Freud than the phantasy life of the child. It is in the real world that children have to maneuver psychically. Rose Edgcumbe (2000) argues,

> Anna Freud's detailed understanding of the many interacting strands in a child's development, and her awareness of the crucial importance of the child's real relationships in facilitating all areas of psychological development, stand in marked contrast to Klein's emphasis on the fantasy life of the child. (p. 57)

Anna Freud, although she knew that phantasies of, say, the mother persist, the child relates to the real mother, not the phantasized version of the mother. But is the child's perception not shot through with phantasies? And don't these phantasies or internalized representations of the mother get in the way of the perception of the real mother? Is it possible to get to—as Kant called it—the thing in-itself or the mother in-herself? Deborah Britzman clarifies this dilemma as she states that Anna Freud's

> interest was in the ego's function of reality testing, and she argued that what it tests is not so much the relation between phantasies and reality but the adequacy of its perceptions, actions, and judgments in the world. (p. 43)

The ego and its "mechanisms of defense" against internal turmoil work to allow the child to see the world and the mother as they are in the real world. Britzman states, "The ego, with the aid of its mechanisms of defense and love from the actual parents, was adept at learning to sublimate instinctual conflict and acknowledge the demands of external reality" (p. 41). But what are the "demands of external reality?" To see things as they are. But questions remain. A postmodernist might suggest that things are not what they seem. If lived experience is perspectival, then people see things through their own perceptual lenses. At any rate, Anna Freud is clearly not a postmodern thinker but rather a modernist thinker. Britzman states,

Anna Freud would center on problems of normal development, and so she was one of the early proponents of the School of Ego Psychology. She believed that development is gradual, in which the ego moves from being the pleasure ego to becoming the ego of reality. (p. 43)

The ego is the agency that allows us to relate to the world, to reality. We need the ego or we would collapse into psychosis. The ego needs its defense mechanisms to fight off conflict and to protect the ego from collapse. Anna Freud (1966/2000) writes,

To these nine mechanisms of defense, which are very familiar in the practice and have been exhaustively described in the theoretical writings of psychoanalysis (regression, repression, reaction formation, isolation, undoing, projection, introjection, turning against the self and reversal), we must add a tenth, which pertains rather to the study of the normal than to that of neurosis; sublimation, or displacement of instinctual aims. (p. 44)

Anna Freud's version of ego psychology attempts to normalize. Eccentricity, difference and alterity play no role in ego psychology. This position is highly problematic because it encourages children to conform, to be normal. But who decides who is normal? Deborah Britzman states, "Anna Freud's analytic technique with children has a normative goal: adaptation to the reality principle, sublimation of the pleasure principle, and an interest in using ego defenses more flexibly" (p. 13).

Anna Freud's work on defense mechanisms—which Sigmund Freud wrote about throughout his work—is important. What one must understand is that, first off, one needs defense mechanisms to survive. At one point in our lives—especially when we are children—defense mechanisms are used to protect the psyche from onslaughts—whether they come from within or whether they are external. Once the defense mechanisms are no longer needed they are still being utilized but now they get in the way of living a full and happy life. A shell-shocked soldier, for example, uses defense mechanisms such as repression during a war because what was experienced was too overwhelming to think through. But what is repressed returns. When the soldier comes home from war these defense mechanisms continue to work but now to the detriment of living. When the soldier experiences a failed repression, psychic trouble is at hand. When the repression was helpful—during combat—later on it becomes an impediment to living. Anna Freud states,

> It is the analyst's business first of all to recognize the defense mechanism. When he has done this, he has accomplished a piece of ego analysis. His next task is to undo what has been done by the defense, i.e., to find out and restore to its place that which has been omitted through repression, to rectify displacements, and to bring that which has been isolated back into its true context. (p. 15)

Children who are abused use defense mechanisms in order to survive the ordeal. But later on during adult life those defense mechanisms are no longer needed but they continue to be utilized. When defense mechanisms are no longer needed they should be given up but often they keep returning and get in the way of adult life. As Anna Freud states in the above citation, the analyst must work to undo those defense mechanisms because they are no longer needed and only get in the way of living a full life.

Child Analysis

For Klein, there was no difference between analyzing a child and analyzing an adult. For Anna Freud, though, children could not be analyzed as if they were adults. A child analysis, then, is different for a child than for an adult. Phyllis Grosskurth (1986) states that Melanie Klein

> then lists the four principal points of Anna Freud's book and proceeds to demolish them one by one: that no analysis of the child's Oedipus complex was possible, as it might interfere with the child's relations with its parents; child analysis should exert only an educative influence on the child, a transference neurosis cannot be effected because the parents still exert a predominant role in the child's life; and the analyst should exert every effort to gain the child's confidence. (p. 168)

Early on in Melanie Klein's career she agreed with Anna Freud on many of these issues and felt that for children the only way to treat them was to help them adapt to reality and to educate them, not analyze them (Petot, 1990). But then Klein changed her position later on. Klein later on believed that children are not that different from adults and should be analyzed just as adults were. It is interesting to note that Sigmund Freud (1965) states,

> The technique of treatment worked out for adults, of course, must be largely altered for children. A child is psychologically a different object from an adult. As yet he possesses no super-ego, the method of free association does not carry far with him, transference (since the real parents are on the spot) plays a different part. (p. 183)

Anna Freud's position is aligned with Sigmund Freud's. But Melanie Klein, for most of her career, believed that children had the same psychic capacity as adults and should be analyzed just like adults. This difference is at the heart of Pearl King and Riccardo Steiner's (1992) book *The Freud-Klein Controversies, 1941–45*. In the British Psychoanalytic Society, it was clear that Klein was on the losing end of this fight. Simply put, most people agreed with Anna Freud's and Sigmund Freud's positions on the differences between children and adults. One simply cannot analyze a child as if he were an adult. Children are not adults.

Psychoanalysis and Education

Anna Freud—who was an elementary school teacher in her early years—felt that child analysis should be about educating children. Rose Edgcumbe (2000) points out,

> All her [Anna Freud] writings make it abundantly clear both that she distinguished the educative role from psychoanalytic treatment, and that her view of education encompasses all the inner developmental processes which can be influenced by the attitudes and demands of important people in the child's life, and therefore truly psychoanalytic. (p. 65)

Edgcumbe captures the slippery slope between psychoanalysis and education. Is psychoanalysis a form of education? Or are these incompatible aims for child analysis? Recall that Anna Freud felt that children could not be psychoanalyzed as if they were adults. But children could be educated. Yet one wonders how education can be psychoanalytic. Alex Holder (2005) writes that Anna Freud's "approach and that of her colleagues was characterized from the beginning by a mixture of psychoanalytic and educative aims" (p. 31). But questions remain. Can education be psychoanalytic or can psychoanalysis be educational? Anna Freud did not collapse education onto psychoanalysis but held them in tension. Deborah Britzman points out, "For Anna Freud, the analyst must win over the child and be prepared to open some possibilities through confidence building, while foreclosing others by rational persuasion and assuming the position of authority" (p. 42). Confidence building is not that different from building a therapeutic alliance with a patient. The patient has to trust the analyst in order to make any progress psychologically. Britzman notes in the above citation that "rational persuasion" is part of the child's analysis. For adults, psychoanalysis has little to do with rational persuasion but rather with working with the irrational, like dreams or parapraxes such as losing keys, forgetting names, and, as Sigmund Freud (1965, pp. 223–224) put it, bungling actions. Anna Freud, as Phyllis Grosskurth (1986) suggests, "had suggested that the role of the analyst should be confined to educational influence" (p. 167). But if the analyst's work is "confined to educational influence," is the analyst doing psychoanalysis at all? Or is the analyst, rather, a teacher? Deborah Britzman writes, "Anna Freud felt that the child could benefit more from the analyst's position as a sort of role model, what she called an 'ego ideal'" (p. 42). In classical Freudian analysis, positive transference is only possible when the patient and the analyst have a certain respect for one another. The analyst serves also as a role model in the analytic situation. This is especially true in the early stages of analysis.

Anna Freud's colleagues—who were educators—were also doing child analysis. Gail Boldt, Paula Salvio, and Peter Taubman (2006) write,

> Analyst-educators, including Anna Freud, Dorothy Burlingham, Eric Ericson, and Bruno Bettelheim, opened schools and worked to influence public practices of education both in child care centers and in elementary and secondary schooling. Although these efforts were undertaken with great hope, they were not long lasting. (p. 2)

Analyst-educators taught what Peter Taubman (2012) calls "disavowed knowledge." Even today professors who work in the area of psychoanalysis and pedagogy are suspect. Part of the problem here is that professors, say, of education are not for the most part psychoanalysts. Deborah Britzman is an exception as she is both a professor of education and a psychoanalyst. As Peter Taubman says, Britzman's work is dedicated to "thinking psychoanalysis and education together" (p. 5). Gail Boldt, Paula Salvio, and Peter Taubman write that thinking psychoanalysis and education together is not new. The above citation points to this fact. Taubman writes

> Deborah Britzman's (1998, 2003, 2006, 2009, 2010) groundbreaking work on psychoanalysis and education has revealed the complicated relationship between these two impossible professions. In several books she has explored how the work of August Aichorn, Siegfried Bernfeld, Anna Freud, Hermine Hug-Hellmuth, Melanie Klein, and, of course, Freud influenced and was integrated into American education. (p. 5)

Today, however, psychoanalysis and education are not examined much in the academy. Peter Taubman points out,

With the exception of a few departments in the humanities, psychoanalysis in the United States has been banished from the academy.....As a form of treatment, psychoanalysis increasingly looks to the pharmaceutical industry and cognitive behavioral therapies to treat the psyche. (p. 1)

Taubman goes on to say, "In the field of education, other than the small field of curriculum theory, psychoanalysis exerts no influence" (p. 1). The purpose of this chapter is to show that in curriculum studies there are many scholars who draw on psychoanalytic knowledge to inform their work. The most influential scholar in the area of psychoanalysis and curriculum studies is Deborah Britzman. Her work is of the utmost importance for students who are interested in the intersections between education and psychoanalysis. It is also important to note that this form of inquiry is not new. It has a history. Elisabeth Young-Bruehl (1988) tells us,

Of Freud's close associates, the one who contributed earliest and most rigorously to both child analysis and psychoanalytic pedagogy was Sandor Ferenczi. He lectured on psychoanalysis and education at the first International Psychoanalytic Congress in Salzburg, 1908. (pp. 159–160)

In the next section of this chapter I will examine the ways in which education and psychoanalysis are similar, the ways in which psychoanalysis and education are different, and the ways in which psychoanalysis and education are at loggerheads. I will be drawing primarily on the work that Deborah Britzman has done to unpack the relationship between education and psychoanalysis.

Deborah Britzman

I would like to highlight the work of Deborah Britzman here. Britzman's contribution to the study of education and psychoanalysis is extensive. I suggest that students read her primary texts alongside this chapter to get a deeper understanding of her work. Here I list Britzman's important books on this topic: *Lost Subjects, Contested Objects: Toward a Psychoanalytic Inquiry of Learning* (1998); *After-Education: Anna Freud, Melanie Klein, and Psychoanalytic Histories of Learning* (2003); *Novel Education: Psychoanalytic Studies of Learning and Not Learning* (2006); *The Very Thought of Education: Psychoanalysis and the Impossible Professions* (2009); *Freud and Education* (2011).

I would like to discuss similarities between education and psychoanalysis. Britzman (2011) points out that Sigmund Freud understood the tension between psychoanalysis and education. In the following citation it seems that Freud tried to drive a wedge between psychoanalysis and education but then also understood that psychoanalysis, as Britzman (2011) reminds, is an "after-education" (p. 12). Britzman writes,

> Though Freud tried to separate the education of children from the work of psychoanalysis even as he oversaw the beginnings of child psychoanalysis in the early twentieth century, he considered psychoanalytic treatment for adults as an "after education," dedicated to the work of self-knowledge. (p. 12)

Freud suggests, as Britzman points out, that adults needed to be educated again because they had been miseducated. This miseducation could be connected to the development of neurosis. Thus there is something about psychoanalytic treatment that is educational. Put differently there is something about education that lands patients in therapy and that therapy is a better form of education because its purpose is to undo the poor education that patients had while growing up.

Britzman (2003) writes that both education and psychoanalysis are born of conflict. She states,

> Like psychoanalysis, education is a theory of conflict and is marked, consequently, by the very processes that it attempts to understand, namely, the vicissitudes of love, hate, and ambivalence in learning and in not learning, and the susceptibility of humans both to the breakdowns and reparations of knowledge and authority. (p. 37)

Both students in educational settings and patients in psychoanalytic settings encounter their own resistances to new thoughts. These struggles are highly emotional and, as Britzman points out, are related to "love, hate, and ambivalence." Going into psychoanalysis means learning new things about the psyche, which is perhaps at war with itself. It is this conflict in the psyche that brings patients into analytic settings. Students in classrooms are also at war with themselves as they encounter new ideas. Often students are highly resistant to anything new. They do not want to let go of old thoughts, of old ideas. So there is often a struggle between the teacher and the student. It seems that learning new things is threatening to the psyche. Britzman (1998) points out that Anna Freud (who was early on an elementary school teacher and later a psychoanalyst) "names the relation between the teacher and the student 'a never-ending battle'" (p. 1). And readers know from our previous discussion in this chapter that Anna Freud "attempt[ed] to consider in tandem the demands of psychoanalysis and the demands of education"

(Britzman, 1998, p. 1). For a time, Melanie Klein also tried to think psychoanalysis and education "in tandem," as Britzman puts it but later on dropped the idea that psychoanalysis and education had the same aims (Petot, 1990). Britzman (1998) points out that remarkably "in the early relations between education and psychoanalysis, analysts in and close to [Sigmund] Freud's circle argued that the dynamical qualities of each field were indistinguishable" (p. 33). What comes to mind here is that, as was stated above, resistance to new thoughts or new ideas is prevalent in both educational and psychoanalytic settings. These resistances emerge in different ways but both point to the same problem: people do not like to learn new things because it threatens the very structure of their psyche.

Britzman (2009) points out other similarities between psychoanalysis and education as she states, "In some sense, what education feels like is as difficult to convey as what psychoanalysis feels like. They have that in common. Their respective emotional situations as well share in the fact that, because they are so needed, both are deeply misunderstood and perhaps feared" (p. xii). What is feared is change. Both education and psychoanalysis can change people. It is this change that people fear. Attempting to understand one's inner world—whether in educational settings or psychoanalytic ones—can be unsettling because there are things about ourselves we would rather not know or acknowledge. Britzman (1998) tells us that according to one Arthur Jersild—an early writer on the connections between understanding the psyche and education—suggested that "the history of education…is in part a history of [people's] efforts to evade or face anxiety" (cited in Britzman, 1998, p. 36). Thus anxiety and fear play roles in both education and psychoanalysis. An interesting question to ask here is whether anxiety causes fear or whether fear causes anxiety. Sigmund Freud, Melanie Klein, and Anna Freud—the three psychoanalysts discussed thus far—all wrote about anxiety and the problems anxiety can cause, especially if it is unconscious.

Following the title of her book *The Very Thought of Education* Britzman (2009) states,

> [The very thought of education] begins with the idea that, like the dream, education requires association, interpretation, and a narrative capable of bringing to awareness, for further construction, things that are farthest from the mind. And whatever education is dedicated to, all education suffers a radical indeterminacy. The approach that can best turn education inside out, in order to understand something of its emotional situation and its inhibitions, symptoms and anxieties, is psychoanalysis. (p. ix)

Freud argued that "what is farthest from the mind" is perhaps the most important psychic information we must access so as to better understand who we are. The very things we do not consider important are the most important things we need to know about ourselves. It is in the not-said that the analysis makes progress. Britzman (2009) points out that psychoanalysis has something to teach education. The issue of anxiety is one that Freud dealt with in some detail. Students must return to Freud to better understand the anxiety education brings. As Britzman points out, education "requires association" (p. ix). In classical Freudian analysis the analysand must be able to freely associate. Freely associating leads us to thoughts or emotions that may be "farthest from the mind" (p. ix). Education, too, can benefit from allowing teachers and students to also freely associate, but often the educational setting does not allow this freedom as lesson plans are highly scripted. But in higher education, it is possible for professors to allow students to freely associate whatever comes into their minds. The problem though is that this is very difficult to do. Psychic censors get in the way of what it is one really wants to communicate.

Britzman (2009) suggests that psychoanalysis is a kind of education. She states,

> The strangest education will take place in the psychoanalytic session: as catharsis, as mystery, as transference and countertransference, and as a love of language. The education we cannot know but that nonetheless insists will be associated with the unconscious. (p. 17)

One of the reasons that psychoanalytic knowledge is strange is because it is primarily unconscious. When we freely associate we really do not know what we are saying. Ideas seem to come to us from some of the "strangest" places. What feels like trivia might allow us access to unconscious materials. This is why a psychoanalytic education is a mystery. But this mystery releases psychic pressure, undoes depression and anxiety in the form of catharsis.

In her book *Freud and Education* Britzman (2011) says, "Though Freud claimed little in the field of education, we notice how the idea of 'education' casts a shadow over his work" (p. 8). Britzman goes on to say that Freud

> wondered whether teachers could in fact prepare children for the harsh realities of the world and the aggression they would inevitably meet; wrote about the love of his teachers and their reminiscent authority; analyzed the frequency of examination dreams and the play of school in nocturnal affairs; and questioned what most affected his education. (p. 9)

So it seems that psychoanalysis and education are inextricably bound. It was Anna Freud who made this connection most clear. Still, as readers will see later in this chapter, many educators think very little about the use of psychoanalytic knowledge in their classrooms, and many psychoanalysts have no use for education. These are different fields, of course. But there are similarities between these fields.

Britzman (2009) points out that transference happens both in the classroom and in the analytic situation. She states, "And yet, as with analysis, much of what goes on in education is the transference, the uncertain exchange of confusion, love and words" (p. xi). When old patterns of emotion get projected onto new situations trouble abounds. Transference is problematic. Old patterns of relating get projected onto new situations. These emotions are inappropriate to the situation. For example, a student hates his teacher. But he knows little about the teacher and this hate is misplaced. The student really hates his father, say, and projects this hatred onto a new figure. Countertransference is a similar problem. The teacher hates the student, yet knows little about the student. The teacher really hates someone else, say, a parent. The student unconsciously reminds the teacher of the hated parent. Transference can also be about love, as Britzman points out above. The same problems occur. For example, the student falls in love with the teacher, but knows little about the teacher. The student really loves his father, say, and projects this emotion onto the teacher. The teacher unconsciously reminds the student of his father. Thus, positive transference (falling in love) or negative transference (hate) occurs in classrooms just as it occurs in the analytic situation. Falling in love with one's analyst or hating the analyst is an example of misplaced emotion. The analyst too could fall in love with her analysand or hate the analysand but these are misplaced emotions. Peter Taubman points out,

> Interest in how transference affects teaching peaked in the 1920s when writers such as Alexander Coriat (1926) and G. H. Green (1922) urged teachers to pay attention to their transferential relations with students....It would not be until the 1980s that transference among students and teachers would again be a focus of curriculum theorists, literary critics, and composition theorists. (p. 55)

One could argue that the transference that occurs in the analytic situation differs from the transference that occurs in classrooms because the transference that occurs in the analytic situation is induced. It is through the transference that the analyst begins to understand how archaic psychic problems are for the analysand. The analyst's task is to help the analysand place these misplaced emotions back where they belong (usually in the family romance or Oedipal situation).

Differences Between Education and Psychoanalysis

Deborah Britzman (2003) writes,

> Formal institutionalized education may be seen as opposing phantasy, but psycho-analysis views phantasy as central to its work and to one's capacity to think. Analytic time is quite different from the ordinary chronology of classrooms, grades, semesters, and years. It is a play between reality and phantasy, between lost time and refound, and between the meeting of the unconscious and the narrative. (p. 3)

Unconscious phantasies drive psychic life. The point of classical Freudian analysis is to make what is unconscious conscious. One does this work by free-ly associating dreams or everyday experience, working through the transfer-ence and attempting to understand one's anxieties, fears, phobias, repetition compulsions, obsessive thoughts, depressions, and paranoias. Conversely, in classrooms the point is to rely on rational thought to understand issues that may or may not have anything to do with the students. Classrooms are driven by the reality principle and on the strength of the ego. Tamara Bibby (2011) argues,

> We need to heed the words of Sigmund and Anna Freud, Susan Isaacs and others: psychoanalysis and education are different projects, they work differently. Psycho-analysis cannot provide a prophylactic for education although it can provide tools and metaphors for thinking about education. (p. 5)

Again, classroom experience is based on reason while analysis is based on unreason, or the unconscious. And as Bibby points out above, education and psychoanalysis are "different projects." Teachers do not psychoanalyze their students and analysts do not (didactically) teach their analysands. Going into analysis is not like going into the schoolhouse. Britzman (1998) reminds us, "The bringing together of education and psychoanalysis has a difficult history, in which each field's consideration of the time of development confounds the desire for any synthesis" (p. 29). Britzman (1998) also states that there is a tension between these two fields. Thus it is unwise to collapse education onto psychoanalysis or psychoanalysis onto education. Rather, scholars must focus on the tensions inherent in their relations. Sigmund Freud (1966a) says,

"I will show you how the whole trend of your previous education and all your habits of thought are inevitably bound to make you into opponents of psycho-analysis" (p. 18). Britzman (1998) asks a similar question: "Why can education not tolerate psychoanalysis?" (p. 29). Formal education is mostly about memorizing disconnected "facts" for tests. Formal education has little to do with students' lives. Formal education is about obedience. Formal education has little to do with repressed sexual desire, anxiety, or depression. Formal education has little to do with emotions. Psychoanalytic knowledge is, as Peter Taubman puts it, disavowed. Exploring inner psychic life unmoors. Repressed memories, transference, and anxiety are uncomfortable feelings; Educators and students might be afraid of their own feelings, they might be afraid to explore these feelings and are perhaps trapped in transferential relations that they have little desire to understand. Psychoanalysis is a threat to formal education. Britzman (2006) tells us that Melanie Klein

> viewed education as an inhibiting force for two reasons. The internal world does not affect itself through rational appeal. But also many of her young analysands were sent to her because their education made them more miserable, compliant, and suspicious of the teacher's intentions. (p. 95)

One has to remember, too, that Melanie Klein, in her early work as a child psychoanalyst, believed that the point of analysis for children should be educative (Petot, 1990), but she eventually dropped this idea. Psychoanalysis is the study of the irrational, not the rational, while education is a study of the rational, not the irrational.

About Freud, Britzman (2011) says,

> He cared a great deal about literature, mythology, and science and advocated the creative work of sublimation and knowing thyself. However, he was suspicious about education and its procedures and felt that certainty and unaccountable belief tended to wreck the creative work of thinking. (p. 11)

Freud considered himself to be a scientist. Most scientists of Freud's generation were guided by reason, clarity, and certainty. Freud was guided by the study of the irrational. Neuroses are irrational. Freud made a science out of studying the unconscious, knowing full well that his colleagues would pay little attention to his work. Britzman (2011) suggests that for Freud, "things mental and unconscious—lost objects—become the elusive ground of psychoanalysis" (pp. 29–30). And students of Freud's work know that throughout his career he changed his positions on many things because he was probably uncertain about how to capture inner psychic life in all of its vicissitudes.

Education at Loggerheads with Psychoanalysis

The aims of education are sometimes at loggerheads with the aims of psycho-analysis. In this section I will explore some critiques of education and show how education and psychoanalysis are at times incompatible. Meira Likier-man (2001) tells us that Sandor Ferenczi

> believed that the conventional education of his day had harmful aspects especially if it proceeded through "the repression of emotions and ideas," or worse through culti-vating "the negation of emotions and ideas." In fact, it seemed inevitable to him that a "…moralizing education based on repression calls forth a modicum of neurosis." (p. 31)

The aim of psychoanalysis is to lift repression and allow for freely expressed emotions. Those who are harmed by education may seek help from psycho-analysts. The purpose of psychoanalysis is to help people undo what damage is done by social institutions such as the school, the family and oppressive culture in general. Oppressive forms of education were a problem in Europe, especially Central and Eastern Europe before the Holocaust (Morris, 2006). North American schools, too, have a long history of oppression. The question becomes why is it that education oppresses? In his book *New Introductory Lectures on Psycho-Analysis*, Freud (1965) says,

> Let us make ourselves clear as to what the first task of education is. The child must learn to control his instincts.…Accordingly, education must inhibit, forbid and sup-press, and this it has abundantly seen to in all periods of history. But we have learnt from analysis that precisely this suppression of instincts involves the risk of neurotic illness. (p. 184)

That education can make us ill is the problem at hand. The purpose of schooling is to civilize the child. And as Freud (1961b) writes in his book *Civilization and Its Discontents* it is the act of civilizing that makes people ill, or discontented. The child who has little inhibition makes trouble for edu-cators. The child must be contained. And it is this containment and con-trol that make children ill. Freud teaches that what is missing in the edu-cation of children is "the part that sexuality will play in their lives" (p. 81).

The purpose of schooling is to erase any trace of sexuality, especially in children. But Freud also teaches that children are polymorphously perverse. That is, children come into the world as sexual beings. And when social mores and institutions like schooling attempt to erase what comes naturally to the child, harm is done. Anna Freud (1979), in her book *Psycho-Analysis for Teachers and Parents*, remarks,

> I maintain that even today psychoanalysis does three things for pedagogy. In the first place, it is well qualified to offer a criticism of existing educational methods. In the second place, the teacher's knowledge of human beings is extended, and his understanding of the complicated relations between the child and the educator is sharpened by psychoanalysis, which gives us a scientific theory of the instincts, of the unconscious and of the libido. Finally as a method of practical treatment, in the analysis of children, it endeavors to repair the injuries which are inflicted upon the child during the processes of education. (p. 106)

Recall that Anna Freud started out as an elementary school teacher so she knew from the inside the damage that schools could do to children. If the injuries to children happen when they are very young, it becomes harder to undo these injuries. Psychoanalysis is not always successful at undoing such injuries. Schooling can cause children to become psychologically arrested, sexually inhibited, and paranoid. Anna Freud seems certain in the above passage that psychoanalysis of the child can "repair the injuries" done to the child. However, sometimes psychoanalysis cannot fix the damaged child. The damage is too archaic and too deep. Sigmund Freud (1965) says, "A moment's reflection tells us that hitherto education has fulfilled its task very badly and had done children great damage" (p. 185). That education has caused "great damage" alarms. Today education still causes great damage but now the damage is done by constant standardized testing of children. The standardization of the child is the aim of public schooling today. The mental strain of constant testing on children causes illness. Deborah Britzman (1998) asks: "How can education recognize and repair its own harm?" (p. 9). Alice Pitt (2003) comments, "From the point of view of psychoanalysis, it seems that education inflicts more harm than good" (p. 12). Sharon Todd (2003) states, "The question is not so much whether education wounds or not through its impulse to socialize, but whether it wounds excessively and how we (as teachers) might open ourselves to nonviolent possibilities in our pedagogical encounters" (p. 20). William Pinar (1975/2000c) comments in his article "Sanity, Madness, and the School,"

> One theme common to almost all criticism is the contention that the schooling experience is a dehumanizing one. Whatever native intelligence, resourcefulness, indeed, whatever goodness is inherent in man deteriorates under the impact of school. The result is the one-dimensional man, the anomic man, dehumanized and for some critics, maddened. (p. 359)

The aim of psychoanalysis is to alleviate psychic symptoms. The aim of schooling is unwittingly to induce a kind of madness.

Curriculum Studies and Psychoanalysis

William F. Pinar

In this final section of this chapter I will explore the work of curriculum theorists who use psychoanalytic theory to inform their work. Historically William Pinar (1975/2000a) was one of the first curriculum theorists—during the early days of the reconceptualizaton—who used psychoanalytic theory to inform his work. The method of currere is partly psychoanalytic. Pinar (1975/2000a), in his piece *Currere: Toward Reconceptualization*, states, "*Currere*, historically rooted in the field of curriculum, in existentialism, phenomenology, and psychoanalysis, is the study of educational experience" (p. 400). In his piece "Search for a Method," Pinar (1975/2000b) fleshes out what currere means. Pinar states that currere

> is (a) regressive, because it involves description and analysis of one's intellectual biography, or, if you prefer, educational past; (b) progressive, because it involves a description of one's imagined future; (c) analytic, because it calls for a psychoanalysis of one's phenomenologically described educational present, past, and future; and (d) synthetic, because it totalizes the fragments of educational experience (that is to say the response and context of the subject) and places this integrated understanding of individual experience into the larger political and cultural web, explaining the dialectical relation between the two. (p. 424)

The method of currere is first and foremost psychoanalytic. Pinar was not the first to bring together psychoanalysis and education, but he was one of the first curriculum theorists—during the reconceptualization—to use psychoanalytic theory to inform his work.

What is striking about Pinar's "Sanity, Madness and the School" and *Currere: Toward Reconceptualization* is that he draws on Carl Jung among others. Not many curriculum scholars have drawn on Jung, even today. Most recently,

Mary Aswell Doll (2011) uses a Jungian theoretical framework (which I will discuss later) in her book *The More of Myth: A Pedagogy of Diversion*. I (2008) also use a Jungian framework in my book *Teaching Through the Ill Body: A Spiritual and Aesthetic Approach to Pedagogy and Illness*.

In Pinar's later work he draws on Freudian and object relations theorists. His book *Curriculum as Social Psychoanalysis*, co-edited with the late Joe Kincheloe (1991), works to broaden the notion of psychoanalysis as it applies to curriculum studies. Many of the writers in the book draw on Freudian theory to flesh out the notion of place. In Pinar's (2001) book, *The Gender of Racial Politics and Violence in America*, he comes back to the idea of using social psychoanalysis to analyze race and gender relations. Pinar states,

> Such knowledge—a curriculum of social psychoanalysis—may be traumatizing, threatening to "shatter the narcissistic unity of the subject," decentering it and displacing it "as ego" (Handelman 1991, 221; Eppert 2000). Such "unheard-of" (Levinas 1991, 148) knowledge can have an important effect. By shattering the narcissistic unity for the (male) subject, subjective space is made for the Other (Handelman 1991). (p. 5)

If there is no "subjective space" "for the other," violence against the other is at hand. Pinar makes a similar argument in his book *Race, Religion, and a Curriculum of Reparation* (2006a) as he states,

> Still, we must re-experience our subjective relation to the internalized father not as disavowed, competitive, and contentious (as "cursed"), but as symbiotic and "incestuous" (homosexual not homosocial). In such an enfleshed restructuring of the inner topography of white masculinity, we might welcome the opposite sex and race within our own psyche (see Geyer-Ryan 1996, 123). (p. 7)

If men do not integrate the father within the psyche, they can make little room for the other—in this case the opposite sex and race. Sexual violence as well as racial violence is a psychological problem brought on because of the inability to integrate troubled relations, especially with parents.

Wendy Atwell-Vasey

Here I will unpack some key ideas in Wendy Atwell-Vasey's (1998) book *Nourishing Words: Bridging Private Reading and Public Teaching*. The main focus of this book turns on the work of Julia Kristeva, a psychoanalyst and linguist. Kristeva is an object relations theorist who is interested not only in the psychological uses of language, but she is also interested in what she calls "pre-linguistic" (p. 57) and pre-Oedipal phases of development. Kristeva—in the tradition of object relations theory—is mainly interested in the relations between the infant and the mother and the very early years of childhood. Atwell-Vasey shows how Kristeva's work informs education. Atwell-Vasey states,

> Kristeva sees the structure of language—rhythms, grammars, syntaxes, and symbols as extensions of existing *body and relational experiences* that have linguistic qualities.... Kristeva helps us see that schools ought to be making use of how students experience language in their bodies and in their social relations. (p. 5)

Although schools ought to care about the embodied and relational use of language, they do not. If anything, standardized testing—which makes up most of public school experience—has little to do with an embodied and relational use of language. The standardization of public school curricula actually works to disembody students and cut off relations not only with peers but with teachers as well. Memorizing disconnected "facts" for standardized tests makes a mockery of language. In fact, Atwell-Vasey states early on,

> A hush falls over the school classroom. The lush word climate that sustains students and teachers in private life somehow turns into a thin and rarified school air. Children find themselves in classrooms in which only a very few and certain words are wanted....Children learn to leave their words outside, in the hall, at home, removing them like muddy boots. (p. 2)

Standardized testing reduces words to bits and pieces of unrelated "facts." The anxiety and fear students must feel entering the schoolhouse erase "the lush word climate" that they experience at home. Atwell-Vasey says, "Words have always been nourishment" (p. 1), but in the context of public schooling words no longer nourish but instead generate anxiety and fear. To fear words is also to lose the ability to speak, write, read, and relate to others. Atwell-Vasey suggests,

> Psychoanalytic discourse challenges the talk we are used to in education, which funnels meaning into static and controlled positions beyond the reach of the projections, introjections, reversals, repressions, and fantasies. (p. 9)

Words are not things, they are symbols of psychic life. Words are clues to deeper meanings, archaic relations, and are highly charged emotionally and intellectually. But schooling has wrecked our relations with words as it serves to cut off any psychic investment we might have not only with words but also with how words build relations. Julia Kristeva, in her psychoanalytic discourse, claims—according to Atwell-Vasey—that the development of language and the use of words spring from the infant's relation to the mother. The mother is internalized and integrated into the personality of the infant. This integration of the mother into the psyche is the beginning of word development. This position is in contradistinction to that of Jacques Lacan. For Lacan, the male child must repudiate the mother in order to develop language. Atwell-Vasey tells us,

> Kristeva's theory of language development rests on the notion that the child experiences the beginning of symbolic life in the regulation of body impulses and desires already within his or her relationship with the mother. (p. 50)

Recall our study of Melanie Klein. For Klein, like Kristeva, object relations have more to do with the unconscious relations not with the father but with the mother. And like Klein, Kristeva is interested in the very early stages of childhood development, in pre-Oedipal and preverbal experience. Atwell-Vasey says, "Julia Kristeva's view is that the prelinguistic body subjectivity we knew in infantile life with a maternal figure serves as a continuing basis for symbolic achievement" (p. 49). "Symbolic achievement" means that the infant develops relations that are ego-syntonic. Without "symbolic achievement" the infant might develop ego-dystonic relations, such as that of a schizophrenic who has little capacity for understanding symbols but rather communicates on a very concrete level.

Atwell-Vasey suggests, "Kristeva asserts that body experiences prefigure the earliest linguistic expressions of sounds, tone, rhythm, and the order and spatiality of syntax. Laughter, cries, intonations, and gestures extend from the traces of body knowledge we develop with the mother" (p. 57). These "traces" are "vocal and kinesthetic fragments" (p. 57). Kristeva argues that these traces emerge in a "psychosomatic space...called a 'chora', the Greek word for womb or space" (p. 57). Thus Kristeva, according to Atwell-Vasey, claims that language and symbol formation emerge in the unconscious relation with the mother, and this unconscious relation is embodied. It is important, then, that Atwell-Vasey contends that Kristeva disagrees with Lacan's basic premise that the "psyche is structured like a language" (p. 50) but rather Kristeva argues that the "psyche and language are structured like a body in a relationship (Oliver, 1993, p. 19)" (p. 50).

Atwell-Vasey contends that for Kristeva, "identity formation" partly has to do with the "ability to reject, or make abject, materials and forces it does not want" (p. 59). This, Kristeva calls the "thetic break" and the "thetic phase" (p. 59). Atwell-Vasey says that "these drives and articulations in the preverbal realm involve our 'abjections' or getting rid of what is not wanted through cries, biting, spitting, expulsions" (p. 59). It is interesting to note that for Kristeva the preverbal period is important to explore if we are to understand the development of the ego, language, and a sense of self. The mother-infant bond is all-important to the development of language. Atwell-Vasey tells us early on in the book that her study of Kristeva can inform "how language arts teaching, or English education...can be realigned to acknowledge that linguistic structure comes from within ourselves, and between ourselves, and not from outside ourselves" (p. 4).

Sharon Todd

Sharon Todd's (2003) book, *Levinas, Psychoanalysis, and Ethical Possibilities in Education: Learning from the Other*, is a groundbreaking study of the complex interconnections between psychoanalysis, ethics, and education. Todd draws on Emmanuel Levinas who was a philosopher and ethicist. Levinas brings to the conversation issues that turn on alterity, difference, otherness, and relationality. What is striking in Todd's work is that she attempts to grapple with Levinas—who was a philosopher—and psychoanalysis. Philosophers, generally speaking, deal with consciousness while psychoanalytic thinkers deal with the unconscious. It is interesting that Todd writes, "What I wish to consider here, however, are the ways in which these two views may be held in tension—without collapsing their significant differences" (p. 13). Thus Todd wants to think philosophy and psychoanalysis together in the context of education and "learning from the other" (p. 10). Todd explains,

> The distinction between learning about and learning from is one Freud made in an essay "On the Teaching of Psychoanalysis in Universities"....With respect to education, both Deborah Britzman and Adam Phillips have written on the significance of this distinction. (p. 10)

Deborah Britzman suggests that learning from the other means learning from the fragility of emotionality (in Todd, p. 10). Britzman writes,

Learning from demands both a patience with the incommensurability of understanding and an interest in tolerating the ways meaning becomes…fractured, broken, and lost, exceeding the affirmations of rationality, consciousness, and consolation. (cited in Todd, p. 10)

Philosophy deals with rationality and consciousness while psychoanalysis deals with irrationality and the unconscious. The question for Todd is how to learn from Levinas and learn from psychoanalysis simultaneously. It seems that Levinas's work is at loggerheads with the work of psychoanalytic writers. Todd shows that these two opposing positions can be thought of together. Todd helps readers understand how to think opposites together. What we glean from studying Levinas can inform educators as well as psychoanalysts on the ethical challenges we face in the 21st century. Rationality and consciousness drive the Levinasian ethic. Todd teaches,

In contradistinction to this, psychoanalysis insists that our relations are indeed laced with threads of affect and psychical complications, where defenses, identifications, and ambivalences continually erupt.…Unconscious slips of the tongue, projected anger, and emotional desire are no strangers to the self-Other relation. (p. 12)

The ethical relation between self and Other—for psychoanalysis—means understanding that affect gets in the way of the ethical relation. If it is the unconscious that drives these emotions, then our ethical encounters too are driven by unconscious desires. It is not so clear, then, what ethics looks like when there seems to be an interminable interruption to relations.

However, Levinas "premises the conditions of ethics—the conditions of a nonviolent relation to the Other—upon a self-Other relation that is free of those screens and filters through which we encounter other people" (p. 12). Levinas—as a philosopher—deals with intellectual constructs that have little to do with emotions, affect or the unconscious as was earlier stated. But he writes about ideas such as alterity, difference, Otherness, relationality and responsibility. The self-Other relation is a nonreciprocal relation whereby it is the responsibility of the self to respect the Other and expect nothing in return. It is up to the Other to respond. When one does respond to the Other one sees God in the face of the other. Violence is unethical because the face of God is in the face of the Other. The Other, for Levinas is an absolute Other. Todd tells us, "Simply put, for Levinas 'the Other is what I myself am not'" (p. 29). Todd teaches, "Levinas is helpful in fleshing out pedagogical encounters, for he centers otherness at the very heart of teaching and learning"

(p. 29). Further, for Levinas the self only becomes a self in relation to the Other. Todd comments, "The Levinasian emphasis on communication... means that subjectivity and responsibility reveal themselves only in relation to an Other and therefore emerge from a signifying encounter with absolute difference that cannot be predicted beforehand" (p. 68). The self is not a stand-alone concept. To be a self, to have subjectivity, means being in relation to the Other. However, for psychoanalysis "when affect troubles the learner's ego...the borders delineating outside and inside become unclear" (Todd, p. 11). Symbiotic relations, projective identification, and introjection also make ego boundaries unclear. Can there really be absolute alterity between people? Perhaps not. But Levinas thinks otherwise.

As against Levinas, Todd argues, "The discourse of ethics and education must grapple with the everyday vicissitudes of unconscious affect in confronting what cannot be known as it explores the conditions for nonviolence" (p. 4). Todd discusses the importance of recognizing that our pedagogical encounters are emotional. And it is the emotion that interrupts the relation between the self and the Other. Todd writes about guilt, love, and empathy (p. 4); she writes about anxiety (pp. 10–11). And as against Levinas, Todd—drawing on the work of Melanie Klein—says, "Moral work is a psychical event" (p. 92). Levinas might suggest moral work is a rational event.

Alice Pitt

Unlike Sharon Todd (2003), Alice Pitt (2003) writes about the intersections between psychoanalytic theory and feminist theory in *The Play of the Personal: Psychoanalytic Narratives of Feminist Education*. Drawing on D. W. Winnicott, Pitt writes about the notion of play. Pitt reminds that for Winnicott "play occurs in an area of life that *is between* reality and fantasy. Play belongs solely to neither realm of experience. Winnicott calls this intermediate space the "transitional spaces" (p. 86). The transitional space—for infants—is the place where they find what Winnicott calls transitional objects. These objects help the infant to individuate from the mother. Adults, too, experience transitional space and use transitional objects to also individuate from oppressing unconscious forces. Pitt writes about "the play of the personal" in the context of doing academic work. It is interesting to note that Pitt asks,

> What do we use the personal to do? I have hinted at two ways in which we use the personal. One way refers to the stories we tell to make good our lives. We use these stories to make sense of ourselves in ways that give meaning to our lives. A second

use is evident in my conversation with the teacher, where we puzzle over the demands made upon teachers and students to use the details of their private lives as curriculum material. (p. 87)

Pitt calls her study an "autobiography of learning" (p. 6). Pitt writes about her experiences teaching feminist studies to resistant students. In order to understand this resistance Pitt—much like Britzman—attempts to think psychoanalytic theory together with education (p. 2). Pitt differs from Britzman here in her work on feminist theory and teaching feminist theory to resistant students. Pitt says, "Using Felman's study of Lacan and Freud's pedagogy and the psychoanalytic theory of resistance, I have explored the significance of learning from students' resistance to knowledge, in particular feminist knowledges" (p. 4). Resistance points to "psychic conflict" (p. 48). Pitt argues that resistance is a way to manage psychic conflict (p. 48). Pitt argues, "Resistance to knowledge is conceptualized as the very grounds of possibility for learning rather than an impediment to it" (p. 73). Resistance to learning tells us something about the difficulties of learning that challenge dominant paradigms. Pitt explains,

When it comes to feminist knowledge, we must remember that such knowledge is by definition oppositional and marginalized within dominant knowledge. We might ask ourselves if forging a relation to feminist knowledge is similar to making a relation to unconscious knowledge. (p. 64)

One might surmise that the repudiation of the mother or the repudiation of women generally has much to do with misogyny. So the repudiation of feminist studies has much to do not only with misogyny but also with patriarchy. In a patriarchal society the study of women encounters resistance on the part of students. Pitt asks: "What do we learn when we conceptualize resistance as a problem of and for interpretation?" (p. 47). Resistance, in general, tells us that something more is going on in the psyche than just not wanting to learn. Resistance could point to deeper psychological regression or even psychological arrest. And again, one might surmise that this resistance has to do with unsolved problems with object relations—and in this case object relations to the mother who is real and yet phantasized. For the infant who has not had a good enough mother—as Winnicott calls it—psychological problems might emerge in adulthood. Students might be resistant to feminist knowledges because they did not have good enough relations with their mothers. These experiences then get transferred later in life to others who unconsciously remind one of the not-good-enough mother. From a Kleinian perspective, one could surmise that students who refuse to learn feminist discourse have never moved beyond the paranoid-schizoid phase. In this phase, recall from our earlier discussions on Klein, the infant hates the bad breast for fear of annihilation. The fear of the mother or her breast is an archaic fear that then gets projected in later life on other mother figures or on other people who unconsciously remind one of the mother. This is called negative transference.

Pitt writes that she "explore[s] the gap between making and missed meaning as a piece of the generative work of thinking about psychoanalysis and education together" (p. 6). "Missed meaning" or the refusal to learn has much to do with psychic regression or with repressed memories. Pitt's book allows us to wonder about all kinds of knowledges that are subject to the refusal to learn. New knowledges encounter fierce resistance because students are threatened by the new. But in the case of approaching feminist knowledge, Pitt suggests that the situation is different in that the resistances are fierce. Again, the problem here is with the deep and archaic hatred of the mother or the hatred of women generally. Pitt draws on the notion of the uncanny to show how psychic events disrupt the good-enough classroom, if you will. Pitt states, "The notion of the uncanny disrupts the dream of learning as a developmental progression through the fantasy of what Madeleine Grumet (1989) has termed 'the beautiful curriculum'" (p. 26). When students are uncannily and unconsciously reminded of their mothers—especially if they had bad relations with their mothers—resistance to feminist knowledges occurs. But not all students had bad relations with their mothers so how to account for the resistance to feminist theory? Men *and women* who live in patriarchal societies unconsciously become misogynist. If we lived in a matriarchal society, things would be very different.

Alan A. Block

Alan Block's (1997) book *I'm Only Bleeding: Education as the Practice of Violence Against Children* is a condemnation of public schooling and the harm it does to children. Block draws upon object relations theory to tease out the violence done to children while in school. Block says early on, "I would like to discuss the violence that is practiced upon the child psychologically by the educational system" (p. 3). That public school is a violent place for children troubles. Block's thesis is bold and it is alarming. Of course—as I discussed earlier in this chapter—from a psychoanalytic perspective school harms psychologically. Block draws on many object relations theorists but D. W. Winnicott helps Block most to drive his point home. Block states,

> As an environment, to use Winnicott's phrases, school is not so much facilitating as discouraging, not so much holding as confining. It does not provide space for the teachers to be good enough so that they might provide space to the education that is good enough for our children. The school's structures choke off the ability to play and replace it with work. Education causes serious damage. (p. 20)

For Winnicott (2010) the mother is to provide a holding environment for the child and she must be a good-enough mother for the child. For Winnicott this means that the mother needs to be there, to be present to the child emotionally and physically. A not-good-enough mother is one who is not there for her child in any sense. Winnicott also talks about the ability to play and suggests that it is the job of the psychoanalyst to bring the child who is not able to play into a psychic space where he or she is able to play. Winnicott says,

> Psychotherapy takes place in the overlap of two areas of playing, that of the patient and that of the therapist. Psychotherapy has to do with two people playing together. The corollary of this is that where playing is not possible then the work done by the therapist is directed towards bringing the patient from a state of not being able to play into a state of being able to play. (p. 51)

Readers will see this theme again in my book (2009) *On Not Being Able to Play: Scholars, Musicians and the Crisis of Psyche*. For me the reference to not being able to play has to do with psychic blocks of musicians and scholars. For Block, not being able to play refers to children who have little opportunity to play in public schooling and how damaging this is psychologically. And not being able to play leads to a sense "of dread in the child" (Block, p. 1). Block points out, "Minimally, the school is a space—an object—that can be used for play and creativity" (p. 19). But there is little play and creativity in schools as the school, Block contends, "has become a training ground for business" (p. 19). Block goes on to suggest,

> If the promise of the school lies in jobs and financial success, then what is the effect on our children when the future offers such limited possibilities for so many of them? What violence do we practice when we prepare them for the future that will never exist? (p. 15)

The "promise of school" should have nothing to do with business. School is not a business. Students should not be treated as if they were workers. But what is even worse is that school treats children as if they are all the same—or should be all the same. The standards movement is about getting children to all think alike and be alike. In fact, Block says, "We spend too much time normalizing and too little time understanding" (p. 21). Standardization serves to normalize children. What happens psychologically to children who do not want to be normalized? At bottom, Block teaches, children are, in reality, ambivalent. Block states, "Ambivalence is the by-product of chaos. Ambivalence confuses certainty and renders it unattainable. And modernity is organized to deny ambivalence and avoid doubt. Children, however, enact the embodiment of ambivalence" (p. 7). Block suggests that schools are driven by the tenets of modernism, even though we live in a postmodern world. The tenets of modernism are order and classification (p. 5). Block says, "The ordering and bureaucratizing of the American public schools is a well-documented narrative...and may be attributed to the moments of modernity" (p. 5). But Block contends that "the child's potential for chaos—its unintegration, to use Winnicott's description...endangers that order" (p. 11). Classroom management is all about keeping children in line, disciplining and punishing them for stepping outside the bounds of order. Perhaps it is this penchant for order and classification that drives children to become "unintegrated" and hence "chaotic," to use Block's terms. A postmodern classroom, as opposed to the modernist classroom, would embrace ambivalence, disorder, chaos, and uncertainty. But public school does not, for the most part, mirror the postmodern era in which we live. Block states, "If the principle of order (and ordering) is the principle of modernity, then the child threatens that order for the child is, finally indefinable except from the perspectives of the adults for whom ordering establishes the world" (p. 13). Psychoanalysis teaches that the psyche is out of order, if you will, because of the unconscious. Alice Pitt (2003) teaches, "Psychoanalytic theories further unseat the authority of the humanist subject [or the subject of modernity] by insisting upon the notion of the unconscious" (p. 49). The unconscious destabilizes. There is no order in the unconscious. And it is the unconscious that drives us to do what we do, to say what we say. Hence, trying to order what is out of order is an impossible and damaging task.

Tamara Bibby

Tamara Bibby (2011), in her book *Education—An "Impossible Profession"? Psychoanalytic Explorations of Learning and Classrooms*, examines teaching and learning psychoanalytically. She draws on Freud, Klein, Lacan, Winnicott, and Bion to explore what thinking means and what classroom relations mean from a psychoanalytic perspective. Bibby is interested in exploring emotions usually ignored by policymakers. Bibby notes,

> Policy metaphors and the trends associated with them have tended to sideline and make it difficult to think and talk about less rational aspects of teaching and learning. These less rational but nonetheless powerful aspects of the learning context include the desire for control and vengeance, resistance, the fear of failure (and success), peer pressure, love and hatred, loss and anxiety. (p. 12)

The word "vengeance" is particularly worrisome in light of school shootings. Although Bibby does not address school shootings, one might psychoanalytically explore the irrationality of these killings. What is it about school that makes kids kill? In the 2011 film *We Need to Talk About Kevin*, a troubled teenager locks students into the gymnasium and kills them with a bow and arrow. Klein intimates that children can show signs of violence at a very young age as they mutilate dolls and so forth. This film is highly disturbing because we see a troubled infant grow up to be a mass murderer. School shootings are not talked about much in the educational literature from a psychoanalytic perspective.

Bibby writes about teaching and learning in the context of psychoanalytic theory. She is interested in the emotions that are connected with teaching and learning. Bibby states,

> The business of learning is dangerous, not only because it is difficult and challenging and thereby risks failure, but also because of its proximity to love (and therefore also to hate, acceptance and rejection). If love is demonstrated by acts of caring, nurturing, feeding, through acts of kindness and the symbolism of gifts, then teaching, which involves the metaphorical exchange of all these goods, is an act of love. (p. 18)

Teaching may be an "act of love" but might also provoke anger and, as Bibby points out, hatred. What do children do with that hatred? Bibby begins this citation by stating, "Learning is dangerous." This takes on a particular meaning in the United States. Again, I am thinking here of the danger of simply going to school, or even to university, in light of school shootings. It is obvious that school shooters are filled with murderous rage. This is something, again, that Bibby does not address. Saying that "learning is dangerous" is not merely a metaphor. Not learning is also dangerous. If teaching is "an act of love" why do some students reject that love? Bibby remarks, "The work of teaching, learning and parenting all arouse strong and conflicting feelings: love, resentment, hate, aggression and gratitude" (p. 29). What do students do with "resentment, hate [and] aggression?" What do teachers do with "resentment, hate [and] aggression?"

Bibby draws on the work of Melanie Klein. Klein's work might help us understand where aggression and even perhaps murderous rage come from. Bibby states,

> Klein suggests that in the early stages of ego formation, defences against anxiety are aggressive and manifest in destructive impulses—kicking, biting and tearing—responses which she describes as 'sadistic.' At this early stage, we need to accept that the child does not have a full picture of (for example) his mother but is attacking parts of her, retaliating in phantasy more than in reality. For Klein, these early defences are constructed against two sources of perceived danger: the subject's own sadism and the object of his sadistic attack. (p. 23)

If the child cannot move beyond the paranoid-schizoid phase, sadism cannot be resolved and carries over into adult life. Sadism, when acted out, can have extremely negative consequences. One must remember that for Klein violence is innate and is not brought about by a bad mother. The child phantasizes bad things that have little to do with the real mother. On the contrary, D. W. Winnicott argues that it is the environment that makes the infant ill. If the mother is not good enough, trouble is on the horizon.

Bibby remarks that for D. W. Winnicott,

> A "good-enough" relationship [between the infant and the mother] can bear the strains of aggression, anger, frustration and hate as well as the satisfaction of love and gratitude. In moving from a state of phantasized omnipotence in which self and mother were one, the child is enabled to bear the ambivalence it feels toward the real-mother who exists "out there" (simultaneously loved and hated), its guilt at the aggression it meted out (phantasy and in biting, pulling, hitting), and its anxiety lest she seek revenge. (p. 48)

Bibby remarks that "later pedagogic relations" (p. 48) reflect the relations between the infant and the mother. The child takes with her to school symbolically the relations she has with her mother and transfers that relation onto the teacher. If the child can psychologically manage ambivalence—as noted by Bibby in the above citation—negative emotions will not be acted out in the classroom. But if the child cannot manage ambivalence, he will more than likely act out his aggression, anger and frustration in the classroom.

Bibby draws on the work of Wilfred Bion to think about the thinking process. What students should be learning in school is how to think but it is not that straightforward, according to Bion. Bibby remarks,

> Central to Bion's understanding of thought and thinking is his suggestion that the thought comes first and thinking develops to process the thoughts. This reverses the usual, rationalist story of thinking conjuring thoughts but it emerges from his understanding of Klein. For Bion, the oscillation between the paranoid-schizoid and depressive positions…demonstrates the development of thinking, a move from "formless chaos to coherence."…If a thought occurs that cannot be tolerated it will be rejected and expelled (the paranoid-schizoid position) but, if it can be tolerated, then there can be a move to the depressive position—a move which *is* thinking. (p. 104)

New knowledge—for a child—is oftentimes not tolerated. What is new can sometimes be threatening. New knowledge for a doctoral candidate, likewise, might not be tolerated again because it threatens to unmoor. If a student is arrested emotionally and stuck in the paranoid-schizoid position, Bion teaches that "formless chaos" is what ensues. Coherence comes only with the arrival of the depressive position. What seems clear to the teacher might only be formless chaos for the student—if that student has regressed to the paranoid-schizoid position.

Bibby reminds us that Freud also wrote about dangerous knowledge:

> The unconscious was a place of great energy and movement—it is dynamic. The dynamism takes two forms. First there is repression, the unconscious presses the unknowable away from our awareness and keeps it there although the thought fights back. The more dangerous the knowledge or thought, the more forcefully it is held down. Second it is dynamic in the generative sense that it causes or generates dreams and phantasies. (p. 7)

Bibby says above that "thought fights back." This might be thought of as the return of the repressed. When the repressed returns it usually does so with a vengeance. Freud, like Klein and Bion, admits that some forms of knowledge are dangerous. For Freud dangerous thoughts that get repressed have something to do with sexuality, incest, childhood traumas, polymorphous perversity, parapraxis. Bibby demonstrates that teaching and learning and life in classrooms are not in any way straightforward. From a psychoanalytic perspective Bibby teaches that our irrational, unconscious, and repressed knowledges affect both teaching and learning.

Peter M. Taubman

Peter Taubman (2012), in his book *Disavowed Knowledge: Psychoanalysis, Education, and Teaching*, writes, "In the field of education, other than [in] the small field of curriculum theory, psychoanalysis exerts no influence" (p. 1). Taubman suggests that one reason psychoanalysis is of little interest to most educationists is that psychoanalytic knowledge is too difficult to manage emotionally. The things one finds out through the study of psychoanalytic theory are too disturbing. Taubman states that even within the field of curriculum theory "it can barely make its voice heard over the cries for social justice and democratic education" (p. 133).

Taubman argues that psychoanalytic theory, broadly speaking, has taken two different directions. Taubman suggests that theorists engage in the "therapeutic project" or the "emancipatory project" (p. 26). Taubman states,

> The therapeutic project focuses on the practical or clinical and aspires either to scientific certainty, so that it can control if not predict its effect, or truth, so that it can rightfully persuade others of its ideals of health, normalcy, or political rectitude. (p. 26)

What comes to mind here is ego psychology. Ego psychology is about adapting to reality, becoming normal. A normalizing psychology is highly problematic. Taubman intimates that ego psychology is problematic because it does not deal with the more disturbing concepts that Freud discusses in his work. Taubman notes, "Heinz Hartmann's ego psychology…understood strengthening the ego in terms of making it more responsive to the demands of the reality principle, which he interpreted in terms of social normativity" (p. 103). But Taubman argues that normativity was hardly Freud's goal. Freud "did not advocate making it [the ego] a muscular organ for social adaptation" (p. 103). Taubman also intimates that the goal of education is also a therapeutic project because it, too, focuses on normalizing students. The standards movement is one of normalization.

Taubman notes that what he calls the "emancipatory project" (p. 28) of psychoanalytic theory is quite different from the therapeutic project. Taubman states,

> The emancipatory project…focuses on all the ways we make sense of or try to understand our experiences, no matter how trivial or traumatic…Such a project aspires to free us from our taken-for-granted views of ourselves and others, to loosen the psychic knots and intellectual ruts we find we are stuck in. (p. 28)

Later in this chapter I will discuss my book (2009) *On Not Being Able to Play: Scholars, Musicians and the Crisis of Psyche*. I examine "intellectual ruts," as Taubman puts it, of both scholars and musicians, and I try to find ways out of intellectual ruts in order to work (either as a scholar or a musician) again.

The emancipatory project has nothing to do with normalization. In fact, it is a project that opens us up to our own strangeness. This strangeness is the unconscious. Taubman says that the emancipatory project acknowledges and respects the unconscious (p. 26). It is the unconscious that makes us strange. The point is not to erase this strangeness but rather to embrace it. However, Taubman points out, "The emancipatory project is often disavowed because it provokes too much anxiety" (p. 26). To acknowledge that we do not understand ourselves, that we are not the masters of our own houses as it were, that our dreams are disturbing, that we are caught up in our own defense mechanisms, that we suffer from all kinds of emotional discomfort is anxious making. Taubman points out, "Knowledge of and from the unconscious disrupts the aspiration to create the smoothly functioning machines with which current educational discourses are so enamored" (p. 23). Human beings are hardly "smoothly functioning machines."

Taubman tells us that psychiatrists embraced psychoanalysis especially after World War II. But this presented many problems. Freud worried that the medical community would misunderstand psychoanalysis and ruin it. American psychoanalysis as practiced by psychiatrists became standardized (p. 100), sanitized (p. 101), and medicalized (p. 101). In the early days of psychoanalysis, women analysts outnumbered men. But after the medicalization of psychoanalysis, men far outnumbered women analysts. Disturbingly, Taubman reports, "The psychoanalysis that emerged in alliance with medicine after the war not only pathologized women, gays and lesbians, not only advocated a normalization of the status quo, but reintroduced a masculine bias to the profession" (p. 101). The medicalized version of psychoanalysis was in sync with what Taubman calls the therapeutic project, which I discussed earlier. "Cure" was the goal of the medicalized version of psychoanalysis and the therapeutic project. Tamara Bibby notes of one of the first patients of psychoanalysis: "Anna O famously characterized her experience of psychoanalysis as a 'talking cure' but we need to be careful how we understand her statement since psychoanalysis does not hold out 'cures' in the medical sense of the word" (p. 3). Taubman says that although Freud early on used Anna O's phrase "talking cure" he eventually abandoned the phrase. Taubman wonders why Freud abandoned this phrase. "Was it that he grew increasingly skeptical of psychoanalysis as a 'cure?'" (p. 45). Recall that for Taubman the emancipatory project of psychoanalysis has no interest in cure.

Psychoanalysis and psychiatry have today grown apart and many psychiatrists are no longer trained in the psychoanalytic tradition but rather are trained to dispense medicine rather than doing any kind of talk therapy (Naomi Rucker, personal communication). Taubman notes that today even psychoanalysts have turned to "the pharmaceutical industry and cognitive behavioral therapies to treat the psyche" (p. 1). One begins to wonder what the fate of psychoanalysis is both as a theory and as a treatment of mental illness.

Gail M. Boldt and Paula M. Salvio

Gail M. Boldt and Paula M. Salvio (2006) have co-edited an important book on the intersections between education and psychoanalysis called *Love's Return: Psychoanalytic Essays on Childhood, Teaching, and Learning*. Here I will focus on three essays from this edited collection. I will explore essays by Paula M. Salvio, Madeleine Grumet, and Jonathan Silin. In the introduction to the book, Boldt, Salvio, and Taubman explain what they mean by the word "love." These scholars write, "These chapters contain difficult questions about love. Accounts of hatred, aggression, trauma, need, and desire appear as love's unwelcomed but inevitable partner" (p. 5). Further, Boldt, Salvio, and Taubman point out,

> Peter Taubman urges us to consider the ways that love is used to mask aggressions, hatreds, and erotics; he describes how using love as a defense against undesired knowledge plays out and in many ways structures life in classrooms. (p. 5)

From a psychoanalytic perspective things are not what they seem. Love is entangled with hate. These writers also make note that the "perplexing questions of love and transference" (p. 3) get played out in classroom settings. The writers in this collection explore especially "difficult relations" (p. 3) in school settings.

Paula M. Salvio

Salvio's (2006) essay titled "On the Vicissitudes of Love and Hate: Anne Sexton's Pedagogy of Loss and Reparation" explores the life and work of the poet

Anne Sexton. (Later in 2007 Salvio published a book on Anne Sexton called *Anne Sexton: Teacher of Weird Abundance*.) The essay that Salvio writes in the collection captures some of the key points she later makes in her full-length book on Sexton.

Here I would like to explore a few key ideas Salvio makes in the collection *Love's Return*. Salvio states: "Anne Sexton is most often remembered as a Pulitzer Prize–winning poet who, in her poetry, 'confessed' the anguish of depression, addiction, and a suicidal mother's love for her daughters" (p. 65). Sexton was a professor at Boston University and, according to Salvio, Sexton's teaching centered on negative feelings in her poetry. Sexton, Salvio tells us, "speaks to her students about the emotions that lie beneath grief—sorrow, feelings of guilt and forgiveness" (p. 80). Salvio's biographic portrait of Sexton is highly unusual in that it deals with emotions most do not like to think about. Sexton committed suicide. This is another issue that educators rarely mention in their work. Most teacher biographies are tales of conquest. But not so for Salvio's work on Sexton. Sexton's life is highly disturbing. However, Salvio writes,

> Anne Sexton offers us a case of a pedagogy of reparation, in part because it presents a teacher engaging in the study of problematic attachments. Her pedagogy is overlaid with emotions that underlie grief—sorrow and feelings of guilt, rage and horror. Finally, Sexton also offers us a way to think differently about what is at stake in discussions about education that hold fast to regressive images of good enough mothers who care for and nurture their students at the expense of their subjectivities. (p. 83)

Salvio problematizes D. W. Winnicott's notion of the good-enough mother. She states that mothers cannot be good enough if they experience extreme emotions like the ones that Sexton writes about. Mothers need the space to experience depression, anxiety, hopelessness, remorse, and so forth. But Winnicott makes little room for these kinds of emotions. Salvio states, "The metaphor of the good enough mother is inadequate for educators because neither the mother nor the teacher can remain continually attuned, placid, contained, or unflappable" (p. 84). Salvio's critique of Winnicott is important because it raises the question of what the good-enough mother means. Salvio's critique of Winnicott is highly unusual. Sexton was never the good-enough mother. Depressed, perhaps psychotic at times, anxious, and suicidal, Sexton's emotions and behaviors raise questions about what the good-enough mother has to do to be good enough. And yet, Salvio claims that Sexton offered students a "pedagogy of reparation" (p. 83). Salvio goes on to say, "Sexton was fearless in her study of the vicissitudes between love and hate and her inquiry into the love that both hurts and comforts us" (p. 79).

Madeleine R. Grumet

In Grumet's (2006) essay, "Romantic Research: Why We Love to Read," she explores the love of working with texts in the context of object relations theory. Grumet sums up object relations theory as she states,

> Object relations theory investigates a child situated within a field of relationships of which the child is a part. It shifts the focus from drives to the social field that surrounds the infant....Object relations theory does not assume that the Oedipal crisis is the only significant moment of psychosexual development. This theory pays attention to pre-Oedipal development. (p. 211).

Grumet suggests that when we read books we are in relation to others. In fact, Grumet points out that books can serve as transitional objects. This Winnicottian interpretation of reading suggests that books move us into another space that at once reminds us of our earliest relations with our mothers or primary caregivers and also moves us away from these early figures. The book serves to transition us away from our mothers and yet remind us of our mothers. Grumet explains, "The overlap of experience that is our early love and identification with our mothers is echoed in our relationship with text" (p. 217). Reading a book, Grumet suggests, "may feel like an illicit intimacy" (p. 216). The reader, in other words, develops a relationship with a text and that relationship is intimate. This private experience, though, is shared in classrooms as teachers read texts with students. Grumet says, "The well-read book provides an extraordinary sense of stability" (p. 215). There is something psychological about reading books. When students tell us that they do not like to read, what are we to make of this remark? Reading is work. Perhaps students who do not like to read, then, do not like to work hard. But Grumet might suggest something deeper. Perhaps students who do not like to read have had negative relations with their primary caregivers. And since books unconsciously remind us of those primary caregivers, reading can only be felt negatively. Some people do not like intimacy either and, according to Grumet, reading is about developing intimacy with texts. If children both loved and hated their primary caregivers so too will they love and hate to read.

Grumet points out, "In the work of Jacques Lacan and in the work of Julia Kristeva, it is the absence of the beloved that creates the space that texts fill" (p. 212). Here, reading has something to do with lost objects. Do we read in order to find those lost objects (or early relations with mothers)? Or do we read to simply find things out? Do we read to cure ourselves of loneliness? Is reading a cure, not in the medicalized sense but in a symbolic sense? Grumet says, "Reading is an essentially romantic process, for it invites us to mingle our thoughts, visions, and hopes with someone else's" (p. 207). Is reading a transferential relation with the family romance otherwise known as the Oedipus complex? We unconsciously choose what we read and transference plays a large role in the way in which we interpret texts (Morris, 2001). The ways in which we interpreted our mothers as children has much to do with the way in which we interpret, say, characters in a novel who remind us of our mothers. At any rate, Grumet says, "What I want to suggest is that we love to read, and that we also read in order to love" (p. 212).

Jonathan G. Silin

In an essay titled "Reading, Writing and the Wrath of my Father," Silin (2006) writes about his struggles with reading and writing. He suggests that as a child he had trouble reading and writing because of his unacknowledged homosexuality. As it was hard for him to accept his sexuality it was equally hard to read and write. Silin comments, "This reluctance to claim my ideas on paper, I now believe, was connected in some complicated and still incomprehensible way to my recalcitrant and unacceptable sexuality" (p. 234). As Silin grew to accept his sexuality, his reading and writing skills improved. In fact, Silin began to love reading and writing after struggling with his sexual identity. Silin tells us,

> As I became a writer, I also became a reader. In his short but memorable essay "On Reading," Proust (1971) described the places and days in which he first became absorbed by books. What remains most vivid about childhood reading, he claimed, is not the text itself but the call to an early lunch when the chapter is not quite finished, the summer outing during which our only desire is to return to the book left hastily aside on the dining room table. (p. 237)

Silin captures Proust's excitement for reading. As Silin matured and began to accept his sexuality he, too, felt excited about reading. Reading involves an immersion into a text. Reading also involves an immersion into the self.

However, if the self is troubled, the reading is also troubled. Reading and writing, then, for Silin are highly psychological acts. Moreover, Silin claims, "Reading can likewise become an act of recuperation" (p. 231). Reading is a way to heal the self, to repair the self. But the act of recuperation involves loss. Silin says, "Learning [which entails reading and writing] may bring with it a loss of connection to people" (p. 239). When young adults go to college they begin to learn a new language and they begin to think differently about the world because of the reading and writing practices instilled in them by their professors. When students return home from college, it seems as if a gap has widened between children and parents. This gap creates a sort of abyss and works to help the young person individuate from her parents. Individuation is a difficult process and involves "difficult emotions" (Silin, p. 239). Learning something new means that something old must be left behind. Silin puts it this way: "Learning a new way of being in the world, a child might also give up an old way" (p. 233). Giving up the old for the new is not an easy process. Students who resist reading new texts do so because texts—in college especially—challenge their belief systems. This is why it is so terribly hard to teach freshmen. Silin remarks, "Learning often involves unspoken forms of loss" (p. 228). Professors might help students work through their resistance to learning. Once this resistance is broken through students might begin to even enjoy reading and writing. Silin puts it this way:

> Literacy, and by extension the curriculum as text, becomes pleasurable when it exceeds social utility, leaves behind the familiar and the well rehearsed, and moves into uncharted territories where loss, discomfort, playfulness—even sexuality—can be fully expressed. (p. 228)

Reading and writing, again, are highly psychological acts. Working to help students "leave behind the familiar" is no easy task. It is easier to do the familiar—because we are comfortable there—than embrace the strange, the new. Embracing the strange means being able to deal with frustration. Silin discusses the work of Deborah Britzman to help us understand what it means to embrace the new. Silin states,

> In her insightful commentary on Freudian pedagogy, Deborah Britzman (1998) suggests that it is the ability to tolerate ambiguity, complexity, and uncertainty that teachers should seek to foster in their students rather than the false notions of truth, knowledge, and linear paths to learning. (p. 233)

Reading and writing involve "ambiguity, complexity, and uncertainty." Students are jolted out of their comfort zones when they understand that learning means more than memorizing so-called facts for a test.

Silin begins his essay by writing about his father who suffers from throat cancer and cannot speak. The importance of writing is driven home when Silin says that the only way his father can communicate is through writing. Silin's short vignette about his father suggests that we should "appreciate the potential of written language for sustaining life and producing social worlds" (p. 228). Like Silin, Salvio (2006), when talking about Anne Sexton, says, "Sexton suggests that she used the act of composing poetry to resist a merger with death" (p. 68). Writing, for some, is a survival tool. But as we know from studying Salvio's (2006, 2007) work, Sexton eventually committed suicide. Sometimes writing is not enough to sustain a life. However, for Silin's father writing sustained him.

Mary Aswell Doll

Mary Aswell Doll is one of the few curriculum theorists to draw on Jungian depth psychology to inform her work. In her book *The More of Myth: A Pedagogy of Diversion*, Doll (2011) examines the intersections among pedagogy, mythology, new science, and depth psychology. Doll divides her book into three parts: "Myth as Psychological Pedagogy, Myth as Ecological Pedagogy and Myth as Cosmological Pedagogy" (p. ix). Doll comments, "Mythic images challenge us to open the landscape of our minds, to probe beneath the surfaces, to re-think, and perhaps, even, to re-member" (p. xvi). In order to "open the landscape of our minds," one must explore the root of the word "psychology," which is psyche. "Psyche," for Jungians, means soul. Academic psychology—to the contrary—is not about soul, it is about the brain. Psychoanalysts who are not of the Jungian bent rarely, if ever, use the word "soul." But for Jungians this is a major concept. Like Freud, however, Jung was interested in exploring the unconscious. For Jung the unconscious is impersonal and sometimes referred to as the collective unconscious. Our dreams are the repositories for the collective unconscious as one can dream of ancient images or artifacts that are buried in the unconscious. Doll points out that for Jung

the psyche: "Among other things appears as a dynamic process which rests on a foundation of antithesis, on a flow of energy between two poles" (p. 350). All descriptors of this place, he continues, must be paradoxical and out of reach of sense perception. (p. 14)

For Freud, these "two poles" would be the two drives of Thanatos (or the death instinct) and Eros (or the life instinct). For Jung, the unconscious, Doll explains, is similar to the image of water. Doll writes,

> Commenting on the connection of water with the unconscious, Jung continues, "a secret unrest gnaws at the roots of our being…Whoever looks into the water sees his own image, but behind it living creatures soon loom up" (1977, p. 24). Jung goes on to describe the quality of the unconscious as "spontaneous," "something that lives of itself," "a life behind consciousness," "an unconscious life that surrounds consciousness on all sides." (p. 27). (p. 11)

Like Freud, Jung taught that what drives a life is not consciousness but the unconscious. If that is the case, then, one is never really certain about anything. We do not know what we are doing because the unconscious—to which we have little access—drives our lives. Doll tells us that for "depth psychology, following Jung…the psyche itself is…absolutely other in the depths of our interior" (p. 19). This Otherness makes us strangers to ourselves and to others. But in the context of schooling, standardization eradicates otherness. Doll comments that Jung was well aware of the problems of standardization. Doll writes, "Carl Jung says, 'in a standardized milieu, it is easy to lose the sense of one's own personality, of one's individuality' (in Sabini, 2005, p. 155)" (p. xvi). In the midst of standardized institutions, Doll suggests that teachers engage in what she calls a "pedagogy of diversion" (p. xvi). Studying mythology is that "pedagogy of diversion" because it is so strange and so Other to our everyday lives. Politically, this "pedagogy of diversion" "eschews" "institutional codes and purposes" (p. xvi). Myths oftentimes escape us. They are hard to follow and sometimes make little sense. But Doll encourages confusion for that is "a path into intrigue" and serves as a "pedagogy of diversion" (pp. xvi–xvii). When studying mythology one is studying what Doll calls "ancient wisdom" (p. xvi). Later in her book she will connect this ancient wisdom with new science. Doll claims,

> String theory, eleven dimensions, force fields of energy: these terms are not the exclusive domain of science, since Orpheus and Taliesin anticipated the strangeness of cosmic energies long, long ago. That these seemingly disparate disciplines should actually share common ground is not only interesting, it is testimony to the wisdom and foresight of ancestral knowledge. (p. xviii)

Jung built his depth psychology on ancestral knowledge as he studied ancient texts and related them to contemporary psychic problems. Although Jung was once part of Freud's intimate circle, his theories were too far afield for Freud to accept them. Jungians today are still on the margins. And in curriculum studies, Doll is one of the few theorists to bring to our attention—through the study of myth—the importance of Jungian depth psychology.

Marla Morris

I (2001, 2006, 2008, 2009) have written several books that draw on psychoanalytic literature to inform curriculum studies. Here, however, I will only discuss one of my books, *On Not Being Able to Play: Scholars, Musicians and the Crisis of Psyche* (2009). The title of the book is loosely based on D. W. Winnicott's (2010) *Playing and Reality*. Winnicott writes, "Where playing is not possible then the work of the therapist is directed towards bringing the patient from a state of not being able to play into a state of being able to play" (p. 51). The question I raise is, what if the musician is never able to play again due to injury or psychic blocks? I ask, "What do you do when you cannot do what you were called to do?" (p. 3). Likewise, I ask what happens to the scholar who can no longer work due to psychic blocks? I state, "This is a theoretical study of play and work, the play of the musician and the work of the scholar" (p. 4). Can the psychologically wounded musician or scholar move from a "state of not being able to play into a state of being able to play" (Winnicott, 2005, p. 51)? Can psychoanalytic therapy help the wounded musician or wounded scholar? This is an open question.

I explain,

> The idea for my book, *On Not Being Able to Play: Scholars, Musicians and the Crisis of Psyche*, came about after reading two groundbreaking texts: Joanna Field's (a pseudonym for Marion Milner) (1957) *On Not Being Able to Paint* and William F. Pinar's (2004) *Death in a Tenured Position*. (p. 3)

Milner suggests that painters who are blocked psychically and cannot paint might try to freely associate while painting. Free association might help the painter unlock a blocked psyche. I state that for Milner "painting is a metaphor for living" (p. 3). When lived experience cannot be freely associated life becomes stultified.

This deadening atmosphere is the academy. Some scholars burn out after they reach tenure and no longer publish. I suggest that these problems are deeper than, say, burn out, or blocked psyches. These problems have to do with repetition compulsion and repression of early childhood memories. I state,

> The connection (between not being able to play and complete inertia) could be symptomatic of an archaic disconnect between m(other) and child. Psychic inertia could be a repetition of a deep unraveling in early childhood object relations. (p. 162)

Psychological problems faced by both musicians and scholars could in fact be archaic. Early object relations—say in the pre-Oedipal period—are not remembered consciously but the repressed returns later in adulthood. The injury that the musician suffers might be caused by overuse but is a symptom of something deeper. The scholar who can no longer write, too, might be repeating an early childhood trauma that happened during the pre-Oedipal period and cannot be remembered consciously. But again, the repressed returns later in life.

The larger thesis of the book is to find "a way out" (p. 8). I suggest,

> One way out of the scholar's dilemma might be in the form of a Parabola. The scholar who gets psychically blocked might turn to music to get unstuck; the musician who can no longer play might turn to scholarship as a way to heal a damaged psyche. (p. 9)

I suggest that if these are untenable solutions, then, one can turn to other art forms, or literary activities to help heal what has been damaged. Influenced by performance artist Laurie Anderson, I contend that other art forms can also serve to heal both musician and scholar. Anderson is a multitalented musician as well as being

> a poet, a storyteller…a visual artist, a cultural critic, a cultural studies scholar…she sings, plays the electric violin, plays keyboards, does multimedia visuals….She combines aesthetics and politics, music and theater, talking and singing. (p. 278).

I comment that career paths do not have to be monolingual (p. 268). The "crisis of psyche" (i.e., not being able to play or not being able to work) does not have to result in psychological inertia. But one must understand at a deeper level what this stultification signifies psychologically before one can find a way out.

REFERENCES

Abiko, T. (2003). Present state of curriculum studies in Japan. In W. F. Pinar (Ed.), *International handbook of curriculum research* (pp. 425–434). Mahwah, NJ: Lawrence Erlbaum.

Abraham, N., & Torok, M. (1994). *The shell and the kernel: Vol. 1.* (N. Rand, Trans.). Chicago: University of Chicago Press.

Abram, D. (1996). *The spell of the sensuous: Perception and language in a more-than-human world.* New York: Vintage.

Adams, H. (2009). *Tom and Jack: The intertwined lives of Thomas Hart Benton and Jackson Pollock.* New York: Bloomsbury.

Adams, P. C., Hoelscher, S., & Till, K. E. (2001). Place in context: Rethinking humanist geographies. In P. C. Adams, S. Hoelscher, & K. Till (Eds.), *Textures of place: Exploring humanist geographies* (pp. xiii–xxxiii). Minneapolis: University of Minnesota.

Adefarakan, T. (2011). (Re)conceptualizing "indigenous" from anti-colonial and black feminist theoretical perspectives: Living and imagining indigeneity differently. In G. J. S. Dei (Ed.), *Indigenous philosophies and critical education* (pp. 34–52). New York: Peter Lang.

Adorno, T. (1997). *Aesthetic theory.* Minneapolis: University of Minnesota Press.

Aizenstat, S. (1995). Jungian psychology and the world unconscious. In T. Roszak, M. E. Gomes, & A. D. Kanner (Eds.), *Ecopsychology: Restoring the earth, healing the mind* (pp. 92–100). San Francisco: Sierra Club.

Alfred, T. (2004). Warrior scholarship: Seeing the university as a ground of contention. In D. A. Mihesuah & A. C. Wilson (Eds.), *Indigenizing the academy: Transforming scholarship and empowering communities* (pp. 88–99). Lincoln: University of Nebraska Press.

Anderson, A. (1998). Cosmopolitanism, universalism, and the divided legacies of modernity. In P. Cheah & B. Robbins (Eds.), *Cosmopolitics: Thinking and feeling beyond the nation* (pp. 265–289). Minneapolis: University of Minnesota Press.

Anderson, B. (2006). *Imagined communities.* New York: Verso.

Anderson, J. G. T. (2013). *Deep things out of darkness: A history of natural history.* Berkeley: University of California Press.

Angod, L. (2006). From post-colonial thought to anti-colonial politics: Difference, knowledge and R.V.R.D.S. In G. J. S. Dei & Arlo Kempf (Eds.), *Anti-colonialism and education* (pp. 159–173). Rotterdam: Sense.

Anijar, K., Weaver, J. A., & Daspit, T. (2004). Introduction. In K. Anijar, J. A. Weaver, & T. Daspit (Eds.), *Science fiction curriculum, cyborg teachers, & youth culture(s)* (pp. 1–17). New York: Peter Lang.

Anzaldúa, G. (2002). Preface: (Un)natural bridges, (un)safe spaces. In G. E. Anzaldúa & A. Keating (Eds.), *This bridge we call home: Radical visions for transformation* (pp. 1–5). New York: Routledge.

Appelbaum, P. M. (1999). Cyborg selves: Saturday morning magic and magical morality. In T. Daspit & J. A. Weaver (Eds.), *Popular culture and critical pedagogy* (pp. 83–115). New York: Garland.

Appiah, K. A. (2007). *Cosmopolitanism: Ethics in a world of strangers.* New York: W. W. Norton.

Arendt, H. (1979). *The origins of totalitarianism.* New York: Harcourt Brace.

Asanuma, S. (2003). Japanese educational reform for the 21st century: The impact of the new course of study toward the postmodern era in Japan. In W. F. Pinar (Ed.), *International handbook of curriculum research* (pp. 435–442). Mahwah, NJ: Lawrence Erlbaum.

Asher, N. (2003). Engaging difference: Towards a pedagogy of interbeing. *Teaching Education, 14*(3), 235–247.

Atwell-Vasey, W. (1998). *Nourishing words: Bridging private reading and public teaching.* Albany, NY: SUNY.

Bachelard, G. (2002). *Earth and reveries of will: An essay on the imagination of matter.* Dallas: Dallas Institute.

Baione, T. (2012). Introduction. In Tom Baione (Ed.), *Natural histories: Extraordinary rare book selections from the American Museum of Natural History library* (pp. ix–xi). New York: Sterling Signature.

Baker, B. M. (1998). "Childhood" in the emergence and spread of U.S. public schools. In T. S. Popkewitz & M. Brennan (Eds.), *Foucault's challenge: Discourse, knowledge, and power in education* (pp. 117–143). New York: Teachers College Press.

Baker, B. M. (2001). *In perpetual motion: Theories of power, educational history, and the child.* New York: Peter Lang.

Balibar, E. (1998). The borders of Europe. In P. Cheah & B. Robbins (Eds.), *Cosmopolitics: Thinking and feeling beyond the nation* (pp. 216–229). Minneapolis: University of Minnesota Press.

Barone, T. (2000). *Aesthetics, politics, and educational inquiry: Essays and examples.* New York: Peter Lang.

Basbanes, N. A. (2010). *About the author: Inside the creative process.* Durham, NC: Fine Books.

Bawarshi, A. (2003). *Genre & invention of the writer: Reconsidering the place of invention in composition*. Logan: Utah State University Press.

Beck, U. (2008). *Cosmopolitan vision* (C. Cronin, Trans.). Malden, MA: Polity.

Bekoff, M. (2010). *The animal manifesto: Six reasons for expanding our compassionate footprint*. Novato, CA: New World Library.

Benhabib, S. (2008). *Another cosmopolitanism*. New York: Oxford University Press.

Benjamin, A. (2006). Introduction. In A. Benjamin (Ed.), *Walter Benjamin and art* (pp. 1–2). New York: Continuum.

Benjamin, J. (1988). *The bonds of love: Psychoanalysis, feminism, and the problem of domination*. New York: Pantheon.

Benjamin, W. (1994). *The correspondence of Walter Benjamin*. (M. R. Jacobson & E. M. Jacobson, Trans.). Chicago: University of Chicago Press.

Benjamin, W. (1999). *The arcades project* (H. Eiland & K. McLaughlin, Trans.). Cambridge, MA: Belknap/Harvard University Press.

Berry, K. S. (2004). Multiple intelligences are not what they seem to be. In J. Kincheloe (Ed.), *Multiple intelligences reconsidered* (pp. 236–250). New York: Peter Lang.

Berry, T. (1990). *The dream of the earth*. San Francisco: Sierra Club.

Berry, T. (1995). The viable human. In G. Sessions (Ed.), *Deep ecology for the 21st century: Readings on the philosophy and practice of the new environmentalism* (pp. 8–18). Boston: Shambhala.

Berry, W. (2002). *The art of the commonplace: The agrarian essays of Wendell Berry*. Washington, DC: Shoemaker & Hoard.

Bettis, P. J., & Adams, N. G. (2009a). Landscapes of girlhood. In P. J. Bettis & N. G. Adams (Eds.), *Geographies of girlhood* (pp. 1–16). Mahwah, NJ: Lawrence Erlbaum.

Beyer, L. E. (2000). *The arts, popular culture, and social change*. New York: Peter Lang.

Bhabha, H. K. (1994). *The location of culture*. New York: Routledge.

Bibby, T. (2011). *Education—An "impossible profession"? Psychoanalytic explorations of learning and classrooms*. New York: Routledge.

Biesta, G. (2009). Deconstruction, justice, and the vocation of education. In M. A. Peters & G. Beista (Eds.), *Derrida, deconstruction and the politics of pedagogy* (pp. 15–37). New York: Peter Lang.

Birkerts, S. (2006). *The Gutenberg elegies*. New York: Faber & Faber.

Blades, D. (1997). *Procedures of power and curriculum change: Foucault and the quest for possibilities in science education*. New York: Peter Lang.

Blades, D. (2001). The simulacra of science education. In J. A. Weaver, M. Morris, & P. Appelbaum (Eds.), *(Post) modern science (education): Propositions and alternative paths* (pp. 57–94). New York: Peter Lang.

Bleich, D. (1999). The living text: Literary pedagogy and Jewish identity. In H. S. Shaprio (Ed.), *Strangers in the land: Pedagogy, modernity and Jewish identity* (pp. 109–132). New York: Peter Lang.

Block, A. A. (1997). *I'm only bleeding: Education as the practice of violence against children*. New York: Peter Lang.

Block, A. A. (2004). *Talmud, curriculum and the practical: Joseph Schwab and the rabbis*. New York: Peter Lang.

Block, A. A. (2007). *Pedagogy, religion, and practice: Reflections on ethics and teaching*. New York: Palgrave Macmillan.

Block, A. A. (2009). *Ethics and teaching: A religious perspective on revitalizing education*. New York: Palgrave Macmillan.

Blumenfeld-Jones, D. (2002). If I could have said it, I would have. In C. Bagley & M. B. Cancienne (Eds.), *Dancing the data* (pp. 90–104). New York: Peter Lang.

Blumenfeld-Jones, D. (2008). Dance, choreography, and social science research. In J. G. Knowles & A. L. Cole (Eds.), *Handbook of the arts in qualitative research* (pp. 175–184). Los Angeles: Sage.

Boldt, G. M., & Salvio M. (Eds.). (2006). *Love's return: Psychoanalytic essays on childhood, teaching, and learning*. New York: Routledge.

Boldt, G. M., Salvio, P. M., & Taubman, P. M. (2006). Introduction. In G. M. Boldt & P. M. Salvio (Eds.), *Love's return: Psychoanalytic essays on childhood, teaching, and learning* (pp. 1–8). New York: Routledge.

Bonnett, M. (2004). *Retrieving nature: Education for a post-humanist age*. Malden, MA: Blackwell.

Bowers, C. A. (1995). *Educating for an ecologically sustainable culture: Rethinking moral education, creativity, intelligence, and other modern orthodoxies*. Albany, NY: SUNY.

Bowers, C. A. (2007). *The false promises of constructivist theories of learning: A global and ecological critique*. New York: Peter Lang.

Brandt, C. B. (2004). A thirst for justice in the arid southwest: The role of epistemology and place in higher education. *Educational Studies: A Journal of the American Educational Studies Association, 36*(1), 93–107.

Breger, L. (2000). *Freud: Darkness in the midst of vision*. New York: John Wiley & Sons.

Brennan, T. (1997). *At home in the world: Cosmopolitanism now*. Cambridge, MA: Harvard University Press.

Brittain, J. (2007). Aristotle: The first philosopher naturalist. In R. Huxley (Ed.), *The great naturalists* (pp. 22–26). London: Thames & Hudson.

Britzman, D. P. (1998). *Lost subjects, contested objects: Toward a psychoanalytic inquiry of learning*. Albany, NY: SUNY.

Britzman, D. P. (2003). *After-education: Anna Freud, Melanie Klein and psychoanalytic histories of learning*. Albany, NY: SUNY.

Britzman, D. P. (2006). *Novel education: Psychoanalytic studies of learning and not learning*. New York: Peter Lang.

Britzman, D. P. (2009). *The very thought of education: Psychoanalysis and the impossible professions*. Albany, NY: SUNY.

Britzman, D. P. (2011). *Freud and education*. New York: Routledge.

Brock, G., & Brighouse, H. (2005). Introduction. In G. Brock & H. Brighouse (Eds.), *The political philosophy of cosmopolitanism* (pp. 1–9). New York: Cambridge University Press.

Buber, M. (2002). *Between man and man*. New York: Routledge.

Butler, J. (1990). *Gender trouble: Feminism and the subversion of identity*. New York: Routledge.

Cahill, S. (2004). Introduction. In S. Cahill (Ed.), *Women write: A mosaic of women's voices in fiction, poetry, memoir, and essay* (pp. xiii–xv). New York: New American Library.

Caine, R. S. E. (2008). Encouraging compassion in education: A non-anthropocentric perspective. In J. Gray-Donald & D. Selby (Eds.), *Green frontiers: Environmental educators dancing away from mechanism* (pp. 184–199). Rotterdam: Sense.

Cancienne, M. B. (2008). From research analysis to performance: The choreographic process. In J. G. Knowles & A. L. Cole (Eds.), *Handbook of the arts in qualitative research* (pp. 397–405). Los Angeles: Sage.

Cannella, G. S., & Viruru, R. (2004). *Childhood and postcolonialism: Power, education, and contemporary practice.* New York: RoutledgeFalmer.

Carlson, D. (2002). *Leaving safe harbors: Toward a new progressivism in American education and public life.* New York: RoutledgeFalmer.

Carlson, D. (2003). Cosmopolitan progressivism: Democratic education in the age of globalization. *JCT/The Journal of Curriculum Theorizing, 19*(4), 7–31.

Carson, R. (1990). *Silent spring* (40th anniversary ed.). New York: Mariner.

Carver, R. (2006). Commonplace but precise language. In D. Gioia & R. S. Gwynn (Eds.), *The art of the short story: 52 great authors, their best short fiction, and their insights on writing* (pp. 104–105). New York: Pearson.

Casemore, B. (2008). *The autobiographical demand of place: Curriculum inquiry in the American South.* New York: Peter Lang.

Casey, E. S. (1996). How to get from space to place in a fairly short stretch of time: Phenomenological prolegomena. In S. Feld & K. H. Basso (Eds.), *Senses of place* (pp. 13–52). Santa Fe, NM: School of American Research.

Casey, E. S. (1998). *The fate of place: A philosophical history.* Berkeley: University of California Press.

Cesaire, A. (2000). *Discourses on colonialism* (J. Pinkham, Trans.). New York: Monthly Review.

Chakrabarty, D. (2000). *Provincializing Europe: Postcolonial thought and historical difference.* Princeton, NJ: Princeton University Press.

Cherryholmes, C. H. (1999). *Reading pragmatism.* New York: Teachers College Press.

Chung, S. K. (2004). Zen (Ch'an) and aesthetic education. In G. Diaz & M. B. McKenna (Eds.), *Teaching for aesthetic education: The art of learning* (pp. 33–47). New York: Peter Lang.

Colebrook, C. (2008). Leading out, leading on: The soul of education. In I. Semetsky (Ed.), *Nomadic education: Variations on a theme by Deleuze and Guattari* (pp. 35–42). Rotterdam: Sense.

Collier, M. (2007). *Make us wave back: Essays on poetry and influence.* Ann Arbor: University of Michigan Press.

Connelly, M. F., He, M. F., & Phillon, J. (Eds.). (2008) *The Sage handbook of curriculum and instruction.* Los Angeles: Sage.

Cronon, W. (1996a). Beginnings. Introduction: In search of nature. In W. Cronon (Ed.), *Uncommon ground: Rethinking the human place in nature* (pp. (23–56). New York: W. W. Norton.

Cronon, W. (1996b). The trouble with wilderness; or, Getting back to the wrong nature. In W. Cronon (Ed.), *Uncommon ground: Rethinking the human place in nature* (pp. 69–90). New York: W. W. Norton.

Cronon, W. (Ed.). (1996c). *Uncommon ground: Rethinking the human place in nature.* New York: W. W. Norton.

Daignault, J. (2008). Pedagogy and Deleuze's concept of the virtual. In I. Semetsky (Ed.), *Nomadic education: Variations on a theme by Deleuze and Guattari* (pp. 43–60). Rotterdam: Sense.

Dalai Lama, D. (1999). Education and the human heart. In S. Glazer (Ed.), *The heart of learning: Spirituality in education* (pp. 85–95). New York: Tarcher Putnam.

Dalton, M. (1999). *The Hollywood curriculum: Teachers and teaching in the movies.* New York: Peter Lang.

Damarin, S. (2004). Required reading: Feminist sci-fi and post-millennial curriculum. In J. A. Weaver, K. Anijar, & T. Daspit (Eds.), *Science fiction curriculum: Cyborg teachers & youth culture(s)* (pp. 51–73). New York: Peter Lang.

Darian-Smith, K., Gunner, L., & Nuttall, S. (1996). Introduction. In K. Darion-Smith, L. Gunner, & S. Nuttall (Eds.), *Text, theory, space: Land, literature and history in South Africa and Australia* (pp. 1–20) New York: Routledge.

Daspit, T., & McDermott, M. (2002). Frameworks of blood and bone: An alchemy of performative mapping. In C. Bagley & M. B. Canienne (Eds.), *Dancing the data* (pp. 72). New York: Peter Lang.

Daspit, T., & Weaver, J. A. (2005). Rap (in) the academy: Academic work, education, and cultural studies. In S. Edgerton, G. Holm, T. Daspit, & P. Farber (Eds.), *Imagining the academy: Higher education and popular culture* (pp. 72–95). New York: RoutledgeFalmer.

Davis, B. (1996). *Teaching mathematics: Toward a sound alternative.* New York: Garland.

Davis, B., & Appelbaum, P. (2002). Post-Holocaust science education. In M. Morris & J. A. Weaver (Eds.), *Difficult memories: Talk in a (Post) Holocaust era* (pp. 171–190). New York: Peter Lang.

Davis, B., & Sumara, D. (2006). *Complexity and education: Inquiries into learning teaching, and research.* Mahwah: NJ: Lawrence Erlbaum.

Dayton, G. H., Dayton, P. K., & Greene, H. W. (2011). Exploration. In M. H. Graham, J. Parker, & P. K. Dayton (Eds.), *The essential naturalist: Timeless readings in natural history* (pp. 91–98). Chicago: University of Chicago Press.

De Cosson, A. F. (2008). Texu(r)al walking/writing through sculpture. In J. Gary Knowles & A. L. Cole (Eds.), *Handbook of the arts in qualitative research* (pp. 277–286). Los Angeles: Sage.

Dei, G. J. S. (2006). Introduction: Mapping the terrain—towards a new politics of resistance. In G. J. S. Dei & Arlo Kempf (Eds.), *Anti-colonialism and education: The politics of resistance* (pp. 1–24). Rotterdam: Sense.

Dei, G. J. S. (2010). *Teaching Africa: Towards a transgressive pedagogy.* New York: Springer.

Dei, G. J. S. (2011a). Introduction. In G. J. S. Dei (Ed.), *Indigenous philosophies and critical education* (pp. 1–13). New York: Peter Lang.

Dei, G. J. S. (2011b). Revisiting the question of the "indigenous." In G. J. S. Dei (Ed.), *Indigenous philosophies and critical education* (pp. 21–33). New York: Peter Lang.

Deleuze, G. (2009). Interviews. In F. Guattari (Ed.), *Chaosophy: Texts and interviews 1972–1977*. Los Angeles: Semiotext(e).

Deleuze, G., & Guattari, F. (1994). *What is philosophy?* (H. Tomlinson & G. Burchell, Trans.). New York: Columbia University Press.

Deleuze, G., & Guattari, F. (2000). *Anti-Oedipus: Capitalism and schizophrenia* (R. Hurley, M. Seem, & H. R. Lang). Minneapolis: University of Minnesota Press.

Deloria, V., Jr. (2007). *We talk, you listen: New tribes, new turfs*. Lincoln: University of Nebraska Press.

Denzin, N. K. (2007). Foreword: A cultural studies that matters. In C. McCarthy, A. S. Durham, L. C. Engel, A. A. Filmer, M. D. Giardina, & M. A. Malagreca (Eds.), *Globalizing cultural studies: Ethnographic interventions in theory, method, and policy* (pp. xi–xv). New York: Peter Lang.

Derrida, J. (1976). *Of grammatology* (G. C. Spivak, Trans). Baltimore: Johns Hopkins University Press.

Derrida, J. (1978). *Writing and difference* (Alan Bass, Trans.). Chicago: University of Chicago Press.

Derrida, J. (1986). *Margins of philosophy* (Alan Bass, Trans). Chicago: University of Chicago Press.

Derrida, J. (1987). *The truth in painting* (G. Bennington & I. McLeod, Trans). Chicago: University of Chicago Press.

Derrida, J. (1988). *The ear of the other: Otobiography, transference, translation* (P. Kamuf, Trans.). Lincoln: University of Nebraska Press.

Derrida, J. (1991). *A Derrida reader: Between the blinds* (P. Kamuf, Ed.). New York: Columbia University Press.

Derrida, J. (1992a). Mochlos; or, The conflict of the faculties. In R. Rand (Ed.), *Logomachia: The conflict of the faculties*. Lincoln: University of Nebraska Press.

Derrida, J. (1992b). *The other heading: Reflections on today's Europe* (P.-A. Brault & M. Nass, Trans.). Bloomington: Indiana University Press.

Derrida, J. (1995a). *Points: Interviews, 1974–1994* (P. Kamuf, Trans). Stanford, CA: Stanford University Press.

Derrida, J. (1995b). *The gift of death* (D. Wills, Trans.). Chicago: University of Chicago Press.

Derrida, J. (1997). *The politics of friendship*. (G. Collins, Trans.). London: Verso.

Derrida, J. (2000a). *Limited Inc.* Evanston, IL: Northwestern University Press.

Derrida, J. (2000b). *Of hospitality* (R. Bowlby, Trans.). Stanford, CA: Stanford University Press.

Derrida, J. (2002a). *Ethics, institutions, and the right to philosophy*. (Trans., Peter Pericles Trifonas). Lanham, MD: Rowman & Littlefield.

Derrida, J. (2002b). *Negotiations: Interventions and interviews, 1971–2001* (E. Rottenberg, Trans.). Stanford, CA: Stanford University Press.

Derrida, J. (2002c). *On cosmopolitanism and forgiveness* (M. Dooley & M. Hughes, Trans.). New York: Routledge.

Derrida, J. (2004). Istanbul, 10 May 1997. In C. Malabou & J. Derrida (Eds.), *Counterpath: Traveling with Jacques Derrida* (D. Wills, Trans., p. 3). Stanford, CA: Stanford University Press.

Derrida, J. (2005). *Rogues: Two essays on reason* (P.-A. Brault & M. Nass, Trans.). Stanford: Stanford University Press.

Derrida, J. (2008). *The animal that therefore I am* (M.-L. Mallet & D. Wills, Trans.). New York: Fordham University Press.

Dewey, J. (2005). *Art as experience.* New York: Penguin.

Diaz, G. (2002). Artistic inquiry: On Lighthouse Hill. In C. Bagley & M. B. Cancienne (Eds.), *Dancing the data* (pp. 147–161). New York: Peter Lang.

Dickstein, M. (1999). Introduction: Pragmatism then and now. In M. Dickstein (Ed.), *The revival of pragmatism: New essays on social thought, law, and culture* (pp. 1–18). Durham, NC: Duke University Press.

Dillard, A. (2013). *The writing life.* New York: HarperPerennial.

Dimitriadis, G., & McCarthy, C. (2001). *Reading & teaching the postcolonial: From Baldwin to Basquiat and beyond.* New York: Teachers College Press.

Doerr, M. N. (2004). *Currere and the environmental autobiography: A phenomenological approach to the teaching of ecology.* New York: Peter Lang.

Doll, M. A. (1995). *To the lighthouse and back: Writings on teaching and living.* New York: Peter Lang.

Doll, M. A. (2000). *Like letters in running water: A mythopoetics of curriculum.* Mahwah, NJ: Lawrence Erlbaum.

Doll, M. A. (2011). *The more of myth: A pedagogy of diversion.* The Netherlands: Sense.

Doll, W. E. (1993). *A post-modern perspective on curriculum.* New York: Teachers College Press.

Doll, W. E. (1998). Curriculum and concepts of control. In W. F. Pinar (Ed.), *Curriculum toward new identities* (pp. 295–323). New York: Garland.

Doll, W. (2005). The culture of method. In W. Doll Jr., M. J. Fleener, D. Trueit, & J. St. Julien (Eds.), *Chaos, complexity, curriculum, and culture: A conversation* (pp. 21–75). New York: Peter Lang.

Doll, W., Jr., Fleener, M. J., Trueit, D., & St. Julien, J. (Eds.). (2005). *Chaos, complexity, curriculum, and culture: A conversation.* New York: Peter Lang.

Donmoyer, R., & Donmoyer, J. Y. (2008). Readers' theater as a data display strategy. In J. G. Knowles & A. L. Cole (Eds.), *Handbook of the arts in qualitative research* (pp. 209–224). Los Angeles: Sage.

Dreyfus, H. L., & Rabinow, P. (1983). *Michel Foucault: Beyond structuralism and hermeneutics.* Chicago: University of Chicago Press.

Dunlop, R. (2004). Red shoes: The woman artist/educator in the ivory tower. In G. Diaz & M. B. McKenna (Eds.), *Teaching for aesthetic experience: The art of learning* (pp. 147–176). New York: Peter Lang.

Eco, U. (2004). *The mysterious flame of Queen Loana.* New York: Harcourt.

Edgcumbe, R. (2000). *Anna Freud: A view of development, disturbance and therapeutic techniques.* New York: Routledge.

Edgerton, S. H. (1996). *Translating the curriculum: Multiculturalism into cultural studies.* New York: Routledge.

Egea-Kuehne, D. (2004). The teaching of philosophy: Renewed rights and responsibilities. In P. P. Trifonas & M. A. Peters (Eds.), *Derrida, deconstruction & education: Ethics of pedagogy and research* (pp. 17–30). Malden, MA: Blackwell.

Egea-Kuehne, D. (2008). Levinas's quest for justice: Of faith and the "possibility of education." In D. Egea-Kuehne (Ed.), *Levinas and education: At the intersection of faith and reason* (pp. 26–40). New York: Routledge.

Egea-Kuehne, D., & Biesta, G. (2001). Opening: Derrida and education. In G. J. J. Biesta & D. Egea-Kuehne (Eds.), *Derrida and education* (pp. 1–11). New York: Routledge.

Eigen, M. (1998). *The psychoanalytic mystic.* New York: Free.

Eigen, M. (2005). *Emotional storm.* Middletown, CT: Wesleyan University Press.

Eiland, H. (2006). Reception in distraction. In A. Benjamin (Ed.), *Walter Benjamin and art* (pp. 3–13). New York: Continuum.

Eisner, E. W. (2002). *Arts and the creation of mind.* New Haven, CT: Yale University Press.

Eisner, E. W. (2008). Art and knowledge. In J. G. Knowles & A. L. Cole (Eds.), *Handbook of the arts in qualitative research* (pp. 3–12). Los Angeles: Sage.

Elabor-Idemudia, P. (2008). The retention of knowledge of folkways as a basis for resistance. In G. J. S. Dei, B. L. Hall, & D. G. Rosenberg (Eds.), *Indigenous knowledges in global contexts: Multiple readings of our world* (pp. 102–119). Toronto: OISE/University of Toronto Press.

Ellis, R. (2011). The first animal book. In T. Baione (Ed.), *Natural histories: Extraordinary rare book selections from the American Museum of Natural History* (pp. 1–2). New York: Sterling Signature.

Eppert, C., & Wang, H. (2008). Preface: Opening into a curriculum of the way. In C. Eppert & H. Wang (Eds.), *Cross-cultural studies in curriculum: Eastern thought, educational insights* (pp. xvi–xxii). New York: Taylor & Francis.

Eppert, C., & Wang, H. (Eds.). (2008). *Cross-cultural studies in curriculum: Eastern thought, educational insights.* New York: Taylor & Francis.

Epstein, M. (2007). *Psychotherapy without the self: A Buddhist perspective.* New Haven, CT: Yale University Press.

Fanon, F. (1963). *The wretched of the earth.* New York: Grove.

Fanon, F. (1965). *A dying colonialism* (H. Chevalier, Trans.). New York: Grove.

Feld, S., & Basso, K. H. (1996). Introduction. In S. Feld & K. H. Basso (Eds.), *Senses of place* (pp. 3–11). Santa Fe, NM: School of American Research.

Feraoun, M. (2000). *Journal 1955–1962: Reflections on the French-Algerian War* (M. E. Wolf & C. Fouillade, Trans.). Lincoln: University of Nebraska Press.

Fernandez, R. (1997). Introduction: From ivory tower to green tower. In P. J. Thompson (Ed.), *Environmental education for the 21st century: International and interdisciplinary perspectives* (pp. xiii–xx). New York: Peter Lang.

Feuerverger, G. (2007). *Teaching, learning and other miracles.* Rotterdam: Sense.

Finley, S. (2002). Women myths: Teacher self-images and socialization to feminine stereotypes. In C. Bagley & M. B. Cancienne (Eds.), *Dancing the data* (pp. 162–176). New York: Peter Lang.

Finley, S. (2008). Arts-based research. In J. G. Knowles & A. L. Cole (Eds.), *Handbook of the arts in qualitative research* (pp. 71–81). Los Angeles: Sage.

Fishman, J. (2001). *Everyone's gotta be somewhere: Savannah columns by Jane Fishman*. Savannah, GA: Pressworks.

Fleener, M. J. (2002). *Curriculum dynamics: Recreating heart*. New York: Peter Lang.

Fleener, M. J. (2005). Introduction: Chaos, complexity, curriculum, and culture. Setting up the conversation. In W. Doll Jr., M. J. Fleener, D. Trueit, & J. St. Julien (Eds.), *Chaos, complexity, curriculum, and culture: A conversation* (pp. 1–17). New York: Peter Lang.

Flinders, D. J., & Thornton, S. J. (Eds.). (2004). *The curriculum studies reader* (2nd ed.) New York: RoutledgeFalmer.

Foucault, M. (1972). *The archaeology of knowledge & the discourse on language* (A. M. S. Smith, Trans.). New York: Pantheon.

Foucault, M. (1979). *Discipline and punish: The birth of the prison* (A. Sheridan, Trans.). New York: Vintage.

Foucault, M. (1983). On the genealogy of ethics: An overview of work in progress. In H. L. Dreyfus & P. Rabinow (Eds.), *Michel Foucault: Beyond structuralism and hermeneutics* (pp. 229–252). Chicago: University of Chicago Press.

Foucault, M. (1988). *Madness and civilization: A history of insanity in the age of reason*. New York: Vintage.

Foucault, M. (1990). *The history of sexuality: An introduction: Vol. 1*. New York: Vintage.

Foucault, M. (1994). *The order of things: An archaeology of the human sciences*. New York: Vintage.

Foucault, M. (2003). *"Society must be defended": Lectures at the College de France 1975–1976* (D. Macey, Trans.). New York: Picador.

Fox, M. (2006). *The A.W.E. project: Reinventing education*. Kelowna, BC, Canada: CopperHouse.

Frank, T., & Wall, D. (1994). *Finding your writer's voice: A guide to creative fiction*. New York: St. Martin's Griffin.

Freire, P. (2005). *Teachers as cultural workers: Letters to those who dare teach, expanded edition* (D. Macedo, D. Koike, & A. Oliveira, Trans.). Boulder, CO: Westview.

Freud, A. (1979). *Psycho-analysis for teachers and parents* (B. Low, Trans.). New York: W.W. Norton.

Freud, A. (1966/2000). *The ego and the mechanisms of defense*. Madison, CT: International Universities.

Freud, S. (1952). *An autobiographical study, the standard edition*. (J. Strachey, Ed. & Trans.). New York: W. W. Norton.

Freud, S. (1959). *Inhibitions, symptoms and anxiety, the standard edition* (J. Strachey, Ed. & A. Strachey, Trans.). New York: W. W. Norton.

Freud, S. (1960a). *The ego and the id, the standard edition* (Rev. ed., J. Strachey, Ed., & J. Riviere, Trans.) New York: W. W. Norton.

Freud, S. (1960b). *The psychopathology of everyday life, the standard edition* (J. Strachey, Ed. & Trans.). New York: W. W. Norton.

Freud, S. (1961a). *Beyond the pleasure principle, the standard edition* (J. Strachey, Ed. & Trans.). New York: W. W. Norton.

Freud, S. (1961b). *Civilization and its discontents, the standard edition* (J. Strachey, Ed. & Trans.). New York: W. W. Norton.

Freud, S. (1961c). *Five lectures on psycho-analysis, the standard edition* (J. Strachey, Ed. & Trans.). New York: W. W. Norton.

Freud, S. (1965). *New introductory lectures on psycho-analysis, the standard edition* (J. Strachey, Ed. & Trans.). New York: W. W. Norton.

Freud, S. (1966a). *Introductory lectures on psycho-analysis, the standard edition* (J. Strachey, Ed. & Trans.). New York: W. W. Norton.

Freud, S. (1966b). *On the history of the psycho-analytic movement, the standard edition* (Rev. ed., J. Strachey, Ed., & J. Riviere, Trans.). New York: W. W. Norton.

Freud, S. (1969). *An outline of psycho-analysis, the standard edition* (J. Strachey, Ed. & Trans.). New York: W. W. Norton.

Freud, S. (1978). *The question of lay analysis, the standard edition* (J. Strachey, Ed. & Trans.). New York: W. W. Norton.

Freud, S. (1980). *On dreams, the standard edition* (J. Strachey, Ed. & Trans.). New York: W. W. Norton.

Freud, S. (2010). *The interpretation of dreams* (J. Strachey, Ed. & Trans.). New York: Basic.

Frierson, P., & Guyer, P. (2011). Notes on the text. In P. Frierson & P. Guyer (Eds.), *Kant: Observations on the feeling of the beautiful and sublime and other writings* (pp. xlii–xlv). New York: Cambridge University Press.

Gadamer, H.-G. (1975). *Truth and method*. New York: Seabury.

Gallagher, K. (2000). *Drama education in the lives of girls: Imagining possibilities*. Toronto: University of Toronto Press.

Gallagher, K. (2007). *The theater of urban: Youth and schooling in dangerous times*. Toronto: University of Toronto Press.

Gard, M. (2006). *Men who dance: Aesthetics & the art of masculinity*. New York: Peter Lang.

Gardner, H. (1983). *Frames of mind: The theory of multiple intelligences*. New York: Basic.

Gawande, A. (2002). *Complications: A surgeon's notes on an imperfect science*. New York: Picador.

Gay, P. (1989a). Introduction. In P. Gay (Ed.), *The Freud reader* (pp. xiii–xxix). New York: W. W. Norton.

Gay, P. (1989b). Preface. In, P. Gay (Ed.), *The Freud reader* (pp. xi–xii). New York: W.W. Norton.

Gay, P. (1998). *Freud: A life for our time*. New York: W. W. Norton.

Gee, J. P. (2007). *Good video games + good learning: Collected essays on video games, learning and literacy*. New York: Peter Lang.

Gere, S. H., Hoshmand, L. T., & Reinkraut, R. (2002). Constructing the sacred: Empathic engagement, aesthetic regard, and discernment in clinical teaching. In E. Mirochnik & D. C. Sherman (Eds.), *Passion and pedagogy: Relation, creation, and transformation in teaching* (pp. 153–176). New York: Peter Lang.

Gilbert, S. M. (2006). *Death's door: Modern dying and the ways we grieve*. New York: W. W. Norton.

Gilman, S. L. (1988). *Disease and representation: Images of illness from madness to AIDS*. Ithaca, NY: Cornell University Press.

Gilman, S. L. (1998). *Creating beauty to cure the soul: Race and psychology in the shaping of aesthetic surgery.* Durham, NC: Duke University Press.

Gilroy, P. (2005). *Postcolonial melancholia.* New York: Columbia University Press.

Giroux, H. A. (2003). *The abandoned generation: Democracy beyond the culture of fear.* New York: Palgrave Macmillan.

Giroux, H. A. (2008). Militarization, public pedagogy, and the biopolitics of popular culture. In D. Silberman-Keller, Z. Bekerman, H. A. Giroux, & N. C. Burbules (Eds.), *Mirror images: Popular culture and education* (pp. 39–54). New York: Peter Lang.

Giroux, H. A. (2010, October). When generosity hurts: Bill Gates, public school teachers and the politics of humiliation. Retrieved from http://www.truth-out.org/

Gogol, N. (2004). *Dead souls.* New York: Everyman's Library.

Goldberg, N. (2005). *Writing down the bones: Freeing the writer within.* Boston: Shambhala.

Gough, N. (2001). Teaching in the *(crash)* zone: Manifesting cultural studies in science education. In J. A. Weaver, M. Morris, & P. Appelbaum (Eds.), *(Post) modern science (education): Propositions and alternative paths* (pp. 249–273). New York: Peter Lang.

Gough, N. (2003). Thinking globally in environmental education: Implications for internationalizing curriculum inquiry. In W. F. Pinar (Ed.), *International handbook on curriculum research* (pp. 53–72). Mahwah, NJ: Lawrence Erlbaum.

Gough, N. (2004). Narrative experiments: Manifesting cyborgs in curriculum inquiry. In J. A. Weaver, K. Anijar, & T. Daspit (Eds.), *Science fiction curriculum, cyborg teachers, & youth culture(s)* (pp. 89–108). New York: Peter Lang.

Gough, N. (2008). Ecology, ecocriticism and learning: How do places become "pedagogical"? *Transitional Curriculum Inquiry,* 5(1), 71–86.

Graham, M. H. (2011). A foundation built by giants. In M. Graham, J. Parker, & P. K. Dayton (Eds.), *The essential naturalists: Timeless readings in natural history* (pp. 1–6). Chicago: University of Chicago Press.

Gray-Donald, J. (2008). Narratives of exploration: Childhood place and the academia of environmental education. In J. Gray-Donald & D. Selby (Eds.), *Green frontiers: Environmental educators dancing away from mechanism* (pp. 14–35). Rotterdam: Sense.

Gray-Donald, J., & Selby, D. (2008). Introduction. In J. Gray-Donald & D. Selby (Eds.), *Green frontiers: Environmental educators dancing away from mechanism* (pp. 1–7). Rotterdam: Sense.

Green, B. (2003). Curriculum inquiry in Australia: Toward a local genealogy of the curriculum field. In W. F. Pinar (Ed.), *International handbook of curriculum research* (pp. 123–141). Mahwah, NJ: Lawrence Erlbaum.

Greenberg, J. R., & Mitchell, S. A. (1983). *Object relations in psychoanalytic theory.* Cambridge, MA: Harvard University Press.

Greene, M. (1995). *Releasing the imagination: Essays on education, the arts, and social change.* San Francisco: Jossey-Bass.

Greene, M. (2001). *Variations on a blue guitar: The Lincoln Center Institute lectures on aesthetic education.* New York: Teachers College Press.

Greene, M. (2004). Carpe Diem: The arts and school restructuring. In G. Diaz & M. B. McKenna (Eds.), *Teaching for aesthetic experience: The art of learning* (pp. 17–31). New York: Peter Lang.

Grody, S. (2007). *Graffiti L.A.: Street styles and art.* New York: Abrams.

Grossberg, Lawrence. (2003). Mapping the intersections of Foucault and cultural studies: An interview with Lawrence Grossberg and Toby Miller, October 2000 by Jeremy Packer. In, Jack Z. Bratich, Jeremy Packer & Cameron McCarthy (Eds.), *Foucault, cultural studies, and governmentality* (pp. 23–46). Albany: SUNY.

Grosskurth, P. (1986). *Melanie Klein: Her world and her work.* New York: Alfred A. Knopf.

Grosz, E. (2008). *Chaos, territory, art: Deleuze and the framing of the earth.* New York: Columbia University Press.

Gruenewald, D., & Smith, G. (2008). Making room for the local. In D. Gruenewald & G. A. Smith (Eds.), *Place-based education in the global age: Local diversity* (pp. xiii–xxiii). New York: Lawrence Erlbaum.

Grumet, M. R. (2004). No one learns alone. In N. Rabkin & R. Redmond (Eds.), *Putting the arts in the picture: Reframing education in the 21st century* (pp. 49–80). Chicago: Columbia College.

Grumet, M. R. (2006). Romantic research. Why we love to read. In G. M. Boldt & P. M. Salvio (Eds.), *Love's return: Psychoanalytic essays on childhood, teaching and learning* (pp. 207–225). New York: Routledge.

Guattari, F. (1995). *Chaosmosis: An ethico-aesthetic paradigm.* Bloomington: University of Indiana Press.

Guattari, F. (2009). *Chaosophy: Texts and interviews, 1972–1977* (D. L. Sweet, J. Becker, & T. Adkins, Trans.). Cambridge, MA: MIT.

Hall, S. (2008). Political belonging in a world of multiple identities. In S. Vertovec & R. Cohen (Eds.), *Conceiving cosmopolitanism: Theory, context, and practice* (pp. 25–31). New York: Oxford University Press.

Hanh, T. N. (2006). *Understanding our mind.* Berkeley, CA: Parallax.

Haraway, D. J. (1989). *Primate visions: Gender, race, and nature in the world of modern science.* New York: Routledge.

Haraway, D. J. (1997). *Modest_witness@second_millennium.FemaleMan_meets_onconmouse: Feminism and technoscience.* New York: Routledge.

Hartmann, G. (1986). Introduction 1985. In G. Hartmann (Ed.), *Bitburg in moral and political perspective* (pp. 1–12). Bloomington: Indiana University Press.

Hayden, M., Levy, J., & Thompson, J. (Eds.). (2008). *The Sage handbook of research in international education.* Los Angeles: Sage.

Hayles, N. K. (1999). *How we became posthuman: Virtual bodies in cybernetics, literature, and informatics.* Chicago: University of Chicago Press.

Hayward, J. (1999). Unlearning to see the sacred. In S. Glazer (Ed.), *The heart of learning: Spirituality in education* (pp. 61–76). New York: Tarcher Putnam.

Heidegger, M. (1962). *Being and time* (J. Macquarrie & E. Robinson, Trans.). New York: Harper & Row.

Hensley, N. (2011). *Curriculum studies gone wild: Bioregional education and the scholarship of sustainability*. New York: Peter Lang.

Heschel, A. J. (1969). *The prophets*. New York: Harper.

Hillman, J. (1995). A psyche the size of the earth: A psychological foreword. In T. Roszak, M. E. Gomes, & A. D. Kanner (Eds.), *Ecopsychology: Restoring the earth, healing the mind* (pp. xviii–xxiii). San Francisco: Sierra Club.

Hofstadter, R. (1965). *Anti-intellectualism in American life*. New York: Vintage.

Holder, A. (2005). *Anna Freud, Melanie Klein, and the psychoanalysis of children and adolescents* (P. Slotkin, Trans.). London: Karnac.

Howard, P. S. S. (2006). On silence and dominant accountability: A critical anticolonial investigation of the antiracism classroom. In G. J. S. Dei & A. Kempf (Eds.), *Anti-colonialism and education: The politics of resistance* (pp. 43–62). Rotterdam: Sense.

Huebner, D. E. (1999). *The lure of the transcendent: Collected essays by Dwayne E. Huebner* (V. Hillis, Ed., W. F. Pinar, Collector). Mahwah, NJ: Lawrence Erlbaum.

Hurren, W. (2000). *Line dancing: An atlas of geography, curriculum and poetic possibilities*. New York: Peter Lang.

Huxley, R. (2007). Unity in diversity. In R. Huxley (Ed.), *The great naturalists* (pp. 7–19). London: Thames & Hudson.

Hwu, W.-S. (2004). Gilles Deleuze and Jacques Daignault: Understanding curriculum as difference. In W. M. Reynolds & J. A. Webber (Eds.), *Expanding curriculum theory: Dis/positions and lines of flight* (pp. 181–202). Mahwah, NJ: Lawrence Erlbaum.

Irwin, R. L. (2004). Introduction: A/r/tography: A metonymic métissage. In R. L. Irwin & A. de Cosson (Eds.), *A/r/tography: Rendering self through arts-based living inquiry* (pp. 27–38). Vancouver, Canada: Pacific Educational.

Jackson, J. B. (1994). *A sense of place, a sense of time*. New Haven, CT: Yale University Press.

Jackson, P. W. (1998). *John Dewey and the lessons of art*. New Haven, CT: Yale University Press.

jagodzinski, j. (1997). *Postmodern dilemmas: Outrageous essays in art and art education*. Mahwah, NJ: Lawrence Erlbaum.

Jameson, F. (1993). Foreword. In, Jean-Francois Lyotard, *The postmodern condition: A report on knowledge* (vii–xxi). Minneapolis: MN. The University of Minnesota Press.

Jardine, D. W. (1998). *To dwell with a boundless heart: Essays in curriculum theory, hermeneutics, and the ecological imagination*. New York: Peter Lang.

Jardine, D. W. (2000). *"Under the tough old stars": Ecopedagogical essays*. Brandon, VT: Foundation for Educational Renewal.

Jensen, D. (2000). *A language older than words*. New York: Context.

Johnsen, M. (2007). *The meaning of the body: Aesthetics of human understanding*. Chicago: University of Chicago Press.

Jung, C. G. (2005). *The nature writings of C. G. Jung* (M. Smith, Ed.). Berkeley, CA: North Atlantic.

Jung, C. G. (2009). *The red book* (S. Shamdasani, Ed.). New York: W. W. Norton.

Justice, D. H. (2004). Seeing (and reading) red: Indian outlaws in the Ivory Tower. In D. A. Mihesuah & A. C. Wilson (Eds.), *Indigenizing the academy: Transforming scholarship and empowering communities* (pp. 100–123). Lincoln: University of Nebraska Press.

Kaneda, T. (2008). Shanti, peacefulness of mind. In C. Eppert & H. Wang (Eds.), *Cross-cultural studies in curriculum: Eastern thought, educational insights* (pp. 171–192). Mahwah, NJ: Lawrence Erlbaum.

Kant, I. (2001). Selections from Critique of Judgment. In A. W. Wood (Ed.), *Basic writings of Kant* (J. C. Meredith, Trans., pp. 273–366). New York: Modern Library.

Kanu, Y. (2006). Introduction. In Y. Kanu (Ed.), *Curriculum as cultural practice: Postcolonial imaginations* (pp. 3–29). Toronto: University of Toronto Press.

Keller, R. C. (2007). *Colonial madness: Psychiatry in French North Africa.* Chicago: University of Chicago Press.

Kempf, A. (2010). Contemporary anticolonialism: A transhistorical perspective. In A. Kempf (Ed.), *Breaching the colonial contract: Anti-colonialism in the US and Canada* (pp. 13–34). New York: Springer.

Kesson, K. (2002). Contemplative spirituality, currere, and social transformation: Finding our way. In T. Oldenski & D. Carlson (Eds.), *Educational yearning: The journey of the spirit and democratic education* (pp. 46–70). New York: Peter Lang.

Kincheloe, J. L. (1997). Home alone and bad to the bone: The advent of a postmodern childhood. In S. R. Steinberg & J. L. Kincheloe (Eds.), *Kinderculture: The corporate construction of childhood* (pp. 31–52). Boulder, CO: Westview.

Kincheloe, J. L. (2002). *The sign of the burger: McDonald's and the culture of power.* Philadelphia: Temple University Press.

Kincheloe, J. L. (2004a). Artful teaching in a "sensational" context. In K. Rose & J. L. Kincheloe (Eds.), *Art, culture, & education: Artful teaching in a fractured landscape* (pp. 1–37). New York: Peter Lang.

Kincheloe, J. L. (2004b). Introduction. In J. L. Kincheloe & S. R. Steinberg (Eds.), *The miseducation of the West: How schools and the media distort our understanding of the Islamic world* (pp. 1–23). Westport, CT: Praeger.

Kincheloe, J. L. (Ed.). (2004c). Twenty-first century questions about multiple intelligences. In J. L. Kincheloe (Ed.), *Multiple intelligences reconsidered* (pp. 3–28). New York: Peter Lang.

Kincheloe, J. L. (2005). Introduction. In P. Freire, *Teachers as cultural workers: Letters to those who dare teach* (pp. xli–xlix). Boulder, CO: Westview.

Kincheloe, J., & Pinar, W. F. (Eds.). (1991). *Curriculum as social psychoanalysis: The significance of place.* Albany, NY: SUNY.

Kincheloe, J. L., & Steinberg, S. R. (Eds.). (2004). *The miseducation of the West: How schools and the media distort our understanding of the Islamic world.* Westport, CT: Praeger.

King, P., & Steiner, R. (Eds.). (1992). *The Freud-Klein controversies, 1941–45.* London: Tavistock/Routledge.

Kirsch, Adam. (2005). *The wounded surgeon: Confession and transformation in six American poets: The poetry of Lowell, Bishop, Berryman, Jarrell, Schwartz, and Plath.* New York: W. W. Norton.

Klein, M. (1940/1975). *Love, guilt and reparation and other works 1921–1945.* New York: Free.

Klein, M. (1946/1984). *Envy and gratitude and other works 1946–1963.* New York: Free.

Klein, M. (1948/1993). *Envy, gratitude and other works.* London: Karnac.

Kridel, C. (Ed.). (2010). *Encyclopedia of curriculum studies.* Los Angeles: Sage.

Kristeller, P. O. (2008). Introduction. In S. M. Cahn & A. Meskin (Eds.), *Aesthetics: A comprehensive anthology* (pp. 3–15). Malden, MA: Blackwell.

Kristeva, J. (2001). *Melanie Klein* (R. Guberman, Trans.). New York: Columbia University Press.

Krugly-Smolska, E. (2001). Bachelard as constructivist. In J. A. Weaver, M. Morris, & P. Appelbaum (Eds.), *(Post) modern science (education): Propositions and alternative paths* (pp. 41–55). New York: Peter Lang.

Kumar, A. (Ed.). (1999). *Poetics/politics: Radical aesthetics for the classroom*. New York: St. Martin's.

Kurzweil, E. (1998). *The Freudians: A comparative perspective*. London: Transaction.

Kusz, K. (2003). BMX, extreme sports, and the white male backlash. In R. Rinehart & S. Sydnor (Eds.), *To the extreme: Alternative sports, inside and out* (pp. 153–175). Albany, NY: SUNY.

Lachman, G. (2010). *Jung the mystic: The esoteric dimension of Carl Jung's life and teachings: A new biography*. New York: Penguin.

Langdon, J. (2009). Indigenous knowledges, development and education: An introduction. In J. Langdon (Ed.), *Indigenous knowledges, development and education* (pp. 1–36). Rotterdam: Sense.

Langdon, J., & Harvey, B. (2010). Building anticolonial spaces for global education: Challenges and reflections. In A. Kempf (Ed.), *Breaching the colonial contract: Anti-colonialism in the US and Canada* (pp. 219–236). New York: Springer.

Lapidus, R. (1995). Translator's note. In M. Serres with B. Latour, *Conversations on science, culture, and time* (p. 205). Ann Arbor: University of Michigan Press.

Laplanche, J. (1999). *Essays on otherness*. New York: Routledge.

Laplanche, J., & Pontalis, J.-B. (1973). *The language of psycho-analysis* (D. Nicholson-Smith, Trans.). New York: W. W. Norton.

Lather, P. (2007). *Getting lost: Feminist efforts toward a double(d) science*. Albany, NY: SUNY.

Latta, M. M. (2001). *The possibilities of play in the classroom: On the power of aesthetic experience in teaching, learning, and researching*. New York: Peter Lang.

Leonard, P. (2005). *Nationality between poststructuralism and postcolonial theory: A new cosmopolitanism*. New York: Palgrave Macmillan.

Leopold, A. (1989). *A Sand County almanac and sketches here and there*. New York: Oxford University Press.

Lesko, N. (2001). *Act your age! A cultural construction of adolescence*. New York: Routledge-Falmer.

Lesser, W. (2014). *Why I read: The serious pleasure of books*. New York: Farrar, Straus & Giroux.

Le Sueur, J. D. (2005). *Uncivil war: Intellectuals and identity politics during the decolonization of Algeria*. Lincoln: University of Nebraska Press.

Levinas, E. (1985). *Ethics and infinity* (R. A. Cohen, Trans.). Pittsburgh, PA: Duquesne University Press.

Levinas, E. (1987). *Time & the other* (R. A. Cohen, Trans.). Pittsburgh, PA: Duquesne University Press.

Levinas, E. (2001). *Existence & existents* (A. Lingis, Trans.). Pittsburgh, PA: Duquesne University Press.

Lewis, P. F. (1979). Axioms for reading the landscape: Some guides to the American scene. In D. W. Meinig (Ed.), *The interpretation of ordinary landscapes: Geographical essays* (pp. 11–32). New York: Oxford University Press.

Lewis, R. (2005). *Gendering orientalism: Race, femininity and representation.* New York: Routledge.

Likierman, M. (2001). *Melanie Klein: Her work in context.* New York: Continuum.

Liston, D. D. (2001). *Joy as a metaphor of convergence: A phenomenological and aesthetic investigation of social and educational change.* Cresskill, NJ: Hampton.

Logue, J., & McCarthy, C. (2007). Shooting the elephant: Antagonistic identities, neo-Marxist nostalgia, and the remorselessly vanishing pasts. In C. McCarthy, A. S. Durham, L. C. Engel, A. A. Filmer, M. D. Giardina, & M. A. Malagreca (Eds.), *Globalizing cultural studies: Ethnographic interventions in theory, method, and policy* (pp. 3–22). New York: Peter Lang.

Lopes, A., C., & Macedo, E. (2003). The curriculum field in Brazil in the 1990s. In W. F. Pinar (Ed.), *International handbook of curriculum research* (pp. 185–203). Mahwah, NJ: Lawrence Erlbaum.

Lorenz, E. (1995). *The essence of chaos.* Seattle, WA: The University of Washington Press.

Luke, C. (2001). *Globalization and women in academia: North/west/south/east.* Mahwah, NJ: Lawrence Erlbaum.

Lyotard, J.-F. (1993). *The postmodern condition: A report on knowledge* (G. Bennington & B. Massumi, Trans.). Minneapolis: University of Minnesota Press.

Macdonald, J. B. (1996). *Theory as a prayerful act: The collected essays of James B. Macdonald* (B. J. Macdonald, Ed.). New York: Peter Lang.

Macdonald, N. (2001). *The graffiti subculture: Youth, masculinity in London and New York.* New York: Palgrave Macmillan.

Macedo, D., & Freire, A. M. A. (2005). Foreword. In P. Freire, *Teachers as cultural workers: Letters to those who dare teach* (pp. vii–xxvi). Cambridge, MA: Westview.

Magee, J. (2007). Alexander von Humboldt: A vision of the unity of nature. In R. Huxley (Ed.), *The great naturalists* (pp. 224–230). London: Thames & Hudson.

Malott, C., & Pena, M. (2004). *Punk rockers' revolution: A pedagogy of race, class, and gender.* New York: Peter Lang.

Manguel, A. (2015). *Curiosity.* New Haven, CT: Yale University Press.

Marcus, L. (1999). Introduction: Histories, representations, autobiographics in the interpretation of dreams. In L. Marcus (Ed.), *Sigmund Freud's The Interpretation of Dreams: New interdisciplinary essays* (pp. 1–65). Manchester, UK: Manchester University Press.

Marshall, J. D., Sears, J. T., Allen, L. A., Roberts, P. A., & Schubert, W. H. (2007). *Turning points in curriculum: A contemporary memoir.* Upper Saddle River, NJ: Pearson.

Martusewicz, R. A. (1997). Leaving home: Curriculum as translation. *The Journal of Curriculum Theorizing, 13*(3), 13–17.

Martusewicz, R. A. (2001). *Seeking passage: Post-structuralism, pedagogy, ethics.* New York: Columbia University Press.

Martusewicz, R. A., Lupinacci, J., & Schnakenberg, G. (2010). Ecojustice education for science educators. In D. J. Tippins, M. P. Mueller, M. van Eijck, & J. D. Adams (Eds.), *Cultural studies and environmentalism: The confluence of ecojustice, place-based (science) education, and indigenous knowledge systems* (pp. 11–27). New York: Springer.

Mayes, C. (2005). *Teaching mysteries: Foundations of spiritual pedagogy*. Lanham, MD: University Press of America.

McCarthy, C. (1998). *The uses of culture: Education and the limits of ethnic affiliation*. New York: Taylor & Francis.

McCarthy, C. (2007). Representing the third world intellectual: C. L. R. James and the contradictory meanings of radical activism. In C. McCarthy, A. S. Durham, L. C. Engel, A. A. Filmer, M. D. Giardina, & M. A. Malagreca (Eds.), *Globalizing cultural studies: Ethnographic interventions in theory, method, and policy* (pp. 123–150). New York: Peter Lang.

McCarthy, C., Durham, A. S., Engel, L. C., Filmer, A. A., Giardina, M. D., & Malagreca, M. A. (2007). Introduction: Confronting cultural studies in globalizing times. In C. McCarthy, A. S. Durham, L. C. Engel, A. A. Filmer, M. D. Giardina, & M. A. Malagreca (Eds.), *Globalizing cultural studies: Ethnographic interventions in theory, method, and policy* (pp. xvii–xxxiv). New York: Peter Lang.

McCarthy, C., Hudak, G., Miklaucic, S., & Saukko, P. (Eds.). (1999). *Sound identities: Popular music and the cultural politics of education*. New York: Peter Lang.

McDougall, J. (1989). *Theaters of the body: A psychoanalytic approach to psychosomatic illness*. New York: W. W. Norton.

McLaren, P., & Houston, D. (2004). Revolutionary ecologies: Ecosocial and critical pedagogy. *Educational Studies: A Journal of the American Educational Studies Association, 36*(1) 27 44.

McLaren, P., & McLaren, J. (2004). Remaking the revolution. In C. Malott & M. Pena (Ed.), *Punk rockers' revolution: A pedagogy of race, class, and gender* (pp. 123–127). New York: Peter Lang.

McNiff, S. (2004). Foreword. In G. Diaz & M. B. McKenna (Eds.), *Teaching for aesthetic experience: The art of learning* (pp. ix–xiii) New York: Peter Lang.

McRobbie, A. (2005). *The uses of cultural studies*. London: Sage.

Memmi, A. (1967). *The colonizer and the colonized*. Boston: Beacon.

Mercury, M. (2000). *Pagan fleshworks: The alchemy of body modification*. Rochester, VT: Park Street.

Merton, T. (1976). *The seven story mountain*. New York: Harcourt Brace Jovanovich.

Metzner, R. (1995). The psychopathology of the human-nature relationship. In T. Roszak, M. E. Gomes, & A. D. Kanner (Eds.), *Ecopsychology: Restoring the earth, healing the mind* (pp. 55–67). San Francisco: Sierra Club.

Meyer, S. M. (1984). *The dynamics of nuclear proliferation*. Chicago: University of Chicago Press.

Miller, A. (2010). Arthur Miller. In, N. A. Basbanes, (Eds.), *About the author: Inside the creative process. Conversations with Alfred Kazin, Arthur Miller, Toni Morrison, Louise Erdrich, Kenzaburo Oe, Doris Lessing, Kurt Vonnegut, Neil Simon, John Updike, Alice Walker, and others* (pp. 159–166). Durham, NC: Fine Books Press.

Miller, J. (2000). *Education and the soul: Toward a spiritual curriculum*. Albany, NY: SUNY.

Mitchell, J. (1998). Introduction to Melanie Klein. In J. Phillips & L. Stonebridge (Eds.), *Reading Melanie Klein* (pp. 11–31). New York: Routledge.

Mitchell, S. A. (1988). *Relational concepts in psychoanalysis*. Cambridge, MA: Harvard University Press.

Mitchell, S. A., & Black, M. J. (1995). *Freud and beyond: A history of modern psychoanalytic thought*. New York: Basic.

Moore, T. (1996). *The education of the heart*. New York: Harper Perennial.

Moore, T. (2005). Educating for the soul. In J. Miller, S. Karsten, D. Denton, D. Orr, & I. C. Kates (Eds.), *Holistic learning: Spirituality in education. Breaking new ground* (pp. 9–16). Albany, NY: SUNY.

Morley, S. (2010). Introduction: The contemporary sublime. In S. Morley (Ed.), *The sublime (Whitechapel: Documents of contemporary art)* (pp. 12–21). Cambridge, MA: MIT.

Morris, E. (2005). *Beethoven: The universal composer*. New York: HarperPerennial.

Morris, M. (2001). *Curriculum and the Holocaust: Competing sites of memory and representation*. Mahwah, NJ: Lawrence Erlbaum.

Morris, M. (2002a). Curriculum theory as academic responsibility: The call for reading Heidegger contextually. In M. Morris & J. A. Weaver (Eds.), *Difficult memories: Talk in a (post) Holocaust era* (pp. 227–247). New York: Peter Lang.

Morris, M. (2002b). Ecological consciousness and curriculum. *The Journal of Curriculum Studies, 34*(5), 571–587.

Morris, M. (2006). *Jewish intellectuals and the university*. New York: Palgrave Macmillan.

Morris, M. (2008). *Teaching through the ill body: A spiritual and aesthetic approach to pedagogy and illness*. Rotterdam: Sense.

Morris, M. (2009). *On not being able to play: Scholars, musicians and the crisis of psyche*. Rotterdam: Sense.

Morris, M., & Weaver, J. (Eds.). (2002). *Difficult memories: Talk in a (post) Holocaust era*. New York: Peter Lang.

Mosha, R. S. (2008). *The heartbeat of indigenous Africa: A study of the Chagga educational system*. New York: Routledge.

Mueller, M. P., & Tippins, D. J. (2010). Nurturing morally defensible environmentalism. In D. J. Tippins, M. P. Mueller, M. van Eijck, & J. D. Adams (Eds.), *Cultural studies and environmentalism: The confluence of ecojustice, place-based (science) education, and indigenous knowledge systems* (pp. 7–10). New York: Springer.

Ng-A-Fook, N. (2007). *An indigenous curriculum of place: The United Houma Nation's contentious relationship with Louisiana's educational institutions*. New York: Peter Lang.

Noppe-Brandon, S., & Holzer, M. F. (2001). Introduction: Maxine Greene and Lincoln Center Institute: Setting the context. In M. Greene, *Variations on a blue guitar: The Lincoln Center Institute lectures on aesthetic education* (pp. 1–4). New York: Teachers College Press.

Nussbaum, M. C. (1997). *Cultivating humanity: A classical defense of reform in liberal education*. Cambridge, MA: Harvard University Press.

Nwankwo, I. K. (2005). *Black cosmopolitanism: Racial consciousness and transnational identity in the nineteenth-century Americas*. Philadelphia: University of Pennsylvania Press.

Oldenski, T., & Carlson, D. (2002). Yearnings of the heart: Education, postmodernism, and spirituality. In T. Oldenski & D. Carlson (Eds.), *Educational yearning: The journey of the spirit and democratic education* (pp. 1–9). New York: Peter Lang.

Olson, R. J. M. (2007). John James Audubon: Artist, naturalist and adventurer. In R. Huxley (Ed.), *The great naturalists* (pp. 233–236). London: Thames & Hudson.

Orelus, P. W. (2007). *Education under occupation: The heavy price of living in a neocolonized and globalized world.* Rotterdam: Sense.

Orr, D. W. (1992). *Ecological literacy: Education and the transition to a postmodern world.* Albany, NY: SUNY.

Orr, D. W. (2002). *The nature of design: Ecology, culture, and human intervention.* New York: Oxford University Press.

Orr, D. W. (2004). *Earth in mind: On education, environment, and the human prospect.* Washington, DC: Island.

Packer, J. (2003). Mapping the intersections of Foucault and cultural studies: An interview with Lawrence Grossberg and Toby Miller, October 2000. In J. Z. Bratich, J. Packer, & C. McCarthy (Eds.), *Foucault, cultural studies, and governmentality* (pp. 23–46). Albany, NY: SUNY.

Paine, R. T. (2011). Inspiration. In M. H. Graham, J. Parker, & P. K. Dayton (Eds.), *The essential naturalist: Timeless readings in natural history* (pp. 7–15). Chicago: University of Chicago Press.

Paley, N. (1995). *Finding art's place: Experiments in contemporary education & culture.* New York: Routledge.

Palmer, J. A. (2003). *Environmental education in the 21st century: Theory, practice, progress and promise.* New York: RoutledgeFalmer.

Palmer, P. (1999). The grace of great things: Reclaiming the sacred in knowing, teaching, and learning. In S. Glazer (Ed.), *The heart of learning: Spirituality in education* (pp. 15–32). New York: Tarcher Putnam.

Pandey, S. N., & Moorad, F. R. (2003). The decolonization of curriculum in Botswana. In W. F. Pinar (Ed.), *International handbook of curriculum research* (pp. 143–170). Mahwah, NJ: Lawrence Erlbaum.

Panichas, G. A. (1977). "Prefatory note." In, G. A. Panichas (Ed.), *The Simone Weil reader.*(pp. xiii–xvi). New York: David McKay Company, Inc.

Penna, L. (2008). Abundance's connection: Three soft experiments to develop an embodied relationship to other-than-human beings. In J. Gray-Donald & D. Selby (Eds.), *Green frontiers: Environmental educators dancing away from mechanism* (pp. 115–131). Rotterdam: Sense.

Perez, D. M. C., Fain, S. M., & Slater, J. J. (2004). Understanding place as a social aspect of education. In D. M. C. Perez, S. M. Fain, & J. J. Slater (Eds.), *Pedagogy of place: Seeing space as cultural education* (pp. 1–5). New York: Peter Lang.

Peters, M. A. (1996). *Poststructuralism, politics and education.* Westport, CT: Bergin & Garvey.

Peters, M. A. (2004). Preface. In P. P. Trifonas & M. A. Peters (Eds.), *Derrida, deconstruction and education: Ethics of pedagogy and research* (pp. viii–ix). Malden, MA: Blackwell.

Peters, M. A. (2009). Introduction: Governmentality, education and the end of neoliberalism. In M. A. Peters, A. C. Besley, M. Olssen, S. Maurer, & S. Weber (Eds.), *Governmentality studies in education* (pp. xxvii–xlviii). Rotterdam: Sense.

Peters, M. A., & Biesta, G. (2009). Introduction: The promise of politics and pedagogy. In M. A. Peters & G. Biesta (Eds.), *Derrida, deconstruction, and the politics of pedagogy* (pp. 1–13). New York: Peter Lang.

Peters, M. A., & Trifonas, P. P. (2005). Introduction: The humanities in deconstruction. In P. P. Trifonas & M. A. Peters (Eds.), *Deconstructing Derrida: Tasks for the new humanities* (pp. 1–10). New York: Palgrave Macmillan.

Petot, J.-M. (1990). *Melanie Klein, Vol. 1: First discoveries and first system 1919–1932*. Madison, CT: International Universities.

Phillips, J., & Stonebridge, L. (1998). Introduction. In J. Phillips & L. Stonebridge (Eds.), *Reading Melanie Klein* (pp. 1–10). New York: Routledge.

Pinar, W. F. (1975/2000a). *Currere: Toward reconceptualization* (pp. 396–414). Troy, NY: Educator's International.

Pinar, W. F. (1975/2000b). Search for a method. In W. F. Pinar (Ed.), *Curriculum studies: The reconceptualization* (pp. 415–424). Troy, NY: Educator's International.

Pinar, W. F. (1975/2000c). Sanity, madness, and the school. In W. F. Pinar (Ed.), *Curriculum studies: The reconceptualization* (pp. 359–383). Troy, NY: Educator's International.

Pinar, W. F. (1994). *Autobiography, politics and sexuality: Essays in curriculum theory 1972–1992*. New York: Peter Lang.

Pinar, W. F. (1998). Introduction. In W. F. Pinar (Ed.), *Queer theory in education* (pp. 1–47). Mahwah, NJ: Lawrence Erlbaum.

Pinar, W. F. (2001). *The gender of racial politics and violence in America: Lynching, prison rape, & the crisis of masculinity*. New York: Peter Lang.

Pinar, W. F. (2003a). Introduction. In, William F. Pinar (Ed.), *International handbook of curriculum research*. Mahwah, NJ: Lawrence Erlbaum.

Pinar, W. F. (2003b). Toward the internationalization of curriculum studies. In D. Trueit, W. E. Doll Jr., H. Wang, & W. F. Pinar (Eds.), *The internationalization of curriculum studies: Selected proceedings from the LSU conference 2000* (pp.1–13). New York: Peter Lang.

Pinar, W. F. (2006a). *Race, religion, and a curriculum of reparation: Teacher education for a multicultural society*. New York: Palgrave.

Pinar, W. F. (2006b). *The synoptic text today and other essays: Curriculum development after the reconceptualization*. New York: Peter Lang.

Pinar, W. F. (2007). *Intellectual advancement through disciplinarity: Verticality and horizontality in curriculum studies*. Rotterdam/Taipei: Sense.

Pinar, W. F. (2009). *The worldliness of a cosmopolitan education: Passionate lives in public service*. New York: Taylor & Francis.

Pinar, W. F. (2010). *The next moment*. In E. Malewski (Ed.), *Curriculum studies handbook: The next moment* (pp. 528–533). New York: Routledge.

Pinar, W F. (2012). *What is curriculum theory?* (2nd ed.). New York: Routledge.

Pinar, W. F., Reynolds, W. M., Slattery, P., & Taubman, P. M. (1995). *Understanding curriculum: An introduction to the study of historical and contemporary discourses*. New York: Peter Lang.

Pitt, A. J. (2003). *The play of the personal: Psychoanalytic narratives of feminist education*. New York: Peter Lang.

Plate, B. S. (2005). *Walter Benjamin, religion, and aesthetics: Rethinking religion through the arts*. New York: Routledge.

Popkewitz, T., & Brennan, M. (1998). Restructuring of social and political theory in education: Foucault and a social epistemology of school practices. In, Thomas Popkewitz & Marie Brennan (Eds.), *Foucault's challenge: Discourse, knowledge, and power in education* (pp. 3–35). New York: Teachers College Press.

Popkewitz, T. S. (2008). *Cosmopolitanism and the age of school reform: Science, education, and the making of society by making the child*. New York: Taylor & Francis.

Porter, N. (2007). She rips when she skates. In A. Greenberg (Ed.), *Youth subcultures: Exploring underground America* (pp. 121–148). New York: Pearson, Longman.

Prose, F. (2007). *Reading like a writer: A guide for people who love books and for those who want to write them*. New York: HarperPerennial.

Purpel, D. (2004). The current crisis in education: Professional incompetence or cultural failure. In D. Purpel & W. McLaurin (Eds.), *Reflections on the moral & spiritual crisis in education* (pp. 17–28). New York: Peter Lang.

Pyle, R. M. (2011). A nat'ral histerrical feller in an unwondering age. In T. L. Fleischner (Ed.), *The way of natural history* (pp. 160–171). San Antonio, TX: Trinity University.

Quinn, M. (2001). *Going out, not knowing whither: Education, the upward journey, and the faith of reason*. New York: Peter Lang.

Rabkin, N. (2004). Introduction: Learning and the arts. In N. Rabkin & R. Redmond (Eds.), *Putting the arts in the picture: Reframing education in the 21st century* (pp. 5–15). Chicago: Columbia College.

Rabkin, S. J. (2011). Eyes of the world. In T. L. Fleischner (Ed.), *The way of natural history* (pp. 103–112). San Antonio, TX: Trinity University Press.

Rasberry, G. W. (2002). Imagine, inventing a data-dancer. In C. Bagley & M. B. Cancienne (Eds.), *Dancing the data* (pp. 105–117). New York: Peter Lang.

Resnik, S. (2001). *The delusional person: Bodily feelings in psychosis* (D. Alcorn, Trans.). London: Karnac.

Reynolds, W. M., & Webber, J. A. (2004). Introduction: Curriculum dis/positions. In W. M. Reynolds & J. A. Webber (Eds.), *Expanding curriculum theory: Dis/positions and lines of flight* (pp. 1–18). Mahwah, NJ: Lawrence Erlbaum.

Riley-Taylor, E. (2002). *Ecology, spirituality, & education: Curriculum for relational knowing*. New York: Peter Lang.

Rinehart, R. E., & Sydnor, S. (2003). Proem. In R. E. Rinehart & S. Sydnor (Eds.), *To the extreme: Alternative sports, inside and out* (pp. 1–17). Albany, NY: SUNY.

Robbins, B. (1998). Introduction part 1: Actually existing cosmopolitanism. In P. Cheah & B. Robbins (Eds.), *Cosmopolitics: Thinking and feeling beyond the nation* (pp. 1–19). Minneapolis: University of Minnesota Press.

Roberts, P. (2003). Contemporary curriculum research in New Zealand. In W. F. Pinar (Ed.), *International handbook of curriculum research* (pp. 495–516). Mahwah, NJ: Lawrence Erlbaum.

Rorty, R. (1998). *Justice as a larger loyalty*. In P. Cheah & B. Robbins (Eds.), *Cosmopolitics: Thinking and feeling beyond the nation* (pp. 45–58). Minneapolis: University of Minnesota Press.

Rose, K., & Kincheloe, J. (2004). *Art, culture, & education: Artful teaching in a fractured landscape*. New York: Peter Lang.

Rosenblum, R. (2010). The abstract sublime/1961. In S. Morley (Ed.), *The sublime: (Whitechapel: Documents of contemporary art)* (pp. 108–112). London & Cambridge, MA: MIT.

Roszak, T. (1995). Where psyche meets gaia. In T. Roszak, M. E. Gomes, & A. D. Kanner (Eds.), *Ecopsychology: Restoring the earth, healing the mind* (pp. 1–17). San Francisco: Sierra Club.

Roszak, T., Gomes, M. E., & Kanner, A. D. (Eds.). (1995). *Ecopsychology: Restoring the earth, healing the mind*. San Francisco: Sierra Club.

Rothko, C. (2004). Introduction. In M. Rothko (Ed.), *The artist's reality: Philosophies of art* (pp. xi–xxxi). New Haven, CT: Yale University Press.

Rothko, M. (2004). *The artist's reality: Philosophies of art*. New Haven, CT: Yale University Press.

Rowlands, M. (2009). *The philosopher and the wolf: Lessons from the wild on love, death, and happiness*. New York: Pegasus.

Roy, K. (2003). *Teachers in nomadic spaces: Deleuze and curriculum*. New York: Peter Lang.

Rudnytsky, P. L. (2002). *Reading psycho-analysis: Freud, Rank, Ferenczi, Groddeck*. Ithaca, NY: Cornell University Press.

Rushdie, S. (2003). *Step across this line: Collected nonfiction 1992–2002*. New York: Modern Library.

Said, E. W. (1994a). *Culture and imperialism*. New York: Vintage.

Said, E. W. (1994b). *Orientalism*. New York: Vintage.

Said, E. W. (2000). *Reflections on exile and other essays*. Cambridge, MA: Harvard University Press.

Said, E. W. (2001). *Power, politics, and culture: Interviews with Edward W. Said* (G. Viswanathan, Ed.). New York: Vintage.

Saks, E. R. (2007). *The center cannot hold: My journey through madness*. New York: Hyperion.

Salvio, P. M. (2006). On the vicissitudes of love and hate: Anne Sexton's pedagogy of loss and reparation. In G. M. Boldt & P. M. Salvio (Eds.), *Love's return: Psychoanalytic essays on childhood, teaching, and learning* (pp. 65–86). New York: Routledge.

Salvio, P. M. (2007). *Anne Sexton: Teacher of weird abundance*. Albany, NY: SUNY.

Sapon-Shevin, M. (1999). A curriculum of courage, a pedagogy of inclusion: A Jewish woman makes her way through academia. In H. S. Shapiro (Ed.), *Strangers in the land: Pedagogy, modernity and Jewish identity* (pp. 275–308). New York: Peter Lang.

Schaller, G. B. (2011). *A naturalist and other beasts: Tales from a life in the field*. San Francisco: Sierra Club.

Scharff, D. (2005). *Object relations: Theory and practice: An introduction*. Lanham, MD: Rowman & Littlefield.

Schlink, B. (1997). *The reader*. New York: Pantheon.

Schubert, W. H. (2004). Foreword. Reflections on the place of curriculum. In D. M. Callejo-Perez, S. M. Fain, & J. J. Slater (Eds.), *Pedagogy of place: Seeing space as cultural education* (pp. ix–xxiii). New York: Peter Lang.

Schubert, W. H., Schubert, A. L. L., Thomas, T. P., & Carroll, W. M. (2002). *Curriculum books: The first hundred years* (2nd ed.). New York: Peter Lang.

Segal, J. (1992). *Melanie Klein*. London: Sage.

Segalla, S. D. (2009). *The Moroccan soul: French education, colonial ethnology, and Muslim resistance, 1912–1956*. Lincoln: University of Nebraska.

Semali, L. M. (1999). Introduction: What is indigenous knowledge and why should we study it. In L. M. Semali & J. Kincheloe (Eds.), *What is indigenous knowledge? Voices from the academy* (pp. 3–58). New York: Falmer.

Semetsky, I. (Ed.). (2008). *Nomadic education: Variations on a theme by Deleuze and Guattari*. Rotterdam: Sense.

Semken, S., & Brandt, E. (2010). Implications of sense of place and place-based education for ecological integrity and cultural sustainability in diverse places. In D. J. Tippins, M. P. Mueller, M. van Eijck, & J. D. Adams (Eds.), *Cultural studies and environmentalism: The confluence of ecojustice, place-based (science) education, and indigenous knowledge systems* (pp. 287–302). New York: Springer.

Serres, M. (1995). *Genesis* (G. James & J. Nielson, Trans.). Ann Arbor: University of Michigan Press.

Serres, M. (2000). *The troubadour of knowledge* (S. F. Glaser & W. Paulson, Trans.). Ann Arbor: University of Michigan Press.

Serres, M., & Latour, B. (1995). *Serres/Latour: Conversations on science, culture, and time* (R. Lapidus, Trans.). Ann Arbor: University of Michigan Press.

Sessions, G. (Ed.). (1995). Preface. In *Deep ecology for the 21st century: Readings on the philosophy and practice of the new environmentalism* (pp. ix–xxviii). Boston: Shambhala.

Shakespeare, T. (2010). The social model of disability. In L. J. Davis (Ed.), *The disability studies reader* (pp. 266–273). New York: Routledge.

Shapiro, H. S. (1999). Introduction: A life on the fringes—My road to critical pedagogy. In H. S. Shapiro (Ed.), *Strangers in the land: Pedagogy, modernity and Jewish identity* (pp. 1–30). New York: Peter Lang.

Shapiro, H. S. (2006). *Losing heart: The moral and spiritual miseducation of America's children*. New York: Taylor & Francis.

Shapiro, H. S. (2010). *Educating youth for a world beyond violence: A pedagogy for peace*. New York: Palgrave Macmillan.

Silin, J. (2006). Reading, writing, and the wrath of my father. In G. M. Boldt & P. M. Salvio (Eds.), *Love's return: Psychoanalytic essays on childhood, teaching and learning* (pp. 227–241). New York: Routledge.

Simon, R. (1999). Election, ambivalence, and the pedagogy of Jewish particularity. In H. S. Shapiro (Ed.), *Strangers in the land: Pedagogy, modernity and Jewish identity* (pp. 309–322). New York: Peter Lang.

Simon, R. I. (2005). *The touch of the past: Remembrance, learning, and ethics*. New York: Palgrave Macmillan.

Simon, R. I., Rosenberg, S., & Eppert, C. (Eds.). (2000). Introduction. In R. I. Simon, S. Rosenberg, & C. Eppert (Eds.), *Between hope and despair: The pedagogical encounter of historical remembrance* (pp. 1–8). Lanham, MD: Rowman & Littlefield.

Sinclair, U. (1906/2006). *The jungle*. New York: Penguin.

Slater, J. J. (2004). The erosion of the public space. In D. M. C. Perez, S. M. Fain, & J. J. Slater (Eds.), *Pedagogy of place: Seeing space as cultural education* (pp. 35–52). New York: Peter Lang.

Slattery, P. (2006). *Curriculum development in the postmodern era*. New York: Routledge.

Smith, D. G. (1999). *Pedagon: Interdisciplinary essays in the human sciences, pedagogy, and culture*. New York: Peter Lang.

Smith, D. G. (2003). Curriculum and teaching face globalization. In W. F. Pinar (Ed.), *International handbook of curriculum research* (pp. 35–51). Mahwah, NJ: Lawrence Erlbaum.

Smith, D. C., & Carson, T. R. (1998). *Educating for a peaceful future*. Toronto: Kagan & Woo.

Smith, L. T. (2007). *Decolonizing methodologies: Research and indigenous peoples*. London: Zed.

Snowber, C. (2002). Bodydance: Enfleshing soulful inquiry through improvisation. In C. Bagley & M. B. Cancienne (Eds.), *Dancing the data* (pp. 20–33). New York: Peter Lang.

Snowber, C. (2004). An aesthetics of everyday life. In G. Diaz & M. B. McKenna (Eds.), *Teaching for aesthetic experience: The art of learning* (pp. 115–126). New York: Peter Lang.

Snyder, G. (1990). *The practice of the wild: Essays*. Emeryville, CA: Shoemaker & Hoard.

Spinoza, B. (2002). *Spinoza: Complete works*. Indianapolis: Hackett.

Springgay, S. (2004). Body as fragment: Art-making, researching, and teaching as boundary shift. In R. L. Irwin & A. de Cosson (Eds.), *A/r/tography: Rendering self through arts-based living inquiry*. Vancouver: Pacific Educational.

Standish, P. (2008). Levinas and the language of curriculum. In D. Egea-Kuehne (Ed.), *Levinas and education: At the intersection between faith and reason* (pp. 56–66). New York: Routledge.

Steinberg, S. R. (1997). The bitch who has everything. In S. R. Steinberg & Joe L. Kincheloe (Eds.), *Kinderculture: The corporate construction of childhood* (pp. 207–218). Boulder, CO: Westview.

Steinberg, S. R. (1999). Foreword. In H. S. Shapiro (Ed.), *Strangers in the land: Pedagogy, modernity, and Jewish identity* (pp. ix–x). New York: Peter Lang.

Steinberg, S. R., & Kincheloe, J. L. (1997). Introduction: No more secrets—Kinderculture, information saturation, and the postmodern childhood. In S. R. Steinberg & J. L. Kincheloe (Eds.), *Kinderculture: The corporate construction of childhood* (pp. 1–30). Boulder, CO: Westview.

Stonebridge, L., & Phillips, J. (1998). Introduction. In L. Stonebridge & J. Phillips (Eds.), *Reading Melanie Klein* (pp. 1–10). New York: Routledge.

Sutton, D. (2007). Pliny the elder: Collector of knowledge. In R. Huxley (Ed.), *The great naturalists* (pp. 38–43). London: Thames & Hudson.

Sylvester, R. (2008). Historical resources for research in international education (1851–1950). In M. Hayden, J. Levy, & J. Thompson (Eds.), *The Sage handbook of research in international education* (pp. 11–24). Los Angeles: Sage.

Tallmadge, J. (2011). Crazy about nature. In T. L. Fleischner (Ed.), *The way of natural history* (pp. 16–28). San Antonio, TX: Trinity University.

Tasar, M. F. (2009). Challenges: Environmental education: A conversation with Annette Gough. *Eurasia Journal of Mathematics, Science & Technology Education*, 5(3), 187–196.

Taubman, P. M. (2012). *Disavowed knowledge: Psychoanalysis, education, and teaching.* New York: Routledge.

Teasley, C., & McCarthy, C. (2008). Introduction: Redirecting and resituating cultural studies in a globalizing world. In C. McCarthy & C. Teasley (Eds.), *Transnational perspectives on culture, policy, and education* (pp. 1–14). New York: Peter Lang.

Thompson, S. (2008). Environmental justice in education: Drinking deeply from the well of sustainability. In J. Gray-Donald & D. Selby (Eds.), *Green frontiers: Environmental educators dancing away from mechanism* (pp. 36–58). Rotterdam: Sense.

Thomson, K. (2007). Charles Darwin: The complete naturalist. In R. Huxley (Ed.), *The great naturalists* (pp. 267–276). London: Thames & Hudson.

Thoreau, H. D. (2000). *Walden and civil disobedience.* New York: Houghton Mifflin.

Tippins, D., J., Mueller, M. P., van Eijck, M., & Adams, J. D. (Eds.). (2010). *Cultural studies and environmentalism: The confluence of ecojustice, place-based (science) education, and indigenous knowledge systems.* New York: Springer.

Todd, S. (2003). *Levinas, psychoanalysis, and ethical possibilities in education: Learning from the other.* Albany, NY: SUNY.

Todd, S. (2008). Welcoming and difficult learning: Reading Levinas and education. In D. Egea-Kuenhe (Ed.), *Levinas and education: At the intersection of faith and reason* (pp. 170–185). New York: Routledge.

Todd, S. (2009). *Toward an imperfect education: Facing humanity, rethinking cosmopolitanism.* Boulder, CO: Paradigm.

Toulmin, S. (1992). *Cosmopolis: The hidden agenda of modernity.* Chicago: University of Chicago Press.

Tracy, D. (1996). *Blessed rage for order: The new pluralism in theology.* Chicago: University of Chicago.

Trifonas, P. P. (2000). *The ethics of writing: Derrida, deconstruction, and pedagogy.* Lanham, MD: Rowman & Littlefield.

Trifonas, P. P., & Peters, M. A. (Eds.). (2004). *Derrida, deconstruction and education: Ethics of pedagogy and research.* Malden, MA: Blackwell.

Trifonas, P. P., & Peters, M. A. (Eds.). (2005). *Deconstructing Derrida: Tasks for the new humanities.* New York: Palgrave Macmillan.

Trueit, D., Doll, W. E., Jr., Wang, H., & Pinar, W. F. (Eds.).(2003). *The internationalization of curriculum studies: Selected proceedings from the LSU conference 2000.* New York: Peter Lang.

Tuan, Y.-F. (1979). Thought and landscape: The eye and the mind's eye. In D. W. Meinig (Ed.), *The interpretation of ordinary landscapes: Geographical essays* (pp. 89–102). New York: Oxford University Press.

Van der Veer, P. (2008). Colonial cosmopolitanism. In S. Vertovec & R. Cohen (Eds.), *Conceiving cosmopolitanism: Theory, context, and practice* (pp. 165–179). New York: Oxford University Press.

Van Eijck, M. (2010). Place-based (science) education: Something is happening here. In D. J. Tippins, M. P. Mueller, M. van Eijck, & J. D. Adams (Eds.), *Cultural studies and environmentalism: The confluence of ecojustice, place-based (science) education, and indigenous knowledge systems* (pp. 187–191). New York: Springer.

Vertovec, S., & Cohen, R. (2008). Introduction: Conceiving cosmopolitanism. In S. Vertovec & R. Cohen (Eds.), *Conceiving cosmopolitanism: Theory, context, and practice* (pp. 1–22). New York: Oxford University Press.

Viruru, R. (2001). *Early childhood education: Postcolonial perspectives from India.* London: Sage.

Wane, N. N. (2008). Indigenous knowledge: Lessons from the elders—A Kenyan case study. In G. J. S. Dei, B. L. Hall, & D. G. Rosenberg (Eds.), *Indigenous knowledges in global contexts: Multiple readings of our world* (pp. 54–69). Toronto: University of Toronto Press.

Wang, H. (2004). *The call from the stranger on a journey home: Curriculum in a third space.* New York: Peter Lang.

Wayne, K. R., & Gruenewald, D. A. (Eds.). (2004). *Special issue: Ecojustice and education. Educational Studies: A Journal of the American Educational Studies Association, 36*(1), 6–9.

Weaver, J. A. (2001). Introduction: (Post) modern science (education): Propositions and alternative paths. In J. A. Weaver, M. Morris, & P. Appelbaum (Eds.), *(Post) modern science (education): Propositions and alternative paths* (pp. 1–22). New York: Peter Lang.

Weaver, J. A. (2004). Curriculum theorists as spawns from hell. In J. A. Weaver, K. Anijar, & T. Daspit (Eds.), *Science fiction curriculum, cyborg teachers & youth culture(s)* (pp. 21–35). New York: Peter Lang.

Weaver, J. A. (2009). *Popular culture primer.* New York: Peter Lang.

Weaver, J. A. (2010). *Educating the posthuman: Biosciences, fiction, and curriculum studies.* Rotterdam: Sense.

Weaver, J. A., Morris, M., & Appelbaum, P. M. (Eds.). (2001). *(Post) modern science (education): Propositions and alternative paths.* New York: Peter Lang.

Webber, J. A. (2003). *Failure to hold: The politics of school violence.* Lanham, MD: Rowman & Littlefield.

Weber, S. (2008). Visual images in research. In J. G. Knowles & A. L. Cole (Eds.), *Handbook of the arts in qualitative research* (pp. 41–53). Los Angeles: Sage.

Weinstein, M. (1998). *Robot world: Education, popular culture, and science.* New York: Peter Lang.

Wells, H. G. (1967). *A modern utopia.* Lincoln: University of Nebraska Press.

Wexler, P. (1996). *Holy sparks: Social theory, education and religion.* New York: St. Martin's.

Wexler, P. (2000). *Mystical society: An emerging social vision.* Boulder, CO: Westview.

Wexler, P. (2008). *Symbolic movement: Critique and spirituality in sociology of education.* Rotterdam: Sense.

White, B. (2009). *Aesthetics primer.* New York: Peter Lang.

Whitlock, R. U. (2007). *This corner of Canaan: Curriculum studies of place & the reconstruction of the South.* New York: Peter Lang.

Wieder, A. (2003). *Voices from Cape Town classrooms: Oral histories of teachers who fought apartheid.* New York: Peter Lang.

Williams, J. (2005). *Understanding poststructuralism.* Stocksfield, UK: Acumen.

Williams, T. T. (2001). *Refuge: An unnatural history of family and place.* New York: Vintage.

Willinsky, J. (1998). *Learning to divide the world: Education at empire's end*. Minneapolis: University of Minnesota Press.

Wilson, S. (2004). Fragments: Life writing in image and text. In R. L. Irwin & A. de Cosson (Eds.), *A/r/tography: Rendering self through arts-based living inquiry* (pp. 41–59). Vancouver: Pacific Educational.

Winnicott, D. W. (2010). *Playing and reality*. New York: Routledge.

Wolin, R. (1994). *Walter Benjamin: An aesthetic of redemption*. Berkeley: University of California Press.

Yagoda, B. (2005). *The sound on the page: Great writers talk about style and voice in writing*. New York: Harper.

Yegenoglu, M. (1999). *Colonial fantasies: Towards a feminist reading of Orientalism*. New York: Cambridge University Press.

Young-Bruehl, E. (1988). *Anna Freud: A biography*. New York: Summit.

Zaretsky, E. (1998). Melanie Klein and the emergence of modern personal life. In J. Phillips & L. Stonebridge (Eds.), *Reading Melanie Klein* (pp. 32–50). New York: Routledge.

Zinsser, W. (1985). *On writing well: An informal guide to writing nonfiction*. New York: Harper & Row.

Zizek, S. (2009). *The parallax view*. Cambridge, MA: MIT.

INDEX

C

X

Y

Z

Studies in the Postmodern Theory of Education

General Editor
Shirley R. Steinberg

Counterpoints publishes the most compelling and imaginative books being written in education today. Grounded on the theoretical advances in criticalism, feminism, and postmodernism in the last two decades of the twentieth century, Counterpoints engages the meaning of these innovations in various forms of educational expression. Committed to the proposition that theoretical literature should be accessible to a variety of audiences, the series insists that its authors avoid esoteric and jargonistic languages that transform educational scholarship into an elite discourse for the initiated. Scholarly work matters only to the degree it affects consciousness and practice at multiple sites. Counterpoints' editorial policy is based on these principles and the ability of scholars to break new ground, to open new conversations, to go where educators have never gone before.

For additional information about this series or for the submission of manuscripts, please contact:

Shirley R. Steinberg
c/o Peter Lang Publishing, Inc.
29 Broadway, 18th floor
New York, New York 10006

To order other books in this series, please contact our Customer Service Department:

(800) 770-LANG (within the U.S.)
(212) 647-7706 (outside the U.S.)
(212) 647-7707 FAX

Or browse online by series:
www.peterlang.com

Lightning Source UK Ltd.
Milton Keynes UK
UKHW051519040822
406850UK00020BA/360